Homemade Bread

Learn the Steps and Have a Variety of Recipes from Around the Globe to Bake Fresh, Healthy and Delicious Bread at Home

By
Timothy Collins

© **Copyright 2020 by (Timothy Collins) - All rights reserved.**

This document is geared towards providing exact and reliable information in regards to the topic and issue covered. The publication is sold with the idea that the publisher is not required to render accounting, officially permitted, or otherwise, qualified services. If advice is necessary, legal or professional, a practiced individual in the profession should be ordered.

- From a Declaration of Principles which was accepted and approved equally by a Committee of the American Bar Association and a Committee of Publishers and Associations.

In no way is it legal to reproduce, duplicate, or transmit any part of this document in either electronic means or in printed format. Recording of this publication is strictly prohibited and any storage of this document is not allowed unless with written permission from the publisher. All rights reserved.

The information provided herein is stated to be truthful and consistent, in that any liability, in terms of inattention or otherwise, by any usage or abuse of any policies, processes, or directions contained within is the solitary and utter responsibility of the recipient reader. Under no circumstances will any legal responsibility or blame be held against the publisher for any reparation, damages, or monetary loss due to the information herein, either directly or indirectly.

Respective authors own all copyrights not held by the publisher.

The information herein is offered for informational purposes solely, and is universal as so. The presentation of the information is without contract or any type of guarantee assurance.

The trademarks that are used are without any consent, and the publication of the trademark is without permission or backing by the trademark owner. All trademarks and brands within this book are for clarifying purposes only and are the owned by the owners themselves, not affiliated with this document.

Table of Contents

INTRODUCTION 9

CHAPTER 1: BREAD – A STAPLE FOOD 11

1.1 Significance of Bread in our lives 13

1.2 Health Benefits of Bread 16

1.3 Importance of Bread in France 22

1.4 Turkish Bread Culture 26

1.5 Importance of Quality of Bread 29

1.6 Factors and Ingredients Involved in Producing a Good Bread 34

CHAPTER 2: FRESH, HEALTHY BREAD 39

2.1 Sprouted Whole Grain Bread 40

2.2 Sourdough Bread 43

2.3 100% Whole Wheat 46

2.4 OAT Bread 47

2.5 Flax Bread 50

2.6 Sprouted Rye Bread 51

2.7 Gluten-Free Bread 54

CHAPTER 3: HOMEMADE BREAD BAKING 56

3.1 Concept of Homemade Bread 58

3.2 Difference between homemade and Industrial Bread 62

3.3 Temperature required to bake a homemade bread 66

3.4 Basics to Bake a Bread at Home 70

3.5 Utensils and Devices Required to Bake a Bread at Home 73

3.6 Requirement of Linear Recipes 77

CHAPTER 4: PROBLEMS AND SOLUTIONS RELATED TO HOMEMADE BREAD BAKING 82

4.1 Difficulties and Obstacles in Right time and Right Ingredients Required to Bake Bread at Home 83

4.2 Organize Kitchen and Grocery List 86

4.3 Linear Process Required to Bake a Bread 88

4.4 Ways to Organize Kitchen 90

4.5 Importance of Old Kitchen Utensils 92

CHAPTER 5: 30 HOMEMADE BREAD RECIPES FROM ALL OVER THE WORLD 94

Recipe 1 94

Recipe 2 96

Recipe 3 98

Recipe 4 101

Recipe 5 106

Recipe 6 113

Recipe 8 121

Recipe 9 125

Recipe 10 127

Recipe 11 .... **129**

Recipe 12 .... **130**

Recipe 13 .... **132**

Recipe 14 .... **134**

Recipe 15 .... **140**

Recipe 16 .... **142**

Recipe 17 .... **143**

Recipe 18 .... **147**

Recipe 19 .... **151**

Recipe 20 .... **153**

Recipe 21 .... **157**

Recipe 22 .... **159**

Recipe 23 .... **162**

Recipe 24 .... **165**

Recipe 25 .... **167**

Recipe 26 .... **169**

Recipe 27 .... **172**

Recipe 28 .... **175**

Recipe 29 .... **178**

Recipe 30 .... **180**

CHAPTER 6: 20 COOL AND STRANGE RECIPES USING BREAD 183

Recipe 1..183

Recipe 2..184

Recipe 3..186

Recipe 4..188

Recipe 5..189

Recipe 6..192

Recipe 7..193

Recipe 8..195

Recipe 9..196

Recipe 10..198

Recipe 11..200

Recipe 12..203

Recipe 13..204

Recipe 14..206

Recipe 15..208

Recipe 16..209

Recipe 17..212

Recipe 18..213

Recipe 19..214

Recipe 20..216

CONCLUSION 219

REFERENCES 220

Introduction

Bread is a staple meal made from a flour and water dough, usually by baking. It has been a popular food in large parts of the world throughout documented history and is one of the pioneer human-made foods, having been of great significance since the dawn of agriculture. Processes such as reliance on naturally happening sourdough microbes, chemicals, industrial-produced yeast, or high-pressure aeration can leaven the bread. Commercial bread typically includes additives to enhance taste, texture, color, shelf life, nutrition, and production ease. Food plays an essential role in religious and secular practices. Bread is one of the oldest foodstuffs prepared. Proof from 30,000 years ago showed starch residue on the rocks used for pounding plants in Europe and Australia. Bread is the staple food of Central Asia, Middle East, North Africa, Europe, and in European-derived civilizations such as those in the Americas, Australia, and South Africa, as opposed to the areas of South and East Asia where noodles and rice are the staples. Usually, bread is made from a wheat-flour dough, which is produced with yeast, allowed to rise, and finally baked in an oven. Adding yeast to the bread explains the air pockets, which are usually found in bread. Many wheat species (including spelled, emmer, einkorn, and Kamut) also make bread from the flour. non-wheat cereals containing rye, barley, maize (corn), oats, sorghum, millet, and rice, have been used to produce bread, but generally in conjunction with wheat flour, with the exception of rye, since they have less gluten. Bread is a symbol of essential needs and living conditions at large in many cultures. For example, a "bread-winner" is the major economic contributor to a household and has nothing to do with the actual supply of food.

Therefore, bread is an excellent source of complex carbohydrates, supplying the body with the energy it needs, and playing a significant role in regulating blood glucose levels. Most forms of bread contain low-value vegetable protein that is low in fat. They also contain B vitamins, vitamin E, and trace elements such as iron, potassium, calcium, and selenium, which are highly supplied throughout the body. Vitamin B significantly contributes to the protein metabolism and cell replacement, vitamin E is an active antioxidant, iron is necessary for growth, and cell oxygenation and potassium for healthy cell function. Calcium contributes to bone density, and it is an essential antioxidant to selenium. For a typical worker, his quintessential prodigy is his right equipment and tools, and this is very true in the bakery industry as well. Bread Baking involves delicious and appealing to the masses and thus needs different materials for the same task. The equipment is highly sophisticated and commercialized, particularly for the company bakery compared to those utilized in the houses and for other personal reasons. With the high-tech equipment, several tasks can be completed in the shortest possible time because they give you an advantage over others in this competition, and bakery equipment will complete the job for you with high quality in the shortest time possible.

Bread baking requires scientific techniques and careful measurements of the necessary ingredients in the various baking products. Special utensils are available which measure the number of ingredients used in each baking process. These utensils include preparing the delicious baked produce. Such equipment includes dry cups for weighing, weighing plates, measuring spoons, and cups for measuring liquids.

Chapter 1: Bread – A Staple Food

The staple food is a food that is regularly consumed and in such amounts, as to constitute a dominant portion of a healthy diet for a given person, providing a significant fraction of the energy needs and usually comprising a substantial proportion of the intake of other nutrients. A staple food of a particular society can be consumed as frequently as every day or every meal, and most people survive on a diet based on just a few staples of food. Particular staples vary from place to place, but generally, foods that contain one or more of the macronutrients needed for survival and health are inexpensive or readily available: carbohydrates, proteins, and fats. Typical examples include roots, tubers, plants, legumes, and seeds. Early agricultural civilizations valued the foods that they defined as staples because they are generally suitable for storage over long periods without decay, in addition to providing essential nutrition. Such non-perishable foods are the only potential staples during shortage seasons, such as dry seasons or cold temperate winters, against which harvest times have been stored. Wider variety of foods can be available during seasons of abundance. For thirty thousand years, bread has been a part of the human diet. In the form of carbohydrates and significant nutrients, dietary fibres, and phytochemicals, it provides energy. Yet there's a lot of misunderstandings around bread. Bread is made from grains of cereals such as wheat, rye, and oats, so its nutrient content is primarily determined by the grain content. Bread's nutritional composition depends on whether the meal used to generate the bread is white or whole meal flour, as well as the inclusion of ingredients such as seeds or fat. Approximately half of our daily energy will come from carbohydrates, mainly starches. Therefore bread is a significant component of a healthy and balanced diet along with potatoes, pasta, and rice. Bread contains many proteins, and only small quantities of fat (unless added during production). EU citizens eat an average of 50 kg of bread per person per year, or around 137 g (3-4 slices of white bread) a day. Consumption, however, varies: German and Austrian people consume the most (80 kg per person per year) and the least (less than 50 kg) in Ireland and the UK. Across the UK and Germany, there is a slight but steady decrease across bread consumption (1-2 percent per year).

An ever more popular assumption is that starchy foods, like bread, are causing weight gain. This belief stems from the increasing popularity of high-protein / low carbohydrate diets that are often effective for weight loss in the short run. However, it is the overall lower energy consumption that contributes to weight loss, rather than the avoidance of carbohydrates. A recent systematic analysis showed that intake of whole grain (such as entire meal) bread was not related to weight gain. This study also found a correlation between dietary trends like processed bread and excess abdominal fat (through consumption of primarily white bread may represent a less healthy diet overall). Another common misconception about bread is that it causes bloating. There's no medical evidence to confirm that in healthy people. However, the ingestion of bread (and other foods containing gluten or wheat) can cause gastrointestinal harm and discomfort in conditions such as coeliac disease or wheat allergy. The number of people perceiving themselves to be allergic to wheat (and other foods) is higher than the real incidence. If an allergy or sensitivity is suspected, professional advice should be obtained and checked. Simply cutting foods can lead to less critical nutrient intakes.

Some of the oldest cooked foods dating back to the Neolithic period, the first pieces of bread were flat, made of a grain-paste made of grains and water from the earth. Bread may have been inadvertently produced by cooking or playing with water and grain flour on purpose. Descendants of these early pieces of bread are now made all over the world from different grains. The simple flat slices of bread formed a staple in the diet of many early civilizations with the Samarians consuming a kind of barley flat cake, and the 12th-century B.C Egyptians. Capable of buying flatbread called from the village street stalls.

Leavened bread, too, can be traced back to prehistoric times. Yeast spores happen everywhere. Dough left to rest will obviously be leavened. Leaving uncooked dough revealing to air for some time before baking may harness airborne yeasts. Parts of the ancient world who drank wine instead of beer used as a source of yeast a paste composed of grape juice and flour that was allowed to ferment, or wheat bran steeped in wine. A slice of dough from the day before was used as a kind of sourdough starter.

1.1 Significance of Bread in our lives

As discussed above, bread is a staple diet prepared by baking a flour and water dough. It is famous worldwide, in every household in Ireland and is one of the oldest foods in the world. The nearly endless combinations of various flours and different component proportions have resulted in a large range of forms, shapes, sizes, and textures available around the world. This may be leavened (aerated) during preparation and baking by a variety of different methods ranging from the use of naturally occurring microbes to high-pressure chemical aeration, or it may be left unleavened. It is possible to use a wide range of additives, from fruits and nuts to different fats, to chemical additives designed to enhance taste, texture, color, and shelf life. Bread can be served at every meal of the day in different ways, eaten as a snack, and also used as an ingredient in other culinary preparations. Bread has come to take on significance as a fundamental food worldwide, beyond pure nutrition, transforming into a staple in religious practices, secular cultural life, and language. Over the ages, bread has been a significant staple food commodity to many cultures. In the Bible, it's called the "men of creation." Since the Neolithic period, humans had eaten some sort of bread, when cereals were crushed and mixed with water to sort a thick paste that could be cooked over the fire. Stone processes were used to break and grind various seeds to extract the inedible outer husks and turn the resulting grain into palatable, flexible foods. While bread is an integral part of our lives, we have to select the type of bread we consume carefully. The healthiest pieces of bread are the dense, chewy forms of whole wheat or whole grain flours made from 100 percent stone ground. These pieces of bread are rich in vitamins and minerals. Slices of bread to avoid include all the easy-to-eat 'fluffy' types or any bread made from processed white flour.

Bread deserves an essential place in the diet, as it is inexpensive, low in fat, and provides a variety of nutrients. Bread is one of the pioneer processed foods – and different types include numerous grains, including wheat, spelled, rye, oats, and barley, as well as seeds such as sesame, sunflower, and linseed. Food products also include unleavened flatbreads such as pita and Lebanese pieces of bread, with or without added yeast, roti, chapatti, and pumpernickel food. Researchers at the Institute of Harvard School of Public Health have discovered a correlation between a whole grain-rich diet and the risk of death. Their findings, published in JAMA Internal Medicine in 2015, showed that whole-grain consumption reduced the overall chance of death in both men and women, mainly from cardiovascular disease. "These results further support current dietary recommendations that recommend that the intake of whole-grain also provide encouraging evidence that indicates a diet enriched with whole grains will bring benefits towards extended life expectancy," the authors of the study wrote. Translation: You're good at grains, so fed up.

Feel down? Keep a sandwich. The carbohydrates raise feel-good neurotransmitter serotonin levels in the brain, which improves the mood and curbs cravings for unhealthier treats, including candy. It's a two-for-one deal: you'll raising your anxiety and tension while slimming your waistline too. There are also advantages to all the grains in whole meal bread. These will improve overall health and lead to reducing the risk of obesity and other risks and diseases. "In their original proportions, whole grains or foods made from them contain all of the essential parts and naturally happening nutrients of the whole grain crop. If the grain has been prepared (e.g., broken, crushed, rolled, extruded, or cooked), the food product should have the same rich nutrient balance that is present in the original seed. "Bread is not only a nutritious food to fulfil the human body, but it is also a spiritual food that also speaks to the spirit of a person. For any religion, it is a sign as it is both a way to preserve the body and a reminder of simple blessings. Bread is called life's workers because it's the most basic food which supports life. A tiny slice of bread can provide nourishment when people can't get other foods. Sometimes, the word "food" is used to mean more than just a piece of bread. It has the whole meal in it. How many times did someone tell you, "Let's break bread together"? Of course, the meal was not confined to bread alone.

Some people wondered if human beings would live on only one food item. The question is valid: eating only one thing will likely save a great deal of time and energy, and potentially a lot of money. Plus, several food products pack a strong nutritious punch. Yet none can contribute anything, which is the crucial explanation of why human beings have evolved to consume a varied diet. For example, potatoes theoretically contain all of the necessary amino acids that you need to survive. Yet all of those amino acids are found in such small quantities that you will ultimately fall into several nutritional shortages, even though you ate much more than a day's worth of calories in potatoes. The same applies to bread, but not all sorts are comparable in nutritious slicing. This carb is produced from the combination of grains and water and some kind of microbe, unlike potatoes or rice, which are stand-alone plants. These fungi, yeast, and other forms of bacteria break down the grains, exposing the nutrients that humans would not usually be able to access inside them. The end product, bread, is much more nutritious than its main ingredient, whole grain, as the environmental news source Grist points out. If you compared the nutritional benefits of porridge, which is basically whole grains soaked in water to traditionally made bread, the latter would come out on top because the oatmeal did not go through the fermentation process, which releases vital nutrients from the grains. However, that is if you have made the conventional way of making the bread. Many pieces of dough made today are manufactured with a blend of white flour and commercial yeast — leaving out all the grains and nutrients they have.

1.2 Health Benefits of Bread

Bread is a staple food in many regions and has been consumed for centuries worldwide. Bread is usually made from flour and water dough and is available in many variations, including sourdough, sweet bread, soda bread, and more. Bread is an excellent item to obtain complex carbohydrates that give our body the energy it needs and plays a significant role in balancing blood glucose levels. Some types of bread, such as granary bread, have a high fiber content which strengthens digestive system activity. Most forms of bread have the inferior nutritional value of vegetable proteins and very few fats. They also contain B vitamins – which all lead to protein metabolism and cell replacement. Vitamin E is an efficient antioxidant capable of dissolving clots formed in the blood, including micronutrients such as iron, potassium, calcium, and selenium, which support our health in several different ways. Iron plays an essential role in the growth and oxygenation of cells. Potassium contributes to the proper functioning of the cells. Calcium contributes to the stability of the bones and their overall strength. We also hear "food is making us fat." While it is groundless to incriminate the bread in such a way, bread only leads to weight gain if eaten in large amounts and if it is part of an unbalanced diet. It should also be remembered that, typically, all types of bread contribute to the same amount of calories. When it contains seeds, sesame, and dried fruit, bread can become a little more fattening. Carbohydrates will be about 50 percent in a healthy diet. So long, so carbohydrates don't just come from bread intake, our daily diet can easily include two slices of granary bread per day. People who consume large quantities of calories, like athletes and kids, will consume even more bread. Bread has a long tradition of being a source of nourishing food. Being the oldest known cooked food, it's no wonder that there are many benefits to bread. An integral part of a balanced diet is the protein tucked away in those grains. Regular bread intake prolongs life and can protect our body against growing diseases. People eat bread for years. The origin of bread in the Fertile Crescent region may be closely associated with the beginning of agriculture. Grain was combined with water and pounded to form gruel. The gruel was then baked into simple flaky pieces of bread on hot stones. The gruel was then exposed to microflora and natural yeasts and fermented before baking.

Nutrition for bread varies according to the type of bread you want to consume. Experts on nutrition and health encourage you to increase your whole grain intake, and choosing a whole wheat bread is typically a right decision. A single slice of whole wheat bread prepared commercially provides approximately 82 calories and about 1 gram of fat but may differ by brand. The installment also provides nearly four grams of protein and 13.8 grams of carbohydrate. However, as it also contains around 2 grams of fiber, you can eat just about 9.6 net carbs per slice. Remember, though, if you make a sandwich with two slices of bread, you need to double those nutritional counts. What about other bread styles, then? Commercially made white bread contains approximately 75 calories and 1 gram of fat. White bread is likely to have 15 grams or more of carbohydrate, and because white bread contains less than one gram of fiber, your net carb intake should be about the same. Rye bread may or may not be made of whole grains, depending on the brand you buy. It can also be made from a combination of processed and whole grains. An average slice of rye bread contains 83 calories, approximately 1 gram of fat, 16 grams of carbohydrates, 1.9 grams of fiber, and 2.7 grams of proteins. The brand and bread variety make a difference in calorie count per slice. When you compare various types of bread, you will find that the installment will vary considerably in size and thickness. Also, note that whole grain pieces of bread tend to be higher in calories, but you get the advantage of insoluble fiber that is essential for digestive health and is not absorbed by the body. To you, the healthiest bread depends on your dietary goals. You may aim to minimize your consumption of sugar or increase your daily fiber. Most eaters of bread tend to eat more protein. Use the nutrition label instead of the statements on the front-of-package packaging to direct your decisions.

Bread mainly gives calories (energy) in the form of carbohydrates. Carbs are a natural source of energy in your body. And you provide your body with fuel for your everyday activities when you eat bread. If you want whole-grain bread, you'll also have nutrients for your organization. Fiber offers many advantages in terms of wellbeing and weight loss. Eating fiber foods will make you feel more relaxed and fuller. Experts in weight loss typically suggest dietarians consume fiber foods to help them eat less and build the calorie deficit required for weight loss. This can also be a good source of micronutrients, including thiamine, selenium, and folate, depending on the bread you purchase. On the commercially baked bread that you see in the grocery store, you can see the term "enriched" during processing enriched foods had nutrients added back in. Very frequently, during the manufacturing process, nutrients were stripped away. Enriched goods are typically made from refined grains, or grains processed in such a way that the entire grain is no longer in contact.

Health Benefits of Whole Grain Bread

Whole grains contain all aspects of the original kernel — bran, seed, and endosperm — in the same proportions, says Keri Gans, a New York City registered dietitian. The bran and grain are taken off in processed food. (Look for the word "whole" — either whole grain or whole wheat.) Always make sure that grain is one of the first three ingredients mentioned on the bottle, advises Wesley Delbridge, RD, a spokeswoman for the Academy of Nutrition and Dietetics. A Whole Grains Council stamp on "whole grain" means that there is at least half a serving of whole-grain inside. And don't be fooled by the healthy-looking bread because it's brown. This might only have molasses or brown sugar to color this.

1. Whole grains consist of a lot of fiber

Fiber is one big reason to consume whole grains. Adults need around 25 to 35 grams of fiber each day, and whole grains contain two forms — soluble and insoluble — that are both beneficial to your health. Within two slices of dark rye bread, you can get 5.8 grams of fiber, but just 1.9 grams of the same amount of white bread. So you can get 5.5 grams of fiber per 1/2 cup of uncooked brown rice compared to 2 grams of uncooked white rice (which isn't a whole grain), and just 0.7 in an instant rice serving. As the fiber digests gradually, it also makes you feel more completely longer. And the health benefits of fiber are well known — it may help regulate blood sugar, minimize LDL, or "poor" cholesterol and minimize the risk of colon cancer. However, not all whole grains are fiber-high.

2. They help with digestion.

Whole grains also have other nutritional benefits. The quality of fiber prevents bowel movements routine (studies have shown that people who consume more fiber need less laxative). And they help avoid diverticulosis, the disease that causes inflammation, constipation, diarrhea, and pain in the colon wall. The tissue is responsible for much of the gain, but whole grains also contain lactic acid in the large intestine, which encourages "healthy bacteria." This species aid digestion, facilitate better absorption of nutrients, and can even improve the immune system of the body.

3. They help drive down cholesterol.

Not only do whole grains help prevent the body from absorbing "poor" cholesterol, but they can also reduce triglycerides, both of which are essential contributors to heart disease. Indeed, whole grains, in general, lower the risk of heart disease. One research showed that women who ate two or three servings of whole-grain bread daily were 30 percent less likely than women who ate less than one serving a week to have heart disease or die from heart disease. "Any type of whole grain, including whole wheat bread, brown bread, rye bread, buckwheat, and millet bread, will bring heart health benefits

4. They decrease blood pressure.

With cholesterol and triglycerides, the heart benefits of whole grains don't end. These are also rising blood pressure, which is one of the most significant risk factors for heart disease. One study showed a 19 percent lower risk of hypertension among men who eat more than seven whole-grain bread breakfast cereal servings a week compared to those who consumed one or less. A women's study found a benefit too. "Eating whole grains rather than refined grains significantly lowers blood cholesterol ... triglycerides, blood pressure, and insulin levels.

5. They can help with weight management.

People who eat plenty of whole grains bread are more likely to keep their weight in check than those who eat refined grains and are less likely to gain weight over time. Women who ate the most wheat bread, brown rice, dark bread, and other whole grains in one study had a 49 percent lower risk of "major weight gain" over time compared to women who preferred doughnuts and white bread. Middle-aged men and women who eat a diet high in fiber weighed 3.35 pounds less over the 12 years than those with whom they went for refined products.

6. They hand out the fat.

Even if eating whole grains bread does not make you lose weight, studies have shown that it will help you to minimize the amount of body fat you have and contribute to a proper distribution of that fat. Eating whole-grain bread will leave you with less abdominal fat — what scientists kindly call 'core adiposity' — which raises your risk of diabetes and other health problems.

7. They make you feel full.

One way that whole grain bread can help you maintain your weight is by making you feel more complete than processed grains like cookies or white bread. "It takes whole grains longer to digest and has a more satiating effect," says Gans, who is also the author of The Small Change Diet. It could also help you maintain track of your pieces. To get the optimum fullness, try rye or protein-packed quinoa.

8. They assist in balancing sugar in the blood.

One of the critical advantages of whole grains is that they help prevent your blood glucose from spiking as opposed to refined grains, which can, among other things, raising the risk of type 2 diabetes. In one study, women who consumed two to three whole-grain servings a day had a 30 percent low-level risk of diabetes than women who ate little or no whole grain bread. One analysis resulted in a 32 percent lower risk of diabetes in people who ate three or more portions of whole grain a day versus a 5 percent reduction in those who ate refined grains. Something as easy as exchanging one-third of cooked white rice serving a day (about two ounces) for brown rice was affiliated with a 16 percent decrease in the risk of type 2 diabetes. "It has been proven that eating whole grains has a protective effect against type 2 diabetes, so they are a good selection for people with pre-diabetes or high diabetes.

1.3 Importance of Bread in France

Bread is so incredibly important to the French people that the average Frenchman was estimated to have taken three pounds a day of bread at the time of the French Revolution in the late 1700s. When stocks of bread ran low, or the quality was poor, the result was riots. There have also been improvements in the language that expressed the value of food, according to the English phrase: "to be the food-winner" has become fashionable to flaunt their victories over French territory. In France, as in most other regions of the world, bread making remained a home-based activity mostly well into the middle Ages. Some families around that time, particularly those without their ovens, started taking their dough to small local bakeries to have the dough formed and baked. As towns and villages sprouted throughout the countryside, bakeries flourished, and home baking drastically decreased. These local bakeries had large wood- or coal-heated brick ovens. A long-handled wooden shovel called a "peel" pushed the dough in and out of the ovens. Many small, independent bakeries still employ wood-fired peel ovens. The French are renowned for their crafty bread. Through using the four essential ingredients of water, flour, yeast, and salt, the French perfected the art of making complex, widely varying bread, given the fact that each loaf contains the same ingredient mix. French law specifies that only the four ingredients mentioned above, along with ascorbic acid and rye flour, can be used for "English "- style bread as such. The French bread is as diverse and creative as the regions in France, by controlling rising times, kneading methods, and using specialized brick ovens. The French boule is a loaf in the shape of a heart, ring. It has a golden, crisp crust on the outside and assembled to retain the delicate, chewy inside, by gently hand-kneading. The legislation was passed in 1920, precluding bakers from operating before 4 am. That made it difficult for customers to make the traditional loaf in time for breakfasts. The larger thinner baguette initially produced in the mid-19th century Vienna solved the problem because it could be prepared and baked much faster. It's become a classic French treat. The baguette is rolled by hand into the typical "wall" shape. The crust is a nice, crispy, golden brown one. The interior is lightweight and chewy. Bakeries throughout France are restoring the art of producing French bread in the traditional style. Many are using the old recipes, baked in wood-fired ovens made of brick and stone once more. The numbers involved in this restoration are rising significantly as a result of increasing demand for authentic bread that bears the flavours and aromas of the tradition of the century.

Bread is an integral part of the diet in France and reigns supreme, especially in the baguette. In a way, this simple stick of bread symbolizes France and is a beloved part of French national culture, immediately recognized by foreigners and idolized by the French. It is both a stereotype and a symbol of authentic French. Anthropologist Abdu Gnaba says of the bread, "it is what distinguishes and characterizes the French." So let's look at the humble food element more closely. Here are some interesting facts: In France, 320 baguettes per second are eaten, resulting in a total of 10 billion a year. Ninety-eight percent of the French population consume bread, and 83 percent consume it regularly. They mash 130 g of bread a day, or 58 kg a year! Eighty-six percent of the population finds bread safe, and 82 percent necessary for a balanced diet. Bread is taken so seriously that a statute, le Décret Pain, was passed in 1993, allowing it to be called a "Maison" baguette. The baguette has to be made exclusively at the premises and not carried in from somewhere else.

Additionally, it could not be frozen, nor could it contain preservatives and additives to be considered "traditional." French are very loyal to their favourite bakery, which may not actually be the nearest; they may go a long way to buy what they think is the best bread. Seventy percent of the bread is still made in bakeries rather than in large factories and is plentiful, mostly merely in a small village. A baguette is baked on the outside and crispy, white and smooth on the inside, to be crusty and golden. If pressed, it should spring back into form when fresh, but due to lack of preservatives, it does not last and is meant to be eaten within a day. However, how people want their bread baked is entirely personal, and you'll find various terms being used by customers to pick their baguette when waiting in line to buy bread. Baguette is normally sliced long and grilled when eaten at breakfast. Prepared in such an accessible format, it's called a "tartine." Jam and butter or honey are spread on the tartine in this situation, which is frequently dunked into a hot coffee/tea or chocolate cup. Another favourite way to eat baguette is with a slab of chocolate wedged in the middle or slathered in Nutella, particularly for children on snacks. Bread is so much an important part of French culture that even the word for "mate/pal/boyfriend" word comes from the Latin cum pane (with bread), which means the person you share bread with. Bread is so significant it has a patron saint, and there are processions, tastings, and other festivities throughout the country every year on the feast day of St Honoré on the 16th of May. The fact that there is a Grand Prix de la Baguette is a favourite reminder of how vital bread is. Twice a year, bakers in Paris compete for the title of the best Boulanger that comes with a financial incentive and the coveted contract to supply daily bread for a year to the President of the Republic.

Some, though not all, reputable artisanal bakeries that employ extended fermentation times increase the quality of a French loaf. When yeast ferments to make bread rise, it creates alcohol, producing aromas and flavour. More time to ferment usually enhances the bread flavour. A perfect loaf relies not only on fermentation but also on wheat, flour, and the baker. The first two elements are the meal mill regulated. Local bakeries have reported using 100% French wheat meal certified to be free from insecticides and quality controlled between the fields in which it grows and the mills in which it is processed. The mills comply with the 'red mark' requirement of the French Ministry of Agriculture, which means superior quality-regulated for lack of additives and adulterants (such as soy or bean flours). Just as local climate and soils form terroir that affects the wine's eventual taste, the characteristics of bread flour depend on the local conditions from which wheat is grown. The gamut varies across France. Powders can be reduced to general types (high, medium, and low protein), but the individual taste also depends on local conditions that cannot be quantified. However, to produce excellent bread, it helps to have a fresh meal of high quality.

1.4 Turkish Bread Culture

"Ekmek" or bread, as it is called in Turkish, is fundamental to Turkish culture, and has always been, arguably. For centuries, nomadic Turks ate bread, and bread is an indelible part of Turkish culture and Turkish cuisine. Nearly every meal that you consume is served with fresh bread, so soaking up the juices or oils of another wonderful Turkish meal is also one of its highlights. Bread is made in vast variations of ways and differs throughout Turkey from region to region. Every country, and sometimes every bakery, has its secrets about how to make the perfect bread, and these secrets are passed from generation to generation. There's an emphasis on freshness in Turkey that you'll find in very few other countries around the world, with bakery lines out the door three times a day as the bread is freshly baked for breakfast, lunch, and dinner. Throughout the Ottoman era, it was assumed that Adam was the defender of Bakers after he mastered how to bake from the archangel Gabriel after being exiled from the Garden of Eden. Yet bread touches upon all cultural aspects. This is connecting nourishment between the wealthiest and poorest in society. It is seen as much more than a "meal" but a cultural commodity. It takes on a virtually holy tone and is often respected for the effort that goes into creating it. Indeed, before putting the bread in the oven, bakers would also invoke God's name, and bread naturally takes on even greater significance during religious festivals. Nearly every religious festival in Turkey, Christian, Jewish or Islamic, features its bread types, each baked and flavoured in different ways. Bread is also used as the poor's meal and the soldier's meal. Peksimet, a hardtack type, was the primary source of food for many soldiers during World War I and the Turkish War of Independence. "Ekmek parasi," or "food money," is the term used to tie the notion of food to life itself for the money one lives off. Bread is sold by government-regulated distributors, with state-determined rates, although private bakers are allowed to sell at whatever price they find acceptable. Flatbreads were widely used by central Turkish Anatolian tribes, with loaves of bread spread on top of each other and rolled up to ensure that the inner layers stayed fresh and that only the outer layers were exposed to the sun. Usually baked on what is known as a "sac" in Turkish, a convex iron grid that is either set over a fire or filled with hot coals, these kinds of unleavened bread. Yet Turkey's types of bread are infinite, with the thickness and weight being a vital differentiator. How the bread is rolled out is also determined by the width. Bread is usually rolled on a long wooden rod called an "oklava" in Turkey. They can be made with various amounts of wheat, barley, or corn, and it is relatively common to mix and match these ingredients. Different flours and different seeds are added, and because bread is so prevalent in each meal, they range from bread intended to be filled, used as pastries, or used as loaves.

There is a reason why Turkey and the Anatolian region are regarded as the "world's breadbasket." Turkey yields some of the world's finest and most diverse bread. Bread is a staple diet, eaten all day, from breakfast to dinner, with every lunch and snack time. Each village, town, and city in Turkey has at least one bakery, and loaves, rings, and dough balls are baked at least twice a day, due to its popularity. In Turkey, a meal without bread is not a meal. To the Turks, eating bread has become a cultural ritual; it's just part of their fabric. Bread has always been known as 'peasant food' because it is simple to make, cheap to produce, and very filling. Yet, in Turkey, bread is for everyone. As much as the rich offer bread to the poor and needy, you will find shoppers of bread placed in bags on walls or hanging from windows. In Turkey, bread is of such value that even tossing bread is an offense, and never should you disrespect the food. No food should ever go to waste, and thus to give food to the hungry. Turkey's wealthier people believe you can never waste bread because you may one day be poor and in need of food, regretting the time you have wasted it. You also hear a Turkish saying, "I'm Turkish, I have to have bread, and I'm Turkish, of course." Eating bread is simply a part of their culture, history, blood, and religion. Given that Islam is such a huge part of Turkish society, it is unsurprising that bread has become such a crucial part of life. Before baking bread, before putting it in the oven, the baker must say the word "Bismillah" meaning "In God's Name" When you can see the bread lying on the table, it should be picked up and put where it can't stand, and you can say "Bismillah" too. It is quite a humbling thought to think that every piece of bread you eat in Turkey has been blessed and cooked in the name of God. So the value of bread is very evident in Islam and Turkey. You should value the bread but particularly during religiously important festivals and days. Under Ramadan's fasting month, the holy month, the famous Turkish bread, pride, is baked every day just before sunset, and millions of Muslims across Turkey are going to rush to their local bakeries to catch a loaf of pride for their evening meal. By adding butter, spices, and fragrant herbs, various flavored bread is made for the many feast days in the Islamic calendar. Bread sprinkled with cinnamon, cumin, saffron, sesame, mustard, and watermelon seeds can be found among other decorations during the festivities. Turkey has two main types of bread, leavened bread baked with increasing agents like yeast and unleavened bread, usually flatbreads. The various doughs, made from a variety of wheat and barley, flours, and seeds, are rolled out with a rolling pin known as an oklava to the desired thickness, usually a long thin wood cylinder. Turkish bread is very precise about the width and thickness of the various types of bread, so oklava rolling is an important part of the process of bread making. Then there are the various ways the bread cooks. Some are cooked in a saucepan as in the western world. Most Turkish bread is cooked on what is known as a 'sac,' a convex iron grid filled with hot coals or put over a pit. Another common method of baking bread is in a tandır oven in Turkey. A tandır oven, which was originally used by families in rural villages, is made of clay and would mostly be kept outside the main house and used mainly for baking bread. Today's technique is based on this theory, using clay ovens or metal replicas, and the dough is always stuck to the tandır's inner wall for cooking. Another notable technique is the baking of pebbles. In an oven, a fire is lit, and pebbles are put on the oven floor. The dough is directly backed onto the hot pebbles. This form of baking is particularly common in the eastern region of Anatolia.

1.5 Importance of Quality of Bread

The consistency of meals in the bread-making process depends on the variety of the grain, all agricultural and climatic conditions including harvesting, and the milling process. In most formulations, Flour is the main ingredient. The most important features of flour are as follows: protein content, in particular gluten quantity and consistency, water absorption ability, and diastatic activity. Flour and water kneading gives the dough a compact, viscoelastic mass that retains the gas produced during fermentation. Consequently, flour is responsible for the bread structure. Bread making quality of wheat flour has long been known to rely on both the quantity and consistency of its gluten proteins. The gluten proteins contribute 80–85 percent of the total wheat protein and are wheat's main storage protein. They belong to the class of seed storage proteins prolamin. Gluten proteins are mostly insoluble in the solution of water or dilute the oil. The distinction can be made between two functionally distinct classes of gluten proteins: monomeric gliadins and polymeric (extractable and non-extractable) glutenins. Gliadins and glutens are typically present in wheat in amounts greater or less comparable. Gluten has a distinct amino acid composition, with Glu / Gln and pro containing more than 50 percent of residues of amino acids. Gluten's poor water solubility is attributed to its poor content of residues from Lys, Arg, and Asp, which together account for less than 10 percent of the total residues of amino acids. Around 30 percent of the residues of amino acids in gluten are hydrophobic, and the residues significantly contribute to its ability to form protein aggregates through hydrophobic interactions and to bind lipids and other non-polar substances. The high content of gluten in glutamine and hydroxyl amino acids (around 10%) is responsible for their water-binding properties. Additionally, gluten polypeptide hydrogen bonding between glutamine and hydroxyl residues leads to their properties of cohesion-adhesion. Cysteine and cystine residues account for 2–3 percent of the total amino acid residues and these residues undergo sulfhydryl-disulfide interchange reactions during dough formation, resulting in extensive gluten protein polymerization. It is agreed that the quality of wheat in bread making is linked to the presence and properties of gluten proteins. It has been stated that the gliadin fraction contributes to the viscous properties of wheat dough and its extensibility. For a long time, the gluten fraction of wheat gluten has been seen as having a prominent role in elastic and dough strengthening. The relative proportions of gliadin and glutenin present in dough affect the physical properties of dough, with higher relative proportions of glutenin providing greater strength to dough.

Furthermore, wheat gluten makes other non-food uses possible, such as films based on gluten and molded biodegradable plastics. Glutenins contribute significantly to the elasticity of dough due to their ability to polymerize extensively through sulfhydryl-disulfide exchange reactions, which takes place during dough formation. Moreover, due to their unique structure and functional characteristics, it is incredibly challenging technically to find alternative ingredients that imitate these properties in bread making. The versatility of gluten protein is essential to the quality of bread. Experiments on fractionation and reconstitution clearly show that the gluten proteins are deciding the variations in bread making results. The output of wheat flour bread is linearly related to the content of flour protein and, therefore, to the content of gluten protein, because this protein fraction increases much more than the non-gluten protein fraction with an increased protein content of grains. When kneading flour with water, gluten proteins allow for the creation of a thick viscoelastic dough capable of retaining gas produced during fermentation and oven-rise, resulting in the traditional fixed open foam structure of bread after baking. Although the rheological properties of the dough, which are essential for making bread, are primarily determined by the wheat gluten proteins, gluten protein matrix interactions with other components of the flour, arabinoxylans, non-gluten proteins that affect their rheological properties. Wheat gluten rheological properties may be changed by adding oxidants, reducing agents, or by adding lipids/emulsifiers or hemicelluloses that may alter the interactions between gluten proteins. Changes in baking consistency, known as maturation or 'aging,' can be improved by chemical 'improvers' that change the physical properties of gluten during fermentation in such a way that bread is obtained of better quality. Matured flour differs from freshly milled flour in having better handling properties and increased resistance to varying fermentation conditions in the dough, and in producing larger volume loaves and more okay textured crumbs.

Baking high-quality products require the right combination of baking ability, a well-balanced recipe, excellent ingredients, consistency, and functionality. The flour requirements have been given considerable attention over the years, but water, the essential ingredient, is too often fails to remember and taken for granted. Water is the second more considerable ingredient in a dough system, which makes it as important to the baker as flour. Some of the time we think "water is water" and it can be used in baking as long as it's potable. It's normal to know that bakers don't pay enough attention to their features and how they can impact the consistency of the finished goods.

Nevertheless, a thorough understanding of this ingredient's functionality in baking may reveal that water quality is just as significant as the quality of the flour. The roles of water in cooking are multiple; some are evident; others are often overlooked by the bakers. For baking, water has to be drinkable irrespective of its sources. Standard tap water can commonly be used to make the dough. They are technically speaking. However, the water quality could have some effects on the characteristics of the flour, the characteristics of the bread, and the proper functioning of individual pieces of equipment. When talking about water quality, three aspects must be taken into account: taste, the content of chemicals, and the content of minerals. An odd bad taste or bad smell found in the water may change the final product's flavor. This could happen at certain times of the year, e.g., after heavy rains or during changing seasons, where water supplies and treatments may differ. It is also a common belief that water from some parts of the world will directly affect the taste of the end products. Water can perform several roles throughout the baking process, from mixing to baking the bread, and through to the bread's shelf life. The water's most significant function could be found in dough mixing. Throughout this first step of the baking process, the position of water will be crucial to obtain the desired properties of the dough. The role of the water during mixing is indeed very critical. An edible consistency dough will result in well-finished product characteristics, whereas a too stiff or too soft dough would possibly need some changes during the baking process. Below we have provided a guide that explains five of the essential qualities in a great loaf of bread that you should be searching for. The bread scoring is intended simply to determine its condition.

Crust

Bread is not a bread worth your time, without a sound, crispy crust. Artisan bread in its crust will have a range of colors, varying from dark brown to a soft dark color. This means the best taste experience you'll get.

Air Pockets

Wheat flour is widely used for making bread as it contains two gluten-forming proteins, but some bakers overwork their dough and end up with a little too dense bread. In fresh bread, what you will be looking for is a range of bubble sizes.

Glossy Interior

Not all bread will look wet inside, but inside, a better bread should have a very glossy finish. So when you press your finger into it, it will spring up.

Flavour

You will be able to detect the flavour before you even bite into a piece if a bread bakery claims to make excellent flavored bread. Any decent bread should have a strong flavour, not like eating dirt.

Finish

Though there's no need for a loaf of bread to look beautiful to be delicious, a pretty bread makes eating even more tempting. An excellent finish or glaze should be an indicator of quality, particularly on sweetbreads.

Always sure that you enjoy the bread you eat, above all else. A great loaf of bread does not mean anything unless you enjoy it. This advice will help you select the best of the best for your palate, with some luck.

1.6 Factors and Ingredients Involved in Producing a Good Bread

There's no reason you shouldn't be able to tell the difference between a loaf of bread and a lovely loaf of bread, whether you're a bread friend or someone who just likes a good sandwich. You may wonder how one loaf of bread is different from any other loaf of bread, but any quality bakery will tell you there is a difference. Although you may not be working in a premium bakery, you may be able to test premium bread like the best of them. Those who understand what good bread is agreed on the qualities that should describe it very carefully and make these qualities a criterion by which any kind of bread can be scored or judged. Many who are not able to make bread and those who have had minimal understanding will do well to have their bread examined by experts or to learn how to measure it on their own. By implementing this method, they would be able to figure out their bread's positive and bad points and then be able to make changes by figuring out the causes of any negative quality. For the beginner to know how to judge her bread's values, she will review the corresponding scorecard and its description carefully. A scorecard analysis will show that for appearance, both external and internal, for lightness, and for taste, a certain number of points are granted to a bread loaf. Enable the loaf to cool thoroughly after baking, to decide these qualities best. Then consider the various points and determine how nearly ideal the loaf is to each of them. Add the numbers that are calculated to demonstrate how the bread performs the result obtained.

The loaf's shape should be uniform and symmetrical to be ideal and rank 5. The size of the loaf is calculated from the standpoint of thorough baking, for which a score of 2 is given. The accurate size that a loaf must be is a complicated thing to say, as the sizes differ considerably, but it should be guarded against a loaf of unequal size, as it will not score well. Bread made in already listed size pans would score high in terms of size. The crust, whose combined characteristics rank 8, should be a coloured golden brown to get 2 for its hue. A pale loaf or one too brown baked does not get the full credit. Unless the correct color spreads uniformly over the entire loaf, the bottom and the sides, as well as the top, two more are applied to the crust's score for color uniformity. A slice of bread will be cut off from the loaf after these points are scored so that the remaining positions can be scored. Since fresh bread does not cut easily, and as a well-cut slice is required for this reason, special care must be taken in obtaining the installment. Then sharpen a broad knife and heat the blade slightly by keeping it close to a flame; then cut a slice from the loaf at least 1/2 inch thick until the edge has had time to cool. The character of the crust, by which its hardness or its tenderness is defined, can be calculated with such a slice break. A score of 2 is given when it is of adequate tenderness or lacks toughness. When it is excellent, the depth of the crust, which depends on the amount of baking the loaf has had, gets a score of 2. Long, slow baking provides a deep crust, which is the desired type; bread baked only for a short period has a thin crust, which is not so attractive and does not rank so well.

The lightness of the bread can be scored easily when cutting the bread. It is measured by the size of the holes and earns a score of 20 if it is good. The holes will be small if the bread isn't light enough, and the bread will feel sturdy and inelastic; if it's too thin, the holes will be broad and coarse. There are many characteristics of the internal presentation, which are ranked next. Ten points are given for even gas distribution, which is determined by the uniformity of the holes. If the kneading has been done correctly and the bread has risen properly, the gas will be distributed evenly through the loaf, resulting in the gaps that make the bread brittle throughout the whole loaf being mostly the same. Such a texture is better than a loaf, which has some major and some small holes. The moisture in the bread is measured by pinching a crumb between the fingers, which earns five if it is of the correct amount. The bread is not moist enough if the crumb feels hard and dry, and if it tastes doughy, then the bread is too humid. The flexibility, for which 5 is given, is calculated by gently pressing the finger into a cut position within the loaf. The bread can be known as elastic if it springs back upon removal of the thumb and does not crack or crumble. Bread is often more flexible compared to cake, a trait that is due to the amount of gluten it contains. It should still be recalled that the elasticity must not be hardness, because if it does, the bread consistency will be affected. The inner part of the loaf should be of even, creamy white to score 15 for color. A plain white or grey hue would suggest poor-quality flour was used, and dark or white streaks in the bread would signify irregular mixing and inadequate kneading. The last thing to score, namely the taste, deserves 30 points. Chew a small piece of bread well, to assess this attribute. If it's neither sour nor musty, it has a sweet, nutty taste and shows that the right amount of salt and sugar has been added in the mixture, it can get a perfect score.

Ingredients Involved in Baking a Good Quality Bread

Yeast

Yeast is the origin of a cycle of bread making. It is an essential ingredient that makes the dough rise and gives its excellent taste and aroma to home-baked bread. To complete the reactions, other parts are added, which results in a perfectly baked loaf of sweet, crusty homemade bread. There are thousands of living plant-like microorganisms in every yeast packet. The yeast emits tiny bubbles of carbon dioxide gas when activated by warm air, and is fed by sugar or starch. This gas is what helps the dough rise, and after baking, gain its light texture.

Flour

Wheat is the most common type of meal used in baking bread. This includes all-purpose food, bread flour, and whole wheat flour. Wheat is rich with gluten, a protein that gives dough strength and elasticity. The gluten forms and spreads to create a network that traps the carbon dioxide bubbles created by the yeast when yeast and flour are mixed with liquid, and then kneaded or beaten. Recipes with whole wheat flour have lower gluten content and make loaves denser. That's why these recipes typically need some all-purpose flour that increases the gluten and makes loaves lighter and taller.

Liquids

Water is an essential liquid because it does two vital things: it dissolves the yeast and kills it. It combines to form a sticky and elastic dough with the flour. Milk, buttermilk, sugar, or juice may be added to improve the texture or taste. For a recipe, only warm liquids can be added to dry ingredients because a too cold liquid slows or prevents the movement of the leaves. A liquid that is too hot will kill the yeast and prevent it from growing. If the yeast is dissolved directly in water, the optimal temperature ranges are 100 ° F–110 ° F; if undissolved yeast is added to dry ingredients, 120 ° F-130 ° F.

Sweetener

Sugar adds vibrant brown color and flavour to the crust of a sandwich. We can also use brown sugar, tea, molasses, and jams.

Salt

Salt is an essential ingredient in bread baking, as it slows the increasing time allowing the dough's flavour to develop and adds to the baked product's taste. We do not suggest omitting the salt in the recycling of yeast for better performance.

Eggs

Eggs give nutritional value to the bread, color, and taste. They also help to make the crumb fine and tender to the crust. Eggs add protein and richness. Many recipes include the use of eggs as a wash, which adds color.

Fat

Butter, margarine, shortening, or oil give flavour and soft, moist bread. Fat slows down the loss of moisture and lets the bread remain fresh longer. When using yeast, fat is heated to air. If the recipe calls for it, do not substitute oil for margarine/shortening.

Chapter 2: Fresh, Healthy Bread

Wheat comprises three components in its standard, fresh-off-the plant form: the germ, endosperm, and the bran layer. The germ contains plenty of vitamins and minerals, while the endosperm is filled with carbohydrates and protein. The bran layer (the gross material, think bran muffin) is made of Trusted Source fiber. Whole-grain flours are made by crushing up whole kernels of wheat; white flours must be "stripped" of all the good things before they are sent to the grinder. Manufacturers extract the bran (along with 80 percent of the fiber and most nutrients) to make white flour, then send the stripped grains through the mill. White flours typically get a dose of B vitamins, folic acid, and iron during processing; this fortification phase eliminates some of the missed nutrient content, but other beneficial compounds, including antioxidants and phytonutrients, are still lacking in the flour. On the other side, wholesome-grain flours are made by grinding the whole kernel. Whole-grain flour retains much of the nutrients that started with the crops. Whole-grain flours also have a lower glycemic index than refined flours, which means they don't increase blood sugar as immediately or as much as they do. According to reputable sources such as the Harvard School of Public Health, products with a higher glycemic index raise the risk for type 2 diabetes and heart disease. Healthy "bread doesn't have to be crumbly and dry. Having a" soaker "for the dough will enhance the texture and even taste. That's when bakers soak all of the flour in liquid before mixing it with the other ingredients. Some whole grain flours are better suited for baking bread than others, particularly if you choose to bake wholly or mainly with entire grains.

2.1 Sprouted Whole Grain Bread

Sprouted bread is produced from whole grains that have initiated to germinate from heat and moisture exposure. Sprouting has been shown to increase the number of certain nutrients and their availability. One study found that pita bread made from 50 percent sprouted wheat flour had more than three times as much folate as pita made without sprouted wheat flour, a vitamin essential to turning food into energy. Studies show that sprouting also increases the antioxidants of grains while reducing anti-nutrients, or compounds that bind to minerals such as iron and block their absorption. Moreover, this cycle breaks down some of the starch in grains and diminishes carb content. Sprouted grains also do not increase blood sugar as much as other grains, making them a safe option for people with diabetes or a decreased regulation of blood sugar. Plus, most sprouted bread is high in protein and fiber. They are, as such, more satisfying than refined bread. Sprouted Whole-Grain Bread offers one slice (34 grams). It contains 80 calories, Protein: 4 grams, Fat: 0.5 grams, Carbs: 15 grams, Fiber: 3 grams. Sprinkling helps to increase the sum of such nutrients and their availability. Bread made from sprouted whole grains are high in fiber, vitamins, and minerals and can affect blood sugar less than other bread.

Everything you might think of like a plant, though, really is a seed. With proper humidity and temperature, whole grain seeds start sprouting into a plant. Compared to bread made from unsprouted grains or plant flours, the sprouting process provides many nutritional benefits.

The sprouting also improves the grains 'nutritional profile, making their nutrients more readily available and likely easier to digest. Sprouted grain bread is nutritionally similar to bread made from whole-grain flours, as they use the whole grain. All kinds of bread are superior to refined wheat bread. Levels in fiber and nutrients are naturally higher, but white flour is also supplemented with vitamins and minerals to reimburse for what is lost during processing. The sprouted grain bread most sometimes contain a mix of whole grains and legumes. Bread is baked from sprouted wheat, barley, lentils, and soybeans. So this type of bread gives you a wider variety of nutrients than whole wheat bread alone. Moreover, the combination of grains with legumes makes the protein full in sprouted grain bread, meaning it contains all nine essential amino acids. The body also becomes easier to use. Sprinkling partly breaks down the starch in the grains, reducing the carb content. One research found that sprouted grain bread had the lowest available carbs, serving 34 grams in a 4-ounce (110-gram) versus 44 grams in a 12-grain loaf. What's more, sprouted grain bread had the lowest glycemic index compared to 11-grain, 12-grain, sourdough or white bread, thanks to its lower carb and higher fiber quality. The Glycemic index is a calculation of how rapidly a diet increases blood sugar. Sprouted grain bread is a particularly good option for people with diabetes or high blood sugar, for this reason. Additionally, during the sprouting process, the grains absorb water, rendering sprouted grains lower in calories than whole grain flours. It could help you lose weight by substituting sprouted grain bread for other forms of bread. Sprouted grains are higher in some nutrients compared with other types of bread, including protein, fiber, B vitamins, and vitamin C. The cycle of sprouting, produces more of these nutrients and also eliminates anti-nutrients which are substances that obstruct nutrient absorption. Studies have shown that whole-grain sprouting is correlated with greater digestibility. The cycle of sprouting breaks down the starch in the grains, making it easier to digest them because they are already partly pre-digested. What's more, they are richer in enzymes than unsprouted grains that help absorb the food you consume from your body. The phytase and amylase enzymes particularly increase during sprouting. Nonetheless, during a high-heat baking process, these enzymes can get deactivated. Therefore some sprouted bread is cooked to retain these enzymes at lower temperatures. A compound called lectin is another substance that affects digestibility. Lectins are a part of the defense mechanism of a plant. Grains are usually rich in lectins related to leaky intestine, chronic inflammation, and autoimmune disease. The plant metabolizes lectins, like seed sprouts. Therefore sprouted grains in lectins can be lower compared to their unsprouted counterparts. One study found that leptin levels in wheat fell by about 50 percent after 34 days of sprouting. To find sprouted grain bread these days are fairly easy. It's available on the market for your local farmers, in a natural food store, or even in a daily grocery store. Most sprouted grain bread can be found in the section of the fridge or freezer. Sprouted grain bread appears to be denser and heavier than flour-made bread, so if you're looking for soft, fluffy bread, it won't fit the bill. It is great for making toast, though. When it's toasted, you might not even note the difference in texture.

2.2 Sourdough Bread

Sourdough is one of the oldest fermentation types of cereals. It is thought to have originated around 1,500 BC in ancient Egypt and remained the standard method of leavening of bread until it was replaced by baker's yeast some centuries ago. Leavened bread is a type of bread whose dough rises as a result of the gas being created as the grain ferments during the bread-making process. Most leavened bread uses industrial baker yeast to assist the rise of the dough. Traditional sourdough fermentation, however, relies on "wild yeast" and lactic acid bacteria, which naturally occur in flour to leaven the bread. Wild yeast avoids acidic conditions more than baker's yeast. That is what helps it to work with lactic acid-producing bacteria to help lift the dough. Sourdough is produced by a fermentation cycle that depends on naturally occurring yeast and bacteria to lift the bread. Fermentation helps to reduce the number of phytats that bind to certain minerals and inhibit their absorption, also known as phytic acids. One study found that fermentation with sourdough helped to minimize phytate content by over 50 percent compared to traditional yeast use. Sourdough may also be simpler to digest than other bread, likely due to its prebiotics and the probiotics that were produced during the fermentation process.

Probiotics are healthy bacteria discovered in your body and some foods, while prebiotics is non-digestible fibers that feed these bacteria. Having enough of each one promotes a balanced gut and digestion.

Sourdough can be made with white and whole-wheat flours. Although growing offers the fermentation-related benefits, whole-wheat sourdough has more fiber, iron, and other nutrients.

Many other fermented foods contain lactic acid bacteria, including yogurt, kefir, pickles, sauerkraut, and kimchi. The mixture of wild yeast, lactic acid bacteria, flour, and water used to produce sourdough bread is called a "starter." The starter leavens the sugars in the dough during the bread-making process, allowing the bread to rise and develop its characteristic flavor. Sourdough bread must ferment and grow much longer than other types of bread, which is what produces its unique texture. The making of sourdough bread remains popular in Mediterranean and Middle Eastern countries, as well as in the US area of San Francisco Bay to this day. Some store-bought sourdough bread is not made using the conventional sourdough process, so their health benefits are diminished. Buying sourdough bread from a farmer's market increases the probability that it will be "real" sourdough bread. While sourdough bread is mostly made from the same flour as other bread types, the fermentation process enhances its nutritional profile in several ways. For example, whole-grain bread contains a large number of minerals, including potassium, phosphate, magnesium, and zinc. The absorption of these minerals is sadly impaired by the presence of phytic acid, commonly known as phytate. Phytates are considered anti-nutrients because they bind to minerals, which reduces the ability of your body to absorb them. Interestingly, the bacteria of lactic acid found in sourdough bread lower the pH of the bread, which helps to degrade phytats. This results in a bread with a considerably lower phytate content than other bread types. One study found that sourdough fermentation could reduce bread's phytate content by 24–50 percent more than traditional fermentation with yeast. Higher levels of phytate improve mineral absorption, which is one reason that sourdough bread is more nutritious than regular bread. Besides, studies have shown that the lactic acid bacteria found in sourdough bread are capable of releasing antioxidants during sourdough fermentation. Sourdough fermentation also raises folate levels in the bread, although some nutrient levels, such as vitamin E, maybe slightly decreased during the process. Finally, the longer fermentation duration of sourdough helps enhance the taste and texture of whole-grain bread. This could make people more likely to go for a whole grain bread, thereby encouraging higher fiber and nutrient-rich bread consumption. Sometimes, sourdough bread is easier to digest than fermented bread with brewer's yeast. Scientists think this may be due partly to the prebiotic nature of sourdough bread and probiotic-like properties. Prebiotics are non-digestible fibers that feed into your gut's beneficial bacteria, while probiotics are beneficial bacteria contained in certain foods and supplements. Eating both frequently will help improve your bowel health and ease digestion. Sourdough fermentation can also cause greater degradation of gluten than baker's yeast. Gluten is a kind of protein established in certain cereals. It may cause digestive problems in persons sensitive to it or allergic to it. Gluten tolerance varies across individuals. Others may not have obvious problems digesting gluten, while in others, it may cause stomach pain, bloating, diarrhea, or constipation. The lower gluten content of sourdough bread can make it easier to tolerate for people who are sensitive to gluten. Research has shown that the process of sourdough fermentation can also help enhance the gluten-free bread's flavor, texture, and nutrient quality. For people prone to gluten, this makes gluten-free sourdough bread a possible choice. Bear in mind. However, that sourdough fermentation does not fully degrade gluten. People who are unable to tolerate gluten or celiac disease should avoid sourdough bread, which contains wheat, barley, or rye. Sourdough bread can have a greater effect than other forms of bread on blood sugar and insulin levels, but the explanation for this is not yet completely understood.

Researchers assume that fermentation with sourdough may alter the structure of carb molecules. It reduces the glycemic index (GI) of bread and slows down the rate at which sugars enter the bloodstream. The GI is a function of how blood sugar influences a diet. Foods with less GI are less likely to produce a spike in blood sugar. Additionally, the lactic acid bacteria present in the dough during fermentation produce organic acids. Some researchers suggest these acids can help prolong the emptying of the stomach and, like vinegar, avoid a spike in blood sugar. The method of sourdough fermentation is also used to produce rye bread because rye does not contain enough gluten to work effectively with the baker's yeast. One research found that participants who ate rye bread had a lower spike in levels of insulin compared to those who got the same amount of traditional bread. Additionally, several other studies measured the glucose response of participants after consuming sourdough bread and fermented bread with baker's yeast. Overall, people who ate the sourdough bread had lower levels of blood sugar and insulin than those who ate the fermented bread with baker's yeast.

2.3 100% Whole Wheat

Whole grains retain all grain, including the germ, endosperm, and bran, intact. The bran, the hard, outer layer, is fiber-high. The bran also contains protein, fat, minerals, vitamins, and beneficial plant compounds, while the endosperm is mainly starch. That is why whole grains, like whole wheat, have higher fiber content and are recognized as healthier than refined grains, which have been formulated to extract bran and germ.

Whole grains have been linked with various health benefits, including a decreased risk of type 2 diabetes, heart disease, and several cancers.

This is important to remember, however, that many manufacturers mark "whole wheat" bread so that they appear healthier, even though they are mainly made from a refined meal. Search for bread that is specified as their first ingredient with 100% whole-wheat or whole-grain flour and do not sneak unnecessary elements such as added sugars or vegetable oil. You can add wheat to any carbohydrate literally, and mark it as a wheat product. You can get whole wheat lucky charms these days-do you believe this makes them healthy? If it is not 100 percent whole wheat, the bread will contain enriched flour, giving you a spike of sugar and a crash with no nutritional value at all. Enriched flour practically means nutrients are stripped off the bread.

2.4 OAT Bread

Oat bread usually consists of a mixture of oats, whole-wheat flour, yeast, water, and salt. Since oats are highly nutritious and are associated with many health benefits, oat bread can be a healthy choice. Oats are exceptionally high in fiber and beneficial nutrients, which include magnesium, vitamin B1 (thiamine), iron, and zinc. The fiber in oats, known as beta-glucan, can contribute to lower cholesterol levels, control blood sugar, and lower blood pressure. A study of 28 studies showed that consuming 3 grams or more of beta-glucan oat a day significantly reduced levels of LDL (bad) and total cholesterol relative to consuming no oats. The study also found that beta-glucan in oats had more potent cholesterol-lowering effects in people with higher baseline cholesterol rates. Only because bread has "oats" or "oatmeal" on its label does not mean it's safe, however. Most oat bread contains just a small amount of oats, and often consist of processed flours, added sugars, and oils.

To vary the diet of patients with celiac disease, oats may be integrated into different food goods. Oats alone is unsuitable for a conventional method of bread making, and the majority of commercial oat bread contain large quantities of wheat flour. In commercial oat bread, the protein network is also strengthened with added gluten. But most of the oat bread currently available are ineffective for patients with celiac disease. However, it is possible to make gluten-free oat bread by using a novel baking technique. Typical, gluten-free bread is starch dependent. The starch bread also lacks cereal flavor, and are weak in providing gluten-containing bread' palatable crumb structure. When oats are combined with other gluten-free ingredients, they can achieve a desirable aroma and taste as well as texture. While often used as whole-grain flakes or flour, oats have a mild, nutty flavor. Recently, baking technology has been further advanced for 51–100 percent oat bread, and the first products have already been marketed. Whole-grain oats may be used to enhance bread taste, as they give the food a pleasant, nutty flavor. Many commercial oat bread only contains a small number of oats, 5–15%. Oats are commonly used as rolled oats in baking, and in bread baking, only a few reports have been reported on oat flour. Oats, as well as other fiber-rich whole grains, are usually harmful to the consistency of the bread.

Dilution of wheat gluten and mechanical disturbance by bran particles in the gluten network decreases the amount of loaf. The use of added gluten or baking enzymes will compensate for at least some of the adverse effects of whole-grain flour on gluten growth. It has been shown that adding gluten improves the structure of mixed oat bread, and transglutaminase has been shown to enhance the protein network in baking oats. The texture's flavor and durability can be improved by using sourdough, which contains yeast or lactic acids.

Oats keep back the staling of bread. This is possibly due to slower oat starch retro gradation and higher water-binding ability of oat flours compared to wheat flours. Oat bread containing 51 percent whole grain oats with decent crumb and crust flavor and texture can be baked by optimizing the process and recipe.

Throughout baking of oat bread, the molecular weight of β-glucan oat decreases. It was due to the presence of endogenous β-glucanases in wheat flour. This would result in lower viscosity without counteracting improvements in insolubility. Considering that high viscosity is considered a key factor in lowering blood cholesterol, optimization of the formula and baking process is required to maintain the health benefits of bread oats. In vitro methods have been developed for predicting the possible gastric viscosity following oat food consumption. In the Netherlands, a bread enriched with oat bran has been introduced to reduce cholesterol. The most visible microstructural alteration that happens during baking is starch gelatinization, while often, the oat starch aggregate structure remains evident in the bread. The level of starch swelling (and amylose leaching) depends heavily on the dough's water content. The starch granules are more bloated, with higher water content, and amylose leaches out. Oat flour is a gluten-free type of whole-grain meal made of whole oats ground into a powder. Oat flour brings more flavor to the baked goods than standard all-purpose flour, but it also brings them a texture that is chewier and crumblier. Since oat flour is gluten-free, you can't substitute it with all the meal in baked goods that need gluten aid for slow-growing, including yeast bread. In a bread recipe, you can replace oat flour with up to about a quarter of the flour, and also raise the amount of yeast in the recipe slightly to help the bread rise. Oat flour is an excellent used in baked goods, such as quick bread and cookies, which do not require gluten to grow.

2.5 Flax Bread

Flax is a fiber and food crop grown in Europe, Asia, and the Mediterranean. Flaxseeds reflect the golden yellow to reddish-brown flax seeds. Such seeds contain phytoestrogens as well as soluble fiber and oil, which are similar to the hormone estrogen. Flaxseed oil contains alpha-linolenic acid (ALA), an essential omega-3 fatty acid. Since 5000 BC, flaxseed was eaten as a meal or used as a medicine. People use mouth-- flaxseed for constipation, colon damage from overuse of laxatives, diarrhea, inflammation of the large intestine lining (diverticulitis), irritable bowel syndrome (IBS) or irritable colon, sores in the large intestine lining (ulcerative colitis), inflammation of the stomach lining (gastritis), and inflammation of the small intestine (enteritis). People also take flaxseed by mouth, which is used for heart and blood vessel disorders, including cardiac failure, high triglyceride rates, high cholesterol, "hardness of the arteries" (atherosclerosis), high blood pressure, coronary artery disease, and metabolic syndrome.

Flaxseed is often taken by mouth for acne, attention deficit-hyperactivity disorder (ADHD), kidney disorders in people with a disease called systemic lupus erythematosus (SLE), menopause symptoms, breast pain, diabetes, obesity, and weight loss, HIV / AIDS, insomnia, malaria, rheumatoid arthritis, sore throat, upper respiratory tract infections (URTI), and cough, bladder inflammation, swollen pro It's also taken by mouth to avoid hemodialysis-related problems. Occasionally, flaxseed is applied to the skin for acne, burns, swelling, eczema, psoriasis, and inflammation soothes. One of the healthiest bread you will consume is flax bread, made mainly from whole-grain flours and flax seeds.

This is because seeds made from flax are highly nutritious and deliver a range of health benefits.

They are primarily an excellent source of alpha-linolenic acid (ALA), an omega-3 fatty acid found in plant foods. A comprehensive analysis of 27 studies showed that high dietary ALA intake was associated with a lower risk of heart disease. Moreover, flax seeds contain compounds called lignans that can act in your body as antioxidants and can help protect against some cancers. In fact, one research in 6,000 postmenopausal women indicated that those who regularly ate flax seeds had an 18 percent lower risk of breast cancer than those who did not eat them. Interestingly, those who consumed flax bread were 23 percent less likely than those who did not eat it to get breast cancer. It's important to remember, though, that this research has been observational. More work is required to understand the relationship between flax seeds and the risk of cancer. Nevertheless, consuming flax bread and other flax seed foods may have additional benefits, such as better digestive health. Check out flax bread made with minimal ingredients, such as whole-wheat and sprouted whole-grain flours, yeast, and water, salt, and flaxseed. Fish oil and oily fish are usually the best food and animal source for heart safe Omega-3 fatty acids, respectively. But this is not a choice for vegans (i.e., animal by-products are a no-go). And flax seeds are. So it's a no-brainer bread with flaxseed is a perfect alternative to your daily loaf. Research shows that flaxseed and flax bread will reduce the risk of booting from heart disease, cancer, stroke, and diabetes.

2.6 Sprouted Rye Bread

Sprouted rye stands out among sprouted plants, and not just because of its dark color. Wheat has a weaker type of gluten, one with less elasticity and protein than other grains.

The flexibility of the sprouted rye and ample nutrients make it a perfect match in most diets, but if you cannot handle gluten, you should avoid that.

Sprouted rye produces less gluten than sprouted wheat. Within its endosperm, it also stores a large amount of fiber, which makes it difficult to separate the bran and the germ. The high fiber and heavy seed coat of rye make it possible to ground it whole, which, when combined with shorter gluten strands, produces a denser bread with more nutrients by weight than bread made from other sprouted grains. The flour soil from sprouted rye has more vitamins and minerals, and higher protein content than the flour soil from unsprouted rye. According to the UC Davis Center for Health and Nutrition Research, sprouted grains can have higher levels of amylase — an enzyme that helps break down starch — than unsprouted grains, so foods made from them may be easier to digest. Though amylase is present in wheat, it is denatured by heat and inactivated.

On the other hand, the amylase in rye stays active during baking, and when you eat rye bread, you absorb more available amylase than when you eat wheat bread. Not only does amylase break down the starch you ingest, but it also breaks down the starch in the bread that contains it; that's why most rye bread mixes wheat and rye flour. Bread made from sprouted rye needs a structural boost, either from flour with healthier gluten, or from extra protein. Sprouted rye has less protein than other sprouted grains, and its gluten in wheat bread does not have as much strength as gluten. You can combine three sprouted-rye parts with 1 part of the wheat flour while making bread with sprouted-rye flour, or add one tablespoon of whey protein concentrate for each cup of sprouted-rye meal.

Ezekiel Bread

Ezekiel's bread is healthy bread. It is a type of sprouted bread, made from a variety of whole grains and legumes which have begun to germinate (sprout).

Ezekiel bread is much richer in nutritious nutrients and fiber than white bread, which is made from processed wheat flour. For several reasons, the bread of Ezekiel is different. While most forms of bread contain added sugar, there is none in Ezekiel bread. It is also made from organic whole grains, which are sprouted. The sprouting cycle substantially modifies the nutrient composition of the grains. Unlike other commercial bread, which consists mostly of refined wheat or pulverized whole wheat, Ezekiel bread includes different varieties of grains and legumes: 4 varieties of cereal grains: wheat, millet, barley, and spelt. 2 Legumes, lentils, and soybeans. All the grains and legumes are riped organically and allowed to sprout before being processed, mixed, and baked to create the final product. Wheat, barley, and spelt all contain gluten, and for people with celiac disease or gluten allergy, Ezekiel bread is out of the question. Although grains such as wheat or corn look outwardly basic, they contain incredibly complex molecular machinery. There are chromosomes, proteins, and enzymes capable of transforming a tiny seed into a whole plant. When the grain receives the right signals, it starts a complex biochemical process. The seed begins to germinate, bursts through the shell, and sends sprouts into the air as well as root into the soil. Eventually, it turns into a plant, with enough water and nutrients in the soil. Somewhere between becoming a seed and a full-fledged plant, a sprouted seed is. Yet one thing you need to bear in mind is that the seed does not sprout unless the conditions are favorable. It will start to sprout, by giving the seed the right signals, primarily hydration (water) and the right temperature. Grains and legumes are simply no exception. Most plants produce chemicals that discourage the eating of animals. Some of these have an anti-nutrient function. Anti-nutrients are substances that can impede nutrient absorption and inhibit digestive enzymes. Soybeans are one such example. They are toxic when raw, because of enzyme inhibitors. Given the fact that most grains and legumes are edible after cooking, cooking does not remove all the negative nutrients. Most non-industrial communities around the world have had no trouble consuming grains. Most of them, however, used conventional preparation methods such as boiling, sprouting, fermenting, and cooking to minimize anti-nutrient counts substantially. While in most people, anti-nutrients do not adversely affect health; they can lead to the lack of vitamin and mineral in people who rely on legumes or grains as a staple diet. Bear in mind that anti-nutrients are not inherently harmful, either. For example, phytic acid is a strong antioxidant which contributes to the beneficial effects of grains and seeds on the health. Several supermarkets and organic food stores are selling Ezekiel bread. By following one of the many recipes listed in this book, you can make your own too. It is, therefore, important to note that wheat is still the ingredient number one in Ezekiel bread. Although sprouting can slightly decrease gluten levels, people with gluten sensitivity need to avoid Ezekiel bread and other forms of sprouted bread containing wheat, barley, or rye. When you are not immune to gluten and are not on a carb-restricted diet, then Ezekiel's bread may be a better option. It's much healthier than 99 percent of the bread on store shelves, which are typically made from processed wheat and also have lots of sugar in them.

2.7 Gluten-Free Bread

Simply put, gluten is a sort of protein found in wheat, rye, and barley. Most frequently, you see this in cereals, bread, and seeds. Gluten is useful for preserving intact elasticity in food when it is fermenting.

Some bakers do use gluten in their bread, as it helps top stick together food items and is chewier.

Demand for gluten-free bread continues to grow, but a slice of gluten-free bread is not safer than a slice of whole-wheat, contrary to common belief. Probably, when you have an allergy, it's best to put the gluten-free bread on the shelf. The store-bought alternatives are mostly made with processed gluten-free grains such as rice flour, cornstarch, and potato flour (meaning they are deprived of fiber and nutrients). They're also strong on the glycemic index, are just as carb-heavy as their counterparts full of gluten, and are sometimes more costly. Gluten inculpation benefits raise cholesterol levels, encourages digestive health, increases energy levels, remove unhealthy and refined foods from your diet (oils, fried foods, bread, and sweets, to name a few). More likely to consume fruits and vegetables as they are all gluten-free. It also decreases the risk of heart disease, other diseases, and diabetes helps avoid influenza and diabetes.

Gluten-free bread, including wheat, rye, or barley, is made without gluten grains. To those wanting to avoid gluten, such as those with celiac disease or gluten allergy, they are a healthy choice. Although the exact ingredients in gluten-free loaves are dependent on the form, they are usually made from a combination of gluten-free flours, such as brown rice, almond, coconut, tapioca, potato, or corn flours. Many wrongly believe that gluten-free bread is safer than gluten-containing ones. Most gluten-free varieties, however, are made from processed flours and high in added sugars, and other needless additives. Some made of almond or coconut flours, such as Barely Bread, tend to be lower in carbohydrates and calories but higher in fiber and protein than wheat or other grain loaves. The higher content of fibers and proteins in these items will help you fill up more than other bread while packing fewer calories and less starch.

Chapter 3: Homemade Bread Baking

Saving money is the most obvious excuse to make your bread- but that's far from the only excuse. Home-baked bread can also be much more tasteful, nutritious and easier to customize to your personal needs. Added to that is the joy of baking. Mixing and kneading can be strangely soothing, and slicing into a fresh-boiled loaf you've made with your own hands is something really rewarding.

According to the Statistics of Bureau Labor, a one-pound loaf of white bread costs around $1.30 at the grocery store. Whole-wheat bread, at about $2 a sandwich, is a little pricier. And if you like seven-grain, sourdough, or cinnamon-raisin fancy breads, you might pay as much as $4 per loaf. Cooking your own bread will drastically cut those costs.

All told, the bread ingredients cost us $1.92 for a recipe which makes two loaves. We're just using a little bit of energy running the oven for an hour, which adds around $0.12 extra to the bill. But with that premium, our homemade bread only costs only $1 a loaf – around half of the store's price for whole-wheat bread. Perhaps you think a dollar isn't all that cheap for a loaf of bread.

After all, you can pick up a store-brand loaf of white bread for about that price at most major supermarkets. And why do you have to go to the trouble of making your own? Imagine a single slice of the one-dollar loaf out of the supermarket to understand why. It's essentially a small, pale sliver, with little substance.

It seems like it weighs less than a single sheet of paper when you pick it up in your pocket. If you pinch your fingers while holding them together, they will go directly through it.

A piece of our homemade whole-wheat bread is nothing like that wimpy, fluffy stuff. It's a chewy, hearty bread you can really sink your teeth into. It is full of nutty, yeasty, whole-grain flavour, with a hint of honey sweetness. And unlike the store-bought stuff, if you try to spread some peanut butter over it, it doesn't fall apart under your knife. Bread should, of course, be purchased at the supermarket with more substance than those squishy, mass-produced loaves. But the good stuff cost a lot more – something like four or five bucks a loaf – so you still have a trade-off between good taste and good price. You get both with home-baked bread. Plus, as a bonus, when it's fresh and warm from the oven, you can enjoy it - a luxury that no supermarket bread will ever offer.

3.1 Concept of Homemade Bread

Living healthy life is really so simple and many of the new bread methods can do all of the bread recipes really easily with minimal effort from you, which is what your family can call you when you serve this up in the midst of beautiful fresh bread smells tickling their noses. Homemade bread is so much more tasteful than store-bought bread, it's not filled with preservatives, and it's straightforward to produce, and it doesn't take too much time, either. Who knows what the store-bought bread really does anyway? We all know that the government is stuffing its pockets with money made from genetically engineered foods that make us sick, and all the new gluten-free goods are now out. Bread usually gets a bad name, as grains are not easy to digest for your body these days. We hear too much about gluten-free foods so we need to ask ourselves if homemade bread is safer for us and better. Well, in this world, a lot of the wheat crops are being genetically engineered to make more money for the people in the food industry but end up harming the general public. Thankfully, we are starting to be more health-conscious and tend to see what we eat, rather than trusting a list of ingredients on the packaging.

Homemade bread is like no other, and here are a few reasons why you should make your bread if you want to save money and eat healthily. When you find it very cheap to buy a loaf, this is a contentious issue.

Yet given its price, cheap bread isn't really such a good buy. Loaded with additives and salt, this cheap, mass-produced bread is far from attractive, and even though you invest in a bread maker instead of baking it by hand, the expense of the bread you regularly bake will soon be recouped as what you turn out to be of far good quality than what you would purchase in the supermarkets.

Take a look at your kitchen's list of ingredients on the bread side. Along with the anticipated flour, yeast, etc., you'll see items described as emulsifiers, typically accompanied by a few long terms that make little sense to anyone, preservatives, and agents of care. Commercial bread on the market needs a lot of preservatives in order to keep it from being dry and moldy. You can purchase more expensive bread that looks higher quality but the fact is that there are still some preservatives in packaged bread. Cook your own bread so you know exactly what's going into it and you can trust in the knowledge that you're offering the best bread you can to your skin. Some of the biggest challenges with bread is that in the shortest period of time, farmers want to produce as much bread as possible. That's what makes the bread more competitive. They cut the time involved to do this by using stuff like dough conditioners (such as azodicarbonamide, the popular ingredient that is also used to make yoga mats) that are linked to various health issues. Home-baked bread can also give more nutrients and less additives than the breads manufactured commercially. The USDA recommends at least 3 oz for consumption of regular whole grains. Commercial bread labels may lead you to believe that they contain more whole grains than they actually do. You should be assured of the amount of whole grains used in the recipe when you cook bread at home. When you suffer from serious food allergies, you should customize your bread recipes to leave offending ingredients out. Also manufactured breads that may not contain the allergen may have been generated on contaminated equipment. Cooking your own bread eliminates almost all cross-contamination possibilities. Many people cannot eat ordinary bread due to food intolerance, such as those with celiac disease, cannot eat anything with gluten. Such specialist products are hard to find and costly to purchase, so making your own is the best way to do so. There are many recipes of bread discussed in the book, and it is easy to adapt the recipes to miss out the gluten. Anyone on a low carb diet would be able to find a recipe for bread that they can adapt to their needs, too; in reality, there is a bread that fits the nutritional needs of everyone. You will have all seen specialist bread for special occasions, and these are invariable expensive. The truth is that they are typically as easy to make as any other bread, and because of budget constraints, you don't have to limit your options by making your own. For example, Stollen is very popular at Christmas, and the homemade recipes for this most delicious bread that originated in Germany mean you can treat yourself to one of the world's best bread.

Walking into a home and smelling bread baking gives you an excellent feeling, which is known to be found in houses that are not being sold by agents of the estate. Homemade bread provides one of the most tempting smells you'll find along with freshly grounded coffee, and feeling good is much more critical than just looking good. You can control the ingredients when you bake your baked bread. You can add elements like flax seeds or quinoa (yes, actually) or oatmeal as you wish. High-quality flours can be picked, and sugar content controlled and what sweetener is used. You may also opt to use less sodium purchased at homemade bread vs. supermarket. When using 100 percent whole wheat flour or other whole-grain flours, you can make a heartier, healthier bread. Whole wheat flour consists of more nutrients and fiber than a processed white meal.

One of the best is the scent of freshly baked bread – there's a reason it's used to selling houses and making you overspend in the supermarket. But it is not just the beautiful fragrance that will inspire you at home to bake it. It's simpler than ever, as you can turn over all the hard work with features such as a 55-minute fast-bake option and a 13-hour delay timer for those tempting loaves early in the morning. Your own bread is also much closer to your wellbeing, above all.

If you've ever looked at the list of ingredients mentioned on a supermarket bread loaf, you're probably going to see some that you don't know. This may include emulsifiers and additives to help make it bake faster, and preservatives to give it a longer shelf life. Bake your own, and you can only use the necessary ingredients and play with a range of flours outside wheat, including rye or spelled. Homemade bread is incredibly adaptable, meaning you can fill it with almost anything you want. Whether you're trying to eat more fruit or cut out gluten, you can cater for your nutritional needs without scouring the shelves for an expensive specialist loaf. And if you don't have time to show and knead the bread yourself, as most of us do. Only safe supermarket bread can be fat-filled to as much as 10.3 g per 100 g. Baking your own provides a very good opportunity to substitute or totally eliminate the saturated fat for healthy fats, such as olive oil. Great news if you're trying to lose weight but still want bread to be a part of your diet. It's not always easy to incorporate a variety of seeds into meals, so homemade bread is a perfect place to sprinkle them without anyone even knowing it. Try sesame, pumpkin, linseed and sunflower seeds in your loaves for a definite hit of dietary fiber, protein, healthy fats, and antioxidants. While you may get cheaper store-bought bread than homemade, you will be better able to monitor the consistency and safety of the ingredients in a loaf that you make at home. Commercial food on the shelf needs a lot of preservatives to prevent it from being stale and moldy. For certain instances, some of the ingredients you cannot even pronounce. You will determine precisely what goes into it when you make your own bread, and the quality of those ingredients. No one can say that it takes more time to make your own bread than to buy it in the supermarket. Yet much of the time isn't spent interacting actively with the ingredients – instead, it's a couple of minutes here and there while waiting for it to rise, which can take a few hours or even overnight relying upon the recipe. When you're already in the kitchen for holiday cooking and baking, adding to your busy schedule a few measures related to bread in between other methods won't add too much time. The taste of freshly baked bread is of no match. The attributes that contribute to the delicious taste are the earthy scent, the bubbly texture and the crispy crust. So once you have perfected a recipe, you can start playing with various surfaces, so coats to be achieved. Store-bought bread won't taste as fresh because it is built explicitly for shelf stability.

3.2 Difference between homemade and Industrial Bread

Homemade bread is much more tasteful than store-purchased bread, it's not filled with preservatives, it's straightforward to produce, and it doesn't take too much time either. Many people in the U.S. consider the bread that was bought at the store as what it would be. The truth, though, is that the bread you can buy at the supermarket looks like and tastes the way it does so it can be made on an industrial scale and last for a long time without going bad. There are two essential reasons for that. The method of industrial-scale is planned to optimize profit while still creating an edible loaf of bread that can be served at dinner. It is achieved by using an unnecessary amount of yeast to produce tons of air bubbles in the bread, hence the "sweet" texture of bread purchased from the supermarket. Because of this abundance of yeast, it also makes the use of poorer quality grains, which means the bread is far from nutrient-rich. Most bread makers in the United States are trade secrets, but the "traditional process" known as the Chorleywood Bread Process is well established in the United Kingdom.

The purpose of this method is to make as cheap a loaf of bread as possible, ignoring taste, nutrition and texture along the way. The other disappointing part of making industrial bread is the presence of a good dose of preservatives. Such preservatives are there for the primary purpose of increasing the bread's shelf life, raising the manufacturer's costs again. Every time you eat a slice of bread purchased from the supermarket, you get a healthy dose of preservatives with each bite.

Along with the fact that homemade bread is so much cheaper to make, the health benefits of buying homemade bread vs. stores are incredibly different. Just a few ingredients are used in homemade bread versus store-bought bread with ingredients that we can't even pronounce. With either a bread machine or a Kitchen Aid mixer with a dough hook, you can easily make homemade bread at home every week. There are so many easy ways to knead bread today while doing other things. Even if you're using the mixer, all you need to do is mix the dough and then pop it up and bake it in a saucepan. The difference between homemade bread and supermarket purchased is that store-bought bread is designed to have uniform substance and texture, to be processed on a massive scale and to have just enough shelf-life to keep you going back to the grocery store. Excessive quantities of yeast help create plenty of bubbles within the bread, adding to the bread's light texture. Grains of a lower quality are often used, and the necessary nutrients may be missing. Commonly, preservatives can be used to help boost the shelf life, reducing manufacturing costs. High fructose corn syrup, calcium dioxide, datem, ethoxylated mono and diglycerides, dicalcium phosphate, sodium stearoyl lactylate, calcium propionate, soy lecithin, ammonium chloride, and ammonium sulphate are some of the products you need to be vigilant of.

Homemade bread has the advantage of having ingredients of high quality, a more robust flavor, taste and texture, and longer shelf life. You put in the right materials in the mix to make the best-tasting bread in the end. You can also create a bread that matches your own health needs and preferences. Depends on where you buy the bread. It's not that nice to have your pure mass-produced supermarket bread. They don't take the time, as food pump claims, to let the dough grow and build flavour. They just want it as fat as they can get on the shelf. A good artisenal bakery is going to take the time to do it right and the bread (for those who don't make their own) is worth every penny. And usually it's not any more costly than things from the store. Most bread makers come with a list of basic recipes and thorough measuring and adding instructions in your ingredients. Click a few buttons after this, and bring your feet up. Your first thought would be to guess how much bread you eat. Is your family going through several loaves a week? Or do you still end up binning the weeks-old bread's moldy remnants? A bread maker is most useful for those who eat a fair amount of bread, mainly because homemade bread doesn't contain the preservatives that are in most loaves sold in shops – meaning you have just a few days to eat it. On the other side, that means you have power over what's going into your food. With a leaner loaf, you can opt to cut sugar and butter, or you can blend it in a different flour, such as whole heat, spelt or rye. Many bread makers come with gluten-free specialist programs too.

The ingredients needed for a loaf of homemade sandwich bread cost about $2 in a recent comparison conducted by saveonenergy.com. Combined with the costs of getting it in the oven, baking your bread is just about $2.20. Now, if you compare this to the cheapest supermarket bread, you can buy that's generally at $3, 5-4 it's clear you're saving money by making your bread. But saving cash shouldn't be your only stimulus.

There is plenty of reason why you should be baking your bread. We all know bread makers are adding preservatives and other unhealthy stuff to the bread. Once we buy from the supermarket, we don't know what was added to the bread. When we were to make our bread, then we would know all the beautiful things that we put into it. The most significant difference between homemade bread and bread manufactured in large quantities in a bread factory is that industrial bread would be baked to a standard texture and taste. Factory-made bread is made on a full scale and must stick to standard recipes. Such recipes often use a significant amount of yeast that helps create plenty of bubbles within the bread. This contributes to the bread's light texture. Most factory bread would also be made with a grain of more inferior quality and also lacks the necessary nutrients. Commercialized bread is manufactured to gain the highest possible profit, which may result in the use of ingredients that are cheaper in more inferior quality. Bread baked at home or in a specialized kitchen has many advantages over commercial bread. Making the bread by ourselves ensures we can use ingredients of good quality to achieve a better flavor, taste, and texture. By adding all the best elements into the dough mix, a higher quality bread will ultimately be created and degusted. Some places you need to be mindful of include these; different flours can function differently. Various flours may have their characteristics, such as whole wheat flour in a recipe that will use less meal than a white meal. You can mix seasonings such as rosemary or oregano into a dough, try playing with a variety of ingredients. Recipes can also be increased, so consider doubling all the ingredients to make two loaves if you adopt a recipe for one loaf. Creating your breadcrumbs is a perfect way to make home-baked bread.

3.3 Temperature required to bake a homemade bread

You first need to grasp the wide spectrum of bread out there to be able to produce bread successfully. You'll need to know the different characteristics of each type of bread and its appearance when making bread. And also how to execute the recipes to get the bread's optimum taste and texture. People have been making bread at home for hundreds of years and in the professional kitchens are very important. Awareness of the baked bread is an age-old tradition dating back to 2000 BC. Before other baking methods started, the Egyptians were the founders of baking fermented bread. Bread was among the earliest foods in New Zealand governed by their Bread Ordinance and Selling of Bread Act of 1863.

New Zealand settlers used two bread baking processes during those days; the Mechanical Dough Production methods and the Bulk Fermentation methods. The latter approach involved allowing the dough to rise for two hours, before it can be broken into the appropriate sizes; a technique that is still valid today. On the other hand, the mechanical Dough Production approach involved stirring the dough at high speed to reduce the amount of time it required to rise to ten minutes. Bread has been baked in the communal ovens, large masonry ovens, or open fire during these days.

The huge masonry ovens yielded great results, but the open fire-baked loaves that were inconsistent in taste, texture, and doneness because it was hard to maintain the appropriate homemade bread temperature. Modern innovations made baking the homemade bread a bit simpler. Bakers can easily control the heat during the preparation, proofing, and baking cycle using electric ovens.

The ThermoPro food thermometers enable bakers to more accurately regulate the temperature to improve the fermentation process and achieve a more consistent texture. Further, the topic deals with all about baked bread.

The Optimal Temperature in Making

a) Proofing Yeast

The temperature at which the dough is made will influence how the yeast proves and the bread's final taste. First, pour warm water into a cup, add sugar, and whisk until it dissolves. Ensure that the temperature ranges from 95 degrees Fahrenheit-115 degrees Fahrenheit. Attach a spoonful of yeast and lift to 110-130 degrees Fahrenheit. Using a higher temperature, for example, 150 degrees Fahrenheit kills the fungus until it proves and temperature below 105 degrees F allows the yeast to prove unevenly, which influences the bread's final taste. Let the blend combination sit for five to six minutes before putting into flour; allow the yeast to dissolve into the water for the first 2-3 minutes while helping the yeast expand for the other three. On the surface, small bubbles will develop; however, if you use musty yeast, it does not affect whatsoever. It explains why the proofing process before adding the flour is essential.

B) Flour Adding

Apply the starch to the mixture and apply room temperature flour and salt. Avoid using freezing flour, because it will take a long time for the dough to rise. For example, whole-grain flour is best stored in a congeler to prevent rancidification. If you are using such flour, removing it from the freezer before the making process to let it warm up to room temperature is advisable.

Use the Thermo Pro TP-03 Wireless Instant-Read thermometer for precision measurement of flour temperature. Many people like to screw the flour through a sieve to lift the temperature. Mix the ingredients to make kneading dough. To produce a smooth and less sticky dough, this process will take 6-8 minutes.

Temperature When the Dough Rises

After kneading the flour, put it in a big, oiled bowl and cover it for one to two hours with a damp towel or wrap to allow the leaves to expand. The optimum fermentation process temperature is within a range of 75-85 degrees Fahrenheit; lower temperatures will enable the dough to ferment for a longer time, while higher temperatures create bland flavor. If you have a proof feature on your oven, you can set it to better results at this temperature. The dough rises faster during cold weather since the air is lighter than when the weather is warmer. This explains why people living in areas of high altitude will be using a small amount of leaven. Knead the dough after the two-hour cycle to get rid of any stray bubbles. After kneading it, you can make a second rise, as there is twice as much yeast in the dough. The second climb is optional and will last 30 minutes to an hour. Knead it over before you shape it.

Shaping the Dough

Once the bubbles are kneaded out, allow the dough to sit a few minutes before baking. This method helps relax the gluten and makes the dough easier to shape. When the famous French bread is being prepared, cut the dough in the middle to make two shapes equal.

Cut the dough for the bread in Italian style, and create oval forms for baking. Make sure to tuck the bottom into the rest of the dough so that when baking, it is not left exposed to produce an even texture.

Place the dough in a bowl and make sure that the side faces smoothly downwards. To prevent sticking, the container should be partially oiled and floured. Cover the containers with a damp towel before putting the dough in the oven to allow it to rise and leave for an hour. Gently poke the dough to the side to decide if it is ready to bake. When it does not suddenly spring back, and the finger leaves a faint mark, then it is ready to bake. To ensure it bakes evenly, the dough should rise reasonably; over-risen dough does not result in a lighter loaf of bread. The flour, on the opposite, collapses and shapes thick, unpalatable bread. As such, if after forming the dough overrises, knead it out and re-form it. Therefore experts advise bakers to use flour that can tolerate several risings before gluten breakdown.

Temperature Required to Bake the Dough

The optimal temperature depends on the type of bread you make. For example, lean-dough bread loaves bake at 190-210 degrees Fahrenheit while denser bread with dough is made at 180-200 degrees F. There are two ways to bake the bread; you can preheat the oven to 475 degrees Fahrenheit for 15 minutes, or place the dough directly in the oven without preheating. If the oven is preheated, ensure that you generate steam by putting a pan filled with water and letting it heat at that temperature (475). Other ways in which the oven produces moisture involves:

Misting spray: the liquid water on the side of the oven and close the door. The heat changes water to steam to increase the level of humidity inside the oven.

Using ice cubes: place a glass or ceramic ice cube bowl inside the oven and leave for 10-15 minutes. Once all of the ice has dissolved, remove the cup.

When the oven is preheated, add two to three cups of water to the saucepan before placing the dough on the baking rack. Leave it to bake for 20 minutes, but after 15 minutes, you can test to gray. If the crust is too brown, heat down to 450 degrees Fahrenheit. When thoroughly cooked, check the loaf's underside to see if it feels soft and hollow; if not, let it in the oven for another five minutes.

The recipe will help you assess the loaf's doneness. Skilled bakers recommend checking the actual baking time a few minutes before it expires, mainly if the crust develops a dark color. The crust will typically have a golden brown color. When you want a smooth, crunchy crust when the bread has baked, turn off the oven and let it for 5-10 minutes without opening the door. The bread that is properly done is firm; if it's too hard, then it's overdone. On the other side, bread that is too spongy is undercooked and can need a few more minutes in the oven.

3.4 Basics to Bake a Bread at Home

You'll need to buy your ingredients when baking your homemade bread. There are several places to purchase parts from, including; the internet is a great place to find the ingredients you need. You can also get your items shipped to your door while shopping online. In fact, you can buy a sourdough starter online if you are making a sourdough and have it shipped. Forget a better idea of the bread selection. You can visit different bread-selling shops, such as supermarkets or specialty bread stores.

A great idea here is to ask the bakers a few questions in order to find out which specific ingredients they use to achieve the quality, texture and taste of the bread you are looking for. Start playing with baked bread by incorporating condiments and sweeteners, and applying different skills to work.

There is a need to learn a variety of methods and resources and to use them to produce various results and types of bread. Finally, homemade bread is simple and easy to make, and is an enjoyable bread baker learning experience. There are several different bread-making recipes, but it's best to start with the basics. A simple method for bread can be built on and improved to the different requirements for bread. Homemade bread is quickly prepared, provides more nutrients, and will result in a particular outcome. Homemade bread has an actuality about them that the commercial bread making machines can't achieve. Also, learning basic skills is necessary, and then creating your recipes.

1. Clean whole grain flour

Without good flour, you can't make good bread. Of course, you can make delicious white flour bread, but you have to go whole to make the most delicious and nutritious loaf. Many people start with whole-wheat flour, but that's just the tip of the iceberg: rye flowers, spelled, einkorn, There are endless possibilities. Regardless of the whole-grain flour you pick, the stronger the meal has been milled more recently as the taste, and nutritional value decreases over time. Bear in mind that whole grain flour would require more space, and ferment more quickly than white flour.

2. A sourdough starter

It is nothing short of magic: the combination of wild yeast and bacteria will make the most delicious bread in the world. Wild yeast (like the commercial type) causes the bread to rise, and the bacteria produce various acids, which make the bread taste wonderful and stay fresh longer. A starter is also effortless to grow: mix flour and water and leave it alone. It does sound too good to be real, right? It's not, but it's needy: for the first two weeks, you have to give your starter some love and keep it every day. Otherwise, making bread cannot grow to be safe and solid, and good.

3. Bowl / tub mixing

You have to turn the dough into something. Bakers would pour their dough into wooden troughs in the olden days. Most bakers today use plastic buckets or tubes. You can track the increasing behavior of the dough if you have one that you can see through, and really hone in on your perfect loaf over time.

4. Bench knife / dough scraper

As a cook is helpless in the kitchen without the knife of a cook, a baker without a bench knife is helpless in the bakery. That's an exaggeration, but when it comes to making bread, a bench knife is a beneficial device. Use your bench knife to break your dough after bulk fermentation, pre-shape your loaves and scrape dough off the table whenever you wish. It'll become an extension of your hand in due time.

5. Thermometer

Fermentation is greatly influenced by temperature, so it is very important to keep a close track of your room temperature, the water you mix into your dough and the dough itself. You can easily incorporate bread baking into your life once you have clear know-how of how your bread dough acts at different temperatures.

6. Scale

They are overwhelmed when most people start baking by weighing ingredients. Okay, as soon as you do so, you know that it really makes it much easier to weigh your ingredients. If you weigh dry ingredients such as flour by volume, you will actually end up with significantly different ingredient quantities. Depending on your method, 1 cup of the meal will weigh as little as 100 grams, or as greater as 175 grams, whereas 100 grams of the meal is 100 grams of the meal — no matter how you scoop it.

7. Proofing basket

After shaping your dough into its final form, you've got to give it a good, comfortable place to relax and mature so it's ready to turn into bread in the oven. Some proofing baskets are filled with linen, others aren't — it's just a personal choice what you do with.

8. Loaf pan

While not what most people think of when they think of "artisan bread," pan breads are a very useful method for taking your loaves — not to mention that using a pan helps you to work with grains that make up a weaker flour, such as einkorn and rye.

9. Razorblade

You execute a final quick act of aggression right before you load your unbaked loaf into the oven: slicing it with a razor. When done well, with grace and faith, this cut helps your loaf to puff whilst in the oven to its maximum potential. Your slash should make for a stunning finished sandwich, while at the same time offering a range of flavors and textures that would otherwise not be without your handiwork. Double-edged razors are much sharper than their single-edged relatives, so be careful to get them. (Of a wooden coffee stirrer you can make a little handle for it.)

3.5 Utensils and Devices Required to Bake a Bread at Home

There is nothing better than baked bread at home. It can be a tasty side item for a meal itself, or a main part of the meal. Some people bake all their own bread, skipping trips to the bread aisles in the grocery store. It can be time taking to do it yourself, but it can also be a fun time spent.

The cycle will go smoothly with the right bread-making equipment and result in tasty, balanced bread loaves. It's important to find a good recipe for bread, and the type of bread will determine the equipment you'll need. Whether you have a kitchen stand mixer, it probably came with a kneading handle, which will take out of the loop a lot of the actual kneading. You might want to make sure the yeast is fresh as you want to avoid getting halfway through the process and finding out that the yeast is old and will not grow. You should check the yeast to make sure it grows and works as normal. If you have a recipe for bread that you want to try, it is an excellent idea to ensure you have all the equipment ready before combining ingredients together. The following lists will help ensure that you will use every piece of bread-making equipment. From there make sure you've got the requisite ingredients. Then you can continue your own bread baking which can be a rewarding experience. These are the devices in your kitchen that you desperately need; the ones you can reach for more often than you thought. Whether you are baking a bread or stirring a batch of cookies, make sure these resources are on hand before you start.

1. Measuring Cups (Liquid and Dry) and Spoons

Baking is all about accuracy, so it's a must to have a complete set of cups and spoons on hand. Don't think you can get through with only one form of measuring cup — you'll need measuring cups to measure all of your ingredients correctly for almost every baking recipe. Keep these devices in an easy place to reach, because you're going to use them all the time. Some measuring spoon sets have a tablespoon, teaspoon, 1/2 teaspoon, and 1/4 teaspoon, while the rest of the measuring cups come in one cup, 1/2 cup, 1/3 cup, and 1/4 cup sets. You can get away with a 1-cup size for liquid measuring cups, but even having 2-cup and 4-cup ones in your cupboard can be helpful.

2. Wooden Spoon(s)

One wooden spoon is enough, but this device is so convenient, getting a few around can often be helpful. Wooden spoons are useful for all kinds of stirring because they are so strong (with only the thickest, hardest doughs you can use them). Only note when you're finished, to hand-wash them so they don't end up broken.

3. Rubber Spatula / Scraper

We bet you reach for your rubber scraper more often than you thought. A method is good for scraping the last bit of batter or dough out of a pan or scraping any of a jar's nooks and crannies. They're also super handy to fold wet and dry ingredients together. Only bear in mind that the silicone scrapers are stronger than rubber to stand up to high heat.

4. Spatula / Metal Turner

There is no better gadget than a good old spatula when you need to move fresh-out-of-the-oven bread to a cooling rack or serve a slice of bread from a 9x13 tray. Using one with a thin metal blade can be especially handy — it will be lightweight enough to slip easily under anything you move without squishing the dough or crumbling your bread.

5. Whisk

Yes, you can use a wire whisk to beat a few eggs together but it's also good for other things. Particularly, it's one of the best ways to thoroughly mix dry ingredients together and is also great for stirring a homemade custard together.

6. Kitchen Scissors

We still have our kitchen shears handy if we are making a meal, baking or otherwise. For so many different ways, they can be useful: snipping fresh herbs, cutting parchment to match an oven, and even opening stubborn packages and containers.

7. Fine-Mesh Sieve

There are various different ways you can put a sieve to work. It's perhaps the most convenient for bakers to sift dry ingredients or to apply a powdered sugar dusting to a finished pan of bread. This is also useful for draining wet ingredients (especially small ones, such as quinoa, which would slip through a standard colander).

8. Chef's Knife

If you only have one knife in the kitchen, make this one. This all-purpose knife is perfect for just about every ingredient your recipe calls for to be cut, diced, chopped, and minced.

9. Paring Knife

Yes, make sure that you've got this little knife in your pocket. It's perfect for peeling and coring foods like apples, so you'll need one at hand — especially if you're making an apple bread. This is also useful to cut other fruits and vegetables, and it is too large for your chef's knife to be used for more delicate work.

10. A standard (13x9x2 inches)

The baking pan is a definite must-have. It can be used for so many sweet things — bread, pumpkin bread, chocolate bread — and, of course, it also has some savory applications. If you want to store your kitchen with only one baking sheet, make this one.

11. Round Cake Pan

Indeed, two of these should be on hand, because you'll need more than one to make a beautiful, towering layer bread. Round pans come in diameters of 8-inch and 9-inch, but most layer bread recipes work for either size (just assure you have two of the same size).

12. Loaf Pan

Banana bread, pumpkin bread, zucchini bread — all our favorite homemade bread recipes involve a loaf pan. If you do want to bake your yeast bread, having two of these pans in your cupboard would be paying off.

13. Wire Rack

No one wants dessert soggy, overbaked cookies, and bread, so make sure that your kitchen has a wire rack on hand. This handy device helps air to flow around the baked goods while they cool, and at room temperature, they can taste just as great as they did fresh out of the oven.

14. Hand mixer/stand mixer

While you don't need to go all-out on a fancy stand mixer, you need at least one hand mixer in your baking machine arsenal. It makes it much simpler and quicker to combine doughs and batters, and it is by far the easiest way to blend ingredients into a dense, firm bread dough without straining your neck.

15. Parchment Paper

If you haven't used parchment paper to bake, start now. Before you start baking bread, spreading a sheet over your pan will make it much easier to clean up and prevent your baked goods from sticking to the bowl. You can also opt for reusable silicone baking mats from the pricier, but parchment paper is more economical and will work as well.

3.6 Requirement of Linear Recipes

Create your baking pantry with the nine important ingredients that you will be using for daily baking recipes. Get ideas to incorporate ingredients for next stage baking too. The comprehensive list of baking ingredients that you can keep in your cupboard, refrigerator, and freezer is limited only by the available space.

So whether you're new to baking, or you're setting up your first kitchen, you'll be pleased to learn that you can narrow the list to only nine important things that you need to keep on hand for regular baking such as cookies, muffins, bread, pies, and pancakes. All after that, so to speak, is the icing on the cake. You can note that the list below is divided by type, such as flour, leavening, sugar, salt, etc. Those are your baking pantry's basic building blocks. When you gain more experience with baking, you'll begin to define what's important for you.

1. Simple Flour

All-purpose flour is appropriately named because it is your baking jack-of-all-trades that can bring out anything from bread to pancakes to muffins. Made from a combination of hi-gluten hard wheat and low-gluten soft wheat, its light and fluffy texture come from milled to extract all the germ and bran from wheat. There is also gluten-free all-purpose flour available from suppliers. Buying small amounts from bulk bins is also safer to avoid having to store leftover items, which may spoil. Using the type of flour mentioned in your recipe for better results before you get a feel for how it works.

- Whole wheat flour preserves the germ of wheat and is frequently used in a recipe to substitute a portion of all-purpose flour to improve the nutritional profile. Whole grain flour also keeps the entire grain kernel, such as wheat, oats, rye, millet, quinoa, barley, or a grain mixture.

- Bread flour consists of more protein and, therefore, more gluten, and is suitable for baking chewy yeast bread.

- Cake meal is lower in protein and gluten than all-purpose flour and is chemically processed and finely ground to make lightly textured cakes.

- Pastry flour is a medium-protein flour best suited to tender pie crusts.

- The self-rising flour has already blended in baking powder and salt. Here's how to make your flour growing up.
- Alternative non-wheat flours from other grains, nuts, and seeds are milled.
- Cornmeal is used for cornbread, crunchy waffles, and pancakes, and so on. Cornstarch is finely ground cornmeal used to thicken sauces and pie fillings.

How to Store Flours

Store flour in airtight containers that are moisture-proof on a clear, shelf or in the refrigerator. Whole wheat flour and whole grain flour damage quicker than all-purpose flour, as it contains more components of wheat grain. To prolong the shelf life, store these flours in a fridge or freezer. Alternative flours also often contain more plant oils, so they should be kept in the refrigerator or freezer after opening, or obey the instructions of the manufacturers for safe storage. Specific leaveners cause chemical reactions that fill batters and dough with the tiny bubbles of gas that because boiled products to rise.

2. Baking Soda

Baking Soda is an alkaline chemical leaveners (sodium bicarbonate) which works by combining it with heat and acid. Acidic ingredients that cause baking soda include fermented dairy products such as buttermilk, sour cream, and yogurt; molasses, brown sugar, cocoa powder (not manufactured in the Netherlands), citrus juice, vinegar, or tartar crème.

- Baking powder is a ready-mixed baking soda with a powdered acid and cornstarch. When you see "double-acting" on the bottle, it means that when it is mixed into the batter or dough, the baking powder forms carbon dioxide bubbles, and again when it's heated. You don't have to add an extra acidic ingredient when baking powder is the only leaveners on your recipe.

- Yeast is a biological leaveners that works much slower than chemical leaveners because it takes time to metabolize and produce carbon dioxide naturally for the yeast cells. Basic bread bakers can store active dry yeast or instant leaven for months in their pantries.

3. Basic Sugars

Granulated sugar is what they mean when the ingredient is mentioned in the recipes. Made from sugarcane juice or beets, this kind of sugar has been stripped of its natural molasses and can be further processed for white appearance. Raw sugar preserves the presence of a tan.

- Confectioner's sugar, or powdered sugar, is ground into ultra-fine particles, and mixed with starch to keep it from baking in its box. Bakers use the sugar of the confectioners in frostings and icings. And a simple dusting of the sugar from candy makers almost always makes it a little prettier.

- Brown sugar is added to molasses and is processed sugar. The amount of molasses in the blend accounts for the variety of white, medium, and dark brown sugar colors and flavor. The brown sugar will clump up and even form crystallized lumps because of its molasses. Storing the correct way to brown sugar will help to avoid that. To measure brown sugar for a recipe, press it into the measuring cup or spoon very tightly until it is wholly compacted and even.

4. Basic Salt

Granulated table salt is what you are going to be using in regular baking. Some bakers prefer not iodized table salt because they can often taste an irritating flavor in everyday baked goods. If you measure salt for a recipe, using table salt.

5. Basic Dairy Unsalted Butter

It is the default baking option unless salted butter is specified on your method. When you're not going to use it all the time, butter can be quickly frozen before you need it. For that creamy texture and taste, which makes your baked goods completely irresistible, you can use butter in batters, pastry dough, and cookie dough as well as in frostings and icings. Discover why butter is better for baking than margarine.

6. Large Eggs

It helps in putting together ingredients. When eggs are identified as an ingredient by recipe authors, it is almost always safe to assume they are thinking about large-size eggs. Hold eggs in the refrigerator. Find out more about eggs and what their labels mean.

7. Milk

Milk gives the moisture to batters. For pancakes and waffles, you may want to keep a quarter of the liquid in the fridge. Whole milk has a more luxurious taste than low-fat milk.

Chapter 4: Problems and Solutions Related to Homemade Bread Baking

To start with, bread baking problems can arise from accidentally killing your yeast using the wrong temperature of the water. If you are hoping to see, the bread dough rises, the water to proof your yeast shouldn't be too hot or cold. To prevent this, your recipe liquid should be warm enough to check on your wrist's inner skin without feeling too hot like you'd be planning for a formula for an infant. Significant issues with bread baking may also involve how much flour you're using for your recipe. When you shape the dough, the weather certainly plays a part in baking bread. More humidity may be in the air, and it may force you to change your bread recipe in the usual way. The critical thing to remember is to apply the flour to your method slowly, instead of pouring much of it in at once. Some days, you'll need less, and others will need more. Your goal to avoid this problem with the amount of flour is to form a dough that is soft and not sticky to touch after kneading it. The stiff dough is because too much flour has been used, the dough overworking or the oven temperature was too low.

Bread with a heavy scent of leaves grows from pouring in too much leaven. You can prevent any of these bread baking issues by correctly measuring the yeast if you don't use enough yeast, the bread takes on a yeasty, sour smell. Bread baking issues with a top crust that crumbles rather than staying intact may be caused by the yeast form you are using. When you're not happy with the quality of your bread, you can have many different reasons for issues with bread baking. For example, if you have too many air holes in the texture or the appearance inside is also uneven, you might have used too much liquid or played too much with the dough.

The quickly cracking taste of bread can be clarified by too much flour, not kneading the dough enough or baking at too low a temperature. Perhaps your bread's surface has a very coarse crumb. This question is probably because the dough isn't kneading enough. Besides working the dough longer, there are a few other ways to deal with this problem of baking the bread. One quick remedy is to try using a foolproof bread processor recipe to make your bread in a food processor. The second solution is getting your kids involved. Children enjoy sticking their fingers in dough and poking at it. You can consider that choice while teaching a useful life lesson for your children. What you bake shows up depends on how your oven is controlled. You may have left the bread in your oven too long if you find that the crust is also brown because you were tied up before you could get there. The oven temperature, however, is likely only high and needs to be lower for your oven model. Forgetting to bake our bread loaves on time is a common problem that happens to the best of us. Often, for the final rising, you can have them in the pans but get busy. The next thing you know is the beautiful high loaf deflates either in front of your very eyes or when it makes it to the oven. You can try scribbling your refrigerator with a note about the time to bake, make someone else remind you, or even set your clock to ring.

4.1 Difficulties and Obstacles in Right time and Right Ingredients Required to Bake Bread at Home

If you want to become a great bread maker, it's essential to know everything you can about some of the problems that you may encounter. These tips and tricks will help you avoid pitfalls when baking bread, ensuring you're going to end up with more carb-o-Licious results.

1. Your dough's not going up.

Your dough has been combined and kneaded; this is the point where you let the dough rise in most recettes. Yet what if he isn't yours? Here are two common reasons why dough is not ripping: stale or inactive is your yeast. Your yeast in your kitchen maybe languished for too long. Or, you may have inadvertently killed the yeast by mixing too hot water — the optimal temperature for water in most bread recipes is about 105-110 F; warm but not dry. Nonetheless, the yeast isn't triggered correctly so that it can do its job. Make sure to look at the expiry date on your yeast for better results, and make sure your water or liquid temperature matches what is listed in the recipe.

2. Your kitchen is pretty cold.

When your kitchen feels more like a fridge that may be the reason why your dough is not growing. In general, at slightly warm room temperature, the bread will rise fastest. This will take a significantly longer time for the dough to build at a cooler temperature. Either leave the dough to grow or move it to a warmer position for a more extended period.

3. Your dough develops a "texture."

Your bread dough develops a kind of crusty coating or "mask," either during the initial rising process or during the proofing phase. This is typical because you didn't cover the dough. Some recipes allow the dough to be covered during both times of growth, and with good reason: you don't want your bread to shape a crust until it bakes.

4. Your bread is rising, and then it is dropping.

The bread is in the oven, and it's beautifully rising and baking, and then, suddenly, it just falls flat in the middle.

Chances are if in the middle of your loaf you found a slope, one of those things was to blame: too much air. If the dough is too damp, it will not properly rise. Seek to reduce the amount of liquid by one or two teaspoons.

5. Way too much leaven.

Carefully read out the recipe. Although most people buy leaves in packets, not all recipes need the entire yeast packet. If you have added too much leaven, it will cause your bread to rise rapidly and then fall.

6. Your bread spreads oddly as you bake.

When your bread comes out of the cooking oven looking to have odd growths all over, chances are you've failed to score it. Not all bread on top needs to be composed; however, many do. It produces tiny "vents" for heat to escape so that the bread can uniformly spread. It can extend in unexpected ways, without scoring the bread.

7. The bread which is excessively thick.

There could be a couple of causes your bread feels like a wall. Here are only a few: Insufficient time to climb or show. Speed over long periods of rising is enticing, and just get your dough in the oven. Yet your bread will end up much flatter and more cumbersome than you would like without the proper time to rise.

Inactive Yeast.

Whether you used too-hot water to kill the yeast, or used old yeast, you may have unintentionally stopped the bread dough from rising properly, which can result in a dense bread loaf. Test the expiry date on your yeast, and use lukewarm water or liquid (105-110 F) in your recipe.

Protein content incorrect in your flour.

When you use a flour that has too low a protein count, it will not respond to the rise as needed. Super-high protein flours (for example, whole-grain flours) will make your bread thicker, too. Be sure to use a good flour when preparing the recipe in question.

4.2 Organize Kitchen and Grocery List

The first step towards successful grocery shopping is to draw up a list of the items you need to purchase. Going shopping without a structured checklist will lead you to wander around the store aimlessly without a thorough plan, just going home with a bunch of stuff you don't need and forgetting the things you're doing. Getting a list of groceries has many advantages, such as keeping you on a safe track and avoiding more trips to the supermarket. It does not have to be firm and tough or time taking to create a structured shopping list. It can be amusing and straightforward. Sure, it's not exactly rocket science to make a simple list of groceries; just jot down a few items you need to store in your desk and bring the list to the store. But a well-organized list will make a big difference if you plan to bake bread, bulk shopping, or only a short time. During your supermarket trip, it will save you time, money, and, most importantly, escape the tension. We've asked some shopping experts for their tips on pre-store planning.

Step 1: Using Last Week's Receipt

Self-proclaimed supermarket guru Phil Lempert suggests beginning the list of groceries this week with receipt from last week's grocery store. Grab your cupboard, fridge, and freezer with that in hand and mark off the things you don't need. Make sure to check in the recesses of the back, as our cupboards appear to have several blind spots.

Step 2: Have a Running List

Somewhere in your house, have a "to buy" list. Use this running list to stay tabs on things you run out of or that need to be replenished.

Step 3: Meal Plan

Meal preparation is the best way to ensure that only the things you need are bought, kept in budget and stayed coordinated.

Step 4: Take Inventory and Staple Items

The first step in making a list of foodstuffs is to go through your pantry and refrigerator and take inventory of any staple products that need replenishment. Eggs, milk, cheese, Granola bars, and other canned goods you currently use must be a priority.

Step 5: Look up Coupons

Look up different coupons and deals that are open to you until the list is more powerful. This way, if you discover and obtain a deal on something that you usually run out of fast, you can save money and stock up.

Step 6: Place by Aisle

Plan your list according to the aisles in your grocery store to make your shopping trip less time consuming and more labor-intensive. If you split your list into pieces, making sure no items go missing is much easier to ensure.

Step 7: Specify Quantity

When creating your list, the quantity of one item is significant. Understanding how much of an issue you need to get in advance is a positive thing.

Step 8: Review your List

Please be sure to go through your list and make any final changes before leaving for the shop. Write out a clear copy of your list where possible.

Step 9: Do not Leave It

Don't leave your list to the counter. Make sure you put it somewhere before you leave for your shopping trip. You should not leave it behind. There are a lot of delicate and sight ways to make sure your list is well organized. Make sure you keep tabs on products that you sometimes run out of, look for coupons, and use our Printable Grocery List whenever possible.

4.3 Linear Process Required to Bake a Bread

In cooking, proofing (also known as proving) is a step in the development of yeast bread, where the dough is permitted to rest and rise a final time before baking. During this period of rest, the yeast ferments the dough and produces gasses, leavening the dough. In comparison, proofing yeast (as opposite to proofing the dough) may refer to the process of first suspending yeast in warm water, which is a required hydration step when baked with active dry yeast. Proofing may also refer to the operation of testing the viability of dry yeast by hanging it with carbohydrates (sugars) in warm water.

If the yeast is still alive, it feeds on the sugar and creates a transparent layer of foam on the water mixture surface. Fermentation rest periods are not always clearly named and may appear as "Allow dough to rise" in recipes. If called, the words include "bulk fermentation," "first rise," "second rise," "final proof," and "made proof."

The process of making leavened bread includes a sequence of alternating work and rest periods. Job times are when the baker manipulates the dough. Several cycles of work are called combining, kneading, and folding, along with sorting, shaping, and panning. Usually, work periods are accompanied by rest periods, which occur when the dough is allowed to sit uninterrupted. Particular rest periods include autolysis, bulk fermentation, and proofing but are not limited to. The initial term for enabling the dough to rise after it has been formed and before it is baked is proofing, sometimes also called final fermentation.

Many pieces of bread continue to mix themselves with an autolyze. It refers to a rest period after the initial mixing of flour and water, a rest period that happens sequentially before yeast, salt, and other ingredients are added. If the rest period allows for improved water absorption and helps balance the gluten and starches.

The autolyze is credited to Raymond Calvel, who suggested it as a way of reducing kneading time and thus enhancing bread flavor and color. Different types of bread would have different process needs. They are usually known as either straight processes or sponge dough. Straight doughs only need a single cycle of mixing. Straight-dough recipes may advise a baker to "punch down" or "deflate" the dough during bulk fermentation. In contrast, artisan bakers may use words such as "stretching," "folding," and "degassing," meaning to remove gas from the bubbles of carbon dioxide that have developed. Sponge doughs require several cycles of mixing. Specialized devices are used to control the fermentation speed and qualities to ensure reliable results and preserve the baking schedules.

A dough proofer is a heating chamber used in baking, which encourages the fermentation of dough by yeast through warm temperatures and regulated moisture content. It's also known as a proofing case, oven proofing, or cabinet proofing. The warm temperatures increase yeast activity, resulting in increased production of carbon dioxide, and a higher, faster rise. The dough is usually allowed to rise before baking in the proofer, but may also be utilized for the first rise, or bulk fermentation. The required proofer temperatures can range from around 70 ° F (21 ° C) to about 115 ° F (46 ° C) (cooler temperatures in a dough retarder are achieved, see below). Commercial bakers usually use big, temperature- and humidity-controlled proofers, whereas home bakers use a variety of methods to build a dry, humid dough-rising climate. Types involve a home oven with a bowl full of water and the pilot light on, hot water in a bowl(the water is regularly drained to stay warm), or a home-made counter top proofer (an electrical appliance).

4.4 Ways to Organize Kitchen

The kitchen is your home area, which is used more often than in most other areas. So it's fair that if your kitchen were more comfortable to use and more organized, your life would feel more comfortable.

Tip # 1: Empty Cabinets

Remove everything from and go through each cabinet. Discard or recycle objects that aren't widely used, duplicate items, missing items, or stuff you've forgotten about. Do that for each office and drawer, forming separate areas for each category on the floor. Be human. Most kitchens have a short storage space, so the goal is to have only the things that you love and use.

Tip # 2: Group as Items

Consider what's best for you in terms of how to group items when your cabinets are all finished. Select and pile all of your baking products together. Filter and put your cooking things together. Group the items you eat from, glassware, holiday, or other seasonal items that are used only once or twice in a year, as well as unique pieces that are used only rarely.

Tip # 3: Organize the Cabinets

Now that you have groups spread out on the floor choose where to store each object. Pieces to cook and bake should be kept close to where you are cooking food. Utensils should also be in the drawer that is closest to the prep area. Glassware can be best in the fridge or sink. Create a coffee or tea station that includes sugar, mugs, and filters and, where possible, position it close to the water source. That means you stop running back and forth around the kitchen for the stuff you just need to make your morning drink.

Tip # 4: Using Clear Containers

Use clear containers to Store Products to streamline the inside of your cabinets. Pack items like sauce mixing packets, gravy mixes, hot cereal packets, and warm chocolate envelopes and place them into small plastic containers to keep them from being scattered all over the kitchen. Using transparent plastic shoeboxes to store food in little boxes like gelatin or a pudding mix.

Tip # 5: Store Containers and Lids Together

Discard lid-free containers and either store the remaining plastic containers with the lids on them, or place the lids in another larger container to hold them all together. Do the same for your pots and pans with the covers. A big, transparent plastic box will keep them on their sides and along nicely. Another choice is to stack them in the cabinet into a wire rack on their hands.

Tip # 6: Use Space Vertically

Place hooks underneath cabinets to support mugs above the countertop, or hang a stemware rack for wine glasses at the same place. This will free up substantial space in the office. You may also hang adhesive hooks to hold devices such as measuring cups, oven mitts, or other kitchen equipment on the inside of cabinet doors or pantry doors. Try hanging pots and pans using the wall space or a ceiling rack. Bear in mind that any room you may use to hang something within a cabinet will free up a flat room.

Tip # 7: Use Drawer Dividers

Drawer divisors to cook utensil drawers and junk drawers. All need a place to keep those little miscellaneous things, but they don't need to be junky and overflowing. Drawer dividers allow you to assign a small spot for each item, and when you need them, you will be able to find things.

4.5 Importance of Old Kitchen Utensils

Few utensils are as essential as the kitchen meals. Utensils we can't prepare, consume or mess about with food- the tools. Some cultures use their hands when consuming more of their food, but you might have heard the concept and purpose of using specific kitchen utensils in case you're not one of them. There is no need to have to be a master chef to know that this way, the right tools and equipment make the cycle of cooking and food consumption easier.

Proper cooking systems are vitally important. To preserve the hygienic climate, it is essential to have a cooking system in place. They increase the pace of the cooking process and make serving the food more accessible. Beginning to think about and prepare the cooking systems, you have to order them for various purposes and your particular needs first. In any kitchen, a good knife is essential.

This is not only essential for the excellent and quick cooking, but also for the safety sake. Wooden utensils are a lot. They're safe and natural items, so they don't leave a scent. They can be used in boiling, baking, stirring, and making salads. Scraping of some kind of food materials from the other utensils is firm and necessary. They are resistant to high temperatures and do not leave scars, and most of the wooden tools also are very inexpensive. Because they are multi-functional, you can still buy some beautiful collection of those for yourself.

Chapter 5: 30 Homemade Bread Recipes from All over the World

Nearly every nation in the world has some kind of bread they claim to be their own. Bread is a staple of cuisines worldwide, from baguettes of France to pita in Mediterranean countries. In their ingredients, they are distinct — some types are made of corn, and others are made of wheat — as well as their shapes — bakers poke holes in Italian focaccia, making in dimples, and French baguettes are often scored at an angle. Such bread is essential and tasty, whether yeasted or unleavened, elegant, or unadorned. The following are the collections of some of the most delicious formulas for bread from around the world, depicting how the bread appears in various cultures across the globe.

Recipe 1

American Sourdough Bread

Sourdough bread is unique in that it uses the naturally occurring yeast from the air to make it rise. There are variations in several countries, but San Francisco has proved to be the source of some of the world's best tangy-flavored bread.

Time to Prep: 20 min. + rise

Bake: 30 min.

Makes two loaves

Ingredients:

Two packets (1/4 ounce each) active dry yeast

1-1/4 cup hot water (110 ° to 115 °)

1 cup Sourdough Starter

Two eggs

1/4 cup sugar

1/4 cup vegetable oil

One teaspoon salt

Six to 6-1/2 cups of all-purpose flour

Melted butter

Directions:

Dissolve the yeast into warm water in a large tub. Add the starter Sourdough, milk, sugar, butter, salt, and 3 cup flour. Play to smooth. Stir the remaining flour in enough to form a soft dough.

Turn onto a floured surface; knead for around 6-8 minutes, until smooth and elastic. Place them in a greased tub, rotating to grease the top once. Conceal and let it rise until doubled in a warm spot for around 1 hour.

Punch-down the bread. Move onto a surface that is lightly floured; divide in half. Mold into loaves. Put in two 8x4-in greased tiles—Pans loaf. Cover and let it rise for about forty-five minutes until doubled.

Bake 30-35 minutes at 375 ° C, or until golden brown. Remove the wire racks from the pans to cool—pinch sugar.

Nutrition Facts: 1 slice: 113 calories, 2 g of fat (0 saturated fat), 12 mg of cholesterol, 79 mg of sodium, 20 g of carbohydrate, and 3 g of protein.

Recipe 2

Italian Grissini Breadsticks

Grissinis are these thin, twisted, and crispy breadsticks, frequently filled with sesame seeds, which you can enjoy as an appetizer with a bowl of soup or wine or as a snack! There are two styles of grissini: Grissini Stirato (Straight Grissini) and Grissini Rubata (Rolled Grissini). There are several flavorings and combinations which can be created to make various kinds of grissini with the same flour. The Grissini can be made very thin and smooth, or slightly thicker and softer. The original Torinese Grissini is made by hand and is slightly thicker and creamier on the face.

The Grissini can be done in many different ways. Pinching off tiny pieces of dough and then rolling them out to form thin ropes would do. These ropes can be twisted a bit to give them a shape. The other approach is to roll the dough into a rectangle and then cut off dough strips that are then moved to form a twisted cord.

The grissini dough is straightforward and is made from flour, yeast, salt, water (or sometimes milk), and some oil. The sesame seeds are optional, so in this recipe, both black and white seeds have been used to give the bread some color. This bread is enjoyable to make with kids and will do a perfect baking project!

Preparation period – 20 minutes plus about 2 hours for rest

Baking period – 12 to 14 minutes per batch

Difficulty level – mild

Ingredients to make Grissinis–makes about 16, 8-inch long Grissinis

All-Purpose Flour – 1 1/2 cup

Milk powder – 1/2 cup

Instant yeast – 1 cup

Sugar – 1 cup

Salt – 3/4 cup

Olive oil – 1 cup

Water (lukewarm) – 1/3 cup (variations could be there)

Milk (for glazing the rolls)

Sesame seeds (black and white)-to sprinkle on top

Procedure to make Grissini:

To make the dough:
- In the mixer bowl, add the dry ingredients (flour, yeast, sugar, salt, and milk powder).
- With the machine running, add the olive oil and the lukewarm water to the dry ingredients and combine to form a soft dough. Slowly, add the water to ensure you are not adding too much.
- Knead the dough using the hook attachment until it forms a very soft dough, which begins to pull out of the sides of the bowl (for about 8-10 minutes). The dough is going to be tacky, but won't be sticky.
- Move the dough to a jar, which is greased. Cover it with plastic wrap and then a kitchen towel. Then hold it for proof (for about 1-1 1/2 hours) in a draft-free place.

To shape the dough:
- Position it on the work surface until the dough has risen, and punch it down a little to get rid of excess air.
- Shape the dough into a 9 x 13 shape using a rolling pin. Seek to keep the edges straight while the dough is rolling, and aim to keep it even in thickness.
- Brush milk on the sides of the dough.

- Sprinkle uniformly over the ring, the sesame seeds. Roll the rolling pin gently over the seeds to keep it from sticking to the flour. If you're not a significant seed fan, just feel free to let them out.
- Slice off about 16 strips from the dough using a pizza cutter. You can even label the lines slightly, and then make the final cut to keep them as even as possible. This also helps in baking.
- Take a strip now and give it a fast twist all along and put it in a baking sheet lined with parchment. Repeat with all the pieces and place them in the baking sheet, slightly spaced.
- Cover with a greased plastic sheet and let them inflate again until they are fluffy, from 45 minutes to an hour.

Bake the Grissini:

- Preheat the oven until 425 F.
- Layer the baking sheet inside the oven's middle rack. Bake for about 12 to 14 minutes, or until golden.
- Let them cool down a bit, and once cool down, enjoy!

Recipe 3

Finnish Pulla Bread

Pulla is a mildly-sweet Finnish bread roll or a dessert bread, flavored with crushed seeds of cardamom and sometimes sliced almonds or raisins. Loaves in the braided form (pitko) are formed from three or more dough strands. The loaves, too, can develop into a ring. Usually, they are coated with egg wash and then sprinkled with white sugar or almonds.

Other types of Pulla consists of little round ones that imitate English scones but have a coating of sugar and butter and larger rolls of cinnamon called korvapuusti.

Usually, the outside has a glossy brown glaze, created by a coating of white egg, milk, or a sugar mixture and brewed coffee.

Usually, Pitko's served in slices. Round Pulla is served as well. In Finland, Pulla is also eaten with coffee. Pulla is also popular in the Upper Peninsula of Michigan and Northern Ontario, regions that have significant Finnish populations in the United States and Canada. There, it is also generally referred to as nisu, an old Finnish word, which means "wheat." Instead, "Korppu" is used to refer to a biscotti-like double-baked breadstick for dunking in coffee, mostly made from "nisu" leftovers.

Ingredients for Pulla Bread:

2 cups plus one tablespoon of whole milk

2/3 cup of granulated sugar

1/2 cup (1 stick) of unsalted butter

Two packets (2 1/4 tsp each) of active dry yeast

6 cups of all-purpose flour

3/4 teaspoon salt

Two teaspoons of ground cardamom

Two eggs, divided

For the icing:

1 cup of powdered sugar

1 to 2 teaspoons of whole milk

Preparation time: 2 hours

Cooking time: 25 minutes

Total time: 2 hours 25 minutes

Yield: 2 Broad loaves

Instructions:

- In a small saucepan of over medium size, place cardamom and two eggs. Stir and add butter until melted. Remove from heat and allow around 115 degrees F to cool slightly, until dry. Stir in the yeast until dissolved. Then let it wait for five minutes until the mixture from the activated yeast is somewhat foamy.

- Combine milk mixture, 2 cups of flour, salt, cardamom, and one egg at low speed until only mixed in a full bowl or bowl of a stand mixer fitted with the paddle attachment. Add three more cups of flour until it has just been added, then stir enough of the remaining 1 cup of flour until the dough pulls away from the sides of the bowl and forms a durable, smooth, elastic and slightly sticky ball. If mixed by hand, use a wooden spoon until a shaggy dough forms. Then turn the dough onto a floured countertop and knead gently until the dough is firm, smooth, elastic, and just slightly faint.

- Smear a full bowl with butter. Form the dough gently into a ball, then put it in a greased pan; turn the dough once to cover. Wrap the bowl with a plastic cover or tea towel and let the dough rise for 1 hour until doubled in a warm spot.

- Punch the risen dough into the tub. Switch the dough to a floured surface lightly. Gently knead the dough for 1 minute, then cover with a tea towel. Let them rest for 10 minutes.

- Divide the dough into six equal parts. Roll each part into a strand that is 15 inches long. Set up lines for three by 3. Pinch ends to seal each group of 3. Braid each grouping gently but tightly to form 2 braided loaves. Pinch each loaf's other end to close the braid and pinch the tucked ends on both sides. Shift each loaf into its sheet of baking paper-lined parchment. Cover with a towel of tea and let it rise for 30 minutes.

- Stove fire to 375 degrees F. Whisk one egg in a small cup, and one tablespoon of milk left. Brush egg washes on each loaf uniformly, over the tops. Bake it for twenty to twenty-five minutes until the loaves are baked and turned brown on top. Switch to a cooling rack to completely cool down.
- Make the icing when the loaves are fresh: Mix powdered sugar and enough milk into a small bowl to create a thick yet drippy glaze. Drizzle glaze uniformly over cooled loaves using a fork or spoon. Enable icing to be set before slicing.
- Enjoy!

Recipe 4

German Pretzels

A pretzel is a type of baked German bread made from dough, usually formed into a knot. The typical pretzel shape is a distinctive symmetrical form, with the ends of a long strip of dough intertwined and then bent in a specific way (a pretzel loop) back into itself. Pretzels come in a large variety in modern times.

Salt is the most popular seasoning for pretzels, complementing the treatment for washing soda or lye, which gives them traditional skin and flavor. Certain other seasonings include cheeses, sugar, cinnamon, chocolate, sweet glazing, seeds, and nuts. Common varieties of pretzels include soft pretzels (that can be consumed immediately after preparation) and hard pretzels (that have a long shelf-life).

Soft Pretzel Recipe

These have a slightly chewy surface, such as would be a decent soft pretzel, while the inside is super soft and buttery. The taste is out of the world. As they are out of the cooking oven, they are bathed in butter. Essentially, the recipe is like hitting the jackpot! They're easier to bake than you think! Don't be afraid to work with the yeast. If you follow the given directions, the recipe would be straightforward.

The following recipe would yield eight soft pretzels. However, if you want to make these for game day or some other event where you would like to feed more people, you can cut the dough ropes into 1-2 inch pieces to make tiny, fluffy pretzel bites!

Ingredients:

2 1/4 tsp of active dry yeast (1 regular package)

1 cup of warm water

One tbsp of unsalted butter, melted

1 tsp of sugar 1 tsp of salt

3 cups of all-purpose flour + up to 3/4 cup more if desired

2 cups of water

Four tbsp of baking soda

One tbsp of coarse salt, to sprinkle on top

Six tbsp of salted butter, melted

Directions:

- Preheat the cooking oven to 475 degrees and put a large baking sheet or two parchment sheets.
- In your stand mixer bowl, blend yeast with warm water and sugar, fitted with the hook attachment. When the mixture is "frothy," the leaven is set. Stir in salt, and melted butter for one tbs. Add 1 cup of flour at a time

until a dough forms and is not sticky anymore. Depending on the temperature variations, you may need more or less. If you press your finger and it falls back into the flour, it's ready to knead. Knead the dough for further five minutes, until it is smooth and fluffy. Give shape to the dough into a round ball and put it back in the bowl for 15 minutes to rest. Prepare a baking soda bath over this time.

- Boil two cups of water in a medium-sized kettle with four tbs of baking soda. Once the baking soda is mostly dissolved, take the mixture off the heat and allow it to fall to a lukewarm temperature. When cooled, pour into a 9x9 baking dish.

- Fifteen minutes of dough rest time will be up at this time. Remove out the dough from the bowl, and slightly flatten with your hand palm. Break the dough into eight bits (like a pizza). Roll each triangle, about 19-20 inches long, into a long rope. Shape the dough into pretzel form and place for 2 minutes in baking soda water. If the stream doesn't fill the whole pretzel, it doesn't touch spoon on top of the regions. After the 2 minutes are finished, either by your hand or with the aid of a fork, carefully pick up a pretzel and put it on a prepared baking sheet. You may need to re-shape a little. Sprinkle with coarse salt over the pretzel when still wet (optional). Repeat these steps until all eight pretzels have been prepared and put on the baking sheet.

- Bake the pretzels for 8-9 minutes until golden or brown—brush (slowly) with six tbs of melted butter, straight from the oven.

- These baked soft pretzels are best served hot and fresh from the oven. These can be placed in an airtight jar for about two days at room temperature. Place them into the microwave and as good as fresh!

Hard Pretzels Recipe

A brief but important note about these pretzels:

They are poached in a baking soda bath for 15 seconds, much like a soft pretzel. The analytical thing to keep in mind here is that baking soda is simply baked soda. And baking soda means it is a soda that has been baked in the oven for about an hour at 250 degrees F. It's an easy task to prepare, but making it more alkaline without having to utilize lye is necessary. That, paired with the bath's brown sugar, is what gives these pretzels their authentic hard pretzely taste, so don't miss that.

Prep Time: 2 Hours

Baking Time: 35 minutes

Total Time: 2 hours 35 minutes

Yield: 24 pretzel rods

Ingredients for the dough:

One cup of lukewarm water (110 to 115 degrees F)

Two teaspoons of light brown sugar, split

One 1/4 teaspoons of active dry yeast

1 1/2 cups of unbleached all-purpose flour

1 1/2 cups of bread flour

1/2 teaspoon salt

For the baking soda bath:

8 cups of water

1/2 cup baking soda

Method:

- **(For baking soda):** Place baking soda on a foil-lined baking sheet and bake for 1 hour at 250 degrees F. This is it!

- Combine 1/4 cup of warm water and 1/2 teaspoon brown sugar in a small pot. Remove yeast and dissolve with a stir. Let sit, until slightly foamy, for 5 to 10 minutes.
- Stir the remaining 1 1/2 teaspoons of brown sugar, flours, and salt into a full bowl of a stand mixer until mixed. Add the mixture of yeast and the remaining warm 3/4 cup water; stir until it forms a dough.
- Knead the dough by hand on a gently floured surface for 5 to 10 minutes until smooth, satiny and elastic; or, knead the dough with the dough hook in a medium speed mixer for 5 minutes until soft, glossy and flexible. Shape the dough into a circular shape and put it lightly greased with oil or cooking spray in a large bowl. Conceal bowl with lightly greased plastic wrap and let the dough rise for about 1 hour, until doubled, in a warm spot.
- Top with two parchment-papered baking sheets. Punch the risen dough down and split it into 24 equal parts. Roll each piece into a rod approximately 9 inches long (1/2 inches wide) and position 1 inch apart on prepared baking sheets. Loosely conceal with lightly oil plastic wrap and allow to rise for 30 minutes.
- In this time, fire up the oven to 350 degrees F.

Prepare the baking soda bath:
- Bring water to a simmer over medium to high heat in a big, deep, and wide saucepan or Dutch oven. Remove baking soda and brown sugar; dissolve and whisk.
- Drop a few dough rods carefully into a simmering bowl. Poach for 15 seconds, remove with a slotted spoon or tongs and return to the baking sheet lined. Repeat with leftover dough rods.
- Clean the rod tops with a wash of the eggs, then sprinkle with water. Bake it for thirty to thirty-five minutes till the

rods are a dark golden brown and hardened, rotating pans halfway through the baking. Switch to refrigeration racks to fully cool.

- Fully refrigerated pretzel rods can be stored for up to 1 week in an airtight container at room temperature.

Nutritional Values of this recipe:

Serves: 24 Servings

Size: 1 Pretzel

Calories per Serving: 64

Percentage of daily value:

1% Total Fat

0.4 g Saturated Fat

0.1 g Polyunsaturated Fat

0.1 g 0% Monounsaturated Fat

0.1 g 3% Cholesterol

7.8 mg 14% Sodium

342.6 mg 4% Total Carbohydrate

12.5 g 2% Dietary Fiber

0.5 g Sugars

4% Protein 2.2 g

Recipe 5

Indian Naan

Naan is a leavened, oven-baked flatbread found primarily in Western Asia, South Asia, Myanmar, and Caribbean cuisines.

This bread is usually made from maida, a refined and powdery Indian white flour, similar to pastry meal. It is most commonly eaten with curry, used to sop all the sauce and pick up vegetables (and meat) instead of a knife. It is sometimes seasoned with nigella seeds — black seeds with a slightly astringent flavor found in Indian grocery stores and are often mistakenly referred to as "onion seeds," "black sesame," or "black cumin."

Simple Naan

This chewy, fluffy bread can be made with simple ingredients at home. You'll want to make it all the time! Not only does yogurt added in the dough make the naan soft and tender, but it also adds great flavor.

What is the difference between naan and flatbread?

Typically Naan has yogurt in it, which gives it a smoother texture, which is perfect for wrapping around sandwich fillings. When fried, Pita bread puffs up, leaving the interior more hollow and perfect for filling. Both are flatbreads, but they have different flavors and different textures.

Required ingredients for this simple naan:

Warm water ½ cup

Instant yeast 2 tsp

Sugar 1 tsp

Olive oil or Canola oil will work) 3 tbsp

Plain yogurt (Greek yogurt or Sour Yogurt can be used as a substitute) ¼ cup

Egg 1

Salt ½ tsp

All-purpose flour 2 ½ cups

Butter 2 tbsp

Yield: 8 servings

Serving Size: 1

Calories: 516

Total Fat: 10g

Saturated Fat: 3g

Trans Fat: 0g

Unsaturated Fat: 6g

Cholesterol: 31mg

Sodium: 186mg

Carbohydrate: 91g

Fiber: 3g

Sugar: 1g

Protein: 14 g

Preparation Time: Twenty minutes

Cook Time: 6 minutes

Additional Time: 1 hour 26 minutes   **Total Time:** 1 hour

How they make the dough?

- In a full bowl, mix warm water, yeast, and sugar and allow to sit for a few minutes.
- Add oil, yogurt, egg, salt, and ample flour to form a smooth, silky dough. Put the dough in an oiled utensil, cover the dough and allow it to rise till doubled.

How to cook naan bread?

- Slice the dough into eight pieces. Roll the single piece into a round shape about 6 inches full, on a lightly floured surface.

- Heat to medium-hot skillet. Attach any palm oil or olive oil. Place a dough circle in the center of the skillet and cook the bottom, until bubbly and golden brown. This takes a maximum of three minutes. Turn the side and cook the other side for 2-3 minutes, or until it is brown or golden.
- Brush the melted butter onto the fresh naan bread.

Note: If you're going to use the naan as a sandwich flatbread right away, you should skip the melted butter, so it's not so messy when you fold it in half and eat it.

How many calories are there in naan?

Every piece is around 230 calories if you prepare it as directed. When you lack the melted butter on top, the calories are about 207 each. When you need to add more than 2 1/2 cups of flour, you'll increase the calorie count, of course.

How long does this bread last?

At room temperature, if preserved in an airtight jar (like a ziplock bag), the naan bread will last 3-4 days on the counter. When you put it in the fridge, it will last for about a week.

Can you freeze naan bread?

Yes, naan can be frozen. It is safe to freeze it before using melted butter to brush it. Let it cool down completely, then cover it in plastic wrap and place it in big Ziplock bags for the freezer. It will last for three months.

How to reheat leftover naan:

Microwave: reheat for around 15-20 seconds in the microwave oven, or more if frozen.

Oven: Spread the bread in a pan of 9,113" and sprinkle with water lightly. Cover the pan with foil made of aluminum—Bake for around 8-10 minutes at 250 °, or until heated through.

Skillet: Heat a low to a medium non-stick skillet. Cook each naan on each side for about 2 minutes, sometimes rotating to ensure it is not burning. Brush it with the melted butter, when it is dry.

What to serve the naan with?

Generally, Naan is great with Asian and Indian foods, but with just about everything, you can eat it. Even with broth, you can also dip it in sauce or hummus, use it to make wraps, or even make personal pizzas as a crust.

Garlic Naan Recipe

Ingredients:

2 cups Flour

1 tsp Sugar

1 tbsp Greek Plain Yogurt

Pinch Salt

2 tsp rising yeast

1/2 cup Warm Water

1/2 tsp Garlic Powder

1/2 butter

1 tbsp Dried fenugreek leaves

However, if you can't get your hands on dried fenugreek leaves, then replace it with cilantro.

Instructions:

- Put your Ghee or Butter melted in a small bowl and set aside.
- Once the dough has increased in amount, put the dough on top and flour the table. Separate the dough into six parts, using a pastry cutter.

- Form each of them into a ball with your hands, then put them on the floured surface and use a rolling pin, roll the dough out into the circles.
- Place a skillet over medium – heat and season the skillet with some ghee/butter with a basting brush.
- Roll out the dough one by one, and place it individually onto the skillet.
- On top of the dough, you will see tiny bubbles forming around 1-2 minutes as the dough starts to take on a light brown color. That is when you want to turn over the dough. But, before that, the dough brush is to be soaked with ghee/butter along with fenugreek leaves attached, then flipped.
- Cook for 1 minute or until golden on the other hand, then move to the serving plate and conceal with a towel to keep warm.
- Repeat steps 3-5 until it cooks all the bits.

Yield: 3   **Serving Size**: 1

Calories: 351 Total

 Fat: 3g

Saturated Fat: 1g

Trans Fat: 0g

Unsaturated Fat: 1g

Cholesterol: 5mg

Sodium: 70mg

Carbohydrates: 4g

Sugar: 2g

Protein: 11g

Sodium: 70mg

Fiber: 4g

Pakistani Roghni Naan Recipe

Ingredients:

2 Cups of flour

One pinch of salt

1 tsp of yeast

2 tbsp of ghee

Sesame seeds as needed

1 tsp of sugar

Roghni Naan Process:

- Add yeast and sugar in 1/2 cup warm water, and mix with a spoon. Hold aside until it is fluffy.
- Stir in milk, salt, ghee, and yeast. Knead it into a soft pastry dough. Keep this dough covered for 3-4 hours in some warm place, or till it doubles its size. Knead it all over again.
- Divide it up into three equal parts. Give it a round naan shape. Use your fingers to form marks on it, then sprinkle sesame seeds over it.
- Apply oil or ghee over the naan with a knife. The cooking oven should be preheated to three hundred and fifty degrees.
- Grease and place naan in the baking tray. Bake for about four to five minutes.
- They can be eaten with any gravies.

Recipe 6

Hungarian Beigli

This poppy seed roll is a pastry bread consisting of a slice of sweet yeast bread with a thick, creamy, bittersweet poppy seed filling. An alternative filling is a minced walnut paste or chestnuts. Beigli is widespread in Central and Eastern Europe, where it is commonly eaten during Christmas and Easter.

Total Time:

Prep: 40 min. + rising

Bake: 30 min. + cooling

Makes four loaves (12 slices each)

Ingredients:

Two packets (1/4 ounce each) active dry yeast

1/2 cup warm 2 percent milk (110 ° to 115 °)

1/4 cup plus two tablespoons of sugar

3/4 teaspoon salt

1 cup butter, softened

1 cup sour cream

Three large eggs, room temperature, lightly beaten

Six to 6-1/2 cups of all-purpose flour

Filling:

1-1/4 cups of sugar

1/2 cup of butter

One large egg

1/2 teaspoon of ground cinnamon

4-1/2 cups California ground walnuts

One large apple, peeled and rubbed

Icing:

2 cups of sugar

2 to 3 tbsp 2 percent milk

Directions:

- Dissolve leaven in warm milk in a large bowl. Stir in the sugar, salt, butter, sour cream, eggs, and flour as per the given quantities. Beat on medium velocity for about 3 minutes until even. Then add sufficient remaining flour to form a soft dough (the dough is sticky).

- Turn onto a floured surface; knead for 6-8 minutes, until smooth and elastic.

- Place them in a greased tub, turning to grease top once concealed and let it rise until doubled, in a warm place, for around 1 hour.

- Alternatively, mix the sugar, butter, egg, and cinnamon in a large saucepan. Cook and mix it over medium heat until the blend is sufficiently thick to cover a spoon back. Take off the heat; whisk gently in walnuts and apple. Cool!

- Punch-down the bread dough. Put onto a side that is lightly floured; divide into four parts. Each roll into a 12x10-inch—right angle. Stretch filling to 1/2 inch of rims. Starting with an extended hand, roll up jelly-roll style; pinch seams to seal. On greased baking sheets, put the seam side down. Cover and let it double, for about 30 minutes, till it doubles.

- Bake for around 30-40 minutes at 350 °, or until lightly browned.

- Lift the wire racks from the pans to cool.

- Combine all the ingredients for icing; drizzle over the loaves.

Nutrition Facts:

One slice: 222 calories

12 g of fat (5 g of saturated fat), 36 mg of cholesterol, 87 mg of sodium, 26 g of carbohydrates (13 g of fiber), 4 g of protein.

Recipe 7

Italian Focaccia

Focaccia is Italian rustic, all-purpose bread; it can be served as a sandwich bread or on the side. It is also highly herbed and can absorb copious quantities of olive oil in its texture.

Total Time:

Prep: 30 min. + raise

Bake: 15 minutes

Makes one loaf (8 wedges)

Ingredients:

1-1/8 teaspoons active dry yeast

Half cup of lukewarm water (110 ° to 115 °)

One tablespoon sugar

One tablespoon Italian seasoning

1/4 teaspoon salt

1/4 teaspoon pepper

1-1/3 to 1-2/3 cups of all-purpose flour

Two tablespoons of oil-packed sun-dried tomatoes, chopped

Two tablespoons of sweet red peppers, drained and chopped

Two tablespoons of ripe olives, drained

5 Greek olives, sliced

Five sliced green olives with peppers, drained

Two tablespoons of fresh parsley

One tablespoon of olive oil

One teaspoon of kosher salt

One teaspoon of Parmesan cheese

One teaspoon of roman cheese, shredded

Directions:

- Dissolve the yeast into warm water in a large tub. Connect the sugar, Italian seasoning flavor, salt, pepper, and 1 cup flour. Beat to smooth. Stir the remaining flour in, enough to shape a healthy dough. Then place in the onions, chili peppers, olives, and parsley.

- Turn onto a floured surface; knead for around 6-8 minutes, until smooth and elastic. Place them in a greased tub, turning to graze the top once. Conceal and let it rise until doubled in a warm spot, about 50 minutes.

- Punch-down the bread. Form in a 9-in. Circle on the baking sheet, greased. Conceal and let rise in a warm area for about 25 minutes, until doubled. Make many dimples over top of the dough with your fingertips. Wash with olive oil. Sprinkle the cheeses and kosher salt.

- Bake for about 14-18 minutes at 400 ° C, or until golden brown. Drop onto a rack of wire.

- Your scrumptious Italian Focaccia is ready!

Nutrition Facts:

One wedge: 118 calories, 3 g fat (0 saturated fat), 0 cholesterol, 418 mg sodium, 19 g carbohydrate, 3 g protein.

Basic Sourdough Focaccia Bread

This very recipe has some plus points over the other version of Focaccia given above.

- First, making a thick crust doesn't require any special equipment — not a Dutch oven or a Baking Steel; not two Pyrex bowls to produce a white, less-thick crust. You already have somewhere in your kitchen a 9-inch oven. Everything you need is this.
- Second, no tricky shaping technique on a floured surface of the work is needed. It is an art to form freestanding sourdough boules, and it requires practice and repetition. Once you get the hang of it, it's a beautiful thing, but it can be frustrating before you do it.
- Third, no scoring is needed. You don't need a razor-sharp lame with focaccia-you use your fingers to dimple the dough.

The recipe below can also be baked in a loaf pan, another excellent choice if you don't want to tackle shaping and scoring, as well as a Dutch oven.

Ingredients:

50 g – 100 g (1/4 to 1/2 cup) active starter

10 g (about 2.5 teaspoons) kosher salt

430 – 440 g water, room temperature

512 g (about 4 cups) bread flour

Three tablespoons extra virgin olive oil, split, plus additional for drizzling

Fine, flaky sea salt

Prep Time: 24 hours

Cook Time: 25 minutes

Total Time: 24 hours 25 minutes

Yield: 1 loaf

Instructions:

- In a full pot, bring the starter, salt, and water in. To blend, swirl with a spatula — it doesn't need to be blended evenly. Stir in flour. Mix until the flour is completely incorporated again.

- Perform one "fold" if time allows: 30 minutes after mixing the dough, hit the bowl, and bring the dough up and down into the middle. Turn quarter turns around the bowl and start pulling this 8 to 10 times.

- Sprinkle with an olive oil spray, then apply to paint. Cover bowl with a tea towel or bowl cover and set aside to rise for 4 to 18 hours (the time will vary depending on the time of year, the strength of your starter and the temperature of your kitchen — in summer, for example, some sourdoughs will double in 6 hours; in winter, they will increase in 18 hours).

- Put two tablespoons of oil made of olives in a nine by 13-inch pan when the dough has doubled. (If you're using a glass pan, you might want to butter it). Drizzle dough with an olive oil spoon. Using your hand to deflate the dough gently, release it from the bowl's sides. Scoop the dough gently into your prepared pan in the middle of the oil bowl. Fold the dough into an envelope form to create a rough rectangle from top to bottom, and from side to side. Switch dough over, so it's down seam-side.

- Brush the dough over with grease. Put on for 4 to 6 hours or until the dough gets puffy and almost doubled.

- Bring the oven to 425 degrees F. Brush with oil softly, then press gently into the dough using all the ten fingers to dimple then stretch the dough to almost match the plate. Broadly brush with sea salt. Place the pan to the oven and bake for about 25 minutes or until golden. Remove the pan from the oven and shift the bread into a refrigerating rack. Cool before slicing, for at least 20 minutes.

Notes:

Time: When your starter is ready to go, this recipe needs an initial rise of 4- 18 hours, followed by a second rise of 4- to 6 hours. After the initial increase (depending on your kitchen's time of year and temperature), you should deflate the dough and put it in the fridge for 8-10 hours (maybe longer) to help with your schedule. Bear in mind that when you remove the dough from the fridge and transfer it to a pan, it will still have to rise for another 5- to 6- hours.

A few thoughts: If you're doing the summer focaccia (northern hemisphere), use 50 g starter and test the dough every few hours. Use 100 g of the starter if you're doing this in the winter, and prepare for a long first rise.

The bath: Chlorine in water can hurt sourdough. Leaving water at room temperature for 24 hours would cause much of the chlorine to escape.

Water quantity: The water may need to be cut back depending on where you live and the time of year. For example, if you live in a humid environment, it would be suggested that you start with 430 g of water. When you don't use bread flour, you might need to cut back some fat, too.

Choosing the bread flour: It is recommended that the bread flour, which appears to be more suitable for people, particularly those living in humid climates, should be used. When you have only all-purpose flour on hand, you can consider reducing the water a little bit — bread flour absorbs slightly more liquid than all-purpose flour.

Herbed Focaccia

This bread is light and full of air, with a beautiful saltiness of olive oil, and those fresh herbs bring the whole loaf to life. Use it as it is, or make delicious sandwiches out of it!

Prep Time: 10 minutes

Cook Time: 22 minutes

Inflation Time: 10 hours

Total Time: 10 hours 32 minutes

Total servings: 10

Ingredients:

2 Cups Bread Flour (or all-purpose)

1 Teaspoon Kosher Salt

1 Cup Hot Water

1 1/8 Teaspoon Instant Yeast

1/2 Teaspoon Granulated Sugar

Olive Oil

1 Teaspoon Fresh Rosemary, Cut (or 1/2 Teaspoon Dry)

1 Teaspoon Fresh Parsley, Cut (or 1/2 Teaspoon Dry)

1/2 Teaspoon Fresh Thyme Leaves, Cut (or 1/4 Teaspoon Dry)

Maldon Flaked Sea Salt

Instructions:

- Mix in the flour and salt in a glass pot. Combine to blend.
- Mix the warm water, yeast, and sugar in a glass measuring cup. Enable yourself to sit for a minute and stir with a wooden spoon into the flour until the dough just gets together.

- Cover the bowl with a tight plastic wrap and place in the refrigerator for 8 hours or until midnight.
- Take the bowl off the shelf.
- Drizzle oil in an 8-inch round cake pan and put the dough in the middle, tucking under ends.
- Cover with plastic wrap and leave for 2 hours to let it rise.
- Heat up to 450 degrees F on the oven.
- When the dough has risen, it will fill the pan. Drizzle with additional oil and press the holes down to the bottom of the pan with your fingertips, but not through the dough.
- Sprinkle over salt and herbs.
- Place in the oven, turn down to 425 degrees F and bake for 22-24 minutes or until golden.

Notes:
- If you do not have fresh green herbs, you can sprinkle Italian Seasoning or use the dry herbs.
- If your leaven is fine, activated yeast will bubble and foam within a few minutes.

Recipe 8

Swedish Tea Ring

A Swedish Tea Ring is a sweet flavored, light bread that is usually made as a tea snack at night or as part of a light breakfast. Nevertheless, it is also eaten as a snack. The preparation is easy to form and doesn't take too long. The dish can be cooked in many ways, and it can have both a mildly sweet and a sweet flavor that is very sugary. The recipe is served in both eggless and with-egg versions.

Egg-based Swedish Tea Ring

Servings: 1 large or too small

Ingredients:

1 cup of milk

1/2 cup of sugar

2 cup of salt

1/4 cup of butter

Half cup of lukewarm water (not hot!)

Two sachets of yeast

Two eggs are beaten

5 to 5-1/2 cups of unsifted flour

Topping:

3/4 cup of sugar

Melted butter

2 tbsp of cinnamon

1/3 cup of raisins or nuts

Frosting:

Icing sugar, cherries, nuts

Instructions:

- Steam milk. Stir in butter and sugar until melted. Cold to lukewarm (tip: be careful, or you'll kill the yeast and cook the eggs, neither are good).
- In a large pot, add water and sprinkle the yeast on top. Stir in the milk and blend properly.
- Beat two eggs, then mix in.
- Season with salt and 2 cups of flour.

- Beat to smooth. Stir in one cup of remaining flour at a time.
- Bring it on a floured surface as it starts to form a ball, and knead for 10 minutes.
- Place it in a greased tub, turn over once in a while.
- Cover with a warm towel. Rest 1-1/2 hours before scale doubles.
- Punch and roll into a rectangle of 14" x 18" and brush it with melted butter.
- Mix cinnamon and sugar and sprinkle. Attach the raisins or nuts (elective).
- Move up from one end, bend into a circle, and tuck ends as best you can together.
- Snip off every 2/3 inch and twist free.
- Place a towel on top and allow size to double. We usually will enable it to go overnight, but if you live in a warmer environment, that may be too long.
- Bake it in a 350-degree oven for 25-30 minutes. Frost and top with cherries.

Eggless recipe for Swedish Tea Ring

Method for the Dough:

1cup Luke warm milk

1/8cup Hanging curd

1tbsp Butter (room temperature)

3tbsps White sugar

1/2tsp Salt

Three 1/4cups bread flour

3/4tsp Active dry yeast

For the Filling:

2tbsp butter (softened)

2tsp Cinnamon powder

3/4cup Brown sugar

2tbsp Raisins

For Icing:

1 cup icing sugar

1/2 tsp Almond Extract

1tbsp Milk, or as needed

Directions:

- Take in a big bowl the milk, hanging curd, butter, sugar, salt, bread flour, and yeast, knead it all like a smooth dough.
- Move to a greased bowl. Cover with plastic wrap and let it grow for around 1 to 1 1/2 hours until doubled.
- Grease 2 baking sheets or use baking paper to line them up. Keep set aside.
- Divide the batter into two. Roll out a single piece into rectangles.
- Cover each dough rectangle with the melted butter, then combine the cinnamon powder, light brown sugar, and raisins in a small bowl.
- Sprinkle on the buttered dough the cinnamon mixture. Roll them up tightly, on the long side, as a log.
- Pinch to cover tops. Stretch and twist to circles, pinch to close ends. Place them onto prepared baking sheets, seam side down.
- Cut 2/3 way through the loaf at around 1-inch intervals, using clean scissors. Spread gently on each cut.

- Conceal each ring with a towel that is clean or greased plastic wrap, and allow the loaves to rise for about 40 minutes until double.
- The oven is to be preheated to 350 F.
- Bake it in preheated, rotate baking sheets for 10 minutes. Bake until the rings are light brown and the filling starts to ooze and bubble, for around 10 minutes.
- Combine sugar, almond extract, and milk in a small mixing bowl until icing is desired consistency.
- Drizzle icing rings over warm water.

Recipe 9

Native American Fry Bread

This bread is a tasty and simple one that derives through contact with Native American people. It did not need yeast – only the powder of flour, salt, and baking from their staple supplies and some oil to fry it. The trick is not to over-knead the dough, so it is difficult – just work it enough to mix it and then leave it for a while to rest. What you are looking for is the frying crispness on the outside and soft texture on the inside.

Native American Fry bread can be slit open and have stew put inside, cut into pieces and used to swab up the gravy from a stew, served as a taco with pulled pork, grilled beef, and assorted vegetables on top or served as a sweet end to the meal with a lump of cream, or double cream plain yogurt, and maple syrup or honey drizzle.

Total time: 35 minutes

Servings: 16 fry bread

Calories: 65 kcal

Ingredients:

2 cups of all-purpose flour

3/4 teaspoon salt

2 1/2 teaspoons of baking powder

1 1/2 cups of lukewarm water. This must be at around 105 F (41C). Mix 2 parts of cold water into one piece of boiling water and prepare it.

1 cup of sunflower oil, canola or coconut are excellent choices

Instructions:

- Combine these three things: the salt, flour, and baking powder in a medium-sized dish.
- Build a well in the center, and add one cup of water, drawing from the sides in the flour.
- When you see it is still too warm, just add the remaining 1/2 cup of water-the the dough will be a little sticky but not messy.
- To blend and smooth out the mix, knead with floured palms.
- Set aside to wait for a few minutes while you make the saucepan where you warm the oil so that the bread can be fry.
- The oil should be an inch deep across the bottom of the pan and should be hot – 350 degrees Fahrenheit on a thermometer or simply, take a tiny piece of dough and place it in the pan – it will instantly start puffing up and sizzling – if it falls to the bottom the oil is not hot enough. You don't want the oil to be consumed by the bread-note: crisp outside, fluffy inside!
- Cook one fry bread for about 2 minutes at a time, then switch over to do the other.

- Remove with tongs, and put to drain the excess oil on a paper towel.
- Serve hot with the various chosen toppings.

Some people prefer larger fry breads-just 5 inches wide are the ones here. If you do not want them to puff up too high in the middle, then with your finger, make a small circle in the middle – they'll still puff up but look more like donuts.

If you want the fry bread to be flatter, then force the dough out thinner – just like the pizza dough – except then they'll be crispier, and the softness inside won't be there.

Recipe 10

The United Kingdom Hot-Crossed Buns

A hot cross bun is a spicy-sweet bun bread, usually made with fruit, marked with a cross on top and traditionally eaten in the United Kingdom, Ireland, Australia, India, Canada, New Zealand, South Africa, the United States and some parts of the Americas on Good Friday. The bun marks the end of Lent, and various parts of the hot cross bun have some meaning, including the cross representing Jesus 'crucifixion, and the spices inside signify the spices used to embalm him at his burial.

Total Time Prep: 25 min. + Raise

Bake: 15 min. + Refrigeration

Makes 2-1/2 dozen

Ingredients:

Two packets (1/4 ounce each) active dry yeast

2 cups warm whole milk (110 ° to 115 °)

Two large eggs

1/3 cup butter softened

1/4 cup sugar

1-1/2 teaspoon salt

One teaspoon ground cinnamon

1/4 teaspoon ground allspice

6 to 7 cups all-purpose flour

1/2 cup dried currants

1/2 cup raisins

One large egg yolk

Two tablespoons water

Icing:

1-1/2 cup sugar

4 to 6 teaspoons of whole milk

Directions:

- Dissolve yeast into the warm milk in a small cup. Combine the eggs, butter, sugar, salt, spices, yeast mixture and 3 cups of flour in a wide bowl; beat until smooth at a medium pace. Add currants, raisins, and ample remaining flour to form a soft dough (the dough will be sticky).

- Put onto a floured part; knead for about 6-8 minutes, until dough is smooth and elastic. Place them in a greased tub, rotating to graze the top once. Conceal with plastic wrap and let it rise until doubled in a warm spot, around 1 hour.

- Punch the dough in. Turn onto a floured surface; break and form into 30 balls—place in 2. Detach from greased baking sheets. Cover with towels in the kitchen; allow to rise in a warm place until doubled, 30-45 min. Preheat the oven until 375 ° C.

- Cut a cross on above of each bun, using a sharp knife. Beat egg yolk and water in a small utensil; brush over tops—

Bake for 15-20 minutes or until golden brown. Lift the racks from pans to wire to cool slightly.

- For the icing, blend sugar from confectioners and enough milk in a small bowl to achieve desired consistency. Pipe a cross over the prepared bread-buns. Serve hot.

Nutritional Values: 1 bun: 171 calories, 3 g fat, 28 mg cholesterol, 145 mg sodium, 31 g carbohydrate, 1 g sugar, 4 g protein.

Recipe 11

Eastern Europe Rye Bread

Countries around the world have their varieties of rye bread, which has been around since the middle Ages due to rye's ability to thrive in poor soils and during drought. It is a perfect bread for a sandwich.

Total Time Prep: 25 min. + Raise

Bake: 35 min. + Refrigeration

Makes two loaves (12 slices each)

Ingredients:

2 Packets (1/4 ounce each) active dry yeast

1-1/2 cup warm water (110 ° to 115 °)

1/2 cup molasses

Six tablespoons butter softened

2 cup rye flour

1/4 cup baking cocoa

Two tablespoons caraway seeds

Two teaspoons salt

3-1/2 to 4 cups all-purpose flour

Cornmeal

Directions:

- Dissolve the yeast into warm water in a deep tub. Shake all-purpose flour in the molasses, sugar, rye meal, cocoa, caraway seeds, salt, and 2 cups until smooth. Incorporate enough remaining all-purpose flour to form a solid dough.
- Turn onto a floured surface; knead for 6-8 minutes, until smooth and elastic. Place them in a greased tub, rotating to grease top once. Cover and let stand until doubled in a warm spot, around 1-1/2 hours.
- Punch-down the prepared dough. Move onto a side that is lightly floured; divide in half. Form each piece into about 10 in. Loaf. Big! Big! Grease 2 baking sheets and sprinkle some breadcrumbs — place loaves on prepared pans. Cover and let rise for around 1 hour, until doubled.
- Bake at three-fifty ° for thirty to forty-five minutes, or when pressed, until the bread sounds hollow. Remove the wire racks from the pans to cool.

Nutrition Facts: 1 slice: 146 calories, 3 g of fat (2 g of saturated fat), 8 mg of cholesterol, 229 mg of sodium, 26 g of carbohydrate (5 g of fiber), 3 g of protein.

Recipe 12

Irish Soda Bread

Irish soda bread is unusual in that it is leavened with baking soda only; historically, no leaven has been used, and it has been as pure as possible. You will find Irish soda bread these days, filled with additions such as cheese, dried fruit, herbs, and seeds.

Total Time:

Prep Time: 15 min.

Bake: 30 min.

Makes eight slices

Ingredients:

2 cups of all-purpose flour

Two tablespoons of brown sugar

One teaspoon baking powder

One teaspoon baking soda

1/2 teaspoon salt

Three tablespoons of cold butter

Two big eggs, room temperature, separated

1/3 cup raisins

3/4 cup buttermilk

Instructions:

- Preheat the oven until 375 °. Whisk the first five ingredients together. Cut in butter until coarse crumbs match the mixture. Whisk one egg and buttermilk together in another tub. Attach the combination to the flour; just stir until moistened. Pour in the raisins.
- Turn the floured surface; gently knead six to eight times. Shape to a 6-1/2-in. Square loaf. Place it on a baking sheet that has been greased. Create a shallow cross on top of the loaf using a sharp knife. Whisk remaining egg; brush over the top.
- Bake, for 30-35 minutes, until golden brown. Move from pan to rack. Serve dry.

Nutrition Facts: 1 piece: 210 calories, 6 g of fat (3 g of saturated fat), 59 mg of cholesterol, 463 mg of sodium, 33 g of carbohydrate (8 g of sugar, 1 g of fiber).

Recipe 13

French Baguette

A baguette is a long, thin loaf of French bread generally made from the lean base dough (the dough is specified by French law, but not the shape). The length and crisp crust make it distinctive. A baguette has a diameter of approximately 5 or 6 cm (2- 2 1/3 in) and an average length of about 65 cm (26 in), although a baguette can be up to 1 m (39 in) long.

Prep time: 40 minutes

Cook time: 30 minutes

Rising: 1 hour 35 minutes

Total time: 1 hour 10 minutes

Calories: 505kcal

Servings: 3 loaves

Ingredients:

1 Cup 1 1/2 12 oz. Water from spring or distilled heated to 115 F

One tablespoon 1/8 oz. Active dry yeast (using instant yeast but using the same procedure).

3 1/4 cups 16 3/4 oz. all-purpose flour

1 1/2 tablespoon 3/8 oz. kosher salt

Vegetable spray (to grease)

1/2 cup ice cubes

Instructions:

- Whisk water and yeast together in a stand-up mixer bowl; let sit, for about 10 minutes, until the yeast is foamy. Add the flour, salt, and mix with a fork until the dough shaped, and all the flour is mixed; let the dough set for about twenty minutes to allow the flour to hydrate. Start mixing the dough hooked with your mixer. Continue kneading for about 10 minutes, until smooth and elastic.
- Sprinkle in the vegetable spray in a large bowl and move the ball of dough to it. Conceal the utensil with plastic wrap and put the bowl in a cold oven.
- Let the dough rest for about 45 minutes until doubled in size.
- Move the dough to a work surface that is lightly floured and form into a rectangle of 8 "x 6." Fold the 8 "sides towards the middle, then fold the shorter sides towards the right, like a T-shirt. Return the dough, seam side down to the greased bowl. Cover with plastic again, and return to the oven. Let it sit until doubled in size, for around 1 hour. Remove the dough bowl from the oven and place a cast-iron skillet or heavy pan on the bottom rack of the oven.
- Burn the stove to 475 F. Move the dough to a work surface that is lightly floured and cut into three equal pieces; form each part into a 14-inch line.
- Flour on a rimless baking sheet with a sheet of parchment paper; put ropes on paper, equally spaced. Lift paper between lines to form plows; put two tightly rolled kitchen towels under long edges of the paper, making the loaves' supports. Cover loosely with plastic wrap; let stay, for about 50 minutes, until they double in size.

- Uncover: remove towels, and flatten paper for loaves to be placed. Slice the top of each baguette at an angle of 30 degrees in four spots using a sharp razor, knife, bread lame, or scissor; each slice should be around 4 inches long. Take out the oven rack with the stone or baking sheet on it and slip the loaves, still on the parchment paper, onto the baking stone or pan using the corner of the parchment paper as a reference.
- Place ice cubes in the skillet or saucepan (this creates steam that helps the loaves to rise until a crust forms ultimately.) Bake the baguettes until brown, dark in color and crisp, for 20 to 30 minutes, then cool until serving.

Notes: Save the bowl-covers shower caps you get in the hotels. They work well as coverings for bowls, and you can save on plastic wrap.

Nutrition: Carbohydrates: 104 g, Protein: 15 g, Fat: 1 g, Sodium: 1173 mg, Potassium: 183 mg, Fiber: 4 g, Calcium: 24 mg, Iron: 6.4 mg

Recipe 14

Polish Bagels

A bagel is a bread product originating in Poland's Jewish communities. It is typically hand-shaped in the form of a yeasted wheat dough shell, which is first boiled in water for a short period and then baked. The effect is a thick, chewy, doughy interior with a dark. At times the exterior part is crisp. Bagels are often decorated with seeds baked on the outer crust, with poppy or sesame seeds being the common ones. Most may have salt sprinkled on their surface, and various types of dough are used, such as whole-grain or rye. Bagels are eaten toasted or untoasted.

Tips for Homemade Bagels:

- **Use bread flour:** The bread flour has a higher protein content, which is equivalent to higher gluten, which is equal to a chewy, but soft bagel. You might go as far as possible for buying a High Gluten flour, but bread flour works well for making this recipe practical.

- **Kneading:** The dough may be mixed and kneaded in a stand mixer. But, you still need a few minutes to knead the dough by hand. You can opt to mix and knead all together by hand. The initial process of adding the flour to the water is an excellent little arm exercise if you process by hand. The dough is rough and sticky and does not quickly blend like a cake batter.

- Kneading by hand, you can prepare for the dough to get to the right texture for ten minutes-which is smooth and elastic. The word elastic when referring to dough is just as you would imagine – that when pushed, poked, or pulled, the dough returns to its original shape – much like a rubber band. To check the dough and know that you kneaded it long enough, simply tap your fingers in it, and the dough fills up the gaps.

- time: 30 minutes
    - time: 25 minutes
    - time: 1 hour
    - time: 55 minutes

Ingredients:

- and 1/2 cups of water, room temperature
- and 1/4 teaspoons (1 packet) active dry yeast (high altitude adjustment: 2 teaspoons)
- tablespoons of brown sugar
- tablespoon of kosher salt

- cups of bread flour
- tablespoon of unsalted butter, melted and cooled slightly
- a teaspoon of baking soda cornmeal (for dusting bagel 'peel')
- big egg, beaten
- toppings: sesame seeds, poppy seeds, sea salt

Instructions:

- Combine 1/4 cup of water and leaven with a teaspoon of sugar spread over the top in a liquid measuring cup. Set aside for 5-10 minutes, before the yeast is smooth and foamy.
- Put the remaining water in a large mixing bowl and whisk the brown sugar in 2 tablespoons. Place two cups of flour and salt into the yeast mixture and stir with a wooden spoon. Keep adding a 1/2 cup of flour at a time and stir until the dough begins to come together as a thick, rough dough. Mixing the dough does need some 'elbow grease' but bringing the dough to the right consistency does not take long. You probably won't need any of the flour.
- Knead the dough – move the dough onto a floured surface (from the rest of the flour you measured), flour your hands and knead the dough for 7-10 minutes until a smooth, soft and elastic dough is present. You'll know that when you put your fingers into the dough, you kneaded the dough long enough and the dough fills up the gaps.
- Brush the melted butter over a large pot. Shape the dough into a ball and put it in the prepared bowl and also brush the butter in a melted form on top of the dough. Conceal the utensil with plastic wrap and a dry

kitchen towel and put the dough in a place which is warm for one to two hours, or until the dough has doubled in size.

- Top 2 half-size baking sheets with a parchment paper (or one full-size). These are going to be used for baking the bagels. Take another sheet of baking, turn it upside down and sprinkle with cornmeal. It is used as the 'peel' to season the bagels before they are moved to their baking sheets for baking.

- Fill a large pot with three-quarters of water when the dough is ready, and turn on heat high to bring it to a boil. The oven should be preheated to 425 degrees. The oven rack is moved to the middle position while using one baking sheet. Adjust the oven racks to the top third and bottom third of the oven, by using two baking sheets.

- Then punch the dough down to remove bubbles from the air. Turn onto a lightly floured surface and cut the dough into eight parts. Not every piece has to be similar, just get as close to the same size as possible. Work at one time with one piece of dough and put a kitchen towel over the other parts.

- You are shaping the bagel – pulling up the sides of the dough all over from the bottom, pinching it all together at the edges – to create a tightly packed ball with a pinched plough at the edges. Flip the pinched top over, so it is on top of your work surface, and stick your index finger in the middle area of the dough ball to create the bagel opening. Make the hole more prominent by using your other index finger to twirl it around your palm. You'll want it to be about 2 inches long because when boiled and cooked, the hole will shrink back slightly.

- Place the bagels in shape on the prepared baking sheets.
- The pot of water will be heating up by this time. To the boiling water, add the remaining two teaspoons of brown sugar and baking soda.
- Drop the bagels two at a time (or three if you have a bigger, more full pot) into the boiling water, and boil on each side for 35 seconds. The bagels will have enough room to float around so they'll be puffing up, so forming their circular shape.
- Remove the bagels from the bowl, and place them on the baking sheet of 'peel.'
- Brush each top with the wash of the egg, and sprinkle with your seasoning option.
- Move the bagels baked in the season to the prepared baking sheet.
- Bake for twenty minutes, or until light brown color emerges on the bagels. When baking on two baking sheets, the sheets rotate halfway round. Switch off the oven when the bagels are cooked, and let sit in the oven for another 5 minutes with the door closed. To cool down, switch to a wire rack.
- The bagels can be kept in an airtight container or Ziploc for up to 5 days at room temperature or place it in a fridge for up to a week. You can freeze leftover bagels for up to 3 months.

Notes:

- Adjustment of high altitude-typically high altitude changes come into play at altitudes above 3,500 feet.
- Reduce leaven to a max of 2 teaspoons. It is going to be less than what is in the yeast boxes, and you'll have

extra that you can recycle. Or you can buy yeast in tiny jars that are kept in the fridge.

- For high altitude changes, more water is used, which is why you can start with all the water and as much flour as required to get to the appropriate consistency of the dough. What a rough, sticky bread!

- In the dough, brown sugar and boiling water bath give the flavor of the donut.

- You can mix them by hand while you are mixing the dough, so you can have control over how the dough is coming together with each addition of flour. It takes a small amount of muscle to mix it, but it will quickly get together.

- If you like better, you can combine the dough in a stand mixer. Using the hook on the dough and mix the dough for 2-3 minutes. You'll also need to knead about 5 minutes by hand on a floured surface.

- There should be warm room temperature when proofing the dough in a friendly environment. Whether you've got a colder house, or it's a freezing day, you're going to want to find a warmer spot, like inside a cabinet or garage. Or even better if you have a box of evidence!

- You will realize that the dough proofing is finished when it has doubled in size and looks spongy as well. You can prove your dough in a full glass or plastic tub so that you can see it.

- While you're making the bagels, when you're splitting the flour, you should only see the right sizes. Others can turn out to be bigger, smaller, or slightly unacceptable, and that's all right! Adds character to a bagel baked in your house.

- In the boiling water bath, the baking soda helps make the bagels chewy. If you want a chewier bagel, you can keep the bagels in the water bath for some seconds longer.
- Enable the bagels to absolutely cool down before serving.

Recipe 15

Slovenia Poteca

Poteca (sometimes written potica or povitica) is a pastry filled and poured with a sweet nut mixture based on the Eastern European yeast. It may be round or in a sandwich, but it is delicious in whatever form you slice it down.

Total Time

Prep: 25 min. + cooling

Bake: 1 hour + cooling

Makes 12 servings

Ingredients:

1 cup butter

1/2 cup 2 percent milk

Three large egg yolks, room temperature

Two packages (1/4 ounce each) active dry yeast

One-fourth cup warm water (110 ° to 115 °)

2-1/2 cups of all-purpose flour

1 1/4 teaspoon sugar

Salt

Filling:

2 cups ground walnuts

2 cups cut dates

1/4 cup 2 percent milk

Three tablespoons plus 1 cup sugar

1/2 teaspoon ground cinnamon

Three big white eggs, room temperature

Confectioner's sugar, optional

Directions:

- Melt the butter with the milk in a small saucepan. Add egg yolks when mixed. Dissolve yeast in warm water in a small saucepan.
- Mix the flour, sugar, and salt in a huge bowl; add butter and yeast mixture. Beat for 3 minutes on medium speed (the dough will be sticky): cover, and cold overnight.
- Combine the nuts, dates, milk, three tablespoons of sugar, and cinnamon in a small saucepan over medium heat. Cook and stir until a paste forms a mixture. Shift to a big bowl.
- In a small saucepan, beat egg whites until soft peaks form. Gradually, beat one tablespoon at a time in remaining sugar, on high peaks until stiff peaks develop.
- Fold into nut mixture.
- Cut dough in half; on a floured surface, roll one portion into a 20-inch square. Spread half the filling over. Roll up tightly jelly- style. Place, seam side up, into a 10-in greased pan. Place, seam side down, over the first roll-up in the pan (layers will bake as one loaf).
- Bake at 350 ° for 60-70 minutes, until golden brown. Leave for 10 minutes to cool completely before removing from pan onto the wire rack. Sprinkle some confectioner's sugar, if necessary.

Nutrition Facts: 1 slice: 509 calories, 26 g fat (11 g saturated fat), 92 mg cholesterol, 182 mg sodium, 66 g carbohydrate (41 g carbohydrates, 4 g fiber), and 8 g protein.

Recipe 16

Italian Ciambella

Ciambella is very chewy, fennel-flavored rings of bread which are beautiful as between-meal snacks. Try this version of sweet Italian bread if the more popular panettone isn't your thing. Ciambella is simple but very satisfying, particularly when dunked in coffee or white wine!

Total Prep Time: 15 min.

Bake: 45 min.

Makes one loaf (20 slices)

Ingredients:

4 cups of all-purpose flour

1 cup of sugar

Two tablespoons of rubbed orange zest

Three teaspoons of baking powder

Three large eggs, room temperature

1/2 cup 2% milk

1/2 cup olive oil

One large egg yolk,

One tablespoon of coarse sugar

Instructions:

Preheat the oven until 350 °. Whisk the flour, sugar, orange peel and baking powder in a big cup.

Whisk eggs, milk, and oil in another pot until combined. Attach the mixture to the flour; just stir until moistened.

Form a 6-in—the round loaf on a tray of greasy baking. Place egg yolk on top; sprinkle with coarse sugar. Bake for forty-five to fifty minutes until a toothpick inserted in the center comes out clean. In the last 10 minutes, cover the top loosely with foil if necessary to avoid over-browning. Remove to wire rack from pan; serve warm.

Nutrition Facts: 1 slice: 197 calories, 7 g (1 g saturated fat), 38 mg cholesterol, 87 mg sodium, 30 g carbohydrate (11 g carbohydrates, 1 g fiber), and 4 g protein.

Recipe 17

German Stollen Bread

Stollen is a fruit bread that includes nuts, spices, and dried or candied fruit, covered with powdered sugar or icing sugar. This is a famous German bread eaten during the Christmas season when it is called Weihnachtsstollen or Christstollen (after Christmas).

This cake-like fruit bread is made of yeast, water, and flour and usually added to the dough with zest. Added in it are the orange peel and candied citrus peel (Zitronate), raisins and almonds, and various spices, including cardamom and cinnamon. Other ingredients may also be added to the dough, such as milk, sugar, butter, salt, rum, eggs, cinnamon, other dried fruits, and nuts and marzipan.

The dough is relatively low in sugar except for the fruits added. The finished bread with icing sugar is the ultimate form. Stollen's standard weight is around 2.0 kg (4.4 lb.), but smaller measurements are common. When it is out of the cooking oven, the bread is slathered with melted unsalted butter and rolled in sugar, resulting in a moister product that keeps better. The middle loop with marzipan is optional. For a superior-tasting bread, the dried fruits are macerated in rum or brandy.

Yield: 1 Big or two small loaves

Prep Time: 1 day

Bake Time: 1 HOUR

Total time: 1 day 1 hour

Ingredients:

Dried Fruits:

2 1/2 cups of dried fruit (raisins, golden raisins, dried currants, dried cranberries)

1/4 cup rum candied zest

1 cup of sugar

3/4 cup water

8 Tbsp zest of lemons and oranges

Dough:

4 cups of flour (all purposes)

1/2 cup of sugar

1 tsp of salt

One packet (1/4 oz.) of yeast

1 tsp of cardamom

One tablespoon of nutmeg

1/2 cup of cinnamon

3/4 cup of milk

One egg

2 tsp of vanilla extract

Instructions:

- Dried fruit: Dunk dried fruit in rum (or orange juice if you want a non-alcoholic version) for at least a few hours (this is best overnight).
- Create Oranges and Lemons Mixed Candied Zest Wash (use organic if you can).
- To zest lemons and oranges, use a Micro plane until you have eight tablespoon
- Put sugar and water in a pan and over medium-high heat, bring to a low boil. Add zest, and cook for 10 minutes.
- Turn off the heat and let it cool down for a couple of minutes. Strain the liquid in a small bowl and let the candied zest cool off.
- Cover and refrigerate with plastic wrap until ready to use.
- Bread Dough: In a stand mixer pot, combine the flour, yeast, sugar, salt, and spices.
- Heat the butter and the milk over medium heat in a small pan. Take off heat when butter is melted, and let cool for 5 minutes.

- Measure the mixture of milk and butter and pour into the dry ingredients. Include vanilla and egg and then mix in a pastry form.

- Knead the dough over low speed for 10 minutes using the hook attachment. Then cover with a towel over the bowl and let the dough rest for at least 10 minutes.

- Move dough to a surface that is lightly floured. Squeeze it into an oval — layer 1/2 of the candied zest over the flour, and chopped or sliced almonds. Fold the dough into half, then the other way in half again. Knead the dough 2 to 3 times to work with the zest and nuts. Push the dough out again and repeat with the remaining zest and chopped almonds.

- A third time, press the dough out and add 3/4 cup of dried fruit. Fold and knead the dough as set out above. A 4th time, press the dough and add another 3/4 cup of dried fruit. Fold again and knead until all is well absorbed into the dough.

- A 5th time press the dough into an oval shape, but this time press down more than the sides in the center so that you create a shallow trough in the middle of the dough. That's how you get the unique shape of Stollen. Put 1/2 cup dried fruit (the place in the middle that you pushed down) to the trough.

- Bend the third of the dough, so the dried fruit you've just added is hidden. Then turn over the dough. Attach the remaining dried fruit to dough trough. Fold the top third of the dried fruit onto the dough.

- Cover the dough with a towel and allow it for 30-40 minutes to rise.

- Preheat the oven to 350 F.

- Move to a lined baking sheet or baking stone. Bake it for sixty minutes, or until the top is golden brown and place in 190 F indoor temperature.
- Let the Stollen take a few minutes to cool, then brush the melted butter over the rim. Sift half of the Stollen's powdered sugar over the top. Pick the remaining butter softened over the top of the bread (on the first layer of butter and sugar). Sift the residual powdered sugar over the top.
- Let the Stollen cool off before they serve. Place in a container that is airtight.
- Stollen is best consumed in just a couple of days.

Notes:

For mini Stollen-split, the dough into two and follow as directed the rest of the recipe.

For Stollen Bites-roll dough into balls of 36 (half the dough) or 72 (all the dough). Don't bite the dough around. Let it get up for 35-40 minutes — Bake for 15-18 minutes on a baking plate, or lined baking dish. Once off the oven, let it cool down for a couple of minutes. Dip every bite of Stollen in butter and then toss it in powdered sugar. Place in a container that is airtight.

Recipe 18

Chapati

It is also termed as roti, shabaati, safati, phulka, and (in the Maldives) roshi. Chapati is an unleavened flatbread originating in India, Nepal, Bangladesh, Pakistan, Sri Lanka, Eastern Africa, and the Caribbean. Chapatis are produced of whole-wheat flour known as atta, mixed with water in the dough, edible oil, and optional salt in a mixing utensil called parat, and cooked on a tava (flat skillet).

It is a popular staple on both the Indian subcontinent and worldwide among expatriates from the Indian subcontinent.

Prepare time: 10 min

Cook time: 15 minutes

Rest time: 20 minutes

Total time: 25 minutes

Servings: 12 Chapattis or Roti's

Calories: 97 kcal

Ingredients:

US Customary — Metric

2 cups of whole wheat flour

1/4 teaspoon salt, optional

Two tablespoons of olive oil, + 1/4th teaspoon of olive oil

1 cup of water, or as required, at room temperature

1/4 cup of whole wheat flour to roll

Optional Ghee

Instructions:

- **To make the dough:** Mix 2 cups of wheat flour, salt, oil in a full bowl with 1/4 cup water. And just continue to knead. Add water in small amounts and start kneading until the dough joins as a ball.
- Apply 1/4th teaspoon of oil to the dough and knead until it absorbs oil.

- If the dough is sticky, sprinkle on the dough around 1/4 teaspoon of wheat flour (or more if needed) and knead again to form a non-sticky dough. The dough should be smooth and supple.
- Cover and set aside the dough for 15-20 minutes.
- **Making the chapatis:** Take a tiny piece about the size of a dough golf ball. Place the piece between your hands' palms, and form it into a ball. Flatten the egg, and cover with flour on both sides.
- Drag the flattened ball out into a circular shape that is uniformly thin (about 7-8 "in diameter). As required, dust more flour to help with the roll.
- Sprinkle the extra flour from the chapati by putting it on one hand's palm, and then turn it on the other hand's palm. Repeat the cycle three to four times.
- **Chapati Cooking:** Heat over medium to high heat a medium-sized pan.
- Place the chapati rolled out into the hot oven. Cook the chapati until tiny bumps begin to appear on the surface (about 1-2 minutes). Flip the chapati onto the opposite side and cook for about 10 seconds before you see cracks.
- Put the pan aside, and cook the chapati on an open flame with tongs. Notice the fire reaches the side that was on top first. Once the chapati has puffed up, turn the other side to cook.
- Take out the chapati from the flame and brush with ghee on both sides and put it in a jar that keeps the chapatis warm until you're ready to eat. Repeat the cycle for the remainder of the dough.
- Grease the chapatis with ghee and eat it warm with curry dal, potato, or chicken.

Notes:

Turn out the next chapati as one cooks in the oven, to fasten the process.

Until cooking, make sure to dust the excess flour off the chapati. This will ensure the chapati stays strong.

Until storing it in an airtight container, let the chapati cool down a bit so that it doesn't get soggy.

For those with a cooktop or coiled stove top induction, here's how you can puff up your roti-once. Both sides are fried; flip the roti onto the pan again. Use a clean towel in the kitchen and push the roti edges (not the middle), and this will create the roti to rise up.

How to make round rotis?

Just flatten the balls until they start rolling.

Roll them in a circular motion, which puts more pressure on the sides than the middle. It takes time to master the circular motion, so then use this method – rotate the dough as you roll them out so that they are spread evenly.

Sprinkle the flour, if the rotis stick to the foundation. Make sure you dust the flour before putting the chappatis in the saucepan.

Other choices: Use a sharp edge plate or bowl – Roll the roti and then use a large bowl or a cookie-like cutter to trim the edges.

Using a tortilla maker – line the press with plastic wrap, add dough, flatten slightly by hand, close the press, and apply pressure with the handle to flatten the dough into thick circles.

Recipe 19

Paska bread

This rich bread, backed by eggs, milk, and butter, has traditionally been made in Poland to mark the end of the fasting of the Lenten.

Total time: 75 minutes

Prep: 20 minutes

Cook: 55 minutes

Serving rate: 1 Paska (12 portions)

Nutritional Guidelines (per serving): 189 Calories, 11g Fat, 16g Carbs, 7g Protein

Ingredients:

1 1/2 cups of milk

1/2 cup of sugar (plus 1/2 teaspoon)

1/2 cup of water (lukewarm)

One pack of active dry yeast

7 1/2 cups of all-purpose flour

(Divided) Three large eggs (room temperature, beaten)

1/3 cup of butter (melted)

1 1/2 teaspoon of salt

Egg wash requirement: 1 large egg (room temperature)

Steps to make it:

- Scald the milk and set aside to cool.
- Dissolve 1/2 teaspoon of sugar in water and sprinkle over the yeast. Mix for 10 minutes and let stand.
- Combine the mixture of yeast with the cooled scalded milk and the 2 1/2 cup flour – play to smooth. Cover and let it rise until bubbly and light.
- Add milk, remaining 1/2 cup sugar, melted butter, and salt, and 4 1/2 to 5 cups of the remaining flour to make a not too stiff and not too loose dough.
- Knead until the dough avoids sticking to the hand and is smooth and satiny (approximately 7 minutes in a mixer, longer by hand).
- Put the dough in a bowl, turn on both sides to grease, cover with greased plastic wrap and let it puff up until doubled. Punch down, and let it come back again.
- For decoration, reserve 1/3 of the dough. Shape the rest into a round loaf and put in a grated 10- to a 12-inch round pan.
- Then shape the allocated dough into choosing decorations — a cross, swirls, rosettes, braiding, etc. — and place on top of the dough.

- Cover the pan with greased plastic wrap, and let it rise to nearly double.
- Stove to be heated to 400 F. Brush the bread with one large egg beaten with two spoons of sugar. Bake in for 15 minutes.
- Reduce temperature to 350 F and bake for another 40 minutes, or until 190 F is registered by an instant-read thermometer. Cover the top of the bread with aluminum foil if necessary to avoid excessive browning.
- Remove from the oven and switch onto a wire rack to completely cool off.

Tip: Some cooks make the decorations from a stiffer, non-yeast, sculpting dough, so the shapes won't bend when baked.

Recipe 20

English Muffins

English muffins are thin, round, flat yeast-leavened bread, commonly sliced horizontally, toasted and buttered. Toasted English muffins, often used as a breakfast food in the United Kingdom and the United States, can be served with sweet toppings (e.g., fruit jam or honey) or savory toppings (e.g., eggs, sausages, bacon or cheese). In several breakfast sandwiches, English muffins are often used as the bread and are an essential ingredient in Eggs Benedict and most of its variants.

Preparation time: 15 minutes

Cook time: 25 minutes

Ready in: 40 minutes

Makes: 12 muffins

Ingredients:

1/4 cup of dry (powdered) milk

1 table cup of sugar (brown or white)

One tablespoon of kosher salt

2 cups plus 2 table cups of unbleached flour

One cup of like warm water (110-115 degrees Fahrenheit or 43-46 degrees Celsius)

1 cup of plain yogurt

1 table cup of unsalted butter, melted

Proofed yeast

Extra butter for greasing

Cornmeal for sprinkling

Phase 1: The yeast to be proofed

Yeast is a living entity and needs to be enabled for the bread to inflate.

Heat 1/4 cup water at approximately 110 to 115 degrees Fahrenheit or 43 to 45 degrees C. It should feel moist and not hot to the touch. Too much hot water will kill the yeast, but the yeast will not be activated if it is too cold.

Stir and add two teaspoons of active dry yeast. Apply 1/4 tea cubit of sugar and flour each.

Let the yeast settle for five minutes or so. It will start foaming and smell like baked bread.

From here, you can move on to the next stage, below.

Phase 2: Mix and bake

In a middle mixing cup or bowl, add the dry ingredients (powdered milk, sugar, salt, and flour).

Then add the wet ingredients (melted butter, tea, and yogurt) and proof yeast.

To knead the dough using a hand or stand mixer, processor, or bread maker, consult the instructions of the supplier. It takes about 5 minutes.

Pour the dough into a medium mixing bowl, cover it with plastic wrap and place in the refrigerator overnight.

The dough will have been "over proofed" by morning, meaning it will have risen entirely and will begin to collapse. Remove the mixing bowl from the fridge and put on the countertop while the muffin rings are being prepared.

Grease the griddle with cornmeal.

Place rings on the griddle and turns heat on low.

Grease 1/4 of a cup. 1/4 cup dough is to be scooped into each loop.

Place a sheet of baking on above of the rings and allow to cook for 6-10 minutes on the first hand, depending on your griddle temperature.

Flip the rings over and cook for about 6 minutes on the second hand, taking care not to burn them.

Switch English muffins to a 5-minute 350 Fahrenheit oven for completion.

Enjoy them warmly or, better yet, let them cool off before they break and toast. Serve English muffins with plenty of real butter, full of nooks and crannies!

Mixing and Baking Tips:

- Plain yogurt gives good "sourdough" taste to the muffins.
- For kneading the dough, you can use a hand blender, bread machine, food processor, or stand mixer. Follow guidance from the manufacturer.
- You have to prove the yeast before kneading (see phase 1, above).
- Over proofing the dough, as is recommended here, makes it rise high and then starts collapsing, giving the English muffins their distinctive texture.
- The condensed milk and warm water can be replaced with 1 1/4 cups of milk.
- You can make the muffins in free-form, but you would need to invest in English muffin rings for perfectly round muffins.
- Do not cause the dough to rise to the rings after pouring it in. It will increase while cooking on the hot griddle.
- You may either use a standard electric or stovetop.
- Cooled, crumbled, and toasted English muffins are best for a crunchy texture.

Recipe 21

Eastern European Challah Bread

Challah is an exceptional and significant bread in Jewish cuisine, usually braided and eaten on ritual occasions such as Shabbat and significant Jewish (other than Passover) holidays. Ritually appropriate challah is made from flour, a small portion of which has been set aside as an offering.

Total Time

Prep: 45 min. + rising

Bake: 30 min. + refrigeration

Makes two loaves (24 portions each)

Ingredients:

2 Packets (1/4 ounce each) of active dry yeast

1/2 teaspoon of sugar

1-1/2 cups of warm water (110 ° to 115 °)

Five big eggs

2/3 cup plus one teaspoon of honey

1/2 cup of canola oil

Two teaspoons of salt

6 to 7 cups of bread flour

1 cup of boiling water

2 cups of golden raisins

One tablespoon of water

One tablespoon of sesame seeds

Directions:

- Mix the yeast with sugar in one cup of lukewarm water in a small pot. Two eggs are to be separated while two egg whites refrigerated. Place the egg yolks and eggs remaining in a large cup. Add 2/3 cup honey, butter, salt, yeast mixture, 3 cups of flour, and staying warm water; beat for 3 minutes at a medium pace. Apply enough remaining flour to form a soft dough (the dough is sticky).

- In a small cup or bowl, put the boiling water over raisins; allow to stand for 5 minutes. Drain off, and brush. Turn the dough over a floured surface; knead for 6-8 minutes, until smooth and elastic. Knead them with raisins. Place them in a greased tub, turning to graze the top once. Cover with plastic wrap and let rise, for around 1-1/2 hours, in a warm place until almost doubled.

- Punch the dough in. Turn on a surface which is gently floured. Divide the batter into two. Divide one serving in six pieces. Each roll into a 16-in. Rope. Place ropes on a greased baking sheet parallel to each other; pinch ropes at the edges.

- Bring the rope to the right and hold it over the two ropes next to it to braid, then slip it under the middle rope and bring it over the last two ropes. Lay down the rope parallel to the other ropes; it's now to the far left. Repeat those steps until you come to an end. As the braid is shifted towards the left, you can pick up the loaf and, as appropriate, make it more recent on your work surface. Pinch ends by sealing and tucking under. Using your fingertips, bring the loaf ends closer together for a fuller loaf. Repeat with remaining dough. Cover with towels for the kitchen; let it rise in a warm place until almost doubled, for around 30 minutes.

- The oven is to be preheated to 350 ° C. Whisk remaining egg whites and honey in a small bowl with water; brush over loaves. Sprinkle the sesame seeds. Bake for thirty to thirty-five minutes until golden brown and bread sounds hollow. Remove to cool from pan to wire rack.

Nutrition Facts: 1 slice: 125 calories, 3 g fat (0 saturated fat), 19 mg cholesterol, 107 mg sodium, 21 g carbohydrate (8 g carbohydrates, 1 g fiber), and 3 g protein.

Recipe 22

Czech Republic Kolaches

A kolach is a type of pastry-bread containing a portion of the fruit that is surrounded by puffy dough. Such small yeasted snacks are often filled with seeds from fruits or poppies. They date back to Bohemia-now part of the Czech Republic. Originating from Central Europe as a semi- wedding dessert and afterward a breakfast item in London (South), they have become famous in parts of the United States.

Preparation time: 3 hours

Cook time: 20 minutes

Total time: 3 hours 20 minutes

Servings: 16

Calories: 316 kcal

Ingredients:

For dough:

1 cup of whole milk

Ten tablespoons butter, melted

One large egg

Two large egg yolks

3.5 cups of all-purpose flour (17.5 ounces) * (up to 4 cups)

1/3 cup of sugar (2.3 ounces)

2 1/4 teaspoons of instant yeast

1/2 teaspoon of salt

For the cheese filling:

6 ounces of cream cheese

Three tablespoons of sugar

One tablespoon of flour

1/2 teaspoon of lemon zest grated

6 ounce of salt

For the blueberry filling:

10 ounces of frozen strawberries, blueberries or cherries

Five tablespoons of sugar

Four teaspoons of cornstarch

For the streusel topping:

One tablespoon of all-purpose flour

Two tablespoons of sugar plus two teaspoons

One tablespoon of unsalted butter cut into eight parts and cooled

For the egg wash:

I egg combined with 1 tbsp of milk

Directions:

For making dough (makes 16 kolaches): Mix milk, butter, and eggs in a measuring cup. Combine dry ingredients in a standing mixer bowl, then add milk mixture and knead for 2 minutes at low speed. Raise speed to medium and continue kneading for 8 to 12 minutes until the dough no more sticks to the side of the utensil you are using. Add ricotta and proceed to combine for another 30 seconds. Cover and cook until required.

Streusel: Add all ingredients in a mixing bowl and mix with fingers. Cover and refrigerate until required.

For fruit filling (sufficient for 16): Combine all ingredients in a safe bowl for microwave and mix well. For around 6 to 8 minutes, microwave on high and stir halfway through the cooking.

To assemble and bake, line 2 parchment-paper baking sheets.

Cut the dough into sixteen pieces of equal size and shape them into balls. Arrange on prepared sheets, cover with plastic, and allow to rest in a warm place for 1.5 hours— Preheat oven to 350 degrees. Flour the bottom of 1/3 cup dry measure or 2 1/4 inch diameter glass and use to make deep indents on top of each ball until the bottom of the measure reaches the baking sheet.

Warmly serve

Recipe 23

South American Cornbread

Cornbread is a staple in the South of America and is suitable for butter absorption. Although there's little or no sweetener in the conventional version, more modern versions incorporate honey, sugar, or even agave.

The honey cornbread is the perfect recipe for cornbread! It's slightly sweet, tender, and delicious.

Course: Side Dish

Cuisine: American

Prep Time: 10 minutes

Cook Time: 20 minutes

Total time: 30 minutes

Calories: 230 kcal

Servings: 10

Ingredients:

One tablespoon butter softened

1 cup of cornmeal

1 cup of all-purpose flour

One tablespoon of baking powder

1/4 cup of sugar

One teaspoon of salt

1 cup of buttermilk

Two eggs

Four tablespoon butter, melted

1/4 cup of honey

Indications:

The oven must be preheated to four hundred degrees F. Use the melted butter to grease a baking pan or cast-iron skillet in 9 or 10 inches long.

Blend the cornmeal, flour, baking powder, sugar, and salt in a big pot.

In the center of the dry mixture, make a well and add buttermilk, butter, and honey.

Filter until just blended-do not overmix!

Pour the batter into the prepared casserole.

Bake it for twenty to twenty-five minutes or until its color turn to a golden brown.

Cool down for 10 minutes or so.

Break it into bits, then eat.

Notes: Simply divide the batter into a greased 12 muffin cup tin and bake for 15 minutes, if you want to make cornbread muffins

Nutrition:

Calories: 230 kcal, Carbohydrates: 34 g, Protein: 4 g, Fat: 8 g, Saturated fat: 4 g, Cholesterol: 50 mg, Sodium: 322 mg, Potassium: 234 mg, Fiber: 1 g, Sugar: 13 g, Vitamin A: 260 IU, Calcium: 88 mg, Iron: 1.4 mg, Dietary calories: 230kcal, Carbohydrates: 34 g.

Recipe 24

Mexican Tortillas

A tortilla flour or tortilla wheat is a type of smooth, thin flatbread made from finely ground wheat flour. It was initially derived from the corn tortilla, a maize flatbread that predates Europeans' introduction to the Americas. Made with a dough based on flour and water, it is pressed and fried, similar to tortillas made from corn. The most straightforward recipes use only wheat, water, fat, and salt, but commercially produced wheat tortillas usually contain chemical leavening agents such as baking powder and other components.

Flour tortillas are usually filled with beef, chopped potatoes, refried beans, cheese, hot sauce, and other ingredients to produce dishes such as tacos, quesadillas, and burritos (a dish originating in Ciudad Juarez, Chihuahua, Mexico / El Paso, Texas).

Prep Time: 5 minutes

Cook Time: 2 minutes

Rest time: 15 minutes

Servings of 12

Ingredients:

6 Cups Bread Flour

4 Teaspoons Baking Powder

3 Teaspoons Salt

2/3 Cup Oil

2 1/4 cups boiling water

Instructions:

- Incorporate the flour, salt, baking powder and oil in a mixing bowl with a standing mixer.
- Switch the mixer to low speed using a dough hook, never fast, and mix until the mixture gets together and looks like moon sand or barely wet sand. In your palm, you can grip it, and it holds together.
- Pour the boiling water at a low level, around 1/2 cup at a time into the mixer. Run the mixer. Keep adding water as you go, before the dough joins in. Let the mixer blend for another 2-4 minutes before the dough is satiny.
- Flour the work surface very gently and pinch balls of dough smaller than your hand palm.
- Keeping the ball in your palm, pinch the dough in the center over and over with your other hand as you shape a rounded side against your hand and a flat side where you pinch.
- Place the entire dough in your bowl and cover it with a moist, humid paper towel or put a lid on the pot. Enable for 10-15 minutes to rest.
- Heat at the medium level the griddle.
- With a rolling pin, dust the work surface gently and roll out the dough balls one at a time.

- Cook the tortilla on the pan that is hot until bubbles start to grow high flip over, and cook again until it shows light browning.
- Remove from heat and serve.

Notes: Before rolling out the dough can sit on the counter for up to 1 hour.

A cooler tortilla is worth it. In the afternoon, you can cook your tortillas, and at dinner, they are still good!

Some pro tips

Bread flour is compulsory. It adds the accurate quantity of gluten and makes it possible to roll out the dough perfectly thin without tearing.

Oil, not shortening, makes tortilla more elastic and still watery (goodbye dry flour tortillas!). You don't need lard or fancy anything. Only plain old vegetables are doing the trick only right!

Boiling water changes the texture of the dough. It's going to be gentle and silky! When it's still hot, your stand mixer can do all the job, so you don't have to be stressed about handling the dough and burning yourself.

Put a towel paper in a Ziploc bag to hold the tortillas, add the tortillas, and put another on top before shutdown.

Recipe 25

Swedish Limpa Bread

Limpa bread is orange-flavored Swedish rye bread with fennel or anise (or both). Toasted with butter, it is excellent but can also be used as sandwich bread.

Complete Time Prep: 30 min. + riser

Bake time: 30 min.

Makes two loaves (12 slices each)

Ingredients:

1/2 cup of light brown sugar

1/4 cup of dark molasses

1/4 cup of butter

Two tablespoons of grated orange zest

1-1/2 teaspoons of salt

One teaspoon aniseed, lightly crushed

1 cup of boiling water

1 cup of cold water

Two packets (1/4 ounce each) of active dry yeast

Half cup or small mug of warm water (110 ° to 115 °)

4-1/2 cups of all-purpose flour

3 to 4 cups of rye flour

Two tablespoons of cornmeal

2 tbsp melted butter

Instructions:

Add brown sugar, molasses, butter, orange zest, salt, aniseed, and boiling water in a large bowl; whisk until brown sugar is dissolved, and butter melted. Remove cold water; let stand until the mixture cools to 110 to 115 degrees.

Meanwhile, mix the yeast in lukewarm water in a large tub. Mix in molasses; blend well. Add 1 cup rye flour and all-purpose flour. Beat for 3 minutes on medium speed. Remove enough remaining rye flour for a steep dough to shape.

Turn onto a floured surface; knead for around 6-8 minutes, until smooth and elastic. Place them in a greased tub, turning to graze the top once. Conceal and let it rise until doubled in a warm spot, around 1 hour.

Punch-down the bread. Put it on a place that is lightly floured; divide in half. In two oval loaves, shape. Grease two baking sheets, then sprinkle with cornmeal lightly — place loaves on prepared pans. Conceal and let rise, for about thirty minutes, till it doubles.

The oven is to be preheated to 350 °. Make four shallow slashes through each loaf with a sharp knife — Bake for 30-35 minutes or until brown or golden. Remove to rack wire; brush with butter.

Nutrition Facts: 1 slice: 186 calories, 3 g of fat (2 g of saturated fat), 8 mg of cholesterol, 172 mg of sodium, 35 g of carbohydrate (7 g of sugar, 3 g of fiber).

Recipe 26

Italian Pane Di Pasqua

Pane di Pasqua is an Italian "Easter bread." This sweet bread is filled with colored whole eggs and is eaten at Easter traditionally as well as other important occasions. Pane di Pasqua (or Italian Easter bread) is just as delicious. Its distinctive form and decorations, coupled with orange and anise flavors, making it best suited for such a special holiday. This Italian Easter Bread is a typically wreath-shaped, fluffy sweet bread with brightly colored eggs baked inside.

Ingredients:

Bread:

1/2 cup warm water

Two packets yeast a little less than two tablespoons

1/2 cup butter

3/4 cups of milk

1/2 cup sugar

Two eggs gently are beaten

1 1/2 teaspoon salt

5-6 cups of all-purpose flour

Zest of 1 lemon

Optional: 5 eggs uncooked

Three teaspoons vinegar

Red yellow and blue food coloring

For the final egg wash: 1 egg

Instructions:

- Mix the yeast in lukewarm water in a large mixing mug or bowl. (Hot tap water, but no colder ones).
- Melt butter in a saucepan. Stir in the milk and heat until dry. Having a drop on your wrist will test it. It should be warm, but it should not feel dry. If it's hot, let it cool down. The hot liquid will diminish the yeast and will not lift your bread.
- Attach the yeast with the milk and butter, and blend.
- Add the sugar, two lightly beaten eggs, salt, and zest of lemons (if used). Combine to blend.
- Apply 5 cups of flour, one cup at a time, mixing each addition in between. The dough is going to get a little sticky.
- Sprinkle onto the counter around 1/2 cup of flour. Turn the dough out and knead onto the floured surface for about 5 minutes. Add extra flour, around 1/4 cup at a time, if the dough is kneading too sticky.
- When you add too much flour, the dough is not going to be light and fluffy. If you have a bread hook mixer, use it to do the kneading.
- Drop the dough into a lightly oiled tub. Cover with plastic wrap, which is finely oiled. Put the dough in a warm area to grow until doubled, 1 to 1 1/2 hours.
- Heat 1 1/2 cups of water while the dough is rising.
- Choose three small tassels. Apply 15-20 drops of color (one red, one yellow, and one blue) to each cup. Add one tablespoon of vinegar to each bowl, then stir and add 1/2 cup of boiling water to each cup.
- Dip the colored eggs, and let them stay as dark as you like. You can mix and match the brown, green, and purple colors too.
- Punch the dough down and break into three equal parts. Wrap each part in a long rope, about 20 inches.

- Braid together the three strands and turn into a circle, pinching and tucking the ends together. Place it on a baking sheet with grease.
- Drive the five-colored eggs gently into the dough. Stick a small cup in the center so that the wreath doesn't close in the middle when it grows.
- Let rise, about forty-five minutes to one hour, until doubled.
- Preheat oven to 350 ° C.
- Remove the bread cup from the middle. Combine the last egg with one teaspoon of water and brush the bread (not the eggs in color). Cover all the dough, even where possible in the crevices between the braid.
- Bake till bread is golden brown for 25 minutes.

Recipe Notes: For the recipe, you'll need a minimum of 8 eggs: 2 are mixed in the dough five-colored and baked on top of the dough one is brushed to make the bread brown and shiny.

Recipe 27

Denmark Julekage

Julekake or julekage is a thick, sweet bread filled with dried fruits and spices with cardamom in particular. During winter holidays it is a staple in Scandinavian households. This bread has a beautiful texture! It's so fluffy, and sprinkled candied fruit makes delicious and beautiful slices.

Ingredients:

4 1/2 teaspoons (2 packs) active dry yeast

Half cup (120 ml) warm water, 105 ° F to 115 ° F

Two cups (480 ml) milk, lukewarm

1/2 cup (98 g) sugar

1/2 cup (113 g) butter, softened

Two teaspoons of salt

One teaspoon of ground cardamom

Two eggs, beaten

7- Cups (840- g) all-purpose flour

1 cup (150 g) golden raisins (sultanas)

1 cup (170 g) mixed candied fruit

Eggs wash (1 egg + 1 tablespoon water)

½ cup pearl sugar

Glaze:

2 cups (227 g) sugar

3-4 spoonfuls of milk or cream

Vanilla extract

Candied fruit for garnish, optional

Instructions

Mix the yeast in lukewarm water in the bowl or mug of an electric mixer and let sit for five minutes until it is foamy. Fit the paddle attachment to the blender and mix in the milk, sugar, butter, salt, cardamom, and eggs. Blend well. (Butter bits are going to float to the surface here, and they're going to look all sorts of wrong– just go with it). Stir in the flour for 3 1/2 cups, and beat well. Stir half the flour in and beat well. Add another three and a half mugs of flour, combine to make the dough fluffy. Cover for 15 minutes, and let it rest.

Fit the dough hook attachment to the mixer. Set a timer, and knead the dough at low speed for 10 minutes. Intermittently, apply the remaining 1/4 cup flour at a time until a smooth, satin, elastic dough forms. You probably don't have to use all the flour. Stop the mixer, then add the fruits. Knead until the fruit is well spread in the dough, again at medium speed.

Lightly grease a large bowl (or wash the mixing bowl, dry and grease) and put the dough inside. Cover with plastic wrap, and let it grow until doubled in a warm place. Punch the dough down and turn up again. Let it rise in bulk until doubled.

Grease 3 round cake pans. Take out the dough onto a lightly floured work surface and knead for a short period (three to four turns) until the dough is not sticky. Split the dough into pieces equal to three. Form each part into a ball of raw material. Using both hands, pick up a ball of dough, and use your fingers. Move the sides of the dough underneath the ball, tuck down the ends, and rotate the ball while you work. Keep repeating the motion until the dough has also rounded together. Place each piece of dough in a prepared saucepan. Cover with plastic wrap and makeup to double stand.

Preheat to 375 ° F on the oven.

Use a pastry brush to coat the cakes with egg wash. Cover with pearl sugar over the top. Bake until golden brown and fragrant, for 25-30 minutes. Turn the bread onto racks for the wire. Let cool down slightly before glazing.

Place the sugar of the confectioners in a large bowl for the glaze and whisk in just enough cream to create a very thick glaze. Ass in the vanilla and whisk well. Glaze generously with additional candied fruit on each loaf and top, if desired.

Recipe 28

Polish Chocolate Babka

Babka is a thick bread. It is a soft dough of yeast filled in layers with fudgy chocolate or cinnamon and baked. Often, it even has a streusel on top. You can remember it as a lovely piece of cake/bread with hundreds of chocolate swirls on your Instagram.

Once you get a bite of this gluten-free Babka bread, you'll wonder what it took you so long to try one. Sweet dough rotated and whirled with a chocolate filling is indeed a heavenly slice!

Course: Breakfast, Dessert

Cuisine: European/ Polish

Type: Gluten-Free

Prep Time: 30 minutes

Cooking time: 40 minutes

Proofing time, resting time: 11 hours

Total time: 12 hours 10 minutes

Servings: 8 servings

Ingredients:

1/2 gluten-free cinnamon roll dough

1/2 cup (1 piece, 113 g) butter

1/2 cup (100 g) granulated sugar

1/3 cup (35 g) cocoa powder

1/4 tsp cinnamon

3 ounces semi-sweet or bittersweet chocolate, minced medium fine

For the syrup:

1/3 cup granulated sugar

1/3 cup water

Instructions:

- Render gluten-free cinnamon roll dough as guided (including 2-hour proofing and overnight chilling).
- Mix sugar, butter, cocoa powder, and cinnamon in a stand mixer bowl (or use a handheld mixer) and whisk through beater for a couple of minutes until creamed and well mixed.

- Take out the dough from the fridge and knead quickly on a lightly floured surface. Roll the dough to a full rectangle, about 10-12 inches (although it doesn't have to be exact). Spread the filling of chocolate to the bottom, leaving a distance of one inch at the top, width wise. Sprinkle the chocolate chopped over the mixture and roll up, pinch seam to close. Place roll on a small baking sheet lined with parchment, seam side down, and cover with plastic wrap. A place for 15–20 minutes in the freezer.

- Line an 8 1/2 by 4-inch loaf pan with an overhanging piece of parchment paper on each long side. Spray with a nonstick spray.

- Remove roll from the freezer and cut down the middle of roll lengthwise using kitchen shears or a very sharp knife to reveal chocolate filling. Twist the two halves together (it is going to get a little messy). Cover with plastic wrap, and give around an hour to grow. It does not double in size, which is useful to perfection.

- Bake for about forty minutes in a three-fifty ° oven. When Babka is baking, add in a small saucepan 1/3 cup of granulated sugar. Little by little, pour 1/3 cup of water around the outer edge of sugar. This helps prevent the development of sugar crystals along the sides of the plate. Bring to a boil for about 3 minutes over medium heat, and boil. Take off heat and allow to cool.

- When Babka has finished baking, remove the pan with a long wooden skewer from the oven and prick. Pour the sugar syrup gradually all over the Babka. Let Babka cool down before serving.

Notes:

Wrap whole Babka in plastic wrap to keep it moist and fresh. Wrap in plastic wrap, then in foil, and put in the freezer to freeze. You can place it in the freezer for three months or so.

For two gluten-free chocolate Babkas, this recipe will double. Use a complete gluten-free ultimate cinnamon roll dough recipe, but split in half and deal with one half at a time. Double filling ingredients, then spread half of the dough over the other half. Increase ingredients of the sugar syrup to 2/3 cup per sugar and water.

Recipe 29

Russian Krendl Bread

Krendl, a Russian holiday bread, is usually reserved for Christmas. This pretzel-shaped sweet bread is filled with dried fruits and makes every celebration a beautiful centerpiece.

Time for Prep: 45 min. + rising

Bake: 45 min. + Refrigeration

Makes 24 servings

Ingredients:

One packet of (1/4 ounce) active dry yeast

Three tablespoons of sugar

3/4 cup warm half-and - a-half cream or whole milk (110 ° to 115 °)

1/4 cup butter, softened

Two big egg yolks

1-1/2 teaspoon vanilla extract

1/2 teaspoon salt

2-3/4 to 3-1/4 cup all-purpose flour

Filling:

1 cup of apple juice

One big apple, peeled and chopped

2/3 cup of finely chopped dried apples

1/3 cup of finely chopped dried apricots

1/3 cup of chopped dried pitted prunes

Five tablespoons of butter

Four tablespoons of sugar

1/2 teaspoon of ground cinnamon

Confectioners' sugar

Directions:

Dissolve the yeast and sugar in a small bowl in liquid water. Combine softened butter, egg yolks, cinnamon, salt, yeast mixture and 1-1/2 cup flour in a wide bowl; beat at medium velocity until smooth. Add enough remaining flour to form a soft dough (the dough is sticky).

Turn the dough onto a floured surface; knead for around 6-8 minutes, until smooth and elastic. Place them in a greased tub, turning to graze the top once. Cover with plastic wrap and allow to rise until doubled in a warm spot for around 1 hour.

Combine orange, apple, dried fruits, two tablespoons butter, and two tablespoons of sugar in a large saucepan for filling. Take to simmer. Reduce heat; boil, expose, for 25-30 minutes or stir periodically until mixture reaches a jam-like consistency. Switch to a bowl, completely cool off.

Punch the dough in. Turn onto a floured surface; roll into a 32x10-in sheet — appropriate point. Melt the remaining butter; scatter over the dough to 1 in of rims. Mix the remaining cinnamon and sugar; sprinkle over the edges — spread mixture with fruit. Roll up jelly-roll style, starting with a long side; pinch seam and seal ends.

Place seam side down on a baking sheet that is greased; turn into a pretzel shape. Cover with a kitchen towel; let it rise until almost doubled in a warm spot for about 30 minutes. The oven should be preheated to 350 ° C.

Bake for 40-45 minutes or until golden brown. Remove from pan to cool wire rack at the time of serving, dust with confectioner's sugar.

Nutrition Facts: 1 slice: 146 calories, 6 g fat (3 g saturated fat), 31 mg cholesterol, 92 mg sodium, 21 g carbohydrate (9 g carbohydrates, 1 g fiber), and 2 g protein, respectively.

Recipe 30

Australian Damper Bread

The staple of a traveler adapted to life on the road. Damper recalls the days of Australia's frontier.

It's an essential blend of water, flour, and salt that can be directly cooked, pressed into a cast iron pan, or even toasted at the end of a stick. Recipes also contain some chemical leavening, butter, and milk these days, transforming the hearty fare in backwoods into a more sophisticated treat similar to Irish soda bread.

Serving: 1 loaf

Ingredients:

2 3/4 cups of all-purpose flour

4 1/2 teaspoons of baking powder

One teaspoon salt

5 1/2 tablespoons of unsalted butter

3/4 cup of cooled water

Golden syrup for serving

Method:

Mix the baking powder, flour, and salt in one big pot. Cut the cold butter into cubes and blend with a dough mixer, a fork, or your fingers. Stir in the water to pull the dough together until the mixture has a coarse texture, with no bits more significant than a pea. If it's too crumbly, add some more sugar. If it's too wet, then apply some more flour. Knead until smooth, and be careful not to overwork.

Preheat the oven to 390 F. Line a parchment paper inside the baking dish, or gently grease.

Form the dough into a circle about seven inches (18 cm) long on a lightly floured surface. Move to bake sheet prepared for use.

Brush a sharp knife with flour and cut eight wedges into the top of the dough, around 1/4-1/2 inches thick. Powder the flour on top of the damper.

Bake in preheated oven for 30-40 minutes, when pressed, until hollow and softly golden. Allow for about 5 minutes to cool on a wire rack before serving. Best of all day, it's made warm or with golden syrup at room temperature.

Nutritional values per serving:

Protein 10.04 g, Fats (total) 3.13 g, Fats (saturated) 1.08 g, Carbohydrates 56.59 g.

Chapter 6: 20 Cool and Strange Recipes Using Bread

Baking is all about creativity. It is an art. Get your inner baker out with these inventive bread recipes. The following bread is cool, strange, and delicious at the same time. You are so going to enjoy them!

Recipe 1

Chocolate chip loaf

The total time for this recipe is 85 minutes, including the preparation and baking time. The method will give one loaf (16 slices).

Ingredients:

3 Big eggs, room temperature

1 cup of sugar

2 cups of sour cream

3 cups of self-rising flour

2 cups of chocolate chips, semi-sweet

Instructions:

- Preheat the oven until 350 °. Beat the eggs, sugar and sour cream until they blend well. Stir in flour, slowly. Fold them into chocolate chips. Move to a fatted 9x5-in. Loaf mold.

- Bake for sixty-five to seventy-five minutes until a toothpick comes out clean. Cool in a saucepan for 5 minutes before moving to a wire rack.

Note: Use 4-1/2 teaspoons of baking powder and 1-1/2 teaspoons of salt in a measuring cup as a replacement for 3 cups of self-rising flour. Combine with an additional 2 cups of all-purpose flour to weigh 1 cup.

Nutrition Facts: 1 slice: 306 calories, 13 g of fat (8 g of saturated fat), 42 mg of cholesterol, 305 mg of sodium, 44 g of carbohydrate (25 g of fiber), 5 g of protein.

Recipe 2

Pumpkin bread

Servings: Makes two loaves

Prep Time: 20 Minutes

Cook Time: 65 Minutes

Total Time: 1 hour 30 Minutes

Ingredients:

2 cups of all-purpose flour, spooned into measuring cup and leveled-off

1/2 teaspoon salt

One teaspoon baking soda

1/2 teaspoon baking powder

One teaspoon ground cloves

One teaspoon ground cinnamon

One teaspoon ground nutmeg

1-1/2 sticks (3/4 cup) unsalted butter, softened

2 cups of sugar

Two big eggs

One can of 15 oz. pure pumpkin (100%)

Directions:

Generously grease two 8 x 4-inch butter loaf pans and flour dust (alternatively, use a baking spray with flour in it).

Combine all these three ingredients; salt, flour, baking soda, baking powder, cloves, cinnamon, and nutmeg into a medium dish. Whisk together as well; set aside.

Beat the butter and sugar at normal speed in a large bowl of an electric mixer until just blended. Blend in the eggs one by one, beating well after each addition. Continue to beat for a few minutes, until very light and fluffy. At this point, the mixture could look grainy and curdled — that is all right.

Add the flour mixture and blend until mixed at a low level.

Place the batter into the prepared pans, divide evenly and bake for 65 – 75 minutes or until clean comes out a cake tester inserted in the middle. Let the loaves cool down in the pans for about 10 minutes, then turn onto a wire rack to cool.

The loaves are fresh from the oven and have a deliciously crisp crust. If they last beyond a day, individual slices can be toasted to get the same fresh-baked effect.

Freezer-friendly instructions: You can freeze the bread for up to 3 months. Cover it tightly in aluminum foil, freezer cover, or place it in a freezer bag after it's thoroughly cooled. Thaw in the refrigerator overnight before serving.

Recipe 3

Carrot bread

Servings: 8
Prep Time: 20 minutes
Total time: 2 hours 30 minutes

Ingredients:

For the bread:

1 1/4 c. All-purpose flour
1 Tsp baking powder
Ground 1/2 tsp cinnamon.
Ground 1/4 tsp. ginger
Ground 1/2 tsp nutmeg.

Kosher salt

Three large eggs

1 c. granulated sugar

Vegetable oil 1 cup

1 tbsp extract of pure vanilla

Rubbed carrots (about 4, medium-sized)

For the frosting:

Cream cheese, 2 tbsp

Melted butter, 2 tbsp

Sifted 1 tsp powdered sugar

Pure 1/4 tsp vanilla extract

½ cup grapes chopped

Toasted pecans 4 oz.

Directions:

- The oven should be preheated to 350 ° C. Grease a loaf pan of 9"-x-5 "with spray for frying, and line with parchment paper. Whisk the flour, baking powder, cinnamon, ginger, nutmeg, and salt together in a medium cup.
- Blend the sugar and eggs in a large bowl until light and fluffy. Pour in oil slowly when whisking until well mixed, then add vanilla. Stir dry ingredients until they are all blended. Wrap in the pecans and raisins.

- Pour batter into the prepared pan and bake for about 1 hour and 10 minutes, until a toothpick added in the center comes out clean. Let it cool down slightly in the oven, then turn to cool on a wire rack.

Meanwhile, make the frosting: Beat cream cheese and butter until smooth in a large bowl using a hand mixer. Add powdered sugar, cinnamon, and 1/4 teaspoon salt and beat.

Spread the frost over the loaf and sprinkle over the pecans that were chopped.

Recipe 4

Almond Bread

Yields: 1 loaf (10 servings)

Ingredients:

Three egg whites

1 cup flour

1/2 cup sugar

4 ounces of whole almonds (skins on)

Directions:

- Beat white part of eggs until they are fluffy.
- Gradually add sugar and beat until consistency with meringue is achieved.
- Cover in whole almonds and flour.
- Place in a lined loaf pan, which is lightly greased.
- Bake in a 40 to the 50-minute oven at 325 degrees.
- Leave in the tin until absolutely cold.
- Take from tin and cover in foil, and store for one or two days in the refrigerator.
- Break the loaf into wafer-thin slices with a very sharp knife.
- Layer on cookie sheets and put for about 45 minutes in a slow oven (250 degrees) until dried out. Insert in an airtight jar.
- This will hold the slices for about three to four months.

Recipe 5

Beetroot Bread

Beetroot is such a versatile vegetable that both sweet and savory dishes can be enjoyed from it. Here is a method of no-knead beetroot bread. This strong beetroot and walnut bread is moist but fluffy, moderately sweet, and has a hint of ginger. Apple juice is used in it instead of milk, and it is milk free. Make this beet bread super nutritious using whole wheat flour or a combination of whole wheat and plain flours.

Ingredients:

270 g of whole or plain flour

180 g of roasted beetroot, peeled weight (approx. 2 small beets)

100 g of peeled pear, cored

Two medium eggs

80 ml of edible vegetable oil

50 g of sugar (0.25 cup)

2 tsp of bicarbonate of soda

2 tsp ground ginger

1/3 tsp fine sea salt

Zest of 1.5 lemon

70 g of walnuts, chopped

80 ml of apple juice

Method:

- Preheat the oven to a gas level of 425 F/ 220 C/ 7. Put the beetroot on a baking tray and bake until tender for 45 minutes. Withdraw from the oven, let it cool, and discard the skin (it should easily peel off). Puree the pear and apple juice and add to the beetroot. You should take the step ahead of time.
- Preheat the oven to a gas mark 4 of 350 F/ 180 C/. Fill a 23 cm bread pan with light grease, line with parchment paper, and set aside.

- Combine the flour, baking powder, soda, ginger, lemon zest, and sodium bicarbonate, and stir thoroughly with a fork. Deposit back.
- Beat the eggs, sugar, and oil together for 2-3 minutes, until smooth. Pour in the beet mixture and blend well.
- Place the walnuts and the flour mixture and just whisk to blend (stop stirring when the dry ingredients are gone). The batter is getting lumpy.
- Move the batter into the bread pan, smooth out the top with a spoon back and bake for 1 hour in the middle of the oven. Extract from the oven and allow to cool for 10 minutes in the pan. Use parchment paper to take the bread out of the oven and place it on a cooling rack. Cool completely before slicing (store the remains in an airtight refrigerator container).

Notes: The beetroot can be baked in advance and refrigerated (overnight) until cooled, until ready to use.

Use whole wheat or white flour, instead.

It's important not to overdo the batter, as your bread can be a bit dense.

Storage: This beet bread can be stored in an airtight jar for a couple of days. You can also freeze the whole sandwich, wrapped in paper or a freezer bag, or freeze individual slices (packed separately) for later enjoyment.

Preparation time requires the time it takes for the beetroot to bake and cool.

Food Serving: 1 serving

Calories: 267 kcal Carbohydrates: 33 g Protein: 6 g Saturated fat: 7 g Cholesterol: 33 mg Sodium: 180 mg Potassium: 338 mg Fiber: 4 g Sugar: 11 g Vitamin A: 55IU Vitamin C: 1 mg Calcium: 69 mg Iron: 2 mg

Recipe 6

Apple Bread

3 cups of all-purpose flour

2 cups of sugar

Two teaspoons of cinnamon

One teaspoon of baking soda

1/2 teaspoon of salt

Four big eggs, room temperature

1 cup of canola oil

1/2 teaspoon of vanilla extract

2 cups of peeled apples (approximately two mediums)

1 cup of peeled walnuts

Directions:

- Preheat the oven to 350 °. Line 2 8x4-in greased loaf pans.
- Whisk the first six ingredients together. Beat the oil, eggs, and vanilla together in another bowl; add to the

flour mixture, stirring until moistened (the batter is thick). Apples and walnuts should then be folded in.
- Move to ready dishes. Bake for 50-55 minutes until a toothpick inserted in the middle comes out clean. Cool down in pans for 10 minutes before shifting to wire racks.

Freeze option: Cover the cooled loaves tightly in plastic and foil, then freeze. Thaw up at room temperature to use.

Recipe 7

Coconut Bread

Ingredients:

Bread:

Two eggs

1 cup of sugar

1/2 cup of vegetable oil

1/2 cup of coconut extract

1 1/2 cup of all-purpose flour

1/2 teaspoon of baking soda

1/2 teaspoon of salt

1/2 cup of buttermilk

1 cup of sweetened coconut

Syrup:

1/2 cup of sugar

1/4 cup of water

1 cup of unsalted butter

One teaspoon of coconut extract

Instructions:

- The oven is to be preheated to 325 degrees F. Grease with parchment paper a 9-inch loaf pan.
- Beat the eggs gently in a large pot. Add in the extract of sugar, olive oil, and coconut and whisk together.
- Whisk together the flour and bake soda, baking powder, and salt in another dish.
- To the egg mixture, add the dry mixture and buttermilk. Continue until firmly combined, then add the coconut and mix until combined. Don't over mingle.
- Pour the batter into the pan, then move to the oven.
- Bake it for about one hour to one hour and 15 minutes until a tester inserted in the center comes out clean. When the bread starts browning too much, cover it thinly with foil.
- Put together the water, sugar, and butter in a small saucepan and put it over medium heat when the bread is almost finished baking. Bring to a boil and let it cook for five minutes. Remove from the pan, and whisk in the extract of coconut.

- Take out the bread from the oven, and poke holes in the bread with a long skewer, leaving the bread in the pan. Pour on the hot bread the syrup.
- Enable the bread to sit for at least 4 hours at room temperature before serving.

Recipe 8

Mint Bread

Ingredients:

1 A cup of water 110 ° F/ 43 ° C hot.

0.25 cup of oil or butter melted

0.25 cup of maple syrup

1.50 tsp of salt

3 cups of bread flour

1 cup of oatmeal

1 cup of mint (cut fresh or dried)

2 tsp of machine yeast

Directions:

1. Place the ingredients in the bread saucepan in the order listed in the ingredients section and choose basic or white, 1.5 loaves, and medium crust.

2. Remove from bread saucepan and cool for 10 minutes on a rack when done. Slice and serve.

3. This bread is perfect as a supplement to lamb, veal, pork or beef with salty or savory dishes, and can also be enjoyed as a snack or as a thin slice with tea.

Recipe 9

Garlic Bread

Garlic bread consists of bread (usually a baguette or sourdough like ciabatta), topped with garlic and olive oil or butter, and may contain additional herbs such as oregano or chives. It is then either grilled or roast until crisp or baked in a traditional or bread oven. It is generally made using a French baguette, or sometimes a sourdough like cyabat. Until frying, the bread is then filled with oil and hained garlic through the cuts. Alternatively, garlic powder and butter are used, or the bread is sliced lengthwise into individually garnished slices.

Total Prep / Total Time: 20 minutes

Makes eight servings

Ingredients:

1/2 cup melted butter

3 to 4 garlic cloves

One loaf (1 pound) of French bread, sliced lengthwise

Two tablespoons of fresh parsley chopped

Directions:

Put together garlic and butter in a small saucepan. Spread on the bread over cut sides; sprinkle some parsley. Put onto a baking sheet, cut the side up.

Bake for 8 minutes, at 350 °. Then bake for about 2 minutes or until golden brown. Break into 2-in — sliced slices. Serve dry.

Garlic Bread tips:

How can the garlic bread be stored?

The remaining garlic bread can be tightly wrapped in foil and stored in the refrigerator for up to 3 days. Bake the packaged bread for about 10-15 minutes at 350 ° to reheat.

What if the garlic is not fresh?

Not a fresh clove of garlic? No problem. No problem! Replace 1/2 teaspoon of granulated garlic for every fresh clove needed in this recipe for garlic bread.

What are some excellent garlic-bread pairings?

Garlic bread is a delicious side that pairs well with marinara-including dishes, much like our best lasagna recipe ever. If you're looking for a lighter meal, serve garlic bread alongside a tomato soup or chopped Italian salad. In any of these recipes, you can use your leftovers, which start with garlic bread!

Nutrition Facts: 1 piece: 258 calories, 13 g fat (7 g saturated fat), 31 mg cholesterol, 462 mg sodium, 30 g carbohydrate, 5 g protein.

Recipe 10

Red Lentil Loaf

Lentils contain the third-highest protein content of any legume, after soybeans and hemp, and are therefore an adaptable and careful addition to many diets, but are particularly useful to meat reductionists and vegetarians. This lentil loaf is highly adaptable and is ideal to use the rest of your vegetable leftover. You can have this loaf as it is, sliced straight from the oven, fry the remaining slices and serve with an egg, or barbecue served in a burger bun.

Ingredients:

200 g of red lentils

400ml vegetable stock

1 tbsp of vegetable oil

One onion, finely chopped

One garlic clove, chopped

One spring onion

1/2 green pepper, chopped

One egg

Salt pepper and other seasoning spices

Method:

1. Put the lentils and stock in a casserole and simmer gently until the liquid is absorbed and the lentils are tender. Strain into a sieve and stand to allow excess fluid to drain
2. While the lentils cook, fry the vegetables until they start turning golden.
3. Position the lentils, cooked vegetables (at this point, add any grated root vegetables), and mix the egg in a bowl — season well with some herbs, spices and salt and pepper.
4. Pour the mixture into a lined and greased 500 g loaf tin and bake for 40 – 50 minutes at GM 5/190C (fan 180C) until raised, brown golden, and firm to the touch.
5. Keep for 5 minutes on the stand.
6. Serve sliced or fry as a burger.

Recipe 11

Cheese Bread

Ingredients:

1/2 cup (120ml) buttermilk, warmed to approximately 110 ° F

1/3 cup (80ml) water, heated to about 110 ° F

2 and 1/4 teaspoons platinum yeast (1 regular package)

Two tablespoons (25 g) granulated sugar

Five tablespoons (72 g) unsalted butter, melted + slightly cooled

One large egg, at room temperature

One teaspoon salt

3/4 teaspoon garlic powder

3 cups (375 g) bread flour

Topping:

Unsalted butter (30 g), melted

Two teaspoons of fresh parsley (or your favorite dried or fresh herb)

1/4 teaspoon of garlic powder

Instructions:

Dough Preparation: In the bowl of your stand mixer fitted with a dough hook or paddle attachment, whisk the warm buttermilk, warm water, yeast, and sugar. Cover, and require 5 minutes to rest.

Stir in butter, egg, salt, garlic powder. Whisk at low speed for thirty seconds, scrape with a rubber spatula down on the sides of the pot, and then add the remaining flour. Beat at medium speed until the dough gets together and pulls away from the bowl's edges. You should mix this dough with a large wooden spoon or rubber spatula if you don't own a mixer.

Knead the dough: Leave the dough in the mixer and beat for another 2 minutes, or knead on a gently floured surface for 2 minutes by hand.

1st Rise: Gently grease a large oil bowl or non-stick spray. Place the dough in the pan and roll it in the oil to cover all sides. Cover the bowl with foil made from aluminum, plastic wrap or a clean kitchen towel. Enable the dough to rise for 1-2 hours or till double in size in a reasonably warm setting.

Grease a 95-inch loaf pan.

Bread shape: Press the dough down to release air. Place the dough on a lightly floured work surface and roll the dough into a nine by 5 inch (approximately) rectangle with a floured rolling pin. Sprinkle the cheese all over the edges, uncovering a 1/2 "margin.

Roll the dough straight into a 15-inch log. Place the log on the surface. Break the log in half lengthwise with a sharp knife.

Cross one half, cut side down, making a circle. Pinch and cover the outer edges as best you can. Cut a few small squares, if you have any remaining cheese, and tuck into the dough. This is just for extra cheesy pockets, optional!

Place in an aluminum foil, plastic wrap, or a clean kitchen towel in the prepared loaf pan. (This move can get some messy!)

Let the covered loaf rest for 30 minutes. It'll rise slightly during this time.

Switch the rack of the oven to the third location underneath. Place a sheet of baking on the lower rack to catch any cheese or butter that may fall off.

The oven is to be preheated to 350 ° F (177 ° C).

Top: Whisk together the melted butter, spices, and garlic powder. Drizzle on top of the flour, or wash.

Bake: Bake until golden brown, and sound hollow at the top of the loaf, about 45-55 minutes when gently tapped. If you discover the top of the loaf browning too soon as it bakes, cover with a foil of aluminum.

Take out the bread from the oven and place it on a wire rack. Cook in the pan for 10 minutes, then remove from the saucepan and place the loaf on the shelf.

Enjoy!

Cover and store the leftovers for two days at room temperature or for up to 1 week in the fridge. Slices of bread taste good when warmed up for 10 seconds in the microwave.

Recipe 12

Orange Bread

This orange bread is a yeast-free loaf, which means no kneading or proofing is mandatory. So if you're looking for a sweet bread recipe that's free of hassles, this is it.

Ingredients:

2 Eggs (small-medium)

1 1/2 cup of granulated sugar (5.3oz/150 g)

Orange (citrus) zest (from 1 citrus three medium orange, juice only

One stick of unsalted butter, softened (2.8oz/110 g)

2 cups of all-purpose flour (10.6oz/300 g)

3 tsp Baking powder

Instructions:

Preheat the oven to 375 ° F/190 ° C.

Whisk the eggs with sugar in a large mixing bowl until smooth and clear.

Add orange zest (from 1/2 orange), orange juice freshly squeezed, and butter softened. Blend with the electric blender.

Sift into flour and baking powder (measure these two ingredients in advance) and blend well with mixer. Load the batter into a loaf tin lined with baking paper (10x4 inch/25x10 cm).

Bake for 1 hour in a preheated oven at 375 ° F/190 ° C or until a skewer inserted is clean.

When finished, pour some more orange juice over the loaf out of the oven. Let it rest on a wired rack for about 10 minutes before being transported. Let the whole thing cool off.

Notes All-purpose meal (US) = Plain meal (UK).

For the batter, you'll need to get 1/2 cup (120ml) of orange juice + around 1/4 cup (60ml) to pour over the baked bread. There should be plenty of 3 medium oranges (150 g each), but if you have dry oranges on the inside, you may want one extra.

Depending on your oven, the baking time will vary slightly.

Recipe 13

Lemon Lavender Loaf

Ingredients:

2 cups of all-purpose flour

1 cup of sugar

Two teaspoons of baking powder

1/2 teaspoon salt

One egg beat gently

One cup of milk or half

1/4 cup of olive oil

Lemon juice and two lemons peel finely rub the lemon peel- save two tablespoons of juice and one tablespoon peel

For icing:

Two teaspoons of dried lavender or two tablespoons of fresh lavender, carefully sliced

For Glaze:

Two tablespoons sugar

2 tbsp butter

1 tbsp lemon juice

Instructions:

- Grease set aside a loaf pan.
- Mix the sugar, flour baking powder, and salt in a big pan or bowl.
- The egg, milk, butter, lemon peel, lemon juice, and lavender are mixed into another cup.
- Load the wet ingredients into the dry ingredients and stir until the batter becomes moist (The mixture is lumpy). Sprinkle some flour into the greased loaf pan.
- Bake for 50 minutes or until clean comes to a toothpick inserted in the middle, and the top of the loaf is broken.
- Cool with glaze for 10 minutes before topping.

For the glaze: Melt butter in a small saucepan with sugar and lemon juice until well mixed.

Pick holes into the top of the lemon loaves and gradually pour over the top of the glaze.

Notes: These can be packed in a freezer bag and frozen for up to 3 months or one week in the refrigerator. For mini loaves, the baking time is reduced to 40 min.

Recipe 14

Caramel Bread

Ingredients:

For the Dough:

1 cup lukewarm water

One packet of instant yeast (about two teaspoons)

Two teaspoons salt

1/4 cup honey or sugar

Four big eggs

3/4 cup butter (melted)

4 1/2 cups of flour (more for dusting)

For the Caramel Sauce:

1/2 cup butter (preferably salted)

1/2 cup Heavy Whipping Cream

1+1/2 cups of brown sugar a hit of sea salt if you want that kind of thing

Instructions:

Make the Dough: Combine all the ingredients of the dough in a mixing bowl, adding the flour last. The mixture will get sticky. Use plastic wrap or a damp towel to cover loosely. Set aside to rise for 2 hours in a warm-hearted spot. Move to the fridge to cool, after it has grown because it is easier to treat.

Roll the Dough: Roll out half of it at a floured surface to a medium thickness when the dough has cooled. Cut it into bits of bite-size, or roll it into balls. Wrap the other half of the dough into plastic wrap and place next time in the freezer.

Cook the Sauce: Melt in a saucepan butter, heavy cream, and brown sugar. Bring to a boil, whisk, and cook for exactly five minutes. Take off the fire.

Assemble: In a pan or pie pan, layer: caramel sauce 1/4 cup, dough, caramel sauce 1/4 cup, crust, caramel sauce 1/4 cup. Reserve the sauce leftover.

Bake: Bake at 350 degrees for twenty-five to thirty minutes, or until the top pieces turn slightly brown. Invert on a serving platter and top with extra sauce, if needed.

Recipe 15

Banana bread

Prep: 20 minutes
Cook: 1 hour 15 minutes
Ready in: 1 hour 20 minutes

Ingredients:

2 Cups of all-purpose flour
One tablespoon soda
1/4 tablespoon salt
1/2 cup butter
3/4 cup of brown sugar
Two egg whites
2 1/3 cups of overripe bananas mashed

Directions:

- Preheat the oven to one hundred and seventy-five degrees Celsius (350 degrees F). A 9x5 inch loaf pan is lightly greased.
- Combine flour, baking soda, and salt into a large pot. Heat the butter and brown sugar together in a separate dish. Bring in the eggs and mash bananas until well combined. Blend the banana mixture into flour mixture; just stir to moisturize. Pour batter into a pan of the prepared loaf.
- Bake for 60 to 65 minutes in a preheated oven, until a toothpick inserted into the loaf center, comes out clean. Let the bread cool down in the pan for 10 minutes, then move onto a rack of wire.
- Serve warm.

Recipe 16

Chicken Bread

Ingredients for the Dough:

6-1/2 Cups Flour

1/2 Cup Flour reserved for kneading

1 Cup Sugar

1 Tbsp Vinegar or Apple Cider Vinegar

1 Teaspoon Salt

3 Tablespoon Butter

2 Tablespoons yeast

1 Cup Water

1 Cup Milk

2 Eggs

For Chicken Filling:

1 to 1/2 lb. boiled boneless chicken cut into bits and pieces

1 Green Pepper

Two tomatoes

One red bell pepper

Some ginger and onion

¼ cup of water

Salt and black pepper to taste

1 tsp curry powder

2 tbsp olive oil

Directions For the filling:

- Dice the peppers, tomatoes, and onions and slim the pepper of the Habanero.
- Preheat the oil in a saucepan, add the diced onion and stir-fry until translucent.
- Remove the hazelnut pepper and sprinkle in the ginger — Mix-fry for about a minute. Add the bell peppers and tomatoes and allow to cook for about 2 to 3 minutes. Add the chicken, spices, and water (1/4 cup) to mix and leave to cook for about 5 minutes. This will make the filling thicken.

- Let it for a minute or two to simmer and turn off the heat.
- Until using it, leave to cool.

To stuff your bread dough: add the flour, yeast, vitamin C powder, salt, sugar, and mix until mixed in a large bowl. Build a hole in the center and add the melted butter, milk, eggs, and.

Mix all together before creating a fluffy and sticky dough.

Move the dough and knead it to a well-floured work surface. Sprinkle a little flour on your work surface at a time each time the dough is sticky until smooth and elastic.

Grease a large bowl with some melted butter or oil, put the dough in the pan, and cover with a thin layer of oil or butter on the top. It would keep a crust from developing at the dough's surface.

Place it in a warm place to grow for 1 hour or until it doubled in size with a tight-fitting lid, a plastic wrap or a damp cloth.

Punch the dough down, then move it to a floured work surface and divide the dough into 4. Roll the dough out to around a quarter of an inch thickness. Place some chicken filling in the middle of the dough from top to bottom, leaving approximately two inches of space at the above and bottom.

Use a pizza cutter or knife to make about 10 to 12 slits of about a quarter to a half-inch long on both sides of the dough and still leave out the 2-inch gap at both the top and bottom of the dough. Make sure that both parties have the same number of stripes.

Fold over the filling on top of the dough and start braiding by crisscrossing the strips you've made (place one piece of dough on one side over another on the other). Continue braiding down the dough before forming the loaf. If you have about two more stripes to go on both sides, fold the bottom portion over the mixture and crisscross the leftover strips over the folded dough and then pinch the dough to secure it.

Use the parchment paper to rise in the pan the braided loaves and leave for another 30 minutes to rise.

Your oven should be preheated to three-fifty degrees Fahrenheit and place a bowl of water in your oven's bottom rack to steam the oven.

Put the bread inside the oven and bake for 20 to 25 minutes, or until the inserted toothpick in the center of the bread comes out clean.

Recipe 17

Mincemeat bread

Ingredients:

2 cups of all-purpose flour

1/2 cup of white sugar

1 1/2 teaspoons of baking powder

1/2 teaspoon of baking soda

1/2 teaspoon of salt

One egg

1/4 cup of vegetable oil

One tablespoon of orange zest

Two tablespoons of orange juice

2 cups of minced pie filling

Directions:

Preheat oven to one hundred and seventy-five degrees C (350 degrees F). Grease a loaf pan, which is 9 x 5 x 3 inches.

Combine the milk, butter, orange peel, juice, and sliced meat together and blend well. Put together baking powder, sugar, flour, and baking soda, and salt; incorporate the egg mixture slowly. Mix until hot. Pour into a packed saucepan.

Bake for about one hour.

Take out the loaf from the oven and cool it on a wire rack.

Recipe 18

Yogurt Bread

Ingredients:

Cooking spray

2 cups sifted all-purpose flour

One teaspoon baking powder

One teaspoon baking soda

One teaspoon salt

3 (6 ounces) vanilla-flavored yogurt containers

1 cup white sugar

Two eggs

One teaspoon vanilla extract

Procedure:

Preheat oven to one hundred and seventy-five degrees Celsius (350 degrees F). Grease cooking spray into a loaf pan.

Add the baking powder, flour, baking soda, and salt in a small bowl.

In a big cup, add the yogurt, sugar, eggs, and vanilla extract. To stop lumps, pour in the flour mixture a little at a time, mixing thoroughly between each addition. Pour batter into the loaf mold.

Bake in the oven that is preheated for about forty-five minutes, until a toothpick inserted in the middle comes out clean.

Recipe 19

Peanut Chili Bread

Ingredients:

50 g tahini

75 g crunchy peanut butter

1 tbsp of cumin seeds

1 tsp of fine salt

Two long red chilies, not too hot

75 g of roasted peanuts

500 g of solid white flour, plus additional

1 tsp of dry yeast

Oil for kneading

Sesame seeds

Instructions:

In a cup, spoon the tahini, peanut butter, cumin, and salt, then add 100ml of hot water. Deseed the chilies, cut roughly, and add the charred pieces to the bowl (leave them on). Add the flour and yeast to 200ml of cold water and peanuts, mix in a soft, sticky dough and leave for 30 minutes. Give the dough a 10-second knead, return the dough to the bowl and leave for an hour.

Break into three, shape into balls, leave for 15 minutes, and then turn into sticks. Pat each stick into an oval (use flour), fold it in on itself a few times, then roll in length to 30 cm. Brush with salt, roll in the sesame seeds, and leave for 45 minutes to rise on a baking tray. Slash the length with a sharp knife, then bake for 30 minutes at 220C (200C fan-assisted)/425F / gas mark 7.

Recipe 20

Date Loaf

This moist date nut bread makes a perfect breakfast or brunch. Walnuts are featured in the method, while pecans are also good. Since it is a quick bread, it needs no yeast or kneading, and it is ready to eat in just over an hour.

This bread is not only tasty, but it even freezes well. Freeze the whole loaf or spread between two thin slices of cream cheese and freeze the "sandwiches" for later enjoyment. Chocolate cream cheese or chocolate-flavored butter is delicious too.

Total time: 70 minutes

Prep time: 15 minutes

Cook: 55 minutes

Yield: 8 servings

Nutrition recommendations: 408 Calories, 15 g Fat, 62 g Carbs, 8 g Protein (per serving)

Ingredients:

1 cup of chopped dates

1 cup of boiling water

One teaspoon of baking soda

1 cup of brown sugar

One egg,

1 cup of chopped walnuts (optional)

1/4 teaspoon of vanilla essence

2 cups of plain baking flour

One teaspoon of baking powder

Directions:

Place the dates in a bowl, boiling water, butter, and baking soda and whisk until butter is melted.

Only set aside for an hour.

Beat sugar, egg, vanilla essence, and walnuts into date mixture (if used).

Sift and mix in flour and baking powder until just mixed.

Pour the mixture into a 22 cm grated loaf tin and bake for 45 minutes in an 180C oven or until the inserted skewer comes out clean.

Before turning onto a cooling rack, leave in the tin for about 10 minutes.

Tips:

To grease the loaf pan, using butter, shortening, or cooking oil. Avoid any oil puddles that form, and make sure there are no butter clumps or shortening. Wiping with a towel of paper helps ensure even coating so that your bread does not stick.

You don't want to overmix the batter like with any shortbread. The final mixing will be only long enough to ensure the integration of the ingredients.

Don't delay getting the batter into the oven. The liquids will trigger the first round of leavening of the baking powder — most of the baking powder is double-acting, and the second round happens in the oven. Effectively function to bring the batter into the oven as soon as possible.

Conclusion

Bread's nutritional composition depends on whether the meal used to generate the bread is white or whole meal flour, as well as the inclusion of ingredients such as seeds or fat. Approximately half of our daily energy will come from carbohydrates, mainly starches. Therefore bread is a significant component of a healthy and balanced diet along with potatoes, pasta, and rice. Bread contains many proteins, and only small quantities of fat. Bread has come to take on significance as a fundamental food worldwide, beyond pure nutrition, transforming into a staple in religious practices, secular cultural life, and language. Over the ages, bread has been a significant staple food commodity to many cultures. Those who understand what good bread is agreed on the qualities that should describe it very carefully and make these qualities a criterion by which any kind of bread can be scored or judged. Many who are not able to make bread and those who have had minimal understanding will do well to have their bread examined by experts or to learn how to measure it on their own. Yeast is the origin of a cycle of bread making. It is an essential ingredient that makes the dough rise and gives its excellent taste and aroma to home-baked bread. Wheat is the most common type of meal used in baking bread. This includes all-purpose food, bread flour, and whole wheat flour. Homemade bread is so much more tasteful than store-bought bread, it's not filled with preservatives, and it's straightforward to produce, and it doesn't take too much time, either. Cook your own bread so you know exactly what's going into it and you can trust in the knowledge that you're offering the best bread you can to your skin. Nearly every nation in the world has some kind of bread they claim to be their own. Bread is a staple of cuisines worldwide, from baguettes of France to pita in Mediterranean countries. A wide variety of bread making recipes are mentioned above.

References

Bread – a nutritious staple: (EUFIC). (2020). Retrieved 2020, from https://www.eufic.org/en/healthy-living/article/bread-a-nutritious-staple

Bread A Staple for Centuries. (2020). Retrieved 2020, from https://www.ewellnessmag.com/article/bread-a-staple-for-centuries

The Benefits of Bread | Eat Bread 90. (2020). Retrieved 2020, from https://www.eatbread90.com/benefits-of-bread/

Healthy Ways to Include Bread in Your Diet. (2020). Retrieved 2020, from https://www.verywellfit.com/bread-nutrition-facts-calories-and-health-benefits-4114942

HuffPost is now a part of Verizon Media. (2020). Retrieved 2020, from https://www.huffpost.com/entry/whole-grains-health-benefits_n_5655022

One-Bowl Chocolate Chip Bread. (2020). Retrieved 2020, from https://www.tasteofhome.com/recipes/one-bowl-chocolate-chip-bread/

Scoring Bread Quality - Bread Making. (2020). Retrieved 2020, from http://www.1920-30.com/cooking/bread/scoring-bread.html

Bread making Quality - an overview | Science Direct Topics. (2020). Retrieved 2020, from https://www.sciencedirect.com/topics/food-science/breadmaking-quality

5 Reasons Homemade Bread is better - Five Spot Green Living. (2020). Retrieved 2020, from https://www.fivespotgreenliving.com/5-reasons-homemade-bread-good/

Starter Sourdough

Learn how to make sourdough to bake bread, loaves, and pizza with over 50 recipes

By

Timothy Collins

© **Copyright 2020 by Timothy Collins - All rights reserved.**

This document is geared towards providing exact and reliable information in regards to the topic and issue covered. The publication is sold with the idea that the publisher is not required to render accounting, officially permitted, or otherwise, qualified services. If advice is necessary, legal or professional, a practiced individual in the profession should be ordered.

- From a Declaration of Principles which was accepted and approved equally by a Committee of the American Bar Association and a Committee of Publishers and Associations.

In no way is it legal to reproduce, duplicate, or transmit any part of this document in either electronic means or in printed format. Recording of this publication is strictly prohibited and any storage of this document is not allowed unless with written permission from the publisher. All rights reserved.

The information provided herein is stated to be truthful and consistent, in that any liability, in terms of inattention or otherwise, by any usage or abuse of any policies, processes, or directions contained within is the solitary and utter responsibility of the recipient reader. Under no circumstances will any legal responsibility or blame be held against the publisher for any reparation, damages, or monetary loss due to the information herein, either directly or indirectly.

Respective authors own all copyrights not held by the publisher.

The information herein is offered for informational purposes solely, and is universal as so. The presentation of the information is without contract or any type of guarantee assurance.

The trademarks that are used are without any consent, and the publication of the trademark is without permission or backing by the trademark owner. All trademarks and brands within this book are for clarifying purposes only and are the owned by the owners themselves, not affiliated with this document.

Table Of Content

INTRODUCTION 7

CHAPTER 1: SOURDOUGH-HISTORY AND FUNDAMENTALS 11

1.1 What is Sourdough? 11

1.2 Tradition and History of Sourdough 16

1.3 Basic Working Principle of Sourdough 20

1.4 Sourdough Hydration Explained (What, Why, How & When) 26

1.5 Sourdough Bread VS. Other Bread 31

CHAPTER 2: BASICS OF SOURDOUGH STARTER 35

2.1 Introduction to Sourdough Starter 35

2.2 Making Sourdough Starter from Scratch 39

2.3 How To Tell When Your Starter Is Ready To Use? ... 42

2.4 Keeping Starter Alive Vs. Getting It Active 44

2.5 Maintaining the Starter 48

2.6 Can Sourdough Starter Replace Yeast? 50

CHAPTER 3: INGREDIENTS AND WEIGHING 54

3.1 Types of Grains and Flour and their life cycle 54

3.2 Process of Leavening 62

3.3 Functional Ingredients and its Preparation 66

CHAPTER 4: EQUIPMENT AND TECHNIQUES 69

4.1 Useful Tools.. 69

4.2 Fermentation and Mixing.. 73

4.3 Dividing and Shaping 76

4.4 Final Proofing, Scoring, and Finishing 80

4.5 Importance of Environmental Condition 83

CHAPTER 5: FACTORS TO CONSIDER WHILE BREAD BAKING 87

5.1 Types of Ovens and other Baking Tools.. 87

5.2 Transforming Dough into Bread 89

5.3 Baking in Professional Oven, Home Oven & Baking without an oven 91

5.4 The Importance of Dough Temperature in Baking (with a calculator) 99

CHAPTER 6: BENEFITS AND ISSUES OF SOURDOUGH BAKING 103

6.1 Sourdough Bread and Health Benefits 103

6.2 Quick Tips for Making the Perfect Sourdough................................ 105

6.3 Problems and Solutions of Sourdough Baking................................ 111

CHAPTER 7: VARIETY OF SOURDOUGH RECIPES 114

7.1 17 Classic Bread Recipes.. 114

7.2 10 Pizza And Other Flat Bread (Focaccia) Recipes 136

7.3 12 Enriched Flours / Whole Grains Recipes 150

7.4 13 Sweet and Savory Treat Recipes 172

7.5 8 Gluten-Free Bread Recipes 191

CONCLUSION 206

Introduction

So, you've heard of sourdough, but you don't understand what it means. You might wish to learn more. You might want to see if that is something you might be interested in. This book will clarify the basics of sourdough and hopefully provide you with enough details to make the decision.

It's the way people used to make "up" bread and other baked goods before those handy yeast packets, or baking powder containers were in the local stores. Before these became available (around 1850), the way to "leaven" bread was to add a bit of sourdough "starter" to the dough and enable it to rise over time.

Since sourdough has long been around, no one knows exactly how it started. Most people assume it started to get ready for baking after somebody mixed flour and water and left the mixture for too long. They found after a while that this started to spread. They realized the bread was easier and lighter to eat when they saw this happening and then baked it down.

People then discovered that if they saved some of the unbaked dough after it had risen, it would rise faster and combine it with the next batch of bread. It could also be split to share this unbaked dough with others, and it became known as a sourdough starter.

Sourdough is a bread that leavens for itself. Also, the originally leavened bread, used by the ancient Egyptians and beloved by many generations before industrialization, made it as simple as a trip to the store to buy yeast. While baking bread with "conventional" yeast involves adding what a concentrated shot of yeast-fungi suspended in animation to a bread dough that is otherwise very un-yeasty is, sourdough profits from the natural yeasts and bacteria present in the air and the flour.

Unwanted microbes can be kept at bay by building a pleasant and comfy atmosphere for ideal yeasts and bacteria in the dough.

The basic baking method for sourdough is to produce a combined bacteria/yeast soup that can then be used similarly to yeast packets. This soup is called a "starter," and is making it unbelievably simple. The method includes combining some flour and water (approximately one dl each) in a jar and then leaving it for about a week at room temperature, "feeding" it about once a day with a little more flour and water. After a few days, a slightly frothy, sour-smelling character will grow on the starter. After this, you can store the starter in the fridge until you want to make bread next time.

You can, of course, order a starter online, or you can get some from a friend. But why should anyone else be having all the fun? The basic idea is to combine water and flour in roughly equal parts together and wait for the yeast to live. In action, there are a few more steps that you can take to increase the probability of success. Every baker has a different idea about what works best to capture wild yeast.

Sourdough is an appealing, tangy flavor, a taste of American gastronomic history, and a popular ingredient in anything from bread and cake to pretzels and pizza crust. Build your starter, and learn how it becomes a part of the family — a living product that thrives on food, water, and love.

Only flour, water, and salt-all the other artificial ingredients used in the commercially processed bread are omitted. Chorleywood processed bread, which is inexpensive, industrially produced, and relies on enzymes, preservatives, emulsifiers, and improvers for fast baking of bread. Those additives are also to blame for the wheat allergy of some people. Is sourdough costly to make?

No. Using ordinary strong flour means that you can make as little as 28p of an 800 g loaf, although it is encouraged to use organic locally milled stone ground flour if they can make sourdough easy.

Stretched over 24 hours, it takes about 15 minutes. Ironically sourdough has a reputation for being complicated, but it's only a matter of knowing how the dough is behaving and what influences influencing it.

Bread has been around for longer than many other products, and sourdough has been around for longer than most other bread — though the word 'sourdough' is a newer concept. The tangy bread has a distinct taste and an airy feel, so you can easily make it at home. Sourdough got its start in the 19th century before commercial yeasts were introduced and mass manufacturing. Traditional recipes had a starter, salt, and flour in them. While this recipe sounds very simple, it gives rise to the complex, tangy flavor we know and love.

A big favorite with innovative craft bakers, sourdough can sometimes appear complicated at home-made bread making. And yet the sourdough concept is clear, and making sourdough-based bread is a fascinating exercise.

This guide discusses the fundamentals of baking sourdough. We are exploring the simple science of sourdough to understand. The section of the Build/Create will show you how to make a start for yourself. In the section of Bake, we put our favorite sourdough bread recipes to work with your starter. The Maintain unit will then cover how to keep your starter alive and safe so that you can bake with it over and over again.

There is nothing like the happiness coming from beginning to finish your sourdough bread: and that means making your starter from scratch. Spend a week feeding, watering, and gradually coaxing water and flour into a bubbling, vigorous, sourdough starter, is worth the minimal everyday effort it takes. And your success is pretty much assured by the easy directions discussed further.

Chapter 1: Sourdough-History and Fundamentals

Sourdough is a bread product made from a long fermentation of the dough using lactobacilli and yeasts that occur naturally. Compared to bread made from cultivated yeast, it usually has a mildly sour taste due to the lactobacilli-producing lactic acid.

Sourdough is a word for a mixture of water and cereal flour (dough or batter) that contains a culture of yeasts and bacteria that occur naturally. It's also sometimes used to name bread and pancakes made using a culture like this.

Sourdough bread is an old favorite with an exciting history behind it that has recently grown in popularity.

This is considered by many to be tastier and safer than traditional bread. Some also say that your blood sugar is more natural to eat, and less likely to spike.

Sourdough is a tricky friend, but it can be extremely gratifying to consider his ability.

While using a sourdough starter is not a prerequisite of the basic concept of bread, we do agree that producing bread using sourdough, rather than commercially manufactured yeast, has benefits.

1.1 What is Sourdough?

Sourdough bread is becoming increasingly popular, and it's not hard to understand why; it's tasty, it keeps well, and it's more nutritious than regular bread.

It is assumed that Sourdough was invented several thousand years ago, and was the critical process used until well into the middle ages to make bread rise. Gradually it was substituted, first by the use of barm leftover from beer making, then by the use of yeasts produced.

Sourdough is a term for a mixture of water and cereal flour that includes a variety of natural yeasts and lactic acid bacteria. It's also sometimes used to name bread made from such a religion.

On the surface of cereal grains, for example, wheat, yeasts, and bacteria suitable for bread production are present in relatively small quantities. They will go up in size and intensity by grinding the grains into flour and enabling these micro-organisms to grow - by adding water, Keep the mixture at the correct temperature and supply food in the form of more flour to build what is known as a 'starter.'

Eventually, enough yeast cells must give off carbon dioxide to make bread rise. The presence of the yeast and the natural enzymes they secrete would have a beneficial effect on the bread's taste, texture, and aroma.

Sourdough refers to both the bread used to make it and the starter. Starter starts with a mixture of flour and air, which can range from a rigid starter made entirely from rye flour and water to an air batter of milk and cornmeal — with plenty of choices in between.

When flour is combined with water, the friendly bacteria (lactobacilli) and wild yeast begin to work together in both the flour and the surrounding area. These tiny living creatures produce by-products inside their flour-and-water slurry (now called starter), which causes bread to rise, giving it a deep, rich flavor.

Sourdough is a bread made from the ordinary yeast and flour-borne bacteria. You'll find three ingredients in traditional sourdough recipes: sourdough starter (which consists of water and flour), salt, and powder. No leaven, no butter, no oils, and no sweeteners. When it comes to bread, it is just as good as you get.

Ask anyone who has eaten sourdough, and they will tell you that what makes it special is the tang. It is believed that the characteristic tartness of sourdough bread comes from the same bacteria that give their pucker yogurt and sour cream too. It is naturally found in wheat flour, along with yeast, and is brought to life when the flour is mixed with water. Here is a very easy description of the process:

Wheat flour + water - > natural enzymes break down starches into glucose (sugar) natural bacteria (tang) + glucose - > natural food for yeast + food - > natural leaven (carbon dioxide) natural leaven + more flour + more water - > natural leaven. .

Nature takes its course, and you have a mixture that contains enough leaven (yeast) to make bread rise over time. Pretty cool, ok? Who knew how to do so little could yield such a stunning performance!

Sourdough is one of the oldest fermentation types of cereals.

It is thought to have originated around 1,500 BC in ancient Egypt and remained the standard type of bread leavening until it was replaced by baker's yeast a few centuries ago.

Leavened bread is a type of bread whose dough rises during the bread-making process with the gas produced as the grain ferments.

Most leavened bread uses industrial baker yeast to assist the rise of the dough. Traditional sourdough fermentation, however, relies on "wild yeast" and lactic acid bacteria, which naturally occur in flour to leaven the bread.

Wild yeast avoids acidic conditions more than baker's yeast. That's what helps it to work with bacteria that generate lactic acid to help the dough grow.

In several other fermented foots, lactic acid bacteria can be found, including yogurt, kefir, pickles, sauerkraut, and kimchi.

The mixture of wild yeast, lactic acid bacteria, flour, and water used to make sourdough bread is called a "starter." In the dough, the starter ferments the sugars during the bread-making process, helping the bread to rise and acquire its characteristic taste.

Sourdough bread must ferment and grow much longer than other types of bread, which is what produces its distinctive texture.

The making of sourdough bread remains popular in Mediterranean and Middle Eastern countries, as well as in the US area of San Francisco Bay to this day.

Some store-bought sourdough bread is not made using the conventional sourdough process, so their health benefits are diminished.

Getting sourdough bread from an artisan baker or from a farmer's market increases the likelihood of it being "real" sourdough.

Sourdough is an ancient type of leavening bread. To leaven the dough, it relies on a mixture of wild yeast and lactic acid bacteria, which are naturally found in flour rather than baker's yeast.

Nutrition quality: The nutritional composition of sourdough bread depends on the form of flour used to produce it — whether whole or processed.

Even the nutrition profile of sourdough resembles that of most other bread.

On average, one medium slice weighing around 2 ounces (56 g) contains (2):

- ✓ Calories: 162 calories
- ✓ Carbs: 32 grams
- ✓ Fiber: 2–4 grams
- ✓ Protein: 6 grams
- ✓ Fat: 2 grams
- ✓ Selenium: 22% RDI
- ✓ Folate: 20 percent RDI
- ✓ Thiamin: 16 percent RDI
- ✓ Sodium: 16 percent RDI
- ✓ Manganese: 14 percent RDI
- ✓ Niacin: 14 percent RDI
- ✓ Iron: 12 percent RDI
- ✓ Sodium: 16 percent RDI
- ✓ Manganese: 14 percent RDI
- ✓ Niacin: 14 percent RDI
- ✓ Iron: 12 percent RDI.

Some store-bought sourdough bread is not made using the conventional sourdough process, so their health benefits are diminished.

Bread can be made using a live sourdough starter only, not inactive dried sourdough powder added solely for flavor and acidity; No commercial yeast or other leavening agents (e.g., baking powder) are used; without any chemical additives; and without the use of other ingredients as a souring agent.

Sour bread sounds strange – I'm not sure I'm going to like it. The sweetness of sourdough bread is largely down to the taste of the maker and may range from an almost imperceptible flavor to a powerful tang. A baker manages his or her starting culture to obtain not only flavor depth and sophistication but also a degree of acidity to his or her taste.

If you've tried sourdough from one baker and didn't especially enjoy it, try a loaf from another. You might find you like it because no two are the same.

1.2 Tradition and History of Sourdough

Bread has been called the workers of life, but bread is not what it was once, nor what it still got the potential to be on the market today as many other food products. Why did you make bread before manufacturing yeast and fancy ovens? And how do flour and water become a beloved commodity around the world?

Bread is older than metal; our ancestors had eaten and baked flatbread long before the Bronze Age. There is evidence of Neolithic grinding stones used for grain processing, possibly for producing a flatbread, yet the oldest bread yet found is a loaf discovered in Switzerland, dating back to 3500 BCE. The use of leavening has been discovered and documented by the Egyptians; there is some debate about how this process has occurred and the extent to which there has been a connection between brewing and bread making, but obviously, without a handy time machine it will remain one of the ancient food historians debating. There is no question that the ancient Egyptians understood both the brewing of beer and the baking process of leavened bread using sourdough, as wall paintings and analyzes of desiccated bread loves and remains of beer indicate.

Wild yeast is used in food preparations in cultures all over the world, which are so overgrown with culture and history that they have been produced long before any written word. The Sudanese, for example, make kisra (fermented dough made with sorghum), the Ethiopians use wild yeast to make injera (teff), Mexicans make a fermented corn drink in the lake, Ghanaian kenkey, and Nigerian use their maize fermentation to make ogi, Indian idli breakfast cakes made with rice, beans or chickpeas, and the Turks make bona '(a fermented drink) usually made with wheat, maize, sorghum, or wheat.

Many historians claim that the Egyptians were the first to discover that flour and water could "come alive" to breed simple dough. There were also bakeries and breweries next door. Someone probably used beer mash in their bread, and thought it was amazing! In time they discovered that one could efficiently produce beautiful loaves of bread by holding a fraction of the next batch's dough. The soured bread had a stronger texture and taste than simple unleavened bread. A similar finding has been made in other regions depending on grains like wheat, barley, and rye. Some starters have been admired over time for qualities such as time to grow and flavor. Families passed beginnings down to the next generation. The bread was a part of local society, from Egyptian pita to German pumpernickel, and Russian black bread.

Although starters made from sourdough and bread made from starters have been around for thousands of years, the word "sourdough" has a relatively short history. It is a term in the US that came into use during the late 1800s California Gold Rush days.

Before going up into the mountains, many gold miners got supplies in the thriving coastal town of San Francisco, and a good start to the bread would have been a critical necessity. Starters from this area have produced bread with a unique and particularly sour tang. Thus the beginners and bread from that region became known as "sourdough." Since then, the term has been extended to mean any natural starter of bread.

In the ancient world, grape juice, wine, beer, and wheat flour porridge (left to go sour) were staples leavening. Egyptian writings describe making bread with such "sours" as early as 4,000 BC. Legend has it that, by the mid-19th century, a crock of starters set sail in the hold of Columbus' ship to the New World, beginners were vital to American prospectors and settlers alike.

By 1849 sourdough had achieved national renown driven by its success with gold prospectors in California. The Alaskan Klondike miners used the fermented dough to make cookies, biscuits, and flapjacks, hanging in a tin above the stove. Many a pioneer family carefully tended a more liquid starter, called the "sponge," as they moved west in their prairie schooners.

Starters fed a lot of families well, moving from friend to friend, and from generation to generation. The sourdough baking has continued to flourish even after the introduction of packaged yeast. Sourdough, with its distinctive taste, has gathered a legion of aficionados — bakers who delight in the starter's mystique and continue to feast on this ancient ingredient with family and friends every day.

The first known civilization that we know was the Egyptians around 1500 BC around that used sourdough. There are no tales about how they first found it, but you may think some of the bread was left out, and some of the wild yeast spores in the air were mixed in the dough at all times, and they realized it rose and became lighter than the traditional flatbread.

The Egyptians often made a lot of beer, and sometimes the brewery and bakery were in the same place. A batch of flour with beer and a light loaf of bread may have been produced, or the wild yeast spores were thick from the brewing and entered the bread dough, causing them to grow considerably more than the normal wild sourdoughs.

They found through trial and error that some of those sourdough cultures worked and tasted better than others. By saving a little raw dough from their baking and adding more flour to it, they could keep this culture alive, and this would create the same taste. This is known as starter sourdough. The strong sourdough culture was very important to daily life, and even the explorers took it as they went on expeditions all over the world.

Some of the Boudin family, who was a well-known master Bakers from France, came to the San Francisco area during the gold-rush days in California. They discovered there was a very distinctive sourdough culture, and they became very popular with this special flavor for their bread. Every morning the miners flocked to this bakery to taste this special bread. Since 1849, they have used the same sourdough culture, which they consider to be a "Mother Dough" and the same recipe, flour, water, a pinch of salt, and some of that "Mother Dough". Their "Mother Dough "is so significant that it was heroically saved by Louise Boudin during the 1906 Great San Francisco Earthquake.

Sourdough came in handy as well 'because old-timers had to cover brown. They rubbed it till soft and dry in the coat, fur side downwards. Many argue that the popularity of starting in the old country or the Klondike age starts in there. A restaurant desiring the authenticity of Alaskan sourdough from the gold rush days recently charged an amount of $600.00 US.

While yeast is still used with rye flours, the sourdough is used to increase acidity, preventing degradation of starches. This use is also seen in other countries with a strong tradition of rye bread, Scandinavian countries, and Baltic States. The Germans, like France, have regulatory defense over what can be sold as sourdough.

In the nineteenth century, the prospectors and explorers in the United States were referred to as sourdoughs as it was a tradition to keep the mother leavening on your head to ensure that she did not freeze in the cold winters. May be it was going to get the yeast going, with the warmth to be more involved and to make better bread rather than as a measure of freezing prevention. As a result, San Francisco's bread was mainly sourdough, with bakeries like the Boudin Bakery still baking today, after being established in the mid-nineteenth century.

1.3 Basic Working Principle of Sourdough

What's so special about sourdough, and how does it work?

Commercial baking yeast is a unified type of the Saccharomyces cerrivasae. This family's yeasts are very specialized. Strains are selected for different end-uses. They are very fast-acting and commercially easy to produce, but they do not adapt well and are intolerant of acidic environments.

A complex mixture of bacteria and yeast is used in typical sourdough. The yeasts in sourdough are strains needed by Saccharomyces, which are S cerrivasae relatives. These yeasts grow on the surface of grains, fruits, vegetables, and even in air and water, naturally. The exact strains of the yeast and bacteria can differ according to the starter's roots.

Yeast and lactobacilli flourish in a harmonious symbiotic partnership in a balanced sourdough-starter. The grains each have a desired carbohydrate fuel. Such carbohydrates are used by yeast for the production of ethanol and carbon dioxide. The bacteria also convert ethanol, which produces lactic acid. Carbon dioxide bubbles get stuck in the stretchy dough, which makes it grow. The acidity that the lactobacilli produce is fine for the yeast but inhospitable for other species. A sourdough starter can be kept at room temperature (if properly fed), and the bread's acidity even after baking serves as a preservative.

A packet of yeast gives rise to dinner rolls. Sourdough starter does the same function — but how? Wild yeast is circling us in the rain. It settles on work surfaces in the oven, and in the ingredients, like flour. Add liquid to flour, and activate this wild yeast, and start creating bubbles of carbon dioxide. This growing army of gas bubbles, effectively trapped in the dough by gluten, is essentially what makes sourdough bread rise.

The signature flavor of sourdough bread comes from pleasant bacteria and yeast, which in rising bread dough produces flavorful lactic and acetic acids. These organic acids differ from mellow to vinegary; managing the balance of these acids, by changing ingredients and rising times in both starter and dough, helps you to make bread with your own favorite flavor.

Unlike conventional yeast bread, sourdough uses a water-and-flour "runner." The starter ferments for a few days; then, the dough is added and left to rise. This process results in a crusty exterior with lots of air pockets and chewy inside. But how it works?

Dough fermentation is a natural bubbly process when yeast and lactobacilli, which is lactic acid, come together. As the starter ferments, additional water and flour are fed to the dough, thereby increasing its thickness. Though the method can sound complex, it's very straightforward indeed.

The bread's "sourness" comes from the acids that the starter creates. The ingredients plus a warm environment build a perfect storm for the starter to ferment and take on the sour flavor of this signature. If you want to make a more sour loaf, find a cool place to raise the bread. Or, use a higher ratio of flour to water when mixing the starter.

Microbiology is related to baking. That may sound like a strange way of looking at it, but it's just a modest exaggeration. Both yeast-leavened pieces of bread owe their shapes and textures to microbial behavior. The yeast used to produce bread can be produced commercially (baker's yeast), or it can be grown in the form of a leaven (sourdough starter) from the world around us. There are several reasons to take advantage of this common choice. Leavens produce bread, which has a flavor depth that commercial yeast-based bread doesn't and is more forgiving due to the longer fermentation time. It takes time to establish a leaven, however, and when you build a preferential use of environmentally friendly microorganisms, you must preserve the culture.

Surrounding sourdough starters are a number of myths and legends, and many of them date well back to the long history of yeast and bread. Before fermentation could be detected by a microscope, no one could have imagined — much less explained — how dough could leaven itself, as if through divine intervention. Today there is an abundance of valuable knowledge about the science of leaven and sourdough bread. And this is significant since having a clear understanding of how the leaven microbes behave will make it easier to work with this preference.

Having Cultured Yeast and Lactic Acid Bacteria: A leaven is favored for making sourdough bread, consisting of a mixture of water and flour fermented with lactic acid bacteria (LAB) and wild leaven. The raw ingredients which go into a sourdough by themselves are essentially flavorless. The sweet-and-sour aromas we love in these bread are by-products of the mutually beneficial battle of the microbes for survival and growth in a dynamic microscopic ecosystem. And the ecosystem's make up evolves over fermentation hours or days.

Unlike commercial baker's yeast, which is yeast strains inside the Saccharomyces cerevisiae family, the yeasts in leaven are numerous, including not only S. Cerevisiae but also a combination of other species, for example, S. Candida tropicalis and Hanensula anomala. A particular combination of yeasts makes each leaven special in flavor — and most importantly, it gives rise to the dough.

While many people believe that their sourdough starter mainly consists of wild yeast, it is far outnumbered in culture by the lactic acid bacteria — LAB outnumbers yeast cells in a mature sourdough starter by around 100 to one. In fact, without the lactic acid bacteria living symbiotically with the wild yeast, a leaven isn't stable.

Unlike yeast, fermentation requires other types of bacteria, too. Many of these bacteria, smaller than yeasts, are members of the Lactobacillus genus, so named because this group's 200-odd species produce lactic acid as they digest sugars. There is much less fermenting power in an individual bacterium than a yeast cell, producing nearly 20 times the amount of lactic acid bacteria such as Lactobacillus Brevis. San Francisco-style sourdough and plenty of other sourdoughs from all over the world derive from L its signature tangy flavor. Francciscensis. Levain also contains bacterial species of the genera Leuconostoc, Pediococcus, Enterococcus, Streptococcus, Weissella, and Lactococcus.

Yeasts and LAB coexist so well, as each can grow side by side and tolerate the defensive mechanisms of the other to some degree. As with yeasts, lactic acid bacteria are selfish when it comes to money. The two work together to poison their surroundings — the poisonous cocktail they make is filled with alcohol and acids that are formed during fermentation. For other microbes, this is a less than warm welcome.

The ethanol the yeasts give off is not much inhibited by the lactic acid bacteria. Some lactobacilli strains are generally more resistant to ethanol than yeasts are. Meanwhile, the LAB secretes acids — notably, lactic acid and acetic acid — that reduce the leaven's pH. (Scientists who compared the pH of commercial yeast-based bread with sourdough bread found that the pH of sourdoughs was much lower: 3.8 to 4.6 versus 5.3 to 5.8 typical of commercial yeast-bread bread.) However, wild yeast species in leaven could live in the increasingly acidic mixture. Certain microbes can invade pure yeast cultures and LAB without each other, and if left unchecked, more alcohol and acid will be produced by both yeasts and LAB than even tolerable.

It helps the sourdough yeasts and LAB like different foods when it comes to peaceful coexistence. Yeasts will allow better use of a large variety of sugars and starches. C. Miller and other yeasts eat glucose and fructose (and sucrose, which enzymes easily break down into these two simpler sugars) very happily. Conversely, sanfranciscensis and other Laboratories favor maltose. Another example of teamwork is that yeast cells also contain amylase, an enzyme that separates complex starches and polysaccharides into sugars that are more digestible for yeasts and their bacterial neighbors.

When bakers build leaven, they manipulate one of the key evolutionary forces — natural selection — by transforming a microbial environment into a tightly regulated bread-making device. The cycle illuminates the yeasts and LAB's amazing ability to adapt to different environmental conditions.

Yeast and bacterial growth depend on three main factors: nutrient supply, acidity, and temperature. Since growth can occur incredibly fast, organisms and strains that are not suited to a specific diet (like flour) can be overwhelmed and die out quickly. That is precisely why the inoculants that some bakers use to jump-start their leaven, such as raisin water, don't make a difference. (We think flour is full of microbes and water works fine.) Additional factors, including hydration, also influence the maturity of a sourdough starter. Leaven can hydrate differently. If you mix water and flour in equal parts together, you will produce a liquid that is highly hydrated leaven. We refer to that as a liquid leaving. The effect would be stiff if you add more flour to the mixture, say 120 percent flour to 100 percent water. We found perceptible variations in pH in our experiments: the more liquid the starter will become, the more acidic it will be. (Thus, if you like your sourdoughs, use liquid leaven.) The crop may also be affected by pollution or invasion of dust particles, spores and the like, which could introduce new microbes.

Most bakers, too, swear by their particular starter. But from a microbiological point of view, if the feeding schedule or temperature is incoherent, the composition of a starter would be very different. If you're not careful, your special starter on day one may be very different from day 20 (or even day 2). And different starters will build surprises if you try to make consistent loaves, which is not a good thing.

A long-lived leaven would almost certainly shift in overtime composition. Think of it as a city; from now on, a great city will be as large as it is today, but its occupants will be different — including those who are descended from the current residents and those who later relocated. Only in a well-controlled sterile atmosphere can the composition of a starter remain the same, more like a laboratory setting than a boulder. The micro-organism population will fluctuate and adapt to whatever food is provided and whatever living conditions it encounters. If one strain considers the atmosphere more welcoming than the rest, it will grow rapidly and crowd its neighbors.

But it's not necessary to lock in a particular population of bacteria. What matters is that a heart-filled colony of yeasts and lactic acid bacteria behave predictably; in other words, it will mature and mature as expected as long as the leaven is fed on the same schedule and maintained at about the same temperature and hydration.

1.4 Sourdough Hydration Explained (What, Why, How & When)

The amount of bread hydration is calculated by percentage. It is a measure of how much water there is in the dough, in comparison to how much flour it has. Depending on the form of flour used, sourdough bread usually appears to have hydration levels from 65 percent to 100 percent. The higher the degree of hydration, the more the crumb texture is transparent, and the thinner and crispier the crust.

When you understand the rates of hydration and how to modify your hydration in order to produce those results for your bread, it can be a real game-changer. But at first, it can be a little difficult to understand. Let's break it up and get into a little more depth. Your dough's hydration level has quite a major effect on the type of bread you end up with. The main factor deciding your bread's texture and look. It will also provide you with a major indication of how the dough will behave during mixing, fermentation, and shaping.

The crumb is in a position to be very small, due to the essence of how sourdough ferments. Thus sourdough bread is typically made from wetter dough than other homemade yeasted bread. It is also necessary to understand how hydration affects the dough so that you can find the optimal amount of hydration to work with.

How lower rates of hydration impact Dough: The lower the hydration, the more rigid the dough is. And it would mean the following for you as a baker: You have to work harder to add all of the ingredients.

It will take the gluten longer to mature (thus can require further kneading). The time it takes to cure will be longer.

The dough will be less sticky, and the handling will be much smoother.

How higher rates of hydration impact Dough: The higher the hydration, the slacker and smoother the dough will become. It would mean: Ingredients will be easier to add as the dough becomes more weathered.

The dough is stickier and more difficult to treat.

The dough will be slacker, and shaping would be harder. (Additionally, additional steps may be needed to develop sufficient dough strength to allow it to rise well).

Kneading is less important and maybe not required at all. This is because the extra wetness allows it easier for the yeasts and bacteria to pass around, thereby allowing them to ferment and grow gluten.

The dough will begin to ferment more easily and will take less time to rise.

So the key take away from dealing with higher hydration dough is that due to the stickiness and slackness, it is more difficult to manage. And gripping and shaping takes more skill. (Tips below on high hydration dough operations).

It is best to start working with lower hydration dough as a beginner sourdough bread baker, and then slowly increasing the hydration as your handling dough experience increases. Yet why bother if it gets harder? Well, higher hydration dough brings some benefits.

How Hydration Rates affect Bread: As mentioned earlier, hydration rates affect not only your dough but also the bread's result.

Here are several of the ways your bread may be influenced if you choose to increase your recipe's hydration level:

• Texture – The higher your bread's hydration level, the smoother the texture will be, and the more flexible the crumb will be (i.e., the bigger holes inside).

- Crust – The sourdough bread crust appears to be very dense and rough, but the higher sourdough hydration has a thinner crust that stays crisp for longer.

- Flavor – Higher hydration loaves tend to have a slightly more refined flavor, whereas lower hydration offers a more pronounced 'vinegary' smoothness.

- Appearance – The higher the loaf's hydration, the less likely it will grow because the dough is much slacker. (If you want a smaller loaf that also has the benefits of a high hydration bread, you can opt to bake it in a loaf tin).

Taking all of the above into account, most people find that learning to work with higher hydration dough is worth the effort. For a thinner crispier crust and a finer textured, more transparent crumb bread, you get a better taste of the sandwich.

What is a reasonable degree of hydration to strive for?

This is one of those kinds of responses that 'it depends.' As already stated, the higher the hydration, the harder it is to handle and form the dough. But a more transparent crumb and thinner crust will reward you.

How high a level of hydration you go, depends on the needs of the eater. It's a delicate mix between how to treat the dough, and how to open your crumb. You may find that you prefer lower hydration for a sandwich-style bread to allow a filling sandwich to hold better. And for instance, a higher hydration bread as a condiment for soup.

There is obviously a limit on how much water/liquid the flour can take. Once, that will depend on the flour you use and how absorbent it is. But levels of hydration can be pushed up to 90 – 100 percent, particularly with whole grain flours.

So how much water does your Dough take?

The only way to tell if the amount of hydration is too high is to check it to see if it responds to your dough. When you can see water pouring out at the top of the dough jar during the bulk ferment, then that is a sign that the flour has consumed all it can and exceeded the upper limit to the hydration point.

Now that you have an idea of what amount of hydration you may want to reach for, we will learn how to measure hydration rates. But let's know a little more about hydration rates for sourdough starters before this.

Sourdough Starter's Hydration Rates: It's very normal to maintain a sourdough starter at 100 percent hydration, which implies using equal quantities of flour and water to feed it. Yet not all this is the case. Some sourdough bakers prefer to keep their sourdough at hydration that is lower or higher than this, and that is why.

NOTE: feedings for sourdough starters should always be performed by weight to keep the hydration rates correct. Feeding sourdough starter by volume would give you too much fluctuation, and accurate determination of the hydration level will be more difficult.

Holding the Starter at a lower degree of hydration: Some bakers prefer a thicker starter (high hydration). A stiffer start means more flour is fed than water, so it's 'stiff.' The lower the starter's hydration point, the stiffer the starter is. Most rigid starters are kept hydrated between 50 and 70 percent.

A stiffer starter feeds the wild yeasts and bacteria through the sugars and starches much slowly, so it can go much longer between feedings. If you can't feed your starter too much, then this is handy.

On the flip side, a stiffer starter will result in more acetic growth, so your bread's flavor will be sourer.

Holding your starter at a higher degree of hydration: Holding your sourdough starter at more than 100 percent hydration helps you to pour the hydration and blend it very quickly into the dough. Many starters with high hydration are kept hydrated at about 125 percent.

These are very quick and easy to feed because the flour absorbs very quickly, but they may also need to eat more often because they eat faster (this is because a wetter starter has more wild yeasts and bacteria movement). Also, higher hydration starters should create a milder tasting loaf, as they tend to prefer more development of lactic acid.

How do you measure rates of hydration in a Recipe?

Now that we know more about sourdough starter hydration levels, we can measure the hydration levels of the sourdough bread we are producing.

Here's a step-by-step rundown on how to measure a particular recipe's level on hydration (we'll follow up with a few different examples, so don't panic if it looks a little insane to start with!):

• Step 1 – Determine how much flour and water your starter contains and take note.

• Stage 2 – Take note of how much water and flour you have in your recipe.

• Step 3 – Add the total amount of flour (i.e., the flour in your recipe, plus the starter flour). Do Water the same. You have two numbers in it now. Complete water quantity and complete flour content.

• Step 4 – The equation for hydration is "Total water" divided by "Total flour" and multiplied by 100. That number is your dough's hydration level in percentage.

1.5 Sourdough Bread VS. Other Bread

The aroma of freshly baked bread is tough to beat — especially when it's the sweet tang of sourdough. A recent increase in popularity has seen this crusty bread, but what is sourdough, and why is it so tasty? Here is what separates sourdough from all the other loaves on the shelf.

Because sourdough is leavened with natural yeast, it creates a crusty yet airy bread loaf rich in flavor. Those signatures help differentiate sourdough from other loaves. But typically, only one or two loaves of sourdough are made at a time because of the bread's long rise time — and the fact that it needs to be made by hand instead of in a machine.

While sourdough bread is often made from the same flour as other types of bread, the fermentation process has many ways to improve its nutritional profile.

For example, whole-grain bread contains a good deal of minerals, including potassium, phosphate, magnesium, and zinc.

The absorption of these minerals is sadly impaired by the presence of phytic acid, commonly known as phytate.

Phytates are considered anti-nutrients, as they bind to minerals, reducing the ability of your body to absorb them.

Interestingly, the bacteria of lactic acid found in sourdough bread lower the pH of the bread, which helps to degrade phytates. This results in a bread with a significantly lower phytate content than other bread types.

One study showed that sourdough fermentation could reduce bread's phytate content by 24–50 percent more than conventional yeast fermentation.

Lower levels of phytate improve mineral absorption, which is one reason that sourdough bread is more nutritious than traditional bread.

In addition, studies show that the lactic acid bacteria in sourdough bread are capable of releasing antioxidants during sourdough fermentation.

Sourdough fermentation often raises bread folate levels, although certain nutrient levels, such as vitamin E, maybe slightly decreased in the process.

Lastly, the longer fermentation duration of sourdough helps enhance the taste and texture of whole-grain bread. This can make people more likely to opt for whole-grain bread, thereby encouraging higher fiber and nutrient-rich bread consumption.

Sourdough bread has higher folate and antioxidant content than other bread. The lower levels of phytate also allow your body to more efficiently absorb the nutrients that it contains. Sometimes, sourdough bread is easier to digest than fermented bread with brewer's yeast.

Researchers think this may be due partly to the prebiotic quality of sourdough bread and probiotic-like properties.

Prebiotics are non-digestible fibers that feed into your gut's beneficial bacteria, while probiotics are beneficial bacteria contained in certain foods and supplements.

Consuming both regularly will help improve your bowel health and ease digestion.

Sourdough fermentation can also more degrade gluten than baker's yeast.

Gluten is found in some cereals. In people who are prone or allergic to it, it can cause digestive problems.

Gluten tolerance varies across individuals. Some have no obvious problems digesting gluten, while others may cause stomach pain, bloating, diarrhea, or constipation.

The lower gluten content of sourdough bread may make it easier to tolerate for people who are sensitive to gluten.

Research has shown that the sourdough fermentation cycle may also help enhance the gluten-free bread's flavor, texture, and nutrient quality.

For people prone to gluten, this makes gluten-free sourdough bread a possible choice.

Bear in mind. However, that sourdough fermentation does not fully degrade gluten. People with a gluten allergy or celiac disease should avoid sourdough bread, with wheat, barley, or rye.

Sourdough bread can have a stronger effect than other forms of bread on blood sugar and insulin levels, but the explanation for this is not yet well understood.

Researchers believe the sourdough fermentation can alter the carb molecules' structure. It reduces the glycemic index (GI) of bread and decreases the rate at which sugar reaches the bloodstream.

The GI is an indicator of how blood sugar influences a diet. Foods with a lower GI are less likely to produce a spike in blood sugar.

Additionally, the lactic acid bacteria present in the dough during fermentation produce organic acids. Some researchers suggest that these acids can help delay the emptying of the stomach and prevent a blood sugar spike similar to vinegar.

The sourdough fermentation method is also used to produce rye bread because rye does not contain enough gluten to work effectively with the baker's yeast.

One research found that participants who ate rye bread had a lower spike in insulin levels compared with those who got the same amount of standard wheat bread.

Additionally, several other studies compared the glucose response of participants after eating sourdough bread and fermented bread with baker's yeast.

Overall, participants consuming sourdough bread had lower levels of blood sugar and insulin than those consuming bread fermented with baker's yeast.

One of the questions asked most often is, why can I digest Sourdough bread, but not ordinary commercial food? There are several explanations for this, and the answer is different for each person.

Simply put, the yeasts released phytase enzymes as the dough acidifies effectively pre-digest the flour, which activates the micronutrients and decreases bloating and digestive distress in turn.

Sourdough bread also requires more time to digest; studies have shown that added rye flour to sourdough will help control levels of blood sugar that help prevent diabetes.

Sourdough is also prebiotic that aids in helping the gut microbiome. But you do need a sourdough starter to get to this beautiful bread!

Chapter 2: Basics of Sourdough Starter

Sourdough starter is wild yeast, grown in a mixture of flour and water. If you've ever dissolved any dried, store-bought yeast in water, and seen it bubble up, you know approximately what a sourdough starter is like. The difference here is that you feed the yeast on more flour and water every so often to keep it running.

So: How can you acquire your starter?

2.1 Introduction to Sourdough Starter

The thing that makes it unique about Sourdough Bread is the Starter that it is made from. Starters are living beings-they feed; they sleep, they multiply and can be very successful if cared for correctly. The starter is tough too-in my own starter's case, it's had a long life (over 20 years), and while it's had a few close shaves, it's lived to tell the story so far!

A starter is a mixture of water and flour that has the yeast required to make sourdough. It keeps the starter alive by feeding it with more flour and water (called "fermenting").

This feeding does many things:

• It feeds the starter yeast and bacteria to keep them alive.

• The bacteria make the starter mildly acidic, which discourages mold and gives its flavor to the baked goods;

• Means that more starters are available to use in the recipes (and to share with others).

The amounts of flour and water used to freshen a starter may vary. Typically equal quantities of flour and water is used, which makes a starter thin enough to pour. There are recipes that use equivalent weights of flour and water, which is around 2 cups of flour for every cup of water. Although you will use any combination, the proportions of flour and water in a recipe need to be changed based on which ratio is used to freshen your starter.

There are many ways to get a sourdough starter:

• If you know someone who has some after they have fermented it, you might ask for a bit of their starter. The good part is, if you have any concerns, you have someone with a sourdough background who can help you out.

• Many companies sell start-ups (an online search will turn up several possibilities). Many of these have been passed down by people for many years from the beginning, and some claim to be "descended" from those used during California or Alaskan Gold Rushes!

• As explained in the next part, you can build your own starter,

Where do I get a sourdough starter by my hands?

If you're fortunate enough to meet someone who's got some sourdough starter, ask them to share with you a cup of sourdough starter. There are several online outlets available if you want to buy a starter.

Most people have memories of being given a batch of bread starter, which grew and grew rapidly and got out of control in their kitchen before they gave up and threw away the whole thing.

Your starter won't take care of your kitchen. It is not a pet that has to be fed twice a day and walked. Sourdough starter is highly forgiving. It can be very painful. It is more like a simple plant in a building.

If you have a sourdough starter that has been built, it is very much to maintain. If you're an enthusiastic baker and want an active start all day long at your disposal, **you can hold the sourdough starter on your counter for the whole day,** but then you'll have to feed it every day. If you're an occasional baker, you should keep your starter in the fridge and feed it every two weeks, at least. Take it out of your fridge every couple of weeks, drain off the greyish liquid pooled on top (or mix it in, it doesn't matter), and then feed your starter. Let it stay bubbly on your counter and then either use it, feed it again or cool it down.

How do you feed your starter sourdough?

You feed your starter with water and flour mixed together. Just pour in: 1 cup flour 2/3 cup water.

Do you need to feed your starter before you use it?

That hinges on the recipe. Generally speaking, if you want a good, high rise, you should feed your starter at least once before baking your bread, particularly if no other leavening agent is included in your recipe. When you decide to make bread, get your starter out the day before and feed it two or three times, waiting for a few hours between feeding, to make sure starter is really healthy before you start to bake bread. Some recipes (like crackers and thin-crusted pizza) call directly from the fridge for an unfed starter. The longer the starter is in the refrigerator, the less active it will be, and the more feedings it will need to revive.

Do you need to discard starter when you feed my starter?

Needless to say, no. At any given time, try to keep about 2-4 cups of sourdough starter on hand. You can normally scoop out a cup or two if your jar gets too full, and make waffles, crackers, or crumpets. You want to make sure your container stays about half empty so it won't leak when fermenting. Also, keeping the start-to-new flour ratio relatively small is a good idea, so your starter remains well-nourished.

A sourdough starter's care and maintenance need a portion of the starter to be discarded when you feed it (we'll get there), so it's pretty easy to grab any off a friend. If no one around you has any, the time and patience is everything you need to make your own — and also flour and water. But here's a reliable shortcut: Using a bit of store-bought yeast, you can also make a sourdough starter.

If there is a shortage of patience (or yeast), you can also buy starters from reputable online sources. You could ask your local bakery to sell you a little bit too. If you love bread but fear gluten, there's even advisable to make a gluten-free starter.

Think of starter sourdough as a perfect leavener and, in many instances, a way to create the wild leaven that naturally occurs in flour and air and convert it into something you can use to make bread (or something else) rise. Wild yeast is more reliable, both in terms of performance and taste, but wild yeast versus wild variety can be thought of as something like the difference between an heirloom tomato and the form of the supermarket. What you lose in color, you also earn inconsistency. Plus, it's kind of a fun, cool hobby wrangling your apartment's wild, wild yeasts like an incredibly unintimidating bounty hunter. But again, if you like, you can use store bought yeast to make a starter too! It is just as well as going to work.

Can I make a sourdough starter, or do I need someone else to take one?

Yeah, you can only make yourself a sourdough starter. It's completely fast! The simplest version needs only water and flour, and time to bake.

How long does a sourdough starter take to produce?

It's just a few minutes to hands-on time. You add flour and water together, and then let it rest at room temperature. Wild yeast will be picked from your environment and given them a healthy, happy place to grow. You'll then be feeding this baby sourdough starter every day. Within about 5 to 7 days, it'll be ready to bake.

2.2 Making Sourdough Starter from Scratch

It takes a portion of time to build your starter, but that's not difficult. This could take about a week until you have a starter ready to use in baking, so don't expect to start this afternoon and serve a wonderful loaf of sourdough bread for dinner!

1. Start with a clean, non-metal (preferably glass) cup and a non-metal mixing spoon. In case they are in touch for too long, metal containers and spoons will give your starter an off-flavor. The container will have a minimum size of 1 quarter so that the starter has space to bubble up and expand.

2. Combine 2 cups of flour and 2 (non-chlorinated) cups of water until you have a smooth paste. Add one packet of dry yeast.

3. To keep out pathogens (other yeasts, mold, etc.) cover the container with a dishcloth or cover, but the cover should not be airtight. This will give off carbon dioxide, which needs to escape when the yeast is running.

4. Leave the container covered in a warm place, free of the draft. Stir the mixture up every day.

5. You can freshen the starter by adding equivalent volumes of flour and water when there is a good sour aroma, and the initial operation has decreased.

6. This process typically takes about one week, but depending on temperatures and other factors, and it can vary.

The starter ingredients couldn't be any simpler: just water and flour.

We would want to start with whole grain (pumpernickel or whole wheat) flour. The wild yeast that gives a sourdough start to its life is more likely to be found in the flora- and fauna-rich environment of whole-grain flour than in all-purpose meal.

As for water, there's no need to use filtered water unless the water from your faucet is handled so heavily that you can smell the chemicals; tap water is perfect. Use room-temperature water from 68 ° F to 70 ° F for better performance. Use lukewarm water; if your house is chilly, if it is dry, use cool water.

- **Day 1**

In a non-reactive dish, mix 113 g (a generous 1 cup) of pumpernickel or 113 g (1 cup) of whole wheat flour with 113 groom temperature (68 ° F-70 ° F) water. Everything works fine; for this reason, it is glass, crockery, stainless steel, or food-grade plastic. Make sure that the container is wide enough to accommodate your starter as it grows; we suggest a minimum capacity of 1 percent.

Thoroughly mix all together; make sure that no dry flour is present anywhere. Cover the container loosely and allow the mixture to sit for 24 hours at warm room temperature (about 70 ° F). A notice on room temperature: The more cold the climate, the more slowly your starter can through. If your home's usual temperature is below 68 ° F, then we suggest you find a warmer place to grow your starter. Seek, for example, to set the starter on top of your water heater, refrigerator, or another device that might produce ambient heat. A decent choice is your switched-off oven — with the light turned on — too.

- **Day 2**

For the first 24 hours, you may see no activity at all, or you may see a bit of growth or bubble. Either way, dump half the starter (113 g, about 1/2 cup); you'll be left with a starter of about 113 g (1/2 cup). Add 113 g (a scant 1 cup) of All-

Purpose Flour (hereafter simply referred to as "flour") and 113 g (1/2 cup) of cool water (if your house is warm) or warm water (if it is cold).

Mix well, cover well and let the mixture rest 24 hours at room temperature.

- **Day 3**

1. You'll probably see some movement by the third day — a bubbling, a fresh, fruity scent, and some signs of expansion. Now it is time to start two feedings every day, as evenly spaced as your schedule allows. Weigh out 113 g starter for each feeding (a generous 1/2 cup until thoroughly stirred). Discard the rest of the starters.

2. Add 113 g of flour and 113 g of water to begin 113 g. Mix starter, flour, and water cover and allow the mixture to rest at room temperature for about 12 hours before repeating.

- **Day 4 + 5**

1. Weigh 113 g starter on day four and discard the remainder of the starter. Repeat feeding routine beginning on Day 3.

2. Weigh 113 g starter on Day 5 and discard the remainder of the starter. Again add the starter with 113 g of flour and 113 g of water. Mix, cover, and allow for 12 hours of rest. The launcher would have at least doubled in volume by the end of day 5. You'll see plenty of bubbles; on the top, there might be some tiny "rivulets," full of finer bubbles. The starter will also have a tangy flavor — slightly acidic but not overpowering.

- **Day 6 + 7**

1. If your starter didn't get up much and didn't have plenty of bubbles, Repeat the discard and feed on day six and day seven every 12 hours, if necessary — as long as it takes to build a vigorous (resurrected, bubbled) start. Conditions vary so

widely that seven days can be too little indeed. The trick is to watch the container for a rapid and continuous rise — at least doubling 6 to 8 hours after feeding. That maybe 7 days or less after you start, or it may be up to a few weeks. Look out for this benchmark, not just the calendar.

2. Give it one last feeding until the starter is ready: Regular 113 g water + 113 g flour. However, if you intend to keep following this guide and bake our Naturally Leavened Sourdough Bread, you'll need to bulk your starter up. Discard all but 189 g, then feed 189 g of water and 189 g of flour. Enable the starter to rest at room temperature for 6 to 8 hours, no matter how much you fed it; it should be healthy, with bubbles breaking the surface.

3. Select the amount of starter your recipe needs — for your crock, pan, or whatever you'd like to store it in the long run; the container doesn't have to be airtight. Feed this reserved starter with 113 g of flour and 113 g of water and allow it to rest for several hours at room temperature before cooling.

4. Store and feed this starter regularly in the refrigerator; we suggest feeding it once a week with 113 g flour and 113 g water.

2.3 How To Tell When Your Starter Is Ready To Use?

The multi-day process involved in making your sourdough starter from scratch results in a strong start that is healthy, bubbly, and ready to lift and flavor bread dough without adding (manufactured) domestic yeast.

How would you know when the starter is ready (i.e., ripe) to use?

When it is very bubbly and doubles in size within 6 to 8 hours of feeding, you're ready to bake with your new starter. (This is why it is useful to feed your starter in a clear, straight-sided container, so it's easy to keep track of its upward progress.) The ripe starter will be vicious, not thin, and if you taste a tiny bit, it'll balance perfectly between rich flavor and acidity.

Why throw away so much starter?

It seems so scrappy. You will end up with a very big starter container very quickly unless you discard the starter at any time. Also, keeping the volume down provides more food for the yeast to consume if you feed it; it doesn't compete with too many other small yeast cells to get something to consume. The feeding cycle finally works perfectly when the starter-to-flour-to-water ratio is 1:1:1 — equal parts, by weight, existing starter, flour added, and water added. Some bakers prefer various ratios, but this is a good starting point.

If you don't want to, you don't actually have to discard starter; you can give it to a friend, or use it for baking.

How to dispose of discard starter:

There are, of course, plenty of other ways to get rid of this.

Scoop it into your bucket or bin if you compost it; the mass of fermenting organic materials will quickly disappear.

If you intend to dispose of it, it is best not to do so in its liquid state, because it may start smelling. Instead, pour it over a piece of parchment or waxed paper and either bake it or let it dry air until it's brittle before throwing away.

You could dump liquid sourdough starter down the drain if you have absolutely no other choice — but do so with caution. You don't want to get your pipes clogged by the start. Place your discard starter in a large bowl and add cold water to the consistency of milk, stirring to thin it; then dump it down the drain, flushing the drain with extra cold water.

Can starter sourdough hurt your septic system?

No, it shouldn't be; it's just organic matter and yeast. But make sure it's thin enough to not clog the pipes again.

How do I understand that my starter is ready to bake bread?

After five to seven days of daily feedings, your starter should be ready to bake. One of these two methods allows you to test the readiness of your starter: It doubles in volume within 4 hours of feeding. A basic test that also sets you up for the very first step of baking bread is to feed your starter first and ensure that it doubles in volume within 4 hours of feeding.

The "float test" passes. The second form is called the float test. Use a cup of cool water, then add around a starter tablespoon. If it floats, then your starter is ready to bake.

What kind of container should I place my starter in?

Any plastic container that is wide enough to hold this amount of flour and liquid would do. You will need a capacity of about one fifth. Using glass with caution — if it breaks, you're going to have to throw your whole starter and start over.

2.4 Keeping Starter Alive Vs. Getting It Active

Know, there is a difference between a starter that is fed only to keep it alive; and a starter that is ready to roast.

Feed it until it doubles in size within 6 to 8 hours of being fed; and appear bubbly and vigorous, with a robust and clean flavor. Measure the amount needed in your recycle, keeping 113 g for the future (and discarding any extra). Feed that retained starter 113 g until cooling.

But how do you find a mature starter? You see bubbles forming on the surface, and it feels very elastic to the touch, it's ready to bake.

If you see some small creases in the top, plenty of foamy bubbles, and the surface of the starter seems to be slightly concave rather than slightly domelike; you'll know it's only barely past its prime. But don't let that deter you; baking with them is still perfect.

Contain Your Starter: What do you do now that you have a starter? Care of the container first. It can bubble up pretty vigorously when you feed an active starter flour, so it's nice to keep it in a box that has enough headroom to allow for that. The clear glass is good, because you can see the rise and fall of the starter, and you can easily see what it is up to.

Second, think about your bread-baking timeline. The best idea if you want to use the sourdough starter early is to keep it on your kitchen counter, or whatever room temperature area is open, and feed it at least once a day to keep those yeasts healthy. Keep the jar in the fridge if you are not ready to bake just yet. That will slow down the yeast operation, and if you want to feed it again, you can neglect it for about a week.

Feed Your Starter: The first five days of a sourdough starter feed are all about producing bulk and enabling the natural yeast. So you'll be adding flour and water at every feeding for the first four days. You will move from merely adding bulk to discarding half of the starter on the fifth day of building a new starter and then feeding the same quantities. This discard is a nice little bonus, since this liquid, besides bread, you can make other small bakes.

Follow the same procedure for days 5 to 7: dispose of half the starter, feed the starter by weight of 4 ounces of each or 3/4 cup meal, and 1/2 cup water — store in a dry, draft-free spot, covering it loosely with plastic or a clean kitchen towel.

How do you feed starters with sourdough? Easy. You add around as much flour and lukewarm water as you have a starter, mix it around, so there are no clumps of dry flour, and let it chill out before things start to bubble up. Just how warm your kitchen is, after this happens, usually two or three hours later, the entire mixture has become more starter. (The colder your oven, the quicker it will ferment.) The rule is to discard part of the starter when you feed it; otherwise, it will only continue to grow and grow and eventually fill your apartment and/or eat whole Manhattan, which isn't the result we're going for. Having a scale to measure the starter-to-flour and water ratios here is helpful, but if you don't have one, you'll be able to measure cups, or even pinch eyeball.

Keep one ounce of starter and feed on one ounce of flour and one ounce of water, since you seldom need a large amount of starter on hand, but various other sourdough luminaries advise different amounts. If you don't have a scale, go to a fourth cup starter in a fourth cup water for half a cup of flour. (Flour weighs less by volume than water or starter.) Only having a small amount is good for maintenance, and because the starter is infinite, if you need more starters, you can always feed it more. (For example, the famous-among-bread-people Tartine country loaf recipe requires just one spoonful of starter for the whole loaf.) A little bit of starter will eat tons of flour and water. When you're feeding it, reseal the container but leave the starter with some air access. Some people are covering it with a tissue. That works for you. When you regularly bake, feed them once or twice a day and set them out at room temperature to keep them healthy. Feed your starter once a week for less frequent baking, and keep it in the fridge.

The only very strict feeding rule is to make sure that you don't feed your starter boiling hot water or overload it with a massively unequal amount of water or flour. Lukewarm or cold are both right. Boiling is one of the few things your starter can actually murder, so avoid that, and you'll be set. If you have the starter in the fridge, let it chill out on the counter with the lid off for an hour or two when you feed it, then screw the lid on and place it back in the refrigerator.

Even if the Much isn't bubbling?

It should have bubbles in it and also smell fresh and fruity. If yours looks a little slow, just keep it out of the refrigerator and step up the feeding schedule. If you feed it for a couple of days to a week every day, it will show signs of life again.

Is My Starter Dead or Go Bad?

If you're taking your starter out of the fridge and an ominous layer of dark liquid is over it, don't despair — that's fine! It is perfectly natural! This is the yeast producing alcohol and doing its thing. Drinking alone is certainly not delicious, but it is not harmful. You may either whisk it in or pour it down from above.

Unless you expose them to high temperatures, the Starter is actually very hard to kill. The only warning you need to throw it out and start anew is if you see streaks of pink or orange in it. That means your starter has developed unfriendly bacteria or mold, and you can't eat healthily, so throw it out similarly if the green is clearly fuzzy. Yeah, that is terrible too. Load this one.

Do I still have a Starter portion to throw away when I feed it?

No! You may send a buddy to discard, to perpetuate the pyramid scheme, the sourdough cults. Or use the sourdough starter you'd throw away to do a recipe, such as waffles, pancakes, pizza dough, or English muffins. The only explanation why discarding the starter is part of the cycle is that an exponential growth curve is unsustainable for something, so you certainly don't need starter gallons and gallons, and your fingertips. But maybe you will?

But I know how to tackle Starter. What am I going to do with it?

Of course, bake bread! You'll want it to be working on baking with Starter. The night before, take your starter out of the refrigerator when you want to bake, feed it, and fire it up in the morning. If it's madly bubbling, you can use it for baking. If not, then you'll feed it again and wait a few hours. There are all kinds of sourdough recipes, but try something low-lift for your first sandwich, like this No-Knead Sourdough Bread. You don't need any special appliances. Getting a Dutch oven helps, but if you don't, you can make loaves in stockpots and on super-hot baking sheets too. Whatever equipment you've got will probably make some bread! Maybe it isn't perfect bakery bread, but who cares as long as it's good. If you get into the habit, at your leisure you'll be making lovely country boules. You're probably going to get crazy into freshly milled flours! Who does know!

2.5 Maintaining the Starter

If you've got your starter going, it's just about keeping them happy. This means freshening and keeping it dry, at least once every few days. Sourdough starters prefer temperatures that are slightly above room temperature, which is why they are kept in the kitchen as usual. Make sure they are not left in direct sunlight, because this may cause the container temperature to get high enough to destroy the starter.

When it comes to containers, holding the starter in a glass jar is safest. Though other materials may be used, they can cause problems. There are a lot of people who will discuss this. You need to gently cover the bag, too. The starter can emit carbon dioxide as it runs, as described earlier, and if the container is airtight, it will build up enough pressure to break the container. Using a lid, not tightened to the full. This will require an escape from the pressure, but hold out stuff you don't want (like bugs!) in your starter.

If you don't want to bake sourdough bread every few days to keep the starter alive, there are other possibilities:

1. You should feed the starter on a couple of days. You can use it in other recipes when your container gets too full. You should throw out the extra if you didn't bake right away.

2. The starter can be kept 1-2 weeks at a time in the refrigerator. At the end of the two weeks, you'll need to take the starter out and feed him. The starter will wait to be fed for two weeks, as long periods of cold slow down the starter.

So, now you've got your starter, it's time to use it! In the last chapter of this book you will get various recipes. Each recipe will use the sourdough starter as one of the ingredients, which means your starter will need freshening every time you use it in a recipe. This trains you for the next time you need to use it.

Once you have produced your starter successfully, you will need to feed it regularly to maintain it. Depending on your schedule and how much you bake, daily feeding could mean anything from twice a day to once a week.

Understand that the less often you feed your starter, the longer it takes for it to be ready for baking. For months on end, if you forget your starter in the refrigerator back, you can always bring it back to life; but it will take almost as long as a new starter is produced from scratch. Feed your room-temperature starter twice a day for better results, and your refrigerated starter at least once a week.

Storage of the refrigerator: Feed once a week Weigh the starter 113 g (1/2 cup); discard the remainder (or bake something with it). Feed this 113 g starter with 113 g of flour and water each. Cap and let it rest on the counter before returning it to the refrigerator until it starts bubbling (1 to 2 hours).

Storage at room temperature: Feed twice a day Starter, which is kept at room temperature, is more active than a refrigerated starter, and thus needs to be fed more frequently. Using the normal maintenance feeding procedure, the room temperature starter should be fed every 12 hours (twice a day): discard all but 113 g, and feed the 113 g starter with each water and flour.

Why the time frames are vague?

Are you looking to be a good sourdough baker? Relax and unwind! In sourdough baking, there are so many variables that there's no way you can monitor them all every time out.

Your starter's vigor, the quality/complexity of your recipe, the dough's hydration, even the outside environment-all combine to decide how much your bread rises, its texture, and how it tastes. Experience is your greatest teacher: the more you bake with sourdough, the more relaxed you will become with his "personality."

However, when you become acquainted with sourdough baking, you will understand it doesn't have to rule your life; feeding at 4 p.m. every 12 hours doesn't mean you have to get up at 4 a.m. if you eat it. And then feed it; 7 a.m. It'll be Okay. And if you skip a feeding day or two (or a week, or two weeks, or), don't worry. You will almost definitely revive your starter by feeding it every 12 hours until it is stable and then putting it back on its daily feeding schedule.

2.6 Can Sourdough Starter Replace Yeast?

Yeah, it does. Standard commercial yeast is also used in preferment such as the Sourdough starter polish for croissant dough is a choice that can live on and on, rising to replace what you have. A really interesting thing about starter sourdough is that instead of (or in combination with) commercial yeast, you can use it.

When we talk about baking bread, we will get deeper into this, but sourdough bread recipes will guide you to use a starter to leaven the bread. You can replace one envelope of active dry yeast with 1 cup of the starter if you want to substitute yeast in a recipe that calls for commercial leaven. But since a starter often contains flour and water, the water needed in the recipe must be reduced by 1/2 cup and the flour by 3/4 cup.

But let's just think a minute about that. You have a recipe that you like, and it uses yeast from the baker. (You love the recipe, don't you? If not, why would you want to keep it all around?) Now you just want to take the baker's yeast and replace it with wild leaven. Easy, huh?

But you're not only adding yeast with sourdough starter, but you're also adding flour, water, bacteria, and the acids they create (this is what makes sourdough sour), alcohol, and other fermentation items. And in doing so, you'll potentially adjust some stuff (for better or worse): dough consistency and strength, fermentation time, price, and, of course, the bread's flavor and texture, to name just a few.

So, what was that original recipe that you liked, anyway? It comes down to this pretty much: if you do it differently, you might well end up with another outcome.

Assuming you're using a scale, understanding your starter's hydration, and beginning with a gram-ingredient recycling recipe. Your original recipe is a "simple dough;" that is, it doesn't have a preference like a polish or a sponge.

How much flour does the starter you'll add, contribute? This is usually between 15 and 25 percent, although it is also higher for rye and whole-grain bread. A good starting point is 15 percent (which is, by the way, Norwich Sourdough's percentage of chosen flour). If you don't like the outcome, the next batch will change it.

Now, look at the formula, which was first. Let's say it's

- 500 g of flour
- 325 g of water
- 5 g of yeast

- 10 g of salt

15 percent of the 500 g of flour is 75 g. So you need to know how much of the 75 grams of flour my starter contains.

Keep a hydration starter of 100 percent, so the calculation is simple. There are equivalent quantities of flour and water by weight in a 100 percent -hydration starter.

So you need 150 grams of starter to get 75 grams of flour, which brings 75 grams of water along with it. If your starter is hydrated differently, you'll need to do some more math.

Now, when you add 75 grams of flour and water to each, by those quantities the flour and water in the final dough. This retains the same ingredients as in the original recipe, minus the yeast in the final dough.

The modified formula is

- 425 g flour
- 250 g water
- 150 g
- 100% sourdough starter hydration
- 10 g salt.

These numbers are the easy part and note that they are just a starting point. A few stuff to remember:

- Sourdough usually requires a higher dough temperature than baker's yeast dough. (Dough temperature is influenced by water temperature.)

- In addition, the dough may require less (or even more) water than its yeast counterpart.

- The dough would almost definitely require a longer fermentation time than the original formula.

- Sour flavor improves with a greater volume of formula starter and longer fermentation periods. Yet fermentation time is decreasing as the amount of starter is increasing. In my experience, increasing starter quantity is having a greater effect on sourness than increasing fermentation time.

• Higher temperature in the dough also reduces the fermentation time. Depending on who you are speaking to, a higher temperature can increase or decrease the bread's sourness. Have fun on that.

• The sourdough acidity makes the dough stronger, with the effect increasing with increasing fermentation time. Initially, you can need to mix the dough slightly less.

• Consider this as an iterative method to get to the result you want, and do what works for you!

Chapter 3: Ingredients and Weighing

There are many ways to bake, and there is no limit to making changes and additions to make delicious food in the recipes. Yet there must always be specific rules to obey to get a flawless desired outcome. You can't mix orange juice with shrimp because it'd taste like feet. Similarly, there are other ranges of variations that we can make in sourdough bread to make it feel good. And for a good loaf of bread, the weight of the ingredients matters a lot. And here are the potential combinations for making delicious bread and the law for weighing the ingredients.

3.1 Types of Grains and Flour and their life cycle

Whole grain flours — mainly wheat or rye — are often used when a new starter is made. They prefer to initially bring more wild yeast to the game than all-purpose flour because they are less processed, and they also provide the yeast with a little more food to feed on.

When you have set up your starter, you don't have to feed it with whole-grain flour; all-purpose flour is perfect. Nonetheless, if you are baking a whole grain loaf, consider using whole grain flour for the final feeding (setting aside some of your initial starters to feed as usual); this will add a little more whole grain to your final loaf, and also speed the starter up a little, due to the extra yeast food in the grains.

What type of meal is best used in sourdough bread? If you're a total beginner, the best choice is organic solid white bread flour made from hard wheat. This flour will:

• Give you the fastest and highest production of gluten • it will be fastest to knead and shape

- It will give the best raise in the oven, but it is also useful to learn about different flours and their properties.

This knowledge will help the sourdough baker expand their baking skills and produce various types of bread.

Here's the complete information to different flours, their properties, their advantages and disadvantages, and how/why to use each in a sourdough bake.

Non-Organic Flour vs. Organic Flour for Sourdough Bread:

We rely on natural organic wild-caught yeasts when it comes to sourdough bread. Therefore it is appropriate to use organic flour to bake sourdough bread whenever possible, as it is natural and chemical-free.

Non-organic flours are also bleached, meaning that they are chemically processed to blanch the flour and age it. Organic flour appears to have higher mineral content, and so sourdough starters are better able to use flour minerals without additional chemical intervention.

Flour styles In Sourdough Bread:

What if you use non-organic flour to bake sourdough bread?

You can use both organic and non-organic flours to bake sourdough bread, and here's what you can expect using non-organic flour:

Giving a less flavored loaf still gave a good rise, and structure to the bread made the sourdough starter smell much more acidic and 'chemically' (rather like nail varnish) sourdough starter seemed less involved.

Using organic flour:

The reasoning is that using organic flour has a slightly different mineral content profile, and does not contain the additional chemicals. So, it offers a more natural and complex variety of flavors when fermented than regular non-organic wheat flour. The truth is, even if using non-organic flour, a solid, mature sourdough starter still bakes good bread. So do not worry too much if you're in a pinch or on a budget. So long as you do your best to feed a high-quality organic flour on your sourdough starter, your starter will be strong enough to always bake excellent bread whatever flour you use for the rest of the bake.

Whole Wheat Flour vs. White Flour:

Using whole wheat flour compared to a white meal, in whatever variety of wheat you use, will have an enormous impact on the bread's flavor. Whole wheat flour has the whole wheat kernel in it. This includes:

The bran–found on the outside of the fiber- and mineral-rich wheat berry. This is the part that gives the most flavor to sourdough

The endosperm – Innermost of the wheat berry rich in starch and makes up mainly of carbohydrates and proteins. This is the part that is essential for the production of gluten in bread.

The germ – A small part of the vitamin-rich wheat berry. This also has left endosperm, depending on how finely it was milled.

You will be offered the use of whole wheat flour in sourdough bread: a much more nuanced flavor profile due to the variety of minerals present in the bran.

Bread has a denser and thicker texture. A thinner, smoother textured bread with a more open crumb (larger holes and a more aerated structure), a milder, simpler flavor profile, the more full you have in your sourdough, the denser it gets but, the more flavor it gets. When using various ratios of whole wheat to white flour, this experience helps you to control the bread and create a loaf that is exactly how you like it in terms of flavor.

Stone Ground Flour vs. Standard Flour:

Stone ground flour has made a comeback in recent years to make Sourdough Bread and shows no sign of slowing down. This is the way flour has historically been milled since the industrial revolution. It consists of two large stones that grind down the wheat berries before they become flour. This produces whole textured wheat flour, which is a processor. When desired, it is then sifted gently to get rid of some of the bran and produce white flour.

Apparently, the vast majority of the flour is roller milled nowadays. It is a faster technique that gives the flour more consistent, finer texture. The wheat berries pass through the center of two large steel rollers and smash as they pass through, crushing and separating the portion of the outer bran as it passes. You are left with white flour, and then some of the bran is further refined and crushed and then added back to the white for whole wheat flour to produce.

Stone ground flour produces a much more flavorful sourdough loaf and is especially suitable for slow fermentation. It provides more nutrients as it retains more of the bran and also because the cycle produces less heat (The heat is consumed by the stone and not by the berry), so the heat does not harm the delicate, healthy fats in the wheat.

As well as that, the flour appears to have a lower Glycemic Index because it takes the body longer to break down, as well as to create a denser crumb because of the preservation properties of the four.

The downside is that stone-ground flour is not as fine in texture, and may make a denser loaf, which may have a harder to handle crust. But several bakers believe that the flavor (and nutrition) that comes from using stoneground flour is something 'out of this world' along the lines.

Use Roller Milled Flour to make Sourdough Bread:

Roller milled flour is much more consistent in its taste, grind, and consistency, so when it comes to sourdough bread, it will give you a more consistent and solid result. If you're new to baking sourdough, it's always best to go with roller milled flour before you get a clear understanding of how the method of making sourdough bread in your kitchen is going.

The drawback to this is that the taste isn't that complex, so it's not as nutritious. For the wheat berry, Roller milling is both physically very harsh and how much heat is produced, so nutrients are lost in the process much more than in stone-ground flours.

Fine Ground vs. Coarsely Ground Flour:

The finer the flour is milled, the more it will grow, regardless of the molding process used. Especially when looking at whole wheat varieties, this is useful to learn, since Perfect whole wheat soil will give you a lighter loaf than just one grazing soil.

In terms of flavor, quality, and workability, freshly milled flour, whether roller milled or stone ground, is a whole different category.

Varieties of Wheat:

In addition to the general knowledge stated about the grain, different varieties of wheat would have different characteristics. It is important to understand these so that you can more effectively experiment with various flours and flavors. Here's a glance of some possible flours you might use for your sourdough bread and what effect they could have on the outcome of your bread.

Strong wheat: This is the most prevalent wheat type in the US. There are a few variants of this type of wheat:

- Hard red winter wheat

- Hard red spring wheat
- Hard white wheat

All these types of wheat (assuming they are white, NOT whole wheat) are, for a few reasons, an excellent choice for a beginner sourdough baker: they all have a high content of protein. They are all solid wheat varieties, producing 'bread quality' gluten. They are easy to manage when used. With many benefits being claimed, such as more nutrients per grain, easier digestibility, and better flavor, ancient grains bode particularly well on slow fermentation by sourdough. Heirloom varieties experiment in baking sourdough bread will potentially add a whole mix of possible complex combinations of flavor to sourdough bread! Here's some background on through, and what you need to know before you use it.

Spelled Flour: Spelt flour is the most popular of the heirloom varieties, and the digestive system is considered to be less harsh. Spelled is available in both whole wheat and white varieties, with a nutty and sweet taste.

- Protein content – 17%
- Strength – Weak on the W index (i.e., not considered heavy wheat)
- Special features – A 100% spelled sourdough bread would be slightly easier to handle than modern wheat.

Spelled is highly extensible (because of its high protein level), but has not much elasticity (because it isn't very strong). This means the dough will stretch out a lot, but it won't spring back too easily. The resulting loaf should have a more compact texture and flatter shape but a wonderful, slightly spicy, nutty flavor.

Also, spelled is less absorbent, and you would need to use less water in the recipe.

Einkorn Flour:

This is the first known cultivated wheat from all kinds of wheat and is the simplest and easiest to digest form. It has a special taste and produces a beautiful golden colored bread.

- Protein content – 18.2 percent
- Strength – Low
- Special Characteristics – While higher in protein than other types of wheat, the composition of gluten is very different; it should NOT be kneaded too much. Otherwise, it will lose its quality and become a big lump of runny mess!

Einkorn helps to offer a more crumbly yet delicate texture to sourdough bread.

Khorasan Flour:

This flour originated in Egypt, is also known as Kamut, which dates back to pharaonic use. It is still growing wheat used in Egypt and its environs. This antique grain has a high count of nutrients and excellent rich flavors.

- Protein content – 16 percent
- Strength – Low
- Special Characteristics – Like spelled, it is stretchy but not elastic, resulting in a fluffy, but very dense texture.

It is more absorbent than modern wheat, and hence more water will be needed for the recipe.

Rye Flour:

Available as dark rye (whole wheat rye) as well as light rye (sifted to extract the bran), Rye flour, and sourdough are like best friends. There is a reason that many artisan bakeries also add rye to their sourdough bread, and that is because rye is like a super food for wild bacteria and yeasts, and is legendary for being the perfect addition to sourdough, creating wonderful complex fruity flavors.

- Protein content – 15%
- Strength – Extremely low
- Special characteristics- Rye contains enzymes, which make it extremely active, meaning fermentation at a faster pace.

Using 100 percent rye with such low strength will make it impossible to knead and will only bode well to pour into a loaf tin, giving you an extremely dense but delicious loaf.

Rye absorbs more water than conventional wheat, so if you add rye to your loaf, you may need to add more water than normal. But it also maintains moisture well, even after it has been baked, which can compensate a bit for the density level compromise.

Measuring flour accurately is necessary for any recipes. But what is the best measuring option? Below are the three basic methods, described from the least accurate to the most accurate, for measuring flour.

Measuring Flour by Volume:

Scooping: While many home cooks scoop flour while baking, the calculation of flour is really not an accurate method.

Why do you stop scooping?

The flour is unevenly packed into the measuring cup by scooping, and each scoop will produce a different volume of the meal.

Measuring flour by volume vs. spooning:

Recipes usually are written in volume. Follow the steps below to spoon in a cup of flour and take the measurements for the most precise volume calculation.

How to Spoon Flour: Begin to loosen any packed areas by stirring the flour.

Using a spoon to gently scoop parts of the flour into a dry measuring cup. Do not use a cup for measuring liquid!

Fully fill out the cup allowing the flour to overfill the cup.

Using one knife's flat side or flat spatula to place the cup over the flour canister to evenly disperse the flour into the cup. Do not push or pile down the flour, because it should be free. Scrape the knife or spatula over the top of the cup to level the meal, with the excess dropping back into the canister of flour.

Measuring Flour by Weight:

As flour varies in volume depending on the grind, the type of grain, and the humidity, weighing meal using a scale provides the best results.

A Calibrated Kitchen Scale can be easily found in kitchen supplies and department stores. If you plan on baking several loaves of bread at a time, you'll want to find a scale that can weigh at least 5 pounds.

Also, note that most weight-including recipes are written in metric units, so you can save hours of math calculations by choosing a scale that can be set to metric or English units!

By carefully measuring flour and other ingredients, beautiful baked goods can be created at home at a fraction of the store-bought cost. Now that you know the fundamentals of measuring flour, you can learn more about various types of meals and how they influence the baking of sourdough. For more tips, keep reading.

3.2 Process of Leavening

Until the commercial production of cultivated dry and fresh baker's yeast, diverse cultures around the world produced homemade leavening bread and other baked goods. Sourdough is one such leavening that home cooks and experienced bakers make use of.

One of the essential aspects of bread making is the method of leavening using leavening agents for the bread. This reaction, in texture and flavor, is an essential part of giving bread its consistency. It's important to understand the workings of this method. In most cultures around the world, the same approach is widely used. It will also be served in some areas such as the unleavened bread in the Middle East.

The following are several measures to help you understand the value of leavening agents for bread-like yeast and tips on how to start using leaven.

The variety of leaving agents used in baking all have properties of their own. This results in different end product characteristics for each leavening agent employed. The taste in sourdough is not created by the yeast that is the lactobacillus (a non-spore-forming bacteria) that the yeast lives with the lactobacillus in the association. The lactobacillus feeds on leftover yeast fermentation materials. It makes the part that's turning sour by lactic acid excretion. This will also stop it from spoiling anything.

A particular strain of yeast is the baker's yeast that is used in bread baking. This is naturally not acidic due to the absence of the lactobacillus and needs to go through the process of forming a sourdough start. Up to the 19th century, all loaves of bread were sourdough before the cycle of growing by microbes was fully understood. Bakers all over the world took upon themselves as soon as this invention was created by the yeast of scientists. Know regarding the different grains used in baking bread.

The Lactobacillus produces the sourdough starter and yeast. This is where lactobacilli and yeast reside, which is close to a mixture of pancake. Manage a sourdough starter continuously by extracting a portion of the starter to be used and adding fresh flour and water back to the mixture. We can hold starters for long periods. In baking families, certain starters have been passed down from generation to generation. Because of the growing ability of sourdough starters, it is possible to buy and develop small parts from specialist suppliers.

A typical method for the production of sourdough in families making bread. Is to get the sourdough packed for the following week and to hold a slice back to use. If you bake once a week, then each week, a small piece of sourdough is kept back and grown for the next week. Starting the previous week, the starter will be saved and mixed with the new ingredients and left to rise.

Built from a flour and yogurt dough, sourdough takes longer to mature and to ferment (8 to 14 days). It is also more spongy, more bubbly, and sourer. It can be maintained and fed forever, with some bakeries taking great pride in their sourdough generation.

Sourdough is used in the recipe at a leavening weight ratio of 30 percent to total ingredients. For example, if the flour, liquids, and other ingredients in a bread recipe exceed 1000 grams, as your leavening agent, you would need 300 grams of sourdough starter. It usually takes a minimum of four hours of that time, but this can be increased if the more pungent, sour note is desired.

One can pick different leavening agents depending on the type of product one wants to get. The choice depends on the shape, structure, weight, color, consistency, and preserving ability desired. Leavening agents most relevant are vapor, soil, biological, or chemical carbon dioxide. Every of these recognizes different mechanisms for leavening.

The term "leavening" is usually incorrectly used as a synonym for "fermentation." Instead, Leavening refers to the great volume expansion of the flour. This is normally completed after frying, as the gas produced in this process is trapped in the dough's knead.

The gas which causes leavening can be derived from: a chemical reaction between salts when using baking powder (chemical leavening); the absorption of air into the dough or water evaporation (physical leavening); or a fermentation process (biological leavening). The latter being the most common micro-organism is the yeast of the brewer (saccharomyces cerevisiae), even though micro-organisms that colonized kneading naturally were usually common. The biga had been exposed to air in the past, and only a portion of it would have been retained and used as a starter for another biga later. Natural yeast (or sourdough) consists of various microorganisms (lactic bacteria and saccharomyces), which can ferment the sugars found in the flour.

Fermentation begins with the addition of a portion of the dough from the previous knead (known as "mother dough"). The dough can be refreshed several times, thus gaining some acidification and leavening ability and the number of micro-organisms that help the dough expand. The number of refreshments and the conditions under which they can be run depending on the product that you want to get, and on how much drive we need to make leavening happen.

The magic of working with mom's dough is to build and maintain a constant equilibrium between the different microbial organisms. It has been scientifically proven that it is not possible to replicate this equilibrium in vitro, but it is merely a gift from Mother Nature. The ability to work with sourdough lies in the ability to maintain balance over time. If the micro flora is too heterogeneous and fragile, yeasts and lactic bacteria begin a fight to win the nitrogen- and vitamin-rich fermentative substrate. The micro flora is healthy and can last over time if favorable and adequately maintained temperature and humidity conditions. External conditions determine not only the ratio of different species but also the quality and quantity of the organic acids produced that can alter the knead rheology. It means temperature, availability of water, oxygen, and free space by external conditions: that is, the system for preserving sourdough.

Holding sourdough in a bag, in a water bath, free or milk, affects the ratio of yeasts to lactic bacteria, and how biga responds in the kneading. Whether you decide to maintain your sourdough depends on the factors affecting the balance. Among them, we can find:

- The texture of sourdough

- The temperature at which sourdough is stored and is fed to the starter

- The quantity of oxygn (redox potential) available in storage (anaerobiosis, oxygenation while feeding biga)

- The ratio of flour to yeasts when feeding biga.

3.3 Functional Ingredients and its Preparation

You can enjoy adding inclusions to your Standard Sourdough Boule to mix it up and add a classic loaf to the attraction. The dried fruit, olives, beans, nuts, cheese, and herbs are some examples of inclusions.

Using baker's percentages to decide how much of the inclusion you have chosen to add to your loaf is a clear guideline.

We like to start with 20 percent and, if necessary, increase or decrease.

An example of this will be a loaf of olives. The Basic Sourdough Boule recipe contains 1000 grams of flour so that you can add 200 grams of olives (1000 grams x 20 percent = 200 grams) to your dough.

Now that you measure the weight of the inclusions that you add to the loaf, you are ready to start mixing.

It is recommended that you add the inclusions while doing the third fold. That is because of two main factors. First, waiting until the third fold gives the dough times to improve its gluten strength without the inclusions being hindered. Some additions at the gluten strands may break, which can weaken them. Second, adding them any later would deflate the dough too much, and there will be not enough time to bounce back afterward.

The mixing process for your dough and the inclusions should be as follows:

1. Mix the starter and the flour, water, and sourdough and blend until mixed. Let them remain there for 30 minutes.

2. Add salt and a small quantity of water, then blend until integrated. Fold first and let sit for 30 minutes.

3. Make the second fold and let it sit for 30 minutes.

4. Attach the inclusions and squeeze in the dough the same way you added the salt before conducting the third fold. Do not worry if they are not distributed very evenly as they will be mixed in even more by the next folds. Take the third fold and let it sit for 30 minutes.

5. Continue as you would the Simple Sourdough Boule with folds and rest, and form.

Baking is the same, but remember that if you have inclusions which contain a lot of moisture, you can need to increase the length of time. If you are uncertain, it is advisable to test the internal temperature. Temperatures should range from 190 ° F to 200 ° F.

Note: If you add an ingredient that contains a lot of moisture, it is a good idea to reduce the amount of water in your dough itself. This is going to ensure your loaf isn't square. Olives are an excellent example of extremely moisture-inducing ingredients.

Examples include:

- Cheese (Cheddar, Feta, Parmesan)
- Dried fruit (Apples, Apricots, Cherries, Cranberries, Dates, Figs, Peaches, Pears, Prunes, Raisins)
- Fresh fruit (Apples, Apricots, Cherries, Cranberries, Figs, Peaches, Pears)
- Crushed grains (Barley, Rye, Wheat)
- Cooked rice (Brown, White, Wild)
- Cooked meat (Bacon, Ham, Salami)
- Nuts (Black, Green, Kalamata)
- Raw or Toasted olives (Black, Green, Kalamata)
- Flours (Corn, Spelt, Teff, Durum, Rye)
- Liquids (Water, Whey, Beet Juice)
- Butternut squash with thyme and saute sage
- Roasted potato and rosemary
- Rye with brotgewurz
- Oatmeal with maple syrup
- Orange zest, anise, and molasses.

Chapter 4: Equipment and Techniques

Consistency is one of the drawbacks of baking at home. It can be hard when the climate of our hectic home kitchens is continuously evolving. Here we have gathered all the tried-and-true methods in one place, and they will help you make your home kitchen bread simpler and more repetitive.

Sourdough baking does not require a lot of extra equipment, but the whole process will be made more accessible by other devices. Let's go over some favorite products for a moment and distinguish the "must-haves" from the "good to have."

4.1 Useful Tools

There are a few resources needed to bake your first loaf of bread. This may sound like a long list, but you already have many of those things in your kitchen — buy what you don't have.

It is to draw your attention to one thing so first: a kitchen scale. If you don't have a cooking scale, you should consider buying one. You can use it in your kitchen for so many things, and it pays for itself again and again. It is highly inaccurate to calculate flour with cups and scoops;

• Cooker hybrid, like a 3qt cabin. Cast iron combination cooker or Le Creuset Dutch oven that can withstand 500 ° F (260 ° C) in the oven, has a lid which can build a strong seal when sealed

- Two medium-sized kitchen bowls to prove the dough
- Bench knife to cut and shape
- Two kitchen towels or tea towels to line the bowls
- Kitchen scale weighing in grams
- Mixing bowl

- Instant-read thermometer
- White rice flour

After all those years of baking, sourdough starter continues to amaze everyone with its production, strength, and resilience every day. The use of glass jars to store your starter helps you to check on the operation of your starter. And they are easy to clean and are safe (i.e., non-reactive) medium to use as well.

Plastic Dough Scraper and Stainless Steel Bench Knife: For effective handling of the dough, these two are a must. You can scoop the dough out of the bowl without deflating it too much with a plastic dough scraper and scrape the dough off your fingers (very useful when dealing with sticky flours such as rye or einkorn). Rinse it with water before using it, to keep the dough from sticking to it.

A bench knife is more durable than a plastic scraper, and it is used to raise, shift, cut, and pre-form the dough. The handling of the bench knife is easy, requiring just a little practice; start using it, and you'll be handling dough like a ninja soon. After each use, wash them well, and store until the next baking.

Digital scale: "Freestyle" sourdough bread baking — that is, making the bread by feeling rather than precisely measuring the flour and water — can be fun to express yourself and very liberating. If you're looking for consistency in your baking, though, a digital electronic scale is worth your time. You can weigh everything that goes into your bread, from flour, water, and salt to starter sourdough and other add-ons.

Few things to note when measuring:

Flour is considered the main ingredient in baking sourdough bread; the proportion of all the other ingredients to flour is called the percentage of the baker, and the water-to-flour ratio is regarded as the amount of hydration of the dough.

Pay attention to the following features when buying a digital scale:

- It should be lightweight
- Durable
- Easy to clean
- Able to carry a decent weight
- The number should be clear when the size of a large bowl is on.

Apron: Handling dough can be very messy from time to time, requiring your hands to be washed regularly (especially if you want to take pictures of your new baking creation too). If you're someone who thinks you can't find a dishtowel when you're most in need, an apron is a way out. One of the favorite kitchen accessories is cotton or linen aprons, as they make you feel decisive, fashionable, and like a smart, experienced housewife. Additionally, resources may be placed in the front pockets of the apron.

Bread Rising Baskets (Bannetons or Brotforms): Bread rising baskets are used to protect the soft dough as it rises; when you place them in the oven, they help the loaves maintain their shape and structure. You can experiment with various glass and plastic containers, and although improvising might be a great temporary solution, the container's material should enable the dough to breathe during its growth. Rising baskets can be used in different shapes (red, oval, rectangular) and materials such as cane, wicker, or wood fiber.

Sprinkle it with water and generously dust it with wholegrain flours before using the growing tub, or line it with a kitchen cloth (which you often dust with flour). This will allow the dough to roll away cleanly.

Baking Stones or Steels: Recall the taste of a pizza cooked in a wood-fired oven, it would lead you to buy a granite baking stone. A baking stone's key advantage is that it mimics the effect of brick ovens by being able to uniformly control and retain a lot of heat, which is ideal for baking pizza and bread, as it helps to produce a deep, crunchy crust. To prevent thermal shock and fracturing of the baking stone or steel, a baking stone should be warmed and cooled along with the oven. Clay baking stones also cost less than granite ones.

Dough Peel: A dough peel (aluminum or wood) will allow you to slide the dough onto the hot baking stone perfectly and easily, whether you are using it for pizza or bread. Make sure you sprinkle it with flour or cornmeal before placing a pizza on a peel to stop the dough from sticking. You may also place a piece of parchment paper underneath it when sliding bread onto a baking stone. After use, dust off or clean off your peel with a wet cloth.

Easy Baking Tins and Trays: The sourdough bread with crispy crust could only be baked in a cast-iron Dutch oven; that's wrong. You can use baking tins and baking trays. You can choose between high-quality enamel vessels in various shapes and sizes and handmade ceramic. When properly cared for, they'll last a lifetime.

You can use tins for baking sandwich and swirl bread, and trays for cinnamon rolls and focaccias. In order to get a crunchy crust when baking in tins and trays, add steam by preheating another, separate tray on the lower rack of your oven in the first minutes of baking. Throw some ice cubes or hot water onto the tray when loading into your bread. The water will evaporate, vaporize, and produce a crunchier layer.

Razor Blades: Inexpensive razor blades that can be bought at any beauty or hardware store are an effective device to score (slash) the bread before baking. By scoring the dough, making a signature bread decoration will spur your imagination. But most importantly, you can monitor how the dough expands in the oven, in which direction, and how much. In the oven, the expansion of the dough is also known as the spring of the oven. The depth and angle of the scores you make will produce different results and impact the magnitude of the oven spring as well.

If you find it too dangerous to keep the razor blade between your fingertips, mount it on a simple wooden handle (such as a coffee stirrer), or use some other scoring device, such as scissors or a very sharp knife. Scoring is the most beautiful when the dough has fermented to perfection.

Bread Knife: A good slice is a regular, nice-looking, and untorn slice of sourdough bread. Investing with a serrated edge in a sharp bread knife is something you'll never regret buying. Your serving plate should look more elegant and delicate.

4.2 Fermentation and Mixing

The very first step in almost every sourdough bread recipe is to add ingredients to make the dough. But recipes seldom go into depth on how best ingredients can be combined. We will clarify methods for mixing the dough here to help you master the sourdough recipes.

The purpose of mixing dough is to blend dry and wet ingredients to create a sticky, tacky dough that will stay together on its own while being manipulated in various ways.

Although mixing dough is a relatively straightforward process, it can have a big impact on your finished product because it is your only real opportunity to make changes before baking to your sourdough recipe. When a dough is formed, it is immune to changes in hydration and ingredient composition, so be vigilant about those variables is extremely necessary when the ingredients are first mixed.

Bread dough simplest form contains only four main ingredients: water, flour, salt, and some kind of leavening agents such as commercial yeast or a natural sourdough starter. There is an endless range of flavoring possibilities beyond those four ingredients. For now, we'll concentrate on using a natural sourdough starter to blend bread dough. The following material is for general use and will refer to almost every sourdough recipe.

There are a few trade tricks that can really make a difference in your finished product when it comes to the technique for mixing good bread dough. Even the sequence in which the ingredients are brought to the bowl will affect the flavor and texture of the loaf. Although several methods are available for mixing dough, these step-by-step mixing instructions should place your dough in good shape to rise well and bake evenly. You will need your ingredients for this process, a large bowl (remember, the dough will expand!), measuring cups or a kitchen scale, clean hands, and a plastic spatula or scraper (optional).

1. Measure water out. Be mindful of the temperature as it applies to your timetable. Remember warmer water = proof for shortness, cooler water = proofing for longer. Remove starter sourdough.

2. Start by adding only one or so tablespoon of the starter: if it floats, your starter is ready to bake with it, and you can add the amount of starter your recipe recommends. You'll have to wait an hour or more to mix your dough, or your starter is just too young to use to bake. If it does not float in water, it will not be able to give the requisite rise to the bread.

3. Break the starter up in the water using your hands to make a murky stream. This ensures an equal distribution of the starter in your bread dough.

4. Add the flour and other ingredients but leave the salt out.

5. Squish the ingredients together, wet and dry. Squeeze the wet and dry ingredients together with your hands or spatula until the flour is fully absorbed, and the dough just stays together-don't over mix! Only add a little more water or flour, depending on how your dough feels at this point.

6. Let the dough take 30-45 minutes to rest. Cover with foil or plastic wrap, to avoid the development of a crust.

7. Dissolve the salt in a bit of warm water and spill it over the surface of the dough. Squeeze your hands into the dough to force the salt down to the rim, pinch the dough together to add the oil. Repeat until the salt feels absorbed, then give the dough a few folds in on itself so that the salt can be spread as uniformly as possible.

8. Keep the dough soft, and either knead or no-knead.

Bulk fermentation (also known as the first rise or main fermentation) is one of the most important steps in baking leaven bread. When mixing ends, it begins right and lasts until the dough is separated and reshaped. The name means exactly what it is: a stage where the dough ferments in a huge, single mass. During this process, fermentation produces organic acids and gasses of carbon dioxide, both of which play an important part in the production of the dough. Organic acids are mainly what gives the flavor and strength of the dough (acids help prepare the gluten network), and carbon dioxide provides consistency and lightness for the dough.

Although much of this research is performed by our friendly yeast and bacteria, the baker still profits from a regular check-in by the dough. Through a series of folds, we help to control dough temperature and strength, and such check-ins also give us the chance to decide how the dough is progressing.

Let the bulk fermentation proceed over 3 to 5 hours at room temperature for a standard sourdough bread recipe. But, essentially, this period is determined by the bread you produce, what the ideal dough temperature reported is, and the temperature at which you hold the dough at.

When to avoid fermentation in bulk?

It takes practice to find the exact point when to stop bulk fermentation. You can learn to read the signs of adequate fermentation with time: dough strength, elasticity, smoothness, gain in volume, and bubbly appearance.

But it can be difficult to make the decision. Cutting bulk fermentation short may mean that your dough isn't fermented enough, and you're moving for an underproof result. If you move the bulk fermentation too far, on the other hand, the dough will be difficult to manage and on the verge of over-proofing. It's got to find a balance.

Look for a dough that had risen dramatically and is much smoother at the end of bulk fermentation than when bulk began. If you pull a little with a wet hand on the dough, you can feel both resistance and elasticity.

Look for lifelines, also. Shake the bowl gently, and it'll jiggle, letting you know the dough has plenty of aeration. These are all fantastic signs the dough has fermented enough and is solid enough for the division.

Strong fermentation, adequate dough strength, finishing bulk fermentation at the right time, and a complete proof – these are all steps needed for a beautiful bread loaf. And as you build a sense of how to deliver on each of these, with every bite, you can taste the difference.

4.3 Dividing and Shaping

There is a stage in the traditional life cycle of baking bread, where the dough has to be shaped into its final shape. But right before that, there is a step which is often ignored but equally important: the pre-shaping of bread dough.

Pre-shaping is just as it sounds; it sets the stage for good final shaping — and a baker will take many approaches. Some people prefer firmly pulling the dough together, and letting it rest with the seam facing up. Others gently pick the dough and make it rest seam-side-down on top for a perfectly smooth surface.

Ultimately it's up to the baker to approach. Let's walk through some factors that can affect how your dough is pre-shaped.

What is it that pre-shaping does?

Most bread recipes need enough dough to make several loaves, but slicing a large mass into perfectly shaped pieces can be difficult on the first attempt. Usually, you'd be left with lumps in different shapes and sizes.

Perform a pre-shape move to add some measure of uniformity to the parts to facilitate the final shaping of those unruly forms. This way, starting from a clear and organized structure, when we begin the final shaping of our dough — whether it's a boule, baguette, or something else.

Pre-shaping also gives us an extra opportunity to add some strength to our dough. When your split dough feels a little loose or slack, you can give it a tighter pre-shape. This simple act will add much-needed strength and stability to a dough, which may otherwise prove to be tricky.

Alternatively, if the dough is extremely thin, likely due to under-mixing or over-hydration, a second pre-shape step may be performed to add more structure to the dough before shaping. It guarantees a high rise in the dough and makes it less likely to fall or spread.

While pre-shaping is not strictly mandatory, it offers an opportunity for your dough to check-in, assess its strength and fermentation activity. It sets the stage for a phase of becoming more streamlined.

Take a very gentle approach to reshape, as with other phases in baking; there is no best way to do something; it depends on your choice and how happy you are with it. It efficiently organizes and strengthens the dough without being too offensive. At the moment, though, it's important to make the call: Is the dough a little on the weak side? If so, pre-shape it more strongly and in more order. Conversely, a very light hand will do if the dough is solid enough.

Think about how long you want to form the final shape after you've prefigured it. If the pre-shape-form interval is low, then gently pre-shape. If it is longer, then more assertively pre-shape.

Why fold and stretch?

Folding by a very basic sequence of acts helps to give energy to the bread dough: spread the dough out and over itself. This stretching and folding act, which only takes a few moments, helps the dough grow the gluten network. Every fold has a significant effect on the strength of the dough.

It also helps to control the dough temperature in the entire bulk mass. This means the temperature of the dough is fairly consistent throughout — no cold or warm spots at either the top or the bottom.

And finally, we have a chance to treat the dough at each package and get a first-hand evaluation of how it develops: is the dough slow because it is cool in the kitchen? This means that we might need to prolong the fermentation in bulk. Is it good enough for pre-forming or requires another set of folds? We have a chance to answer those questions by interacting with the dough in this way and to change course as appropriate.

How do I fold in and stretch?

This method works best when performing a series of fast folds and then letting the dough rest. If you attempt to execute another package too fast, you will find that the dough is too small. Stretching would be difficult, and may even break. Consider spacing out each set by 30 minutes for most dough (with the first collection that occurs 30 minutes after bulk fermentation begins).

How to fold bread dough: There are several ways to fold bread dough, but it's your choice to do it in the bowl directly. Next, get a small water-filled cup, and place it next to your bulk container. To avoid unnecessary sticking, dip your hands in the water before folding.

A simple stretch and fold performed with wet hands to prevent sticking.

Four times, you'll do the same up-and-over motion, turning the bowl after each fold. Use two wet hands, and take the side of the dough farthest from you, then raise it and down to the side nearest to your neck. After that, rotate your container 180 °, wet your hands again if necessary, and do the same stretching and folding. Next, rotate the container 90 °. Take the side of the dough away from you; move it back and forth again to the side of the container nearest to your neck. Rotate your bowl to 180 ° and do the same fold one last time.

Gently pick the dough up in the middle to finish the package and let the ends fall just under a little bit. It helps keep the middle of the dough clean.

How many fold-up sets are needed?

There is no single answer on how many sets the needs for your dough. When mixing your dough by hand, it can be done by two to four pieces. Flour form and hydration in the recipe, of course, also play a major part in answering this issue. Generally speaking, the slacker the dough, the more folds we need to strengthen it fully.

There are also other types of dough that do not need to be folded for. For example, you should probably skip folding with a 100 percent rye bread, since the gluten properties in the rye do not reinforce wheat gluten in the same way. Also, if your dough is very rigid and has poor hydration — or if it has been mixed and kneaded before bulk fermentation to maximum growth — there is no need to impart additional strength via folding.

4.4 Final Proofing, Scoring, and Finishing

The final proof is a repetition of the fermentation of yeasts, which allows relaxing and expanding of the molded dough portion. A piece of dough that has gone through the sheeting and molding process is degassed and lacks in length. Once baked, the final proofing produces an aerated dough of optimal shape and volume.

Proofing happens in a controlled environment of warm and humid conditions. In general, the proofing temperature is higher than the fermentation temperature at around 32–54 °C (90–130 °F). In the final proof, three basic factors are important:

1. Temperature-It is recommended a range of 35–37 °C (95–100 °F). Temperature and time variables work closely together.

2. Humidity – 85–95 percent relative humidity (RH). If humidity is too high, humidity condensation may occur on the dough, resulting in a tough crust and surface blistering in the finished bread. If the humidity is too low, dry skin on the dough may form, preventing expansion and causing discoloration of the crust.

3. Time-The time for proofing will be 60–65 minutes — over proofing results in light crust colored loaves, coarse grain, weak texture, and an acid overtone taste. Under-proofing produces limited loaf length, shell tops, insufficient flow, and bursting at the sides.

Starch is converted to sugars by enzyme action during final proofing. The sugars feed the yeast, and the yeast uses the carbohydrates to produce carbon dioxide and alcohol in the absence of oxygen. Within the cells produced in the protein matrix, the carbon dioxide is stored, allowing the cells to grow and the dough to expand.

Value of the final proof: Yeasted dough must undergo a final proof after forming to recover volume and extensibility before baking. Acids are produced by yeast operation during final proofing and contribute to the production of flavor. Adequate proof time is required; otherwise, the pieces of the dough cannot relax sufficiently, which can lead to poor volume and dense texture.

The final period for the proofing differs depending on various dough forms. Ultimate proofing time for quick mixing dough is quick, up to 1 hour. Ultimate proofing time takes between 1 and 2 hours for enhanced and intensive mix dough. Proofing times for bread leavened only by a sourdough starter are also longer.

Time and temperature of testing are defined by the strength of the flour, the composition of the dough, the degree of fermentation, the care obtained by the dough during mixing, and the type of product. Calculation of the loaf's height is sometimes used to assess when the dough is adequately proven. The dough expands by a factor of three or four during the proofing to reach its final volume. Another way to determine when the final proof is complete is to test the dough for spring. Press the dough gently, and when it springs back, it is ready to be baked.

Pre-shaping steps for bread dough:

The aim of pre-shaping is to take each piece and form it into a loosely round form with just enough outside tension. The round will maintain its shape on the surface of the work but not be so tightly pre-shaped that the outer "head" begins to break. Avoid pre-forming when you find that the surface is smooth without creases and is fairly uniform all over — if you're too rough with pre-forming, you'll end up with a denser loaf of broth.

Turn the dough over a floured work-board. Then brush the dough with flour on top and break it into parts according to the desired weight of the dough.

Move the blade against the dough, and roll it gently over the work surface as you move. Each of your hands works in unison: as you drive the blade into the dough, your empty hand tugs the dough under. The movement is swift and gentle; then, take your blade and hand out of the dough when it comes to rest on the work board. Repeat this motion with your blade and send it over and over, turning the dough gently every time. Through the move, you will find that the dough tightens further as it snags the surface of the dry work, and you hurry it along. This stretching on the outside of the dough will be noticeable as the skin stretches slightly and becomes taut.

Continue with these motions till the dough is in a loose, round shape. Neither clear seams nor bulging sides should be present. Start gently rounding the dough if there is, and smooth the top. The trick is finding the balance between just enough and not enough stress.

After all of your dough pieces have been pre-shaped, let them rest on the bench before shaping.

Until final shaping: bench rest. If you had to shape your dough immediately after pre-shaping, it would be too tight and could break. After giving the dough time to rest, you give it time to relax and spread in what's called the "bench rest." This gives the uniform pieces extensibility, allowing us to manipulate them into their final form.

Bench rest can usually range from 10 minutes to 45 minutes. The length depends on how solid your dough has been and how closely you have pruned it. The closer the pre-shape, the lengthier the bench can rest before relaxing enough.

Fast cut the bench rest when you notice your dough spreads easily. Then, either take a second pre-shape step or continue straight away with the final shaping.

Conversely, if you stop shaping your dough, consider giving it more time to relax and rest.

Pre-shaping, as with most aspects of baking, requires time and special consideration. If you look closely, we can see how each movement brings order to pieces that once were shaggy parts. This paves the way for a more effective shaping and a greater consistency in baking.

What's the easiest way to get your pre-shape working? Find a recipe for bulletproof bread, double the ingredients, and perform. There is no substitute for building the confidence and intuition which comes with repeated training.

4.5 Importance of Environmental Condition

When you consider the kinds of baked goods found around the world, you will find that the regional environment influences their characteristics. Crusty bread, for instance, tends to come from more arid areas, while softer bread also comes from more humid regions. Given the access a bakery has to the finest available ingredients, it cannot import the environment from the country of origin of a nice. Climate management methods can be used to establish the optimal conditions, however.

Storage: The need for sufficient levels of relative humidity begins in the storage room before the baking starts. If relative humidity levels are lower and temperatures are warmer, many ingredients perform their best and retain their consistency. Otherwise, the ingredients will decay faster as they oxidize, increase the weight of the water, and become susceptible to growth in the mold. Conversely, certain foods, such as fruit or icing, need higher relative humidity levels, or they will desiccate.

Also critical are the conditions under which you store and treat the baked goods, as temperatures and humidity levels influence the finished products and their shelf life. Excessively humid conditions soften crisp crusts, cause crackers to lose their crunch, or prevent the drying of dough, which is important for pasta. If the temperature control fails in the field, the products will quickly grow mold. Goods that customers consider to be soft and moist, such as cakes and sweet rolls, dry out excessively arid conditions.

Although a bakery might be utilizing refrigeration and HVAC systems, condensation due to the moisture that freshly baked goods give off or condensation from oven exhaust might not be adequately prevented. Bakeries, therefore, benefit from the use of independent climate control technologies, which allow them to track and regulate the conditions in individual areas.

Dough Proofing: The yeast is adaptive to its surroundings as a live organism. In flour, temperatures, and relative humidity levels, the water content influences how it ferments. As proof of dough, yeast produces carbon dioxide, which causes the dough to rise, have a distinctive aroma, and change the gluten in it. Bakers also use dough fermentation rooms or proofing cabinets, or proofers, to gain greater control over how yeast performs. Dough fermentation rooms need at least 75 percent of relative humidity. The relative humidity of the proofers is at least 80% to prevent skin from settling on the dough during the final stages of the proofing. Generally, the lower humidity makes the crustier bread as it bakes. Technologies for climate control integrated into the proofing areas maintain the temperature and humidity levels needed for the baked goods concerned. This is particularly beneficial during warm days when proofers appear to retain more heat.

Baked goods require more than putting the dough in the oven, as the quantity of water vapor in an oven influences baking times and the finished product. Forced convection ovens with lower temperatures have relative humidity levels of 30 to 60 percent. Natural convection ovens with higher temperatures have humidity levels of 90 to 95 percent. Baking times are longer when the humidity levels are higher, leading to the gradual evaporation of moisture and gluten coagulation in the crust. Arid conditions will over-bake the products and make them too tough. The best type of oven and level of humidity depends on the product at the problem.

When your bakery conditions are of higher quality, you can produce higher yields, experience less food waste-related losses, and promote greater customer satisfaction.

Monitoring factors that affect the growth of microorganisms:

- Time

It will take several days of daily feeding to create a starter or rehydrate a dried starter. When ready to use, it will bubble and grow and produce a surprisingly sour scent.

- Temperature

The fermenting microorganisms are more viable at temperatures that are comfortable for you, at normal room temperature (around 70 ° F). Fermentation slows at cooler temperatures, and when too hot for your comfort happens too fast or even ceases.

- Moisture

Water mixed with flour provides the atmosphere required to grow wild yeast and bacteria. Hold the starter covered loosely to prevent the production of mold.

- Acidity

Beneficial lactic acid bacteria (LAB) produce lactic acid, which increases acidity and safely lowers the pH below 4.6. This rapid acidification of the sourdough starter will help limit the production, including mold, of harmful microorganisms.

- Nutrients

Periodic periods of feeding are required. Removal of some starter for optimum microbial growth with each new introduction of flour and water assists with nutrient access. Flour type may also influence the production of the microbial and the final product.

- Oxygen

Carbon dioxide is created by fermenting the sourdough starters. To release the gas safely, the starter should be loosely covered, but the culture does not require oxygen.

- Changes made to high altitude

Remember that low humidity and low pressure at higher altitudes influence the preparation of the food.

Chapter 5: Factors to Consider While Bread Baking

Creating sourdough bread is one of the most enjoyable baking activities you might embark on at home. The entire cycle from building a starter to baking your first loaf may seem daunting, but to demystify the period, this book is the simple sourdough bread guide. Not only does Sourdough taste incredible, but wild yeast (starter) also turns flour into a tasty, nutritious source of food. When you're just getting started baking sourdough, be prepared to fall in love. Baking sourdough bread is something that is so profoundly satisfying. From watching the fascinating cycle of fermenting wild yeast to shaping and scoring your loaves, making a sourdough is a beautiful act of love and devotion.

Baking sourdough takes a few days, even though your actual time in the kitchen is limited.

5.1 Types of Ovens and other Baking Tools

The core of a bakery is its oven, and when deciding what sort of oven to buy, you'll have plenty of options available. Like purchasing a commercial mixer, it is essential to think about what product types you are making and what amounts, as these factors will affect which type of oven is better for your needs. No matter what sort of oven you end up installing, knowing about all types of the oven is good.

Convection Ovens:

Convection ovens are the most popular pieces of commercial bakery appliances. They're doing a fantastic job of baking a range of items quickly and uniformly. The use of internal fans to disperse the air produces even browning effects that can be replicated. Of the types of ovens usually used in a bakery, the most popular and the least expensive is the convection oven.

Some high-end convection ovens in the bakery boast steam injection and other specialist features that can take the baked goods to the next level.

Deck Ovens:

Artisan-style bakers or those who make bread of different types also choose a deck oven. Their stone cooking decks are heating up, giving a distinctive, crispy character to the crust while retaining a soft and moist interior. A deck oven takes up considerably more space compared with a convection oven, so bear that in mind when space is small. However, they last a long time and work without much trouble due to their reasonably simple nature and few moving parts. There are both single-deck styles and multi-deck styles.

Roll-In Rack Ovens:

In principle, a roll-in rack oven is similar to a roll-in refrigerator or cabinet proofing. You can wheel a pan rack full of products straight into the oven to bake. To better outcomes, some models will "grab" the pan rack and rotate it during the baking process. The benefit of this design is savings in time and energy due to less handling of the items.

When you have a roll-in Proofing Cabinet, you can save even more time. In that case, you can load the pans full of products onto the rack, prove them, roll them into the baking oven and roll them out for cooling once the baking is finished! If this style is considered, make sure that you have roll-in oven racks designed for this use; not all racks have high-temperature casters.

A rolling oven has large rotating trays that can be filled with the food, similar in design to a rotisserie-style oven at a deli or store. They have very high potential and potential for production, but they are also very costly. Make sure that your production and budget needs will warrant purchasing one of those units.

5.2 Transforming Dough into Bread

It all starts with the dough when you make good bread or some other baked good. Getting the dough correctly prepared is key to the finished product's consistency and texture. Although the activity of a very small or artisanal type may choose to mix its bread dough by hand on the table of a wood-topped baker, most commercial bakeries would want at least one, if not several, dough mixers.

Professional mixer: Mechanical planetary mixers are available in a stunning variety of sizes, from small 5 qt. Up to 100+qt countertop models. Most bakeries of mid to large size would have many large floor units and may benefit from the compact design of a countertop unit, which can quickly and easily mix up small batches of icing or fillings. The most critical aspect is adapting the mixer's strengths to what you'd like it to do with.

Dough Dividers and Sheeters: Dough dividers are advanced pieces of commercial baking equipment that carry a large batch of dough out into uniformly formed and weighted balls of dough for consistent results when producing pies, bread or even pizza crusts. Dough sheets take a dough ball and roll and stretch it to the size and thickness you specified. It increases the consistency of the dough crusts in your pie and pizza.

Dough dividers and dough sheets are excellent labor savers and help you make your production more reliable. You'll want to understand the return on investment, however, because they can initially be bulky and expensive to buy. As a result, higher-volume businesses use them the most frequently.

Holding/Proofing: You cause it to rise before baking when proofing bread dough. Since dough rises best in dry, humid conditions, you'll probably want to invest in some cabinets for proofing. To obtain reliable, repeatable results, these advanced pieces of equipment achieve the ideal temperature and humidity levels. Suffice it to say that large amounts of varieties and styles of cabinet proofing are available.

Purchase Criteria:

- Size: Full-height, height 3/4, height 1/2.

- Interior configuration: fixed wire slides, lip load slides, shelves, universal slides.

- Door setup: glass or solid doors, full door, or split door.

You can buy cabinets that are exclusively built for proofing or models that also include a hot keeping function. Such hybrid keeping and proofing cabinets give you the flexibility of two different pieces of equipment in one footprint; you can prove dough and keep hot and ready to sell or serve the finished product or other foods in the same cabinet!

Retarder/Proofer: You can refrigerate the dough if you wish to slow down the growth. Yet when they are allowed to rest at higher temperatures than a commercial refrigerator, certain forms of dough turn out better. Maybe you may like to find a retarder in this situation. The most flexible retarders are usually combination units that, when you are ready to do so, can turn over to proofing the dough. These retarder/proofer combinations are perfect labor savers, as you can put your dough in them overnight, program the device to start proofing and at a certain point, and have them tested and ready to bake exactly when you're done. Many advanced models also merge the capabilities of the retarder/proofer and the convection oven into one!

If you want to play with various varieties of flour to customize your loaf, here is a quick guide:

– Chewy with more transparent crumb & thicker crust: Omit the all-purpose flour in the dough and then substitute it with all bread flour.

– Even softer with finer crumb & thinner crust: take the bread flour out of the dough and replace it instead with all-purpose flour.

– Darker crust: Many people prefer darker & more caramelized crust. If that's your choice, you'll want to bake your bread at a higher temperature after you've taken it off the Dutch oven for the second baking point. Baking your loaves at 425 ° F, instead of 400 ° F, will result in a darker crust.

5.3 Baking in Professional Oven, Home Oven & Baking without an oven

Baking bread is trickier than you'll learn from the recipe books! But it's also easier. You can transform a well-made and well-formed dough into something special by professional use of the oven with a bit of thermal understanding.

That's why you have to read this to understand how you want to get the tests.

It's down to getting to do what you want to do. Let's break it into categories of bread types and uses it for the bread you produce:

• Smooth, thin crust. Suitable for sandwiches or other uses where hard chewing is not necessary. Social occasions, for example, where bread can be eaten in other people's company, and conversation is important. And there's crunching down!

• The crust is thin yet crisp. Suitable for picnic bread, finger foods, or times when it's important to appear, but where the bread has to keep its shape.

• Crust is dense and chewy. Perfect for occasions when a clear point needs to be made by the bread and when presentation and color can be robust. For example, this kind of bread suits Mediterranean and Italian feasts, or when it is used to dip into soup or other liquids and needs to stay together.

There are a few other specifics too-the thickness of the bread will come into it, whether it is tall or low, and the overall bread volume being baked; for example, one loaf or two. The oven itself would make a major difference - gas and electric heat are very different forms - how much space is in the middle around the outside of the bread.

A good bit of that is either common sense, or trial and mistake, but people still have issues with these things, so this section is intended to be a bit of a guide to saving from ever happening a few dodgy loaves. Nothing is more disappointing than to have a sourdough lovingly tended for a whole day, to ruin it in the oven. Then as you get a little bit more advanced, the fine detail will raise your bread's finish.

Crust: Management of the crust is primarily related to moisture, and also to the time in the oven. It has very little really to do with the temperature.

In general, you need steam in the first half of the baking cycle to position the crust correctly.

Like most domestic ovens as a default setting, place a small bowl of water on the oven floor before turning on the oven. Instead, after the oven has reached the target temperature, it requires an additional ten to fifteen minutes to evaporate the water. At the very least, it will keep the air moist in the oven.

As my normal ambient temperature, work with 180 degrees Celsius, but if you bake directly on the sole, get around 220 C on the baking surface. Baking temperatures can be altered for several reasons:

- The amount of bread in the oven relative to the oven's total efficiency. When the oven is pretty full, since it's going to be exposed to the elements, you could find a slightly lower temperature works better. If you have a rough crust, that could well be the explanation for it-just lop off 10 degrees at a time and see how it goes. Add about 10 minutes to the overall baking time, though as well.

• If you have a big oven with just a small loaf in it, the reverse is true, because it is a long way from the sun. Nonetheless, remember to shorten the baking time a bit.

• Convection furnaces are cooler than still-air ones.

• Crust considerations-see below for different crusting techniques.

Using the bowl of water as your means to get the steam going in the oven for a fluffy, light crust. In reality, you want a higher oven temperature and a shorter baking time. Approximately ten degrees cooler, combined with about ten minutes less in the oven, would do the trick.

If a thin, crisp crust is desired, heat the oven above the ideal temperature to around 30 degrees Celsius and let it stay there for at least 15 minutes to stabilize and steam the walls. Then spray the sidewalls with a mist spray gun just before you load the oven. That will cause a fair bit of steam to be in the oven. Load your bread quickly and close the door. Remove to target temperature immediately, and bake as natural.

You'll achieve a fine, thin-crust, and golden color if you do these two things together.

If you're after a thicker crust, you'll want, in a general sense, a drier oven. In the beginning, you can want to spray the walls only and leave the water bowl out. Alternatively, you can use the bowl for the first half of the bake, then pull it out halfway. In general, however, wipe a good 20 degrees off the temperature (or more) after around ten minutes in the oven, and bake for an additional 20 minutes to a long half-hour.

You are unlikely to burn the bread at low temperatures, so keep baking until the crust is the way you want it. Italian bakers often bake for an hour and a half at a pace as low as 120 degrees to get a very thick crust.

Knocking the bread: If the bread is cooked, a hard knock on the crust will give a hollow sound. Otherwise, it'll sound more like a dull thud.

When you've educated your nose, you'll also be able to detect if the bread is baked. That's from experience, so it's dependable. Many bakers who have worked in bakeries for years still possess this ability, although they will not be in a position to articulate exactly what they do.

A healthy oven technique is basically about practice, meaning trial and error. However, if you work from these instructions, while at first, they can seem a little counter-intuitive, you may find that you are going to master your oven quickly. The temperatures mentioned will vary a little. Be consistent; above all, with your approach-if, you change things, change one thing at a time; otherwise, you won't know which change worked!

Follow these measures to bake your sourdough bread in a Dutch oven:

Cover with cornmeal on the bottom of your Dutch oven. Let it rest and rise again by placing the dough inside. This time, for a shorter duration, it will become, about 1-2 hours. When the dough is slightly puffy, you'll know it's ready. Factors like the temperature of your dough and the surrounding atmosphere can influence its rate of growth, so keep your mind open.

Make a shallow slice about 2 inches long at the center of the dough, using a serrated knife. It will help stretch the dough and avoid the steam.

Having a Dutch baking oven ensures you can bake the sourdough bread outdoors. At around 400-420 F, the bread can be baked in an oven for 40 minutes. This temperature

can be reached by using 40 charcoal briquettes (give or take-just hold a thermometer around if necessary). Bake for an hour or until a dark, golden brown above the briquettes.

Please remember that some of the briquettes will lose heat or die-off along the way. Keep a thermometer handy for better performance in deciding the temperature of the Dutch oven. Add or remove briquettes where appropriate. If the sourdough is cooked, let it cool and then enjoy!

Why bake in a Dutch bread oven?

Baking sourdough loaves in your Dutch oven should provide a way for the dough to steam as it bakes. This helps to shape a crusty loaf with a hot, tender center.

You'll need to find some way to catch steam around your bread when it's baking without the Dutch oven. If you've got a big roasting pan, you might try that. And if anything else fails, try a sheet of cookies with a roasting pan lid over it.

Make a delicious, crusty recipe for bread from scratch also needs baking in a Dutch oven. What if you don't have one? No worries-we've protected you with these simple replacements for Dutch oven!

Steam baking: The idea is to create steam around the dough as it bakes. Most of the ovens have no big seal. Thus it is less than desirable to spritz the bread in the oven as it bakes. You need continuous steam around the loaf for the best crust and texture, while it bakes for the first 15 to 20 minutes.

Baking sourdough hearth bread in bread pans: Bake one loaf at a time, if you have a big Dutch oven. In the recipe card, follow the instructions.

Place them on a cookie sheet if you cannot fit the bread pans into your Dutch oven.

You'll need a lower space, as well—Preheat to 400 ° F. 15 Minutes. Bake 30 to 40 minutes more with reduced heat to 375.

For steam, fill a pan with water (like a roasting pan) on the shelf below the pots.

Sprinkle the unbaked loaves with water liberally before putting them in the hot oven.

Ignore the instructions on the recipe. Do the thump check to ensure it's completed.

When talk about a Dutch oven alternative for bread, what is really talking inside your oven build steam?

In crusty bread baking right down to the point where the loaf has browned and set, steam is important. Whenever this happens, it is time to remove steam from the equation (too much steam will make your crust dense and tough!) Do this by removing the cover for the last 10-20 minutes of baking time. You will either remove a cover, remove a dish of water or track the water amount that you use so that it evaporates in time to allow the bread to crisp up.

Option 1: Two Cast Iron Skillets + Ice Cubes

Preheat two cast iron skillets (we suggest one 8" to 12" skillet for the bread itself, and one 6" to 8" skillet for holding the ice cubes we'll use to build steam) in the oven while it's heating until baking. Place the smaller skillet directly below the large skillet onto a separate oven rack.

Note: The directions usually advise you to preheat the Dutch oven if you are using a Dutch Oven Bread recipes. If you use this process, simply preheat the cast iron skillet!

Take 8-10 ice cubes from the freezer when it's time to bake and get them ready to go.

Remove the large cast-iron skillet from the oven using oven mitts. Bring your bread gently down into the hot skillet (do not burn yourself!).

Put the mitts back on your oven, then place the hot skillet carefully back into the oven.

If the bread is in the oven, dump your ice cubes into the second hot skillet quickly (but carefully!), and close the oven door.

When it reaches the hot oven, the ice will steam, producing the steam you need for a crispy crust. After 20ish minutes the water from the ice cubes will evaporate completely, leaving your bread in a steam-free oven for a large crispy crust to finish the baking.

Note: This ice cube method is NOT recommended with hot glass or ceramic baking dish, because the extreme temperature difference will cause such materials to crack. Use a heavy metal baking dish instead if you don't have a spare cast iron skillet.

Option 2: Oven-Safe Pot and a Tight Lid or Sheet Pan

Bake crusty bread with oven-safe pot and sheet plate! If you have a secure, oven-safe lid in your bowl, please feel free to use that instead of a sheet pan. Instead of a standard baking dish, use a stockpot since typical casserole dishes are typically too small to bake crusty bread ineffectively: the bread will both reach the baking sheet on top and flatten out into a sad glob, or it will rise so high that it raises the cookie sheet off the platter and releases all steam.

Be sure to use a pot or dish which is at least 4 inches deep to give the bread space to rise as it bakes for better performance. A 5- or 6-quarter casserole or stockpot is going to do a fantastic job – just make sure it's oven-safe. If you're using a standard stainless steel pot, you can skip the pre-heating phase here.

A steel pot can heat up much faster than a cast-iron skillet or a Dutch oven, and since it does not disperse heat as evenly, it is more likely to burn the bread's bottom if it is preheated.

Instead, place your shaped loaf directly in the cold pot when you're ready to bake, then put it in your hot oven and immediately cover it with your baking sheet.

Bake as instructed by your recipe and remove the baking sheet during the last 10-20 minutes of baking.

Option 3: Baking Steel or Pizza Stone and Water Dish

Last but not least-bake your bread on a good old pizza stone or steel baking and make steam using a dish of water. Like the Dutch ovens, the heat is well conducted by baking steel and distributed uniformly for a uniform bake.

Preheat your baked steel for 45 minutes to 1 hour before baking, for better results.

Fill a small baking platter with water to generate steam (1 cup is normally plenty) and put it in the oven, on a rack directly below your baking stone or steel, 5-10 minutes before you put your bread in the oven. Place your bread on the baking steel when you are ready to bake and bake as instructed.

Remove the water dish from the oven carefully for the last 10-20 minutes of baking (if you're following a Dutch oven bread recipe, take the water dish out when it asks you to remove the Dutch oven lid!) Don't worry about trying to pour off the water when it's still hot, just put the baking dish on the stove or a trivet and let it cool off.

Ways to Build Steam in Your Oven:

This is not an infinite of all the ways without a Dutch oven to bake crusty bread:

• Fill a clean water spray bottle. Sprinkle many water pumps right into the oven as you place the bread on a pizza plate, baked steel, or even a preheated sheet pan, and then again in the oven after 5-10 minutes. It just doesn't give you the same crispy, crunchy crust as some of those other techniques!

• Place an upside-down oven-safe mixing bowl over bread that you bake on a pizza or steel baking stone. This technique does a fantastic job of generating steam and making a crisp crust, but attempting to raise a big bowl off a flat surface while wearing oven mitts is incredibly difficult, not to mention being much harder to burn yourself unintentionally.

• Pour the water right into a hot cast iron skillet when putting your bread on a pizza stone or steel baking. Some bakers recommend pouring very hot water in a preheated saucepan to build steam, and some recommend pouring COLD water into a preheated saucepan, either from a bowl or from a long funnel.

5.4 The Importance of Dough Temperature in Baking (with a calculator)

Many bakers will say you don't need a thermometer, and you don't need to track the dough temperature. People baked bread before the thermometer was invented. Nonetheless, investing in a few basic resources with similar processes helps you eliminate the guesswork and take steps towards greater consistency. Another is a decent standard thermometer.

As your baking intuition grows over time, reliance on these devices subsides, but still, take a minute to check the dough temperature right at the start of bulk fermentation. Why? It gives an intuitive understanding of how bulk progresses.

Monitoring dough temperature is a simple matter: place your thermometer in the center of dough mass and record the temperature. If you feel your dough temperature can swing dramatically during bulk, take its temperature whenever you stretch and fold; this is a good time to check in with the dough and evaluate the development and progress of the dough. Although assigning hard numbers for how long bulk fermentation will last for a specific dough is extremely difficult, the following table is an example of how a range of final dough temperatures may affect bulk length. Remember that this table is just for illustrative purposes, my attempt to provide a snapshot of how things could change with varying temperatures. The table assumes that all other variables are equivalent to bake-to-bake (hard to ensure!).

Typical Bulk Fermentation Period with Temperature:

75°F (24°C) 4.25 – 4.5 hours

78°F (25°C) 4 hours

80°F (26°C) 3.25 – 3.5 hours

Measuring Necessary Water Temperature: By conducting a few simple calculations, we can easily determine how much to heat (or cool) our water to the DDT formula. In the following example, we measure what our water temperature must be to achieve a 78 ° F (25 ° C) FDT.

Ingredient	Measured temperature
Leaven 75°F (24 ° C)	75°F (24 ° C)
Flour	70°F (21 ° C)

Room temperature	75°F (24°C)
Friction Factor	zero

Practical Tips for Consistency:

We strive for a dough temperature around 24°C/75°F to achieve reasonable bulk fermentation and proofing times. This temperature provides a good balance between pace and taste. Using the following techniques, you can hit and sustain your dough's temperature:

• Invest in a good digital thermometer.

• Use warm winter water or cool summer water to achieve the right temperature.

• Water temperature depends on room temperature and other components temperature. In winter we also need really hot water to get the poolish and new flour up to 24C. However, by using a lower preference for the final dough ratio, water around 30C is always enough to hit 24C.

• Attempt to keep the dough intact. Often we place a bowl of dough on top of the oven with a tea towel and a folded towel. A preheated and turned off oven to about 30C (use a thermometer to check the temperature inside, as your dial on the oven might not be very helpful) will work well.

• Some people create their fridge, using an old refrigerator or kitchen cabinet. Using a 40W or 100W light bulb on the cabinet bottom (warm air rises from bottom to top!), you can easily heat your cabinet inside. To regulate the temperature, you can use a simple mechanical thermostat.

• If you don't have the means to regulate your dough's ambient temperature, you should make your dough a few degrees colder in summer and a bit warmer in winter to account for the rise or decrease in temperature.

• Water and flour are thermally distinct. In bread baking, this translates into twice the effect of water on dough temperature. This is taken into account in most of the bread recipes' dough calculator.

Chapter 6: Benefits and Issues of Sourdough Baking

After baking with sourdough for a while, you'll learn all kinds of little tricks to produce different results and make sourdough work for you. You will also appreciate the wellness benefits.

Below are some tips for baking sourdough bread with some common problems when baking.

6.1 Sourdough Bread and Health Benefits

Sourdough Breaks down Gluten. The longer time required to lift sourdough bread makes protein breakdown (gluten in wheat) into amino acids, making digestion easier. This gluten breakdown is why certain people with a gluten allergy can tolerate sourdough wheat bread.

Sourdough Naturally Preserves the Bread. The lactic acid produced during fermentation produces a lovely tang in the bread and predigests the grain for you. Acetic acid helps hold bread longer by inhibiting mold growth.

Sourdough is Sustainable. One of the best aspects of the sourdough cycle is that it helps you to make bread with the easiest ingredients you can make yourself. Instead of buying a yeast packet for every bread loaf, just add your home-made starter. Recall no more buying yeast!

Since sourdough bread goes through a fermentation process, many of the simple sugars in the grain are eaten up in the process. This method encourages blood sugar bread. The fermentation process also increases bread in nutrients, particularly B vitamins.

Lastly, the bacteria in sourdough help activate phytase, an enzyme that breaks down phytic acid, an anti-nutrient present in all grains and seeds2. This helps your body to retain minerals better because phytic acid will bind them and take them out of your body.

You know yogurt and kefir's health benefits, right? Imagine the advantages, fresh and warm from the oven, buttered.

It's not quite like that, but it's similar!!

Lactobacillus: Lactobacillus in yogurt, kefir, sour cream, buttermilk, etc. It ferments the mixture of flour/water, producing lactic acid, a catalyst that significantly increases the micronutrient profile. Simply put, all the nutrients present in whole wheat flour are bigger, and now your body can use them better.

Fermentation alone is perfect for the digestive system. The Lactobacillus helps feed the healthy bacteria in your digestive system to keep battling the bad guys. Recall a healthy gut means a healthy body—much of your immune systems in your digestive tract.

Phytates: A cool thing about the long soaking necessity of sourdough is that it breaks down many of the phytates that bind the amazing minerals in grains. Our bodies will snatch those nutrients and actually use them!

The Science behind Soaking Grains:

With those nutrients readily available, starch digestion is much easier on your body. In reality, the natural bacteria that work with the natural yeast predigest the starch for you. Sourdough's benefits make your tummy full.

Glucose: Remember how normal yeast feed on glucose? With a large portion of the glucose consumed in the fermentation process, sourdough does not cause a spike in your blood sugars like white bread sometimes consumed. The long cycle also breaks down several gluten proteins into amino acids, making sourdough bread tolerable for those prone to gluten!

One last clean tidbit: sourdough bread is less likely to stalk, holds much of the moisture as it ages, and helps avoid mold development! Now, that doesn't mean your sourdough won't go stale and never grow mold. But it's good to know that the artisan loaf you treated at the farmer's market won't go too far.

6.2 Quick Tips for Making the Perfect Sourdough

There are countless self-proclaimed sourdough experts out there, each eager to share the "key" to sourdough. Often these "secrets" are contradictory. Sourdough is an environment of immense confusion and firm ignorance.

"Science" bakers argue that sourdough bread cannot be made without a detailed understanding of the symbiotic relationship between yeast and lactobacilli. Simultaneously, for centuries, people made bread with wild yeast — so how difficult could it be?

Look at everything you learn about sourdough as one approach. There are as many ways to continue, nurture, and bake as there are world bakers. The knowledge you read here works well for us, and hundreds of thousands of happy bakers have shared our expertise.

Make your sourdough starter work before you start baking sourdough. If your starter doesn't rise after each feeding, there's no bread you've put in.

Two critical factors initially influence starter activation: flour type and temperature. Whole grain flours ferment faster, and the starter grows faster at higher temperatures (the optimal starting temperature is 25-27 ° C/77-80 ° F). The most favorite starter sourdough bread is whole grain rye flour. Rye flour is rich in sugars and yeast feeds on amylase enzymes that break down starches into simple sugars.

1. Water will make a big difference

A recipe may say, 70% hydration, but your flour could only accommodate 60% hydration, or 80% hydration. What you want when combining flour, water, and the sourdough starter is the consistency of the dough that feels perfect-both stretchy and elastic (the dough's ability to bounce back). There are examples, of course, including baking focaccia. Because it's baked in a tray, and shaping is simple, hydration can be higher than average.

What makes it stretchy and elastic? That's gluten. Gluten contains two proteins, glutenin, and gliadin. Glutenin is responsible for elasticity and stretchability.

Gluten in flour is just a potential for elastic and stretchy bread. Once the water is applied to the flour, gluten strands are formed. What makes the flour absorb various water quantities? Also, it's gluten. The more gluten in the grain, the better the grain, the faster the fermentation, and vice versa. The tricky part is understanding how much water the flour absorbs.

Too much water in the flour form elastic flour to the runny dough. On the other side, more water in the dough and you can go from close to open crumb. It's about your hands holding and thinking. What wonderful learning to feel the dough between fingertips.

2. Wear Dough, Forget TV

Samuel Fromartz, a journalist and an enthusiastic home chef, wrote it. "Time was their most important tool: time to let the dough gently come together, time to let fermentation work its magic, and power to be driven by nothing but the demands of the bread itself."

It's always asked: How long do you leave the dough to rise? The response will be: I'll do nothing until it's completely fermented. That's why it's important to observe and feel the dough and move to the next step based on how the dough tastes, looks, and smells, rather than the time and rising times of the recipes. Five hours can mean three or seven hours in your kitchen.

How's the perfectly fermented dough? When we look at the first rise (bulk fermentation), you're looking for airy, bubbly, solid, and live dough, which has also increased in volume.

None of this is straightforward, but it is further exacerbated by the fact that the baker needs a sound understanding of what is probably the most challenging element of bread making — fermentation. If you misjudge this — and fermentation is truly a judgment call — then the defects will be magnified in any other phase of the method. Then repeat it.

3. Its Quick, Just Planning

You often leave your dough to rise 12 hours in the refrigerator when you sleep, or you're at work, or your dough needs a 5-hour rise, but you don't have time for that. The truth is that sourdough baking isn't an all-day task. It takes as little time to mix and knead the dough. The rest, it's the bacteria and yeasts that do their job, and we're doing our job.

4. Don't Confuse

What if I left my three-day fridge starter, he'd die? What if I don't let the dough rise for three hours? If I skip one stretch and fold, will my bread be good? How if I knead my dough 4 minutes instead of 6? May I use a rye starter instead of a grain starter?

5. Learn one recipe before continuing

The most important step is not to give up, because after all, it's not the recipe you master, but the fermentation understanding. When you understand the basic concepts of fermentation and know when the dough is ready for the next step, you're on a highway to apply this expertise to every sort of recipe, and you're innovative without any constraints.

And that's sourdough baking's charm.

6. Don't miss the Autolyse

To Autolyse, mix a recipe's flour and water and let it sit for a while before adding starter and salt. Autolysis is not a required step, but once your dough reaches a higher degree of hydration, having longer autolysis can be the difference between a well-managed dough and a dough lying in a mess pond!

7. Retard the dough to make the flour easier to treat by placing it in the freezer, making it easier to deal with. During the last (or all) step of bulk fermentation, you can retard it to make handling and shaping easier. You may also pause the dough during the second rise. This will help keep it better when pulling it out of the proofing tub.

8. Flour the Proofing Basket well to avoid sticking. So your dough will be stickier, you'll need to flour the proofing basket very well. You want to stick to the proofing basket after all the hard work and effort you put into making your bread. Using a coarse grain like dark rye or whole-grain seems to work best, but many bakers do use rice flour because it's nice to prevent sticking.

9. Using Wet Hands. Use damp hands while handling dough is a game changer while dealing with wet dough. It will not stick to your hands, and you can concentrate instead of handling the dough!

Dip your entire hand in a bowl of water and sprinkle the excess or spray water on your hands just before treating. If required, even during dough handling, you can do the same again to stop more sticking.

10. Use a Dough Scraper for lower hydration dough, but a Wetter dough needs a dough scraper to stretch the hands. Wet the dough scraper like you would your hands, and use the dough scraper as the primary contact for your dough.

TIP: Can be handled with 2 dough scrapers, one in each hand.

11. Uncover the Dough halfway through the bake. Higher hydration dough creates a thinner crust in the oven. To keep it nice and crispy, remove the cover or steam source halfway through the bake to ensure it crisps nicely.

12. To help slack Dough stand tall, pre-shape the dough. Pre-shaping is not mandatory for lower hydration dough. But before it's the final form, a hot, slack dough will enjoy a pre-shape. It will help to improve the loaf's structure and allow it to be taller.

Leave 20 minutes to an hour between pre-shape and final shaping to help calm the dough. You'll also find that shaping is simpler in the final form if it's pre-made!

13. Perfect your first loaf, particularly if you're new to baking with sourdough. Start with an easy-to-use flour and get perfect first, before starting experimenting with other flours. Healthy starting flour is organic white bread flour. This flour is fairly easy to handle, giving you a good loaf of sourdough bread with a high rise and open crumb. When you feel comfortable with making this loaf style and understanding its actions, you can try other flours.

14. Get to Know Your Flour. When working with a new flour type, use the above guide to understand its specific characteristics, and change your recipe accordingly. For example, if the flour is more absorbent, be ready to add extra water to the mix and note how much water you've added. If it's more involved, remember how much faster it fermented. Taking notes ensures that for every loaf of sourdough you produce, you will be able to look back and see what influenced the bread.

15. Use a little at a time. Using different flours would probably be harder to use than ordinary flour. So one way to ease the learning curve is to add to your regular loaf a bit of the new flour (maybe 10 percent) and write down the difference it made. The more alternative flour you apply, the better you'll learn to manage different flours.

16. Use Loaf Tins to handle. If you end up with a dough that's especially hard to handle, use a greased loaf tin for baking your bread instead of a banneton. A loaf tin can help sustain the bread's structure and cause the bread to grow up rather than outward.

17. Sourdough is not always savory. Making sour bread takes some effort. If you have no 8- to 24-hour lead time to let the bread rise, add a pinch of instant yeast. You'll still get sourdough's nuanced flavor but much quicker rising time.

18. Bake bread on a baking stone whenever possible. Heat the oven stone to an hour. Often check the doneness loaf. There are a few ways to check whether a loaf is baked:

- Thump Check. Flip the hot loaf over with your finger. Sounds flat, it's over.
- External Temperature Test. Monitor internal temperature using an instant-read thermometer. When the loaf is between 190 ° and 210 ° F, cooked through.

6.3 Problems and Solutions of Sourdough Baking

Some commonly asked questions and problem occurring during sourdough baking are:

What if I forget it?

When sourdough starters are neglected — left on the counter or in the refrigerator for long periods without being fed — the yeast and bacteria run out of food, and their populations die slowly. Essentially, your starter is dying a slow death; the longer it stays unfed, the easier it will be to revive it and prepare it for baking. Regular feeding will avoid this situation. When you forget your starter for a moment, a series of daily feedings will restore your health.

What's "true" flavor?

Sourdough starter can smell strongly sour but "clean" without spoilage overtones or strange chemical smell (think acetone). Although sourdough's scent can literally make you draw back from its power, it shouldn't be distasteful.

When tossing it out?

If your starter is ignored for an extended time, the liquid on top appears to change from transparent to black. That's OK; pour the liquid back into the starter and feed the meal it desperately craves. But if your starter displays clear mold signs, or an orange or pink tint/streak, or smells — well, putrid — throw it out; it's been infiltrated by toxic microorganisms, and it's time to start over.

What if I leave town for a long time and can't feed my starter?

There's no question! By spreading your starter in a thin layer on a parchment or foil-lined sheet plate, you can dry it out. Hold the dried starter in a jar and rehydrate by dissolving the dried starter in warm water and feeding it at regular intervals as you would normally. Men resuscitated starters 4,500 years ago!

What if my starter wasn't bubbly?

A brand new starter takes three days to show signs of life — a bubbled surface and a sour scent. If, after day four, you still see no movement, consider shifting your starter to a slightly warmer kitchen area. Keep your eyes in the starter for any orange or pink stripes, this is a warning that the starter has gone wrong, and you should toss it.

For the first few days, you find some liquid sitting on top of your starter, don't worry. Mix the liquids in the starter and feed as normal, but make sure you feed your starter every 24 hours and stash your starter in a warm place.

Sure, I've got a bubbling starter. What's it?

It's amazing! Your starter is almost ready to bake — make sure it passes the above double or float test before you start baking. You can leap straight into full loaves baking or dip your toe into the sourdough game by trying English muffins or focaccia with sourdough starter. Don't forget to keep up with your daily feeding, or safely store it — more on that below.

How many starters can I use to bake?

Most sourdough recipes, from bread to biscuits, require 1 to 2 cups of starter (our classic sourdough recipes use even less), so you can get two loaves of sourdough every few days with regular feedings. Or you can put your starter in the fridge once it's set up, and bake it once a week.

How can I keep my starter alive? So long will I feed it?

When your sourdough starter is built (about 7 to 9 days after starting and daily feedings), you can slow feed once a week (or less) by placing the starter in the long-term fridge. Feed your refrigerator once a week if you intend to bake regularly. Otherwise, the sourdough starter will live happily between feedings in the fridge for months. If you stash your starter long-term, be sure to give it a few feedings at room temperature before using it.

I forgot to feed my starter. Is it dead?

That's a common issue! Mild negligence won't harm your starter, like saying skipping a feeding or accidentally feeding your starter. A little brown or gray liquid on top is a warning that an underfed starter is not a dead one, and the liquid can be stirred right in and then fed. Nevertheless, high heat exposure and long room temperature neglect can destroy your starter. Any starter that develops mold or has pink or orange hue must be trashed.

Someone gave me a starter. What am I doing now?

Most likely, a gifted starter has been fed recently and can either be stored in the fridge before you're ready to use it, or you can set a feeding schedule to make sure your kitchen starter is satisfied. It may ask the giver, how much and when they feed this particular starter, but a general thumb rule is an equal starter, flour, and water at each feeding.

I've got a happy, thriving starter. I'm feeling a million dollars! How am I doing now??

Congratulations to you!! You'd feel like a million bucks; you've successfully captured wild yeast and evolved it into a living, developing yeast colony that will feed you and your family in bread. That's magic.

Chapter 7: Variety of Sourdough Recipes

Until now, we have covered most aspects of sourdough bread and its starter. Now, it's time to test the skills we've learned in this book's previous chapters.

Below are some yummy and nutritious sourdough bread recipes with simple instructions. Let's try and have fun baking them.

7.1 17 Classic Bread Recipes

1. Classic Loaf:

Ingredients:

- 500g/1lb 2oz white bread flour + extra for dusting
- 2 tsp. **brown sugar**
- 300g/10½oz **sourdough starter**
- 2 tsp. **salt**
- Flavorless **oil**, for greasing

Instructions:

In a tub, mix the flour, sourdough starter, and 250ml/9fl oz. water. Stir in the sugar and salt. Turn on to a surface and knead for 10 minutes or until the 'windowpane effect' (where the dough can be stretched until it becomes so thin that it is transparent) is achieved.

Put the dough in a lightly oiled tub, cover with a damp tea towel and leave for 2½–3 hours to show. You will not find a rise in the dough as much as you will with regular, yeasted bread, and it will take much longer.

Turn the dough out onto a knockback and board. Portion the dough into two and form two loaves in the shape of a sphere. Flour generously, and put each loaf seam-side up in a tub, lined with a soft cloth or a heavily floured tea towel – without the cloth, the loaf would stick in the tub, and you won't be able to turn it out. Leave another 2½ hours to prove.

Preheat Oven to Fan/Gas 8, 230C/210C. Place a couple of ice cubes or cold water in a baking tray, and put steam in the bottom of the oven. Turn the loaves out onto a hot baking stone or baking tray. Using a small, sharp knife score on top of the loaf two or three times and put it in the oven. Bake for 35 minutes until a good crust is formed, and when tapped on the surface, the loaves sound hollow.

2. Simple Bread:

Ingredients:

- 375g/13oz **white flour**, plus extra for dusting
- 7.5g **salt**
- 250g/9oz **sourdough starter**
- 130-175ml/4-6fl oz. tepid water
- Olive oil, for kneading

Instructions:

For a large mixing bowl, add the flour, the starter, and salt. Add a little water at a time, and combine to make a soft dough with your hands (you do not need all the water).

Cover a chopping board with olive oil or work the top, then tip the dough on it and knead the dough 10-15 minutes or until smooth and elastic.

Put in a lightly oiled bowl and cover with a fastener. Leave to rise for five hours in a warm spot, or till at least double in size. Knead the dough till it is smooth, then knock out the dirt. Roll up the flour into a ball and dust.

Tip the dough into a floured round bannet or proving basket and leave for 4-8 hours to rise. Place a half-filled tray on the shelf of the bottom oven, and preheat the oven to 220C/425F / Gas 7.

The risen dough gently tips onto a lined baking tray. Bake the loaf at this heat for 30 minutes, then heat down to 200C/400F / Gas 6 and bake for another 15-20 minutes. Lean on a rack to lean off.

3. Classic Sourdough Bread:

Ingredients:

- 1 cup (8 ounces) sourdough starter
- 5 to 6 cups All-Purpose Flour
- 1 1/2 cups (12 ounces warm water
- 1 tablespoon salt
- 1 tablespoon sugar (optional)
- Cornmeal to sprinkle on pans

Instructions:

Pour the starter cup into a large mixing bowl. Attach the hot water and about three cups of flour. Beat stiffly. Cover the sponge with plastic wrap and put it to work away. This can be a very flexible period but allow at least 2 hours and up to 8 hours. Longer time at low temperatures can give rise to a more sour taste.

Take off the plastic wrap after the dough has bubbled and spread. Blend in the salt, sugar, and 2 cups of flour leftover. Mix until the dough combines and knead until the dough is smooth and elastic, with your hands, a mixer, or a bread machine. Just add enough extra flour to prevent the dough from getting stuck. Put in a lightly oiled bowl, cover and allow to rise for 1 to 2 hours until doubled.

Divide the dough halfway through. Shape into an oval-shaped loaf, and position on a slightly grated baking sheet sprinkled with cornmeal.

Cover and let it rise until doubled (could take up to 2 hours).

Place a pan full of hot water onto your oven's bottom rack. Preheat 450 ° F. Remove the cover, slash and bake, until golden brown, for about 20 minutes. Remove from the oven and refrigerate on a shelf.

Yield: two mini loaves and nine rolls-OR-four mini loaves-OR-18-20 rolls

4. Ancient Bread:

Ingredients:

- Strong bread or pizza flour, for dusting

Leaven

- **50 g** (2 tbsp.) **active sourdough starter**
- **75 g** (½ cup) bread or pizza flour
- **80 g** (80 ml/⅓ cup) lukewarm water

Dough

- **700 g** (4⅔ cups) bread or pizza flour + extra for dusting
- **2½ tsp.** fine sea salt
- **500 g** (500 ml/2 cups) warm water

Instructions

Combine the sourdough starter, flour, and water in a medium dish to make the leaven and mix until well mixed. Cover with plastic wrap and stand overnight at room temperature (12 hours). The leaven would have grown and been very bubbly when ready to use.

Move the leaven to a wide pot to make the flour. Apply half the water and use a spatula or balloon whisk to break up the leaven until it is almost smooth. Stir in the remaining vapor. Mix the flour and salt, add to the leaven mixture and stir the wooden spoon into a very shaggy and mixed dough. Cover the plastic bowl, leave for 1 hour in a dry, draught-free location.

You must spread out and fold the dough instead of kneading. Leave it in the bowl to fold the dough and pick up the dough's top side, raise it, and fold it back into itself. Turn a quarter turn on the bowl and repeat three times more, turning the bowl after each fold. Cover with plastic wrap, hold 30 minutes in a warm, draught-free spot.

Repeat this folding process five times more (which will equal 6 folds), resting the dough in each fold for 30 minutes. The dough will be loose and shaggy when you begin this phase but will get less as you continue to fold and rest. Having completed all six folding and resting phases, the dough will be very smooth, spongy, and elastic.

If the dough has been folded a total of 6 times, cover and place for 1 hour or until slightly puffed in a warm, draught-free position.

Turn the dough gently out of the bowl onto a well-floured board. Using a sharp knife or a pastry scraper to cut the dough in half, being careful not to deflate the dough. Using well-floured hands or a pastry scraper to shape each portion of the dough into a loose circle. Cover every dough with an upturned bowl (width enough, so the dough has space to rise) (see picture 10) and leave for 1-2 hours or until well puffed to rest on the bench.

Dust 2 generously with flour, clean, loosely woven cloths or tea towels, and rub the flour into the cloth with your fingers. Place two round dough proofing baskets or colanders with the cloths 22 cm (top measurement).

Dust one of the portions of the dough with flour on top. Flip it over, and then use a similar folding motion to form a circular loaf, pulling the edges of the dough into the center so that the dough surface below is tight to help shape it, only folding six times to help hold as much air as possible. Turn the loaf softly over again (so that the surface is smooth) and use your hands to shape and level the round, extending the dough's top surface toward its base. Repeat with the remaining portion of the dough. Stab the top and sides of the loaves with a little more flour, then turn each upside down into your lined basket or colander. Fold the tea towels over the dough loosely over the overhanging sides.

Place each loaf in sealed plastic bags in its baskets or colanders. Set aside for 2-3 hours in a dry, draught-free place to prove or until well risen.

Preheat the oven to 240oC (fan-forced at 220oC). Line two heavy, non-stick baking paper baking trays. Place loaves gently over lined trays. Use a sharp knife to score loaves' surface, around 1.5 cm deep. Place loaves in the oven, throw a big handful of ice cubes into the bottom of the oven and shut the door promptly. Bake for another 20 minutes.

Swap the trays in the oven, reduce the oven to 220 ° (200 ° C fan-forced) and bake 15-20 minutes or until deeply colored, and the loaves sound hollow when knocked on the surface. Move the loaves to a wire rack and set aside before slicing to cool.

5. Sourdough Beer Bread Recipe:

Ingredients:

- 12 ounces beer (room temp)
- 1 cup sourdough starter
- 1/2 cup sugar
- 5 cups bread flour (approximately)

Instructions:

Preparing the Bread Dough: This recipe needs only four ingredients, so you'll be spending more time kneading the dough than mixing it.

Put the can of beer and starter sourdough in a wide tub. Remove the sugar until it dissolves.

Mix the flour in enough to shape a dough that you can knead with your hands.

Turn the dough out and knead the dough onto a floured surface for about 10 minutes. Add flour, one tablespoon at a time, thus kneading to the touch until the dough is no longer sticky. It's time to relax and wait for your dough (or "proof' in bread baking lingo) to rise. Like most bread, this sourdough with a little kneading and shaping in between needs to go through two stages of proofing.

Place the dough in a bowl and turn over the dough to grate the rim.

Cover with a kitchen towel or plastic wrap and let it sit in a dry, draft-free location for about 1 1/2 hours or until doubled in size.

Roll the dough out, knead on a floured surface for 5 minutes. Divide the dough into half, and shape a loaf every second. Grease two pans of bread, and place loaves in the pots.

Cover with a towel and allow for about 45 minutes, or until it has doubled. When your dough has proven, it is ready to bake for the final time. Your kitchen will fill quickly with the lovely scent of freshly baked bread (and, of course, a touch of hops mixed in).

Baking the bread: The oven is preheated to 350 F. Bake the bread for about 45 minutes or, when pressed, until the bread sounds hollow. Remove the loaves and let them cool off on a rack or towel. The loaves can be bagged and frozen for subsequent use.

6. Sourdough Rolls:

Ingredients:

- 450 grams bread flour
- 250 grams milk (at room temperature)
- 150 grams active sourdough starter
- 50 grams butter (softened)
- 35 grams of sugar
- 10 grams of salt
- 1 large egg

Instructions:

Collect materials—grease a baking pan measuring 9 x 13 inches.

Put all the ingredients in a stand mixer bowl that is equipped with a dough handle. Mix at low speed until mostly combined, around 2 minutes, then turn to second or third speed (must be vigorous but not quick) and mix for 4 to 5 minutes more. The dough should be fluffy and smooth. If it's a little sticky, it's perfect.

Move the dough to larger, shallower bowl using a dough scraper. Cover with a damp towel or plastic bag over the pot.

Rest for 20 minutes, then take a stretch and fold to the dough. Ferment the dough at room temperature for 4-5 hours then refrigerate for 12 to 16 hours.

Divide the cold dough into twelve parts, approximately 80 g each. Form each piece into a ball and place them in the prepared pan in a single layer. Cover and let it grow in a warm place for about two hours (around 80 to 85 F is optimal, but time above 65 F is also fine) until the dough has increased to approximately 1 1/2 times its original volume.

Oven preheats to 425 F. Bake well for 20 to 30 minutes or until browned. Serve warm, if you want to. Enable to cool before being processed.

7. Sourdough Banana Bread:

Ingredients:

- 1 ripe banana (about 140 grams)
- 130 grams of sugar
- 140 grams cold discard **sourdough starter**
- 30 grams of olive oil
- 20 grams of butter (melted)
- 10 grams blackstrap molasses
- 1 large egg
- 1/8 teaspoon vanilla extract
- 1/2 teaspoon ground cinnamon
- 75 grams of bread flour
- 1/2 teaspoon baking powder
- 1/2 teaspoon baking soda
- 1/4 teaspoon salt
- 60 grams of walnuts pieces

Instruction:

Oven preheats to 350 F. Add the banana and sugar into a large mixing bowl and mash with a fork or whisk. It's cool if there are any tiny bits, there's no need to purée the banana.

Stir in starter sourdough, olive oil, butter, molasses, sugar, cocoa, and cinnamon. Whisk to merge. If you like, you can use an electric mixer, but whisking by hand will do the job easily.

Combine bread flour, salt, and baking soda in a cup. Mix well.

Add the dry ingredients until the walnuts are fully mixed. Stir in to distribute a few more times.

Butter, and gently flour a loaf pan of 8 x 4 inches. Add the batter to level the top, and spread. Bake until the loaf center temperature reaches 200 F for about 45 minutes.

Let it cool before turning onto a refrigerating rack. Before serving, allow to cool completely.

8. Sourdough Bagels:

Ingredients:

- 110 grams sourdough starter
- 165 grams of water
- 330 grams bread flour
- 25 grams of honey
- 8 grams of **sea salt**
- 1 tablespoon baking soda
- Optional: Sesame seeds, poppy seeds, onion, etc.

Instructions:

Stir in a wide bowl with the sourdough starter, water, milk, honey, and salt. Stir to combine with a spoon, then knead the dough with your hands until well combined, about five minutes.

Use a damp towel or plastic bag to cover the pot, and rest for 30 minutes. Stretch out the dough and fold. Have another 30 minutes to rest. Divide the dough into 6 pieces, which weigh about 100 grams each.

To form the bagels, roll each lump into a rope about 12 "long. Moist both ends of the rope gently, then force them tightly together, so the rope forms a closed loop. Don't just put in the tips. Let the ends overlap so that you get a nice tight seam.

Line a parchment-paper sheet plate. The paper is finely greased with spray oil. Place the bagels on the parchment and use plastic wrap to protect them.

Allow for about 90 minutes to rise, then place them in the refrigerator and leave for overnight.

Oven preheats to 500 F.

Take the bagels off the shelf. Put to a boil a big pot of tea. Stir in the baking soda. Poach the bagels for 2 minutes, and flip through halfway. With a wire spider or slotted knife, detach and return to the greased sheet tray. If desired sprinkle with toppings.

Bake for about 15-18 minutes until golden. Cool on a rack of wire.

9. Sourdough Loaf:

Ingredients:

- 15 ounces/425 grams bread flour
- 1/3 ounce/9 grams salt
- 10 ounces/285 grams **sourdough starter**
- Olive oil (for greasing)

Instructions:

In a big, roomy mixing bowl, add the flour and salt. Build a center well, and add the starter. Mix flour and starter to make a loose dough by dipping the flour into the middle. With this, you should use your hands. Add warm water if the mixture is dry until a smooth, slightly sticky dough is formed.

Sprinkle gently with a little flour on your worktop. Tip the dough onto the work surface and knead the dough until smooth, silky and elastic. Note: Sprinkle with a little more flour if the dough is sticky. Sprinkle with some olive oil if too warm, and start kneading. You should predict about 12 to 15 minutes of kneading.

When the dough is smooth, silky, and elastic, a large mixing bowl of olive oil should lightly grease. Tip the dough with a film / plastic wrap fastener into the tub.

Place the bowl in a comfortable, not cold, draught-free position and leave until the dough has doubled in size, for up to 6 hours. Leave it overnight if you wish, but in a cooler space, this will cause the bread to rise very slowly.

Turn the dough onto a floured surface until it has doubled. Knock out the bread dust, and gently knead the dough for just a few minutes. Wrap the dough into a ball, dust with flour, and put in a bannet or mixing bowl. Cover with a towel for tea. Again place in a cool, not cold spot and leave for 8 hours to rise slowly.

Heat the oven until 475 F. Place a roasting tin on the lowest shelf of the oven, filled with ice cubes. The steam produces a perfect crust on your loaf.

Strip a baker with grease-proof paper and graze very lightly with a little olive oil. Place the raised loaf gently onto the sheet (don't worry if you lose any air from the loaf while you do this, it'll be back in the oven). Place in the heated oven center and cook 30 minutes, then lower the temperature to 400 F and cook for another 20 minutes or till the bread sounds hollow when tapered on the surface, and the loaf is golden brown.

Place the loaf on a cooling rack before eating, and leave to cool completely. The sourdough will maintain for up to a week. Do not bring it in any plastic, because it softens the crust. Place in a paper bag or bread bin. This way, the bread holds well and is always nice when toasted, even after a week.

10. Amish Sourdough Bread:

Ingredients:

- (1/4 ounce) packaged yeast
- 2 teaspoons salt and sugar each
- 7 cups flour
- 1 cup sourdough starter (room temperature)
- 1 1/2 cups water (110 to 115F)
- 1/2 teaspoon baking soda

Instructions:

Dissolve the leaves in hot water.

Stir the flour, salt, sugar, and sourdough starter in 2 1/2 cups.

Combine the flour with 2 1/2 cups of baking soda; stir in the sourdough mixture. Mix with a spoon and add in as much 1/2 to 1 cup flour as you can.

Knead in enough of the remaining flour on a lightly floured surface to make a fairly compact, smooth and elastic dough (total for 6 to 8 minutes).

Form into a ball and put it into a grated tub. Turn once and cover with plastic wrap or clean sheet. Let it rise in a warm place, 1 to 1 1/2 hours, or till the volume doubles.

Punch down and halve the flour. Cover for 10 minutes, and let rest.

Grease 6-inch round loaf baking dish or two 9 x 5-inch loaf pans. Dough shape into the desired form. Create a smooth knife with X shaped slashes. Cover and let rise approximately 1 hour, or until doubled.

Oven preheats to 400 F. Bake 35 to 40-minute loaves. Cool on rack wire.

Serve, and have fun.

11. Landbrot - Wheat Sourdough Bread:

Ingredients:

For Freshening the Sourdough:

- 1/2 cup sourdough culture (active)
- 1 handful of flour (add until stiff)

For Leaven Build:

- 3 tbsp./1.3 oz. sourdough mixture
- 1/2 c./4 oz. water
- 1 1/3 c./5.8 oz. **whole wheat flour**
- 2 1/2 tbsp./0.6 oz. flour (white)

For Final Dough:

- 2 3/4 c./22.4 oz. water
- 3 c. + 2 tbsp./14.4 oz. whole wheat flour
- 2.5 c. - 2 tbsp./11 oz. flour (white)
- 1 tbsp./20 g. salt

Instructions:

Start by Freshening the Sourdough

Collect materials.

Keep your sourdough starter 100% hydration or higher. That means add flour and water to make a thick batter for a pancake when you feed it. Take a half cup or so of sourdough culture to start this bread, and add flour until the batter is very steep.

Add the flour to an active crop, that is, one that was fed recently and did not just come out of the fridge. Make the dough stiff.

Cover and hang out for 4-6 hours on the table.

Create the Leaven:

Use three tablespoons of the fresh, sourdough crop (or weigh 1.3 oz.) and add 1/2 cup water and 1 1/2 cup (total) flour in a bowl, stirring until smooth. Cover this dough and hold it for about 12 hours on the table.

Attach 2 3/4 c on the next day. Water, 3 c. (22.4 oz. + 2 pc. Whole wheat flour (14.4 oz.) and 2.5 c. -- 2nd T. White flour (11 oz.) to a large mixing bowl and stir until all the flour is wet. Cover and allow to "autolyze" this dough for 20 minutes to an hour.

Sprinkle the salt, and add several pieces of the "leaven." Mix in a mixer for 2 to 3 minutes, or 5 minutes by hand. The dough is pretty loose.

Bulk fermentation is at room temperature for around 2 1/2 hours. You'll fold the dough 2 times during this process.

Flip the dough on a floured surface to fold. Fold horizontally in thirds (like a letter), then spread out the dough and fold vertically in thirds (folding step by step here).

The dough of bread now weighs about 3 1/2 pounds. You might make smaller loaves out of it, but we made one big loaf for the pictures.

Shaping and final proof:

The dough is shaped in a loose, round shape. Place in a well-flown proofing tub, seam-side down, or an oiled, floured cup.

Loosely cover the bread, without the dough touching the cover. A box of cardboard will fit perfectly.

Let this dough rise 2-2 1/2 hours at room temperature.

Preheat to 440 F, and ready the oven for steam, about an hour before baking. Sprinkle with flour or cornmeal or semolina. Unmold the dough on to the parchment from the proofing basket. The dough is already really moist and sticky, so try not to deflate it.

Quickly push the baking sheet into the oven or transfer the dough onto the baking stone using the parchment paper. For baking use steam, as mentioned here.

Bake for 15 minutes, then lower to 420 F and bake for around 60 to 75 more minutes until baked. With an instant-read thermometer, check the bread and ensure the indoor temperature is at least 195 F.

Let the bread cool down on a rack for several hours. The longer the bread remains, the stronger the flavor. You could be freezing that bread.

12. Stuffed Italian Sourdough Loaf:

Ingredients:

- 1 large sourdough boule
- ¼ lb salami
- ¼ lb prociutto
- 3 tablespoons giardiniera
- ½ cup lettuce
- ¼ cup fresh basil
- ¼ lb provolone
- ¼ lb mozzarella
- 1 tablespoon oil

- 1 tablespoon balsamic vinegar

Instructions:

Cut a wide hole carefully into the top of the boule; set aside the cut-out bread. Hollow out the boule (you can save the dough inside and make crumbs for your bread if you wish).

Layer the other ingredients of the sandwich inside and finish with oil and vinegar.

Place the sandwich back on top bread and slice it into quarters.

13. Basic Sourdough Bread:

Ingredients:

- 1/2 cup milk
- 2 tbsp. shortening
- 2 tbsp. sugar
- 1 tsp. salt
- 1 cup sourdough starter
- 2 to 3 cups flour (bread)

Instructions:

Scald the milk and shorten in a small saucepan. Set aside and allow to cool down until torrential.

Add sugar and salt in a large saucepan. Pour in warm milk and shortening until cooled. Remove until sugar dissolves.

Mix the starter in.

Add 1/2 cup of flour until the dough is too thick to mix with the wooden spoon.

Turn dough on floured board and start kneading for 10 minutes, adding flour when the dough becomes sticky.

In a greased bowl, put the dough and grease the dough. Cover for 90 minutes and let it rise in a warm spot. Punch the dough in. Cover the bowl, let it rise again for 30 minutes.

Turn on board, knead for 3 minutes or so.

The dough is molded into a round loaf. Place on baked grated board. Cover and let grow for 60 minutes until double in size. Preheat 400 F.

Slash an X to the top with a sharp knife — Bake for 40 minutes or when tapped on, until bread sounds hollow.

14. Potato Flake Sourdough Starter and Bread:

Ingredients:

For the Starter:
- 1 cup of warm water
- 1/2 cup sugar
- 1 package (2 1/4 teaspoons) dry **yeast**
- 3 level tablespoons instant potato flakes

For the Starter Feeder:
- 1 cup of warm water
- 1/2 cup sugar
- 3 tablespoons instant potato flakes

For the Bread:
- 1 cup starter (see notes below)
- 6 cups bread flour
- 1 tablespoon **salt**
- 1/2 cup sugar
- 1/2 cup oil
- 1 1/4 cups warm water

Instructions:

Note: although this recipe has several steps, this bread is broken down into workable categories to help you organize your cooking and preparation better.

Gather the ingredients for Starter.

Blend the warm water, sugar, yeast, and potato flakes in a small cup. Let them ferment for two days on the counter.

Feed with feeder for starters (down). If someone else gives you a starter, you can skip this move. Gather the ingredients for the Starter Feeder.

Mix the warm feeder water, sugar, and potato flakes in a small cup. Attach to the starter, then combine well. Let it stay for 8 hours on the countertop. Refrigerate for 3 to 5 days, then dark.

Feeding the Starter: After using 1 cup of the starter for bread (see below), dump all but one cup of the rest of the starter and cool down.

When you're ready to make more bread, or add the starter feeder mixture once more every 3 to 5 days. Remove well and leave overnight or all day at the counter (about 12 hours), then refrigerate.

Bread: Add 1 cup starter, salt, sugar, oil, and warm water to a wide bowl or mixer. Blend well. Knead for 5 to 10 minutes using a dough hook or by hand until smooth and elastic.

Place the dough in a greased bowl. Cover and let it grow overnight or all day (around 12 hours) in a warm spot.

Just punch it down. Knead to a floured surface to keep any bubbles out of the air.

Spray 3 loaf pans with a cooking spray and split the dough equally between the 3 pans (shaped into a loaf). Let rise, loosely sealed, for 6 to 8 hours.

Bake for 25 to 30 minutes, at 350 F. Clear from the oven and pan and cool on a wire rack.

15. Extra-Tangy Sourdough Bread:

Ingredients:

- 1 cup (227g) ripe (fed) sourdough starter
- 1 1/2 cups (340g) lukewarm water
- 5 cups (602g) All-Purpose Flour, divided
- 2 1/2 teaspoons salt

Instructions:

Combine the flour starter, water, and 3 tassels (12 3/4 ounces, 362 g). Strongly beat throughout 1 minute. Cover for 4 hours at room temperature. Cool overnight, for about 12 hours.

Attach the remaining 2 cups of flour (8 1/2 ounces, 241 g), and the salt. Knead together to form a smooth dough. Enable the dough to rise in a covered bowl until light and airy, with bubbles of visible gas. This can take up to 5 hours (or even longer), depending on how active your starter is, depending on the vigor of your starter. Gently deflate the dough once an hour for better results by turning it onto a lightly floured work surface, extending and folding the edges into the middle and turning it over before returning to the pot. Adding these folds gives you a deeper picture of how the dough progresses.

16. Brioche:

Ingredients:

- Flour (strong light sifted or white) 500 grams 17.65 oz. 100.00%
- Sugar 30 grams 1.06 oz. 6.00%
- Salt 10 grams 0.35 oz. 2.00%
- Eggs (3 eggs) 200 grams 7.06 oz. 40.00%

- Starter (100% hydration) 250 grams 8.83 oz. 50.00%
- Butter 300 grams 10.59 oz. 60.00%
- Milk 200 grams 7.06 oz. 40.00%

Instructions:

Slice butter into 1 cm cubes and soften at room temperature for a few hours. Mix to combine all ingredients except butter, form a stiff batter (adjust the quantity of milk if necessary) Remain for 10 minutes before continuing to mix for 10-15 minutes.

The dough may begin to resemble a soft bread but does not have the same degree of elasticity in the soft butter until no lumps remain (now is the time to add dried fruit if you wish).

Place your dough in a covered container Rise in a cool spot, 8C to 15C, for around 15 hours OR Rise at room temperature up to 150 percent of the original size, then refrigerate until the dough is hardened.

Remove dough from cool place. Scale and form into balls to fill small forms (muffin tins are fine) up to 75% of the size of the form AND / OR shape into loaves for larger tins or specialty shapes.

Rinse at room temperature until 150 percent to 175 percent of the original size. Blend the whole egg and brush gently over raised shapes Bake in a moderate oven (215C) for 20 minutes for small brioche, for 45 minutes for larger brioche.

17. San Francisco style sourdough bread:

Ingredients:

- MAKES 1 LOAF (65,2% HYDRATION)
- Starter (233 g total weight)
- 264 g bread flour
- 50 g spelled flour (pref. whole grain)

- 204 g water
- 9 g salt

Instructions:

Making the Loaf:

So, it's probably somewhere in the afternoon on day 3 of the recipe (17.00 h if you stick to my time table). Remove the starter from the refrigerator and launch the dough immediately. Combine the starter with 204 g of water and play for 1 minute to release the rigid starter. Add flour and salt and knead (we use a spiral blender) for 3 minutes. Cover the mixer bowl and let it rest for 15 minutes.

Take out the dough and fold it (full letter fold, left over right, right over left, bottom over the top, top over bottom). Leave covered to sit on your bench for 15 minutes. Take a second stretch and fold. Return to the (greased) pot, cover, and let stand at room temperature for 40 minutes. Now put the dough in your refrigerator and leave for 15 hours (yes, you can sleep, the yeast cells in your dough will possibly do some hibernation of their own in the refrigerator, the bacteria will remain more active in this colder environment and continue to develop acetic acid, which, If all goes well, give the sour taste to your bread. It's now day 4 of SF sourdough ma. If you think it has risen enough, use your finger to make a very small tooth in the dough. If the tooth remains, the bread is ready to be baked, and if the indentation disappears, the dough needs a little more time.

Preheat your oven to 235C/455F (what amount of heating your oven depends on how long it takes to heat your oven, some take 30 minutes, others, with stone floors, take up to two hours. Preparation time from this point before the bread goes into the oven is 3 hours. Now your loaf is ready for the oven. If you're trying to generate steam with a baking tray, you may want to set your oven temperature a little higher, because you're going to lose some heat in the process.

Your loaf should be ready for 45 minutes of baking. Switch to the rack and let it cool. This loaf is also very well contained in the freezer. But please make sure that you eat at least some of it while it's new!

7.2 10 Pizza And Other Flat Bread (Focaccia) Recipes

1. Sourdough Flatbread:

Ingredients:

- 180 grams bread flour
- 120 grams of warm water
- 60 grams sourdough starter
- 15 grams extra virgin olive oil
- 5 grams of sea salt

Instructions:

Load all of the above ingredients into a medium bowl (a glass bowl is perfect so you can detect fermentation bubbles). Thoroughly blend. The dough looks rough and shaggy, fluffy and sticky.

Cover bowl with a towel or plastic bag and rest 20 minutes.

Then stretch and fold the dough as follows. Moist your hand with sweat, scoop your hand under the dough and gently grab one side of the lump. Extend the dough in your hand away from the main mass, then fold it over. Do this motion three or four more times on various dough sides.

Then turn the entire dough mass so that the folds face down against the bowl's rim. Note the shaggy dough is considerably smoother, which is the target. If the dough looks shaggy, use a visual aid and try again.

Rest for another 20 minutes, stretch and fold again.

Cover again, cure at room temperature for 3-4 hours. Your dough can not rise dramatically, but you can see bubbles forming on and below the surface (which you can see if your dough is in a glass bowl). If you don't see bubbles, boil until you do.

A job surface gently flourishes. Invert the bowl above the floured area, waiting for the bowl to release itself. Divide dough into two. Using exactly the same technique as earlier stretch and fold (minus wet hands), form pieces into circles.

Cover the inside of two round, one-pint storage containers (preferably lids) with oil and put a seam-side dough ball in each. Cover with plastic wrap.

Refrigerate 24 hours before using it. Dough stored in the refrigerator will start to produce flavor, with a shelf life of one week or more.

Take the dough out from the fridge to make pizza, and put on a well-floured surface. Coat the dough lightly with flour, too. Kindly flatten and stretch the dough into a thin circle about 12 inches in diameter.

Attach sauce, toppings, and bake according to your preferred process. Immediately serve.

2. Sourdough flatbread pizza

Ingredients:

- 1 1/4 cup all-purpose flour
- 1/2 +1 tbsp. cup Water
- 1/4 cup sourdough starter
- 1/2 tsp. onion powder
- 1/2 tsp. garlic powder
- 1/2 tsp. salt

- 2 tbsp. extra virgin olive oil
- 14.5 oz. can of diced tomatoes
- 1/2 tsp. oregano
- 1/2 tsp. sugar
- 2 tbsps. chopped fresh basil
- 1 pinch salt
- 1 tbsps. tomato paste
- 2.5 tbsps. balsamic vinegar
- 4 oz. ball of fresh mozzarella slice
- Any topping

Instructions:

Put flour, starter, salt, onion and garlic powder and water in a mixing bowl with a dough hook attachment, then blend at low for 8 min. Cover and let sit at 100 degrees for 15 min, or put in the oven.

For sauce preparation, heat 2 tbsps. of oil in a small saucepan. Once heated, add tomatoes to a boil, then add 2 tbsps. of balsamic vinegar, later reserve rest. Add remaining ingredients in the sauce — Cook over low heat for 10-15 min.

Heat oven to 550 with the inside cookie sheet. Sprinkle the flour on a piece of large parchment paper.

Rub some oil on hands and start stretching the dough in the shape of a rectangle with your hand, put it on paper, and continue stretching until you can't. If you keep pushing the flour outward, it will be easier.

When ready, top bread with optional sauce, cheese, and topping. Use the parchment to slide flatbread on the cookie sheet, bake for 5 min, remove the parchment below, and continue baking for 10-15 minutes. Melt 1 cup of butter and add 1 cup of parmesan cheese, salt pinch, and 1 cup of parsley. Brush on the crust of a flatbread.

In a non-stick skillet, heat 1/4 cup of oil on medium heat, make sure that the oil is very hot, break two eggs directly in the oil, fry for 2-3 min. Cover with cheese, arugula, and balsamic vinegar and drizzle. Cut, and have fun.

The sauce is perfect for 2 folding broth. Makes 1.5 tassels. Strong dry yeast is used. Get it as slim as possible.

3. Easy Sourdough Flatbread:

Ingredients:

- 2 cups sourdough starter
- 1 teaspoon garlic powder
- 1/2 teaspoon salt
- 1 teaspoon Italian seasoning
- 2 tablespoons olive oil
- 2 cloves garlic, minced
- 1/4 cup fresh herbs, like rosemary, sage, basil or oregano

Instructions

Preheat a 400-degree pizza block, or cast-iron skillet.

Pour the starter mixture into thin, flatbread shapes onto the preheated block. Drizzle with a spoonful of olive oil.

Add chopped garlic. For about 10 minutes, bake at 400 degrees or until cooked through. Drizzle with the remaining olive oil and the fresh chopped herbs. Sprinkle with extra salt, to compare.

Slice them and add to a nice basket to take to a party, or just enjoy it as it is!

4. Sourdough Flatbread Pizzas:

MAKES 2 TO 4 SMALL FLATBREADS

Ingredients:

- 1/2 cup recently hydrated **sourdough starter (here's how)**
- 1 tsp. salt
- 2 ½ cups flour
- 1 cup of water

Instructions:

Mix the starter sourdough, sea salt, and water together. Cover with 2 1/2 cups of flour. Knead the dough for around 5 to 8 minutes, then add more flour, if needed, a little at a time. The flour required will depend on the sourdough starter's degree of hydration — the ratios of flour to water used when feeding the starter.

Let the dough sit for a total of 6 to 8 hours, or overnight. When ready to make, heat the oven to 450 ° F.

Divide the dough into between 2 and 4 balls.

Roll the dough out on a lightly floured surface. Move to a cookie sheet or pizza plate.

Bake on the crust for about 6 minutes. The crust is removed from the oven. Attach the desired toppings and bake until the brown crust and the cheese (if used) melts. About 6 to 8 minutes.

5. Starter Sourdough Pizza Crust/Grill bread/Skillet Flatbread:

Ingredients:

- **1 cup** sourdough starter (unfed/neglected is the best here)
- **1 teaspoon** sugar

- **1 cup of** warm water
- **1.25 cups** all-purpose unbleached flour (for the first ferment)
- **0.75 cups** mix of whole-grain flours: buckwheat, spelled or "mixed-grain" are excellent choices, whole wheat flour is just fine too (for the first ferment)
- **1 cup** all-purpose flour (for final dough)
- **1 tablespoon** salt
- **1 cup** high gluten or bread flour (for final dough)
- **1 tablespoon** olive oil
- Toppings, extra olive oil for brushing on grilled dough

Instructions:

In a wide bowl, stir the starter, 1.25 cup all-purpose flour,.75 cup of grain flour and warm water until uniform. Cover for 2 hours using a damp towel. Hopefully, when your starter starts, you'll see some bigger bubbles, but if you don't, and you're fairly positive in your starter, it should work out perfectly. If not, leave it for long before the starter wakes up.

Stir the starter down, then add the remaining flour, salt, sugar, and olive oil. Here, you may stir dried herbs or small seeds. Mix the ingredients into a ball of dough, which might require more flour, until it's too hard to mix.

Knead about 6 minutes on a floured countertop until it is firm and a uniform texture. Seek not to add too much flour, but you may need to add a decent amount to prevent it from being too sticky depending on the ambient humidity, the initial starter, etc. Tacky is perfect, not sticky.

Refrigerate overnight in a big bag-assume minor expansion.

Take out from your refrigerator about 30 minutes before baking/cooking. It's going to be loose and gentle, but it's OK!

Let it arrive at room temperature (even a little cool is good because when you start working with it, it will warm up).

Divide into 5-6 pieces and keep covered until required. At this level, the parts you don't need can be frozen. When you are used to the dough, it will be easier to work with smaller bits.

Use a 475-500 degree oven with a preheated cook surface (pizza stone, robust upside-down cookie sheet) for oven pizza. This dough seems to need to cook a little longer because it does not rise because high. Stretch and pull the dough onto a well-floured surface in an even thin circle. Switch to a well-dusted pizza peel / make-shift peel with cornmeal or semolina. Top with a quick olive oil brushing and toppings (go easily over the watery ones), then move the pizza to the oven. Bake for 15 minutes or until the dough is fully cooked and put on tops.

Divide the dough sections into 3 smaller pieces for skillet flatbreads. Get a medium-hot, cast-iron skillet (not smoking). Roll each piece (do not work too far ahead or the dough gets too spread out) to 1/8-1/16 inch thick on a floured surface, rotating the dough a few times using a rolling pin. You can add dried spices and herbs, seeds, etc. during the rolling process. Slap the dough onto the hot skillet, cook and flip until browned (2 to 3 minutes). Store unfilled bread in the fridge, and cook it on a dry skillet.

Grilled pizza: have all the ingredients right next to your grill to top the pizza ready. You will be operating on a medium-hot grill (for 3-4 seconds, you will be able to keep a hand above the grate). Make sure the grills are clean and good. Dip the dough into a little olive oil and spread it to the medium-hot grill with your hands as you gently pull or stretch into a thin crust shape. Don't want to take a few minutes to push the dough. Let it cook on edge, and caramelize, then release.

Make sure the top side gets a good brushing of olive oil. Flip, then work quickly with your at-hand sauce, cheese, and everything you don't need by cooking (it won't get it in the grill) to top the pizza. Close your grill and cook for about 5 minutes (except when you smell burning). You can do this one at a time, and when they are all done, reheat the pizzas in the grill at once. But if you barbecue, it might be hot out, and you don't need piping-hot pizza!

6. Sourdough Pizza Crust:

Ingredients:

- 1 cup (241g) sourdough starter, unfed/discard
- 1/2 teaspoon of dry or instant yeast
- 1/2 cup (113g) warm water
- 2 1/2 cups (298g) All-Purpose Flour
- 1 teaspoon salt
- 4 teaspoons Pizza Dough Flavor, optional

Instructions:

Until measuring 1 cup (241 g) in a large mixing bowl, place any liquid on top of your refrigerated starter back in it.

Note: This is a good chance to feed the rest of your starter if needed.

Connect the warm water, flour, salt, yeast, and Dough Flavor pizza (if used). Mix to blend, then knead with the dough hook in a mixer for around 7 minutes, until the dough wraps around the hook itself and cleans the bowl edge.

Place the dough in a greased tub, cover and let the dough grow to nearly double in bulk. Depending on the starter's stamina, this will take 2 to 4 hours. Place in a warm place for a faster rise, or double the yeast.

Divide the dough in half for two thin-crust pizzas, and shape each one into a flattened disk. Brush two 12 "ringed pizza pans with olive oil and brush to cover the base. Put the dough in the pans, cover and let rest for 15 minutes. Press the dough gently to the edges of the pans after this rest. If it begins to shrink again, before proceeding, cover and let rest for 15 minutes.

7. Sourdough Nan Flatbread:

Ingredients:

- 275g organic all-purpose flour (2 heaping cups) I often substitute in a portion of whole-grain flour.
- 200g sourdough starter (2/3 cup stirred down)
- 75g yogurt (1/4 cup)
- 125g milk (~1/2 cup)
- 5g salt (1 tsp.)
- OIL OR BUTTER FOR YOUR ROLLING PIN
- FLOUR FOR YOUR COUNTERTOP
- OPTIONAL: Minced garlic and cilantro or other herbs that can be added to the dough until it rolls flat, or mixed with melted butter and brush on the flatbreads after frying.

Instructions:

Mix all ingredients in a tub, then hand-knead for a couple of minutes. If the dough is too wet, add extra flour or more milk if it is too warm. · Cover the dough and allow it to increase by 70-100%. It can take several days in the fridge or 4-8 hours at room temperature (or more), depending on the temperature and ripeness of the starter.

Scrape and de-gas the dough onto a floured countertop and divide it into eight parts. Cut the dough like a cookie. It is a perfect time to add chopped garlic, chives or herbs if you wish. However, keep the pieces small so as not to split the dough as you roll it out.

Round the triangles into 8 spheres, keep track of which ball you made first, so this will be the first dough you fry. You will need about 10 minutes between making the first ball and attempting to roll it flat to relax again in the gluten.

Heat a larger cast iron pan or a 10-inch to "hot." By trial and error, you can get to the right temperature for your pan and burner.

Roll out the first ball to a height of just under 1/4 inch. Flourish your counter very softly and oil my rolling pin very slightly.

Switch the dough to the frying pan, and cook for 1-2 minutes on each hand. Flip as the top and sides of the dough bubbles curl under. You're hitting brown spots, so change the heat accordingly.

To cool down, put the cooked nans on a rack. You will have time when frying another dough to roll one. Once all the nans are cooked and cold, cover or wrap them to keep them from drying out. Use melted garlic-and-herb butter to brush them when they are warm if you like

The nans in the toaster can be frozen and reheated.

8. Sourdough Focaccia:

Gives: 3 small flatbreads

Ingredients:

- 1 tsp. salt
- 1/2 cup water
- 1 cup sourdough starter
- 2-3 cups flour (white or whole wheat)
- 2 cloves garlic, minced
- 3 tbsp. olive oil
- 1 tsp. dry/fresh thyme
- Coarse salt (optional)

Instructions:

Mix the sourdough starter with the water the night before you go bake the bread. At this point, change the amount of water (e.g., 2 or 3 cups) if you intend to double or triple the recipe. Stir in enough flour to make a solid batter (about 1 cup). Cover with a towel and leave for the night.

The mixture of starter, water, and flour will be foamy in the morning. Stir it in. Add the salt, thyme, 2 tbsp. of olive oil, and the remaining flour and make a soft dough. Knead a couple of minutes.

Dab olive oil on a foil-coated baking sheet (more calories but more tasteful!) with vegetable spray or grease tape. Oil your hands gently and divide the dough into three rounds. Place them onto the prepared baking sheet into ovals. Cover with a towel and let them rest for about 20-30 minutes at room temperature.

Mix in a small cup, the remaining olive oil, and garlic.

Oven preheats to 400 F (220 C). To make tiny dimples, expose the flatbreads and gently press your fingertips into the dough. Smear the mixture of olive oil and garlic uniformly over the broth. If necessary, sprinkle with coarse salt.

Bake for 20-25 minutes until brown and golden. Cool at room temperature and put in.

9. Sourdough pita:

Ingredients

- **500g** wheat (bread/plain) flour
- **20g** sourdough culture (100% hydrated, equal parts flour and water)
- **9g** (sea) salt
- **280g** water
- **15 g** olive oil

Instructions:

Build the dough in a free-standing mixer by kneading all the ingredients for 4-5 minutes (by hand for 8 to 10 minutes). Drape the dough in a greased tub, cover with Clingfilm and let stand for up to 24 hours at cool room temperature (18 – 20 ° C/64 – 68 ° F). 24 hours' work beautifully sourdough culture to achieve the desired dough and the production of taste. Yet each culture is different and can behave differently, so you have to give it a couple of attempts to find your own optimum.

You divide the dough into 8 equal parts (slightly more than 100 g each) and shape it into balls for the next stage. Cover and let relax for 10 minutes while the oven is preheated as hot as possible. Most ovens go up to 250 ° C/480 ° F, but it's much cooler if yours goes up to 300 ° C/570 ° F. Make sure that the stone or rack you're going to use is also in the oven when you're preheating because you want your bread baked on a hot surface directly.

You can preheat your household oven to a traditional setting of 300 ° C/570 ° F and just before you put the first pita in the oven, turn to the convection setting (which goes up to 250 ° C/480 ° F). It's kind of a trick to get the best out of both environments, get the oven as hot as possible first, and then the hot air helps with the puffing up part.

Now take a dough ball and shape it gently by hand to the shape of a disk. Take a disk and roll out the disk with a rolling pin to a diameter roughly two to three millimeters thick. This second shaping part can also be done by hand. Just roll from the middle to the edges and turn the dough a couple of times, so it can roll out evenly and round.

Now 'throw' on the hot rack or stone, a rolled-out disk. Be fast, so your oven isn't falling too far in temperature. Naturally, you can bake many at once, but it's best to first do a trial version of one pita to see how that comes out. Now watch it puffing up, and after 3 to 4 minutes, take it out. Repeat with other balls.

You should keep the pitas baked warm between two tea towels (this way, they'll stay warm for quite a while). Fresh and warm are better consumed, but you can freeze the remaining pitas (not more than a few weeks). Thaw them in your toaster, and give them a minute. Very yummy!

10. Sourdough Tortillas:

Instructions:

- Starter – 9 oz. / 255g @ 166% hydration
- Oil – 1 oz. / 28g
- Hot water 130F+–11 oz. /314g
- Salt – .4 oz. /11g

- All-Purpose Flour- 1 lb. 11 oz. /765g

Instructions:

Weigh the starter in the bowl first, and then the oil and salt. First, add the flour and hot water. Get your hands inside the bowl and mix the dough with your hands very well. The dough has an unusual feel and appears wetter than its hydration of 54.7 percent. When the dough has been well coated, cover the bowl and let the dough sit for 20 minutes.

Now break the dough into 12 bits that weigh about 4 oz. each. Roll the dough out into small balls. Cover with a slightly damp tea towel, the dough bits. Steam a medium-heat heavy bottom 12" skillet; don't let it smoke. Then take each ball one at a time and sprinkle the surface with flour and roll the ball out to around 5 inches with perfect timing.

Then let it rest while rolling one or two balls to the size of 5 inches. Now go back to the first ball that had an opportunity to rest and roll it out (sprinkle flour as necessary to prevent the dough from sticking) to a circle about 10 inches in diameter.

Turn the dough into your hot, heavy Tramontane skillet until you achieve this, and let the dough bubble up on one side, then turn it over again and let it bubble on the other. You shouldn't cook the tortillas too long, or they get like a cracker or carton. When your lovely tortilla has been finished, place it on a plate and cover it with a kitchen towel to keep warm and fluffy. Then put the next tortilla in the saucepan.

Roll out a few tortillas and have them cook in line; it takes a bit of timing to keep it all going. The purpose you roll the dough out in two stages is that if you want to roll the dough quickly out to 10 inches, it will resist your efforts, so the rest time helps the gluten relax for the final stretch again! The thick tortilla is made of 4 oz dough balls.

If you want a thinner tortilla, use 3.5 oz. of dough and roll it out to a circle of 10 inches in diameter, it will be nearly seen through. After you have finished frying up your lovely stack of tortillas, serve them with fresh butter, beans, and everything else that completes your meal.

7.3 12 Enriched Flours / Whole Grains Recipes

1. Rye Sourdough Loaf:

Ingredients:

- 225 grams/8 ounces bread flour
- 9 grams/1/3 ounce salt
- 225 grams/8 ounces rye flour
- 1 cup of water
- 285 grams/10 ounces **sourdough starter**

Instructions:

Place the two flours in a wide baking dish, add salt, and blend together. Create a wide well in the center and add the dough for the starter. Draw the flour into the center using a fork, and mix gently. Then mix the starter and flour together and water at a time to make a sticky dough.

Then knead the bread with a dough hook in a mixer, or tip the dough onto a lightly floured workstation and knead until a smooth, elastic dough is present. If the dough is warm, add more water, too wet, and sprinkle with a little flour, in the machine for about 10 minutes, 12 to 15 minutes by manual.

If the dough is ready, a mixing bowl with a bit of olive oil should lightly grease. Scoop the dough into the pot, cover with a film/plastic wrap, and put the bowl in a cool spot, not cold and free of drafts. Let the dough double in size, or for up to 6 hours. Keep it overnight if you want to; the dough must be in a cooler space allowing the bread to rise very slowly.

Tip the dough onto a gently floured surface and shake the bread air out. Knead the dough gently for a couple of minutes, then roll the dough into a ball, Lightly dust with flour, and put in either a flowered bannet or a mixing bowl lined with a floured tea towel. Cover with plastic bowl or bannet and put it in a cool, not as cold position as before and leave for 8 hours to rise gradually.

Heat up the furnace to 220 C/475 F / gas 6. Place half-filled with boiling water in an ovenproof bowl on the lowest shelf of the oven. The steam from the water gives the loaf a lovely crust.

Top a baking sheet with greaseproof paper, which is lightly oiled. Tip the loaf onto the sheet from the banneton or bowl (don't worry if you lose a bit of air from the loaf when you do so, it will fall back in the oven). P oven and loaf it. Cook for 30 minutes, then drop to 200 C/ 400 F/ gas 6 and cook until the loaf is golden brown. The crust should be smooth, and when tapped on the foundation, the bread sounds hollow.

Place the loaf on a cooling rack before eating, and leave to cool completely. Rye sourdough can be used like any other bread, and freshly baked and spread with butter is, of course, delicious.

The sourdough can sustain for up to a week. Do not position it in any plastic, because it softens the crust. Place the loaf in a paper bag or a bread tub instead. The bread keeps well and is still nice toasted even after a week.

2. Grilled Herb and Butter Sourdough Toast Recipe:

Ingredients:

- 1 **sourdough loaf** cut in half lengthwise
- 1/2 cup/120 mL room temperature unsalted butter

- 2 teaspoons/10 mL **paprika**
- 1/2 teaspoon/2.5 mL dried oregano leaves
- 1/2 teaspoon/2.5 mL garlic powder
- 1/4 teaspoon/1.25 mL cumin
- 1/4 teaspoon/1.25 mL cayenne
- 1 teaspoon/5 mL sea salt

Instructions:

Combine the butter with the garlic, oregano paprika, cumin, cayenne, and oil.

Spread the sourdough loaf into the cut leg. Preheat the heat to medium-high grill.

Place aluminum foil on the grill and put the bread upside down on the buttered side grill. Close the lid and cook until the butter is melted for 5-7 minutes. Take off grill, slice, and serve.

3. Rye Bread with Sourdough:

Ingredients:

For the Rye Sponge:

- 2 1/4 cups/300 grams **rye flour**
- 2 Tbsp. /30 grams **sourdough starter**
- 1 cup of water

For the Final Dough:

- 2 3/4 cups/340 grams bread flour
- 2 tsp. /12 grams of salt
- 3/4 cup/200 grams water
- 1 tsp. /4 gram **instant yeast**
- 2 tsp. /7.5 grams of malt powder

- 1 Tbsp. barley malt syrup (or light **molasses**)

Instructions:

Sift through a sieve (1 millimeter or 1/32 inch mesh) if you have a sack of whole-grain or stone-ground rye flour, and use the sieved part for this dough. Retain the bran for the crust and large bits of broken rye. For 2 1/4 cups of rye flour (300 grams), sew another cup or so. Should not sieve if you have a medium or a light rye flour.

Mix the rye flour with a cup of water (250 grams) and about 2 tablespoons of rye starter (30 grams) that may come straight from the fridge. Feed the battery, and then return to the fridge while you are at it.

When the three ingredients are thoroughly wetted, cover with a lid or plastic and allow to ferment for 16 hours at room temperature (about 75 F). If it is less than 75 F, you may have needed it to ferment a little longer.

In the wet, sticky dough, you won't see any physical change, but you can smell a good, sourdough smell.

Use the full rye sourdough and add the remaining ingredients. Mix on low with a dough hook with a stand mixer for about 7 minutes.

Turn on a clean plate, and knead with your wet hands many times. The dough is strong but oily, and it will prevent the hands wet from sticking too badly. Form into a sphere, place it in a bowl, and cover at room temperature with a damp cloth for 30 minutes. You could see some upsurge.

For rolls: Shape dough into 100 gram balls on a lightly floured surface, flatten to rectangles and shape into 4-inch baguettes. Dip the rolls into tea, then roll into the leftover rye bran or simply roll in some flour for a rustic look. Does 11 rolls.

Split the dough into two segments and shape into boules for bread or a batard.

Let the bread or rolls rise on parchment paper, covered with a damp cloth, for 70 minutes.

Preheat oven to 450 F for 60 minutes, ideally with a baking stone. Slash rolls or razor blade pizza.

Slide the parchment, if necessary, with the rolls onto the baking sheet. Bake for 25 to 30 minutes (bread 40 to 50 minutes) with steam (5 minutes of steam), and turn the temperature down to 400 F as soon as you place the dough in the oven.

Cool bread for dry crusts on shelves, and eat or freeze as you want. When cut into thin slices, the rolls form perfect cocktail bread.

4. German Dinkelbrot: Spelt and Rye Sourdough Bread

Ingredients:

Sourdough:

- 1/2 cup/50g rye flour
- 1 to 2 teaspoons/5ml **sourdough starter** (active)
- 3 tablespoons/40ml water
- **Porridge:**
- 3/4 cup/85g cracked rye
- Optional: 2 teaspoons/5g diastatic barley malt
- 3/4 cup/170ml water

Soaker:

- 1 1/2 cups spelled (flakes)
- 1 1/4 cups/290ml water
- 4 teaspoons/24g salt

Final Dough:

- All sourdough (less than 1 to 2 teaspoons for next batch)
- All of the soaker
- All of the porridge
- 6 3/8 cups/730g whole-spelled flour
- 1 tablespoon/10g vegetable oil
- 1 1/8 cups cold water
- 20 grams fresh yeast)

Instructions:

The Day before Baking: Blends the sourdough ingredients together until the paste becomes rigid. Cover, and let it stay at room temperature overnight.

Combine the crushed rye, water, and diastatic barley malt in a small saucepan at about the same time, bring to a boil and simmer for two hours, always stirring. It will be dark brown, and a little sweet by the time you cook it. You can let it sit on the table or in the fridge overnight.

Put the soaker ingredients in a pot, and quickly mix. Cover at room temperature and let stay overnight. You can also start that just three hours before the final dough is mixed.

Baking Day: Put all the ingredients in a big bowl for final dough. (If you use active dry yeast, dissolve part of the water before adding it. If you use it immediately, add it directly to the bowl.) Knead with the dough hook in the mixer for eight minutes at the slowest speed, then two minutes at the second-lowest speed.

Let it rest twenty minutes, then knead five minutes slow and two a little faster again.

Let it rest a decade. The dough will clear the bowl's rim and look homogeneous (no big pieces of grain) but not shiny.

Divide the dough into two parts, approximately 1 3/4 pounds each. Shape into loaves (round or long as you like). Place them on paper to parchment.

Wash with water over the loaves. As in the photograph ("S" for spelled), you can decorate with a little flour using a stencil, if you wish.

Let the loaves sit for an hour and preheat the oven to 450 F/230 C. Cover with a plastic wrap or tub, so they do not dry out.

Use a baking stone in the oven if you can, and set the oven up for steam. See in the oven this detail about steam.

Turn the loaves onto the mortar for baking. Its okay to always pass them on the parchment paper, and you can delete it in baking for around 20 minutes as soon as the loaves firm up.

Bake the loaves for at least one hour, or until the bread's internal temperature reaches 190 F/87 C or more. Turn the loaves halfway through, and on the one hand, they don't go over gold.

Cut, and cool before slicing for two hours.

5. Polish Sourdough Rye Bread:

Ingredients:

For the Sourdough Starter:

- 4 tablespoons flour (medium rye)
- 3 tablespoons milk (warm)

For the Bread:

- 4 cups flour (medium rye)
- 4 cups flour (all-purpose)
- 1 tablespoon salt
- 1 package/2 1/4 teaspoons yeast (instant)
- 2 tablespoons butter (softened)
- 2 1/2 cups water (warm)
- 1 large egg white (room temperature, beaten)
- 1 tablespoon caraway (seeds)

Instructions:

Note: The different steps of this recipe are grouped into workable categories to help you organize your cooking and preparation better.

Make the Starter: Combine the 4 tablespoons of rye flour and milk together in a small tub.

Cover with plastic and set for two days or until it smells pleasantly sour in a warm place to mature.

Combine 4 cups of rye flour and all-purpose flour, salt, yeast, butter, water, and starter to make the Dough In a large pot. Knead it by computer for 7 minutes or by hand for 10 minutes.

Place the dough in a clean, greased bowl, cover with plastic and enable it to grow until it doubles about 1 hour.

Punch the dough down, knead it for 1 minute, and then split it in half.

Heat the oven to 400 F. Shape and Bake.

Cut each dough in half on two baking sheets lined with parchment. Cover with oiled plastic each round and allow to rise for 30 minutes or until almost doubled.

Brush egg white to the raised rounds and sprinkle with caraway seeds. Bake for 40 minutes or until 190 to 195 F registers instant-read thermometer and bread sounds hollow when pressed.

Slide the bread round off the baking pans and cool down on a wire rack.

Slice, and take advantage!

6. Eastern European Black Bread Recipe:

Ingredients:

Soaker:

- 2 1/4 ounces cracked rye
- 4 ounces cool water

Rye Sour:

- 9 ounces whole rye (pumpernickel) flour
- 8 ounces of water
- 1/2 ounce ripe sourdough starter

Dough:

- 6 ounces of water
- All of the soaker
- All of the rye sour
- 7 1/2 ounces ripe sourdough starter
- 1 1/2 teaspoons blackstrap molasses
- 4 1/2 ounces high-gluten flour (14% protein)

- 8 ounces whole rye (pumpernickel) flour
- 1 teaspoon whole fennel seed (coarsely ground)
- 2 teaspoons instant yeast (not rapid rise)
- 2 teaspoons salt
- 1 tablespoon cocoa powder

Instructions:

Note: This bread dish is broken down into workable categories, and there are several steps to this recipe to help you prepare your preparation and baking better.

The cracked rye and water in a small, non-reactive jar for the Soaker Combine.

Cover and let sprinkle overnight. Combine the rye flour, water, and starter for the Rye Sour, and blend until smooth.

Stab the surface with rye flour, cover, and let stand for between 12 and 15 hours.

For the oven, Dough Heat up to 500 F. Coat with vegetable spray over the Pullman pan and lid. Only sprinkle the saucepan with rye flour.

Using the paddle attachment to combine all the ingredients in a stand mixer bowl (or a big pot, if mixed by hand). Switch to the hook and knead for 4 minutes. Raise the pace for another 4 minutes to medium, and knead on low. The dough is getting sticky.

Move the dough to the prepared Pullman saucepan and level it off. Slide the lid onto the pan and brush with rye flour.

Let it rise for 45 to 50 minutes, or until it is 1 inch from the tip.

Put into the oven and bake for 15 minutes. Reduce heat to 400 F and bake for another 15 minutes.

Remove the cap, raising the temperature to 325 F and bake for about 45 minutes, until done.

Remove the bread from the oven and switch it right away from the pan onto a wire rack to cool down completely. Since black bread appears to have a rubbery interior, it needs to sit 24 hours before slicing.

7. Rye Pumpernickel with Sourdough:

Ingredients:

For the Sourdough Starter:

- 1 tablespoon refreshed sourdough culture
- 2 1/2 cups or 270 grams whole rye flour
- 1 1/4 cups or 270 grams of water

For the Rye Soaker:

- 1 cup rye berries

For the Old Bread Soaker:

- 3 3/4 cups or 180 grams old bread

For the Final Dough:

- 1 3/4 cups or 224 grams **bread flour**
- 2 teaspoons (6 grams) **instant yeast**
- 1 3/4 cups or 224 grams cracked rye
- 1 tablespoon (17 grams) **salt**
- 1 1/2 tablespoons or 36 grams) dark **molasses**

Instructions:

Prepare the day before gathering the ingredients for Sourdough Starter and Rye Berry Soaker.

If you haven't refreshed your starter in the fridge for a while, do so 2 days before you decide to bake. It's better to have rye sour, but if you just have wheat flour, it will work too.

Mix the whole rye flour, water, and set up your sourdough starter in a bowl until all the flour is soft. Cover it tightly so it can't dry out and leave for 16 to 18 hours at room temperature. This sourdough will produce a certain scent of sourness.

Place the rye berries in a saucepan, cover with 2 inches of water and leave overnight at room temperature.

Gather the ingredients for the Dough. Boil the rye berries in the pan the next day (add water as needed) and simmer until the berries are tender, for 30 minutes to 1 hour. Drain and put away.

Place old bread in a pot, including crusts, and pour the boiling water over it; leave for a few minutes or longer. When it is soft bread, it will quickly fall apart; if it is old pumpernickel, softening will take longer.

Squeeze out the bread water (it may look like bread pudding or clay) and set aside.

Place all of the Final Dough ingredients in the bowl of an electric mixer fitted with the dough hook and blend for 10 minutes at the lowest level. Add water or flour as needed to form a slightly sticky dough ball. The amount will vary depending upon how much water was in the soaked bread and berries.

Knead on the counter to make final changes for a few minutes. Form into a ball and let it rest for 1 hour at a warm spot.

Preheat oven to 350 F, ideally placed inside the oven with a baking stone or another type of heat retention. 2 or more bread pans or Pullman pans with oil and flour.

Divide the dough to match your bread shapes as needed. Shape the dough into loaves and placed it inside the pans.

Dust with flour, cover and allow to rise in a warm spot for 30 minutes.

Cover the loaf pans with tightly packed, oiled aluminum foil.

Bake the bread in the oven using rising temperatures for several hours, slowly. Starting midday is best so that the bread can sit overnight in a warm (but switched off) oven.

Place inside the oven and bake at 350 F for 1 hour.

Turn down the oven to 325 F and bake 30 minutes.

Place the oven down to 300 F and bake for 1 hour.

Set the oven to 275 F and bake 2 hours.

Set the oven to 250 F and bake 2 hours.

Set the oven to 225 F, then bake for 1 1/2 hours.

Set the oven to 200 F, then bake for 1 1/2 hours.

Switch off the oven and leave the pans in the oven until morning (the oven stays warm). The bread had been about 16 hours in the oven. Leave wrapped in cotton or linen for an additional 24 hours before slicing.

8. Black Forest Bread - Schwarzwaelder Kruste:

Ingredients:

Starter:

- 1/2 cup/118 g lukewarm water
- 1/2 cup/58 g rye flour(medium)
- 2 to 3 tsp. sourdough starter from the refrigerator
- 1/2 cup/58 g rye flour(light)

Sponge:

- 1 1/5 cup/270 g water
- 1/8 tsp. /1 g salt
- 1/4 tsp. yeast (instant, or 1 g. fresh)

- 3 1/4 cup or 388 g flour (bread)

Final Dough:

- All of the sourdough and sponge
- 3 1/4 cups flour (bread)
- 1/3 cup/40 g rye flour (light)
- 10 g. fresh or 1 tsp. /4 g instant yeast
- 2 tsp. /10 g lard (or shortening)
- 1/3 cup/40 g rye flour (medium)
- 1 1/3 cup/300 g water
- 3 tsp. /14 - 21 g salt

Instructions:

In the original recipe, the rye flour called for is "Roggenmehl 997," which ranges between light and medium flowered rye. Replace all light flour or some medium flour if you wish.

Prepare the Day before Baking Sponge and Sourdough: This takes just a few minutes and is getting easier, the more you do it. If you bake bread a lot, invest in a scale so you can use the measurements by weight to be very precise.

Mix the sourdough starter ingredients together by hand until a ball is shaped.

Cover the battery and leave for 12 to 18 hours at room temperature. One may feed the starter on rye or white flour. The starter should have been fed recently, so feed it once before beginning this recycle If it's been in the fridge for a month.

Blend the sponge ingredients together by hand. When fresh yeast or non-instant yeast is used, dissolve the yeast in a little water before adding it.

Once the dough comes together to shape a ball, at room temperature, let it sit for two hours.

Then roll the dough into plastic wrap and put it for 10 to 16 hours in the refrigerator. All sections can also be refrigerated for up to 48 hours, if appropriate.

Baking Day: Combine the sourdough, sponge, and other ingredients in the mixer for about eight minutes at low with a dough handle.

Turn a notch to the speed and continue to mix for four minutes.

Turn on a floured surface, then knead several times. If the dough is too soft, add flour. It should be supple but not soft that when you let it go, it instantly loses form on the surface. Let it stand up for 30 minutes, sealed.

Punch it down, then allow it to rise for 15 minutes. This assumes an approximate dough temperature of 74 F. If your dough gets colder, then let it rise a little longer. The dough is NOT going to double in size.

Cut the dough into two round loaves, pull the dough around to form a "boule," and spread the "head" gluten to the bottom. Should not pinch the underside absolutely closed, because this will be the appealing surface in the oven.

Place the dough round in a rye-floured bread basket or flour-lined cup, with the seam side down.

Let the bread rise for 60 minutes. Even if not doubled in volume, you will see an appreciable increase.

Heat the stone in the oven at least 30, better 60 minutes, to 475 F. The stone should be on the middle rack to hold the hot water pan.

Unmold the bread (seam-side up) onto the peel or back of a cookie sheet of a cornmeal-strewn baker and move to the hot plate.

Open the oven door after two minutes, and add a cup of hot water to the hot water pan. If you can, add steam by sprinkling water on the walls.

Turn Oven Temperature down to 400 F after 10 minutes. Bake another 40 minutes.

An oven a crack to let out the remainder of the steam for the last 20 minutes. Bread should have at least 190 ° F indoor temperature.

Enable the bread to completely cool until slicing or freezing.

9. Easy Lithuanian Dark Rye Bread:

Ingredients:

- 2 cups milk (scalded)
- 2 tablespoons butter
- 2 tablespoons sugar
- 1 teaspoon salt
- 1/2 cup water (lukewarm)
- 1 package **active dry yeast**
- 4 cups **dark rye flour**
- 2 1/2 cups **whole-wheat flour**
- OPTIONAL: 2 tablespoons caraway seeds
- 1 large egg white (beaten)

Instructions:

Pour in cold milk over medium heat in a heavy-bottomed saucepan. Stir it regularly with a wooden spoon or silicone spatula until the scalding temperature of the milk exceeds

180 F. Remove the scalded milk from oil, and cool to 110 F. For milk, this is done to denature proteins that can prevent the production of gluten and keep the dough from rising.

Garnish the scalded milk over butter, sugar, and salt in a wide bowl or stand mixer. Remove to cool.

In the lukewarm water dissolve the yeast. Attach the yeast mixture to the milk mixture and 3 cups of rye flour. Thoroughly beat, then, if using, beat in the remaining rye flour and caraway seed. Cover position the dough in a warm spot (70 to 75 F) and allow the dough to rise until it doubles. It can take quite a long time, as only rye flour is being used. Prepare for a couple of hours, and know it can take up to 12 hours.

Attach the flour and knead until smooth. It helps to wet your hands because this is a sticky and dense dough. You're not going to grow the springy consistency that you get with wheat dough, so don't keep adding flour in the hope of achieving that quality.

Divide the dough into two round or oblong loaves in half.

Place the loaves on pans lined with parchment. Cover with plastic wrap and let it expand until doubled (1-4 hours, but this will change again). Brush white with broken egg.

Oven preheats to 450 F. 15 Minutes to bake the loaves. Reduce heat to 350 F and bake 35-45 minutes longer, or until 190 F is registered by an instant-read thermometer.

Switch the loaves from the pans onto a wire rack to fully cool off.

Slice the loaves, and have fun!

10. Dark Rye Sourdough:

Ingredients:

- 12 oz. Organic Dark Rye Flour
- 4 oz. Canadian Strong White flour

- Ladleful active sourdough starter
- Half-pint approx. cold and just-boiled water (mixed 50:50) with a slug of cold-pressed rapeseed or olive oil added

Instructions:

Start early at night: place the flours in the bowl and blend. Add the starter ladleful. Set the mixer to go and add much of the oil and warm water. If required, add the remaining water and more to shape the dough. Knead 4 minutes in the mixer. It would feel pretty much like an unappetizing putty glob!

Shape on a lightly floured board into a ball, place the dough ball in a lightly oiled bowl with a small room to rise, and cover it with a lid or plate. Leaving for about 4 hours before bedtime.

A banneton slightly flourishes. Turn the dough out, form it, and place it (top side downwards) in the banneton. Within a plastic bag, sit banneton and leave overnight (or around 8 hours). Just before you get up, set the oven on the timer to heat up to 220 degrees (fan).

Turn loaf out onto the baking tray in the morning, and bake 30 minutes.

11. Weekend fruit & nuts loaf:

Soak fruit version 1

- 200 g HOT water
- 50 g rum
- 150 g dried dates
- 100 g dried figs
- 50 g raisins
- 50 g dried sour cherries

- 50 g dried apricots

Soak fruit version 2

- 200 g HOT water
- 100 g raisins
- 200 g dried pears
- 50 g rum
- 100 g dried sour cherries

Ingredients:

- Makes 2 loaves, each about 530 g
- 75 g bread flour
- 175 g whole rye flour
- 100 g rye sourdough starter (100% hydration)
- 4 g salt
- 1 g ground cloves
- 4 g ground cinnamon
- 200 g fruity water
- 400 g soaked mixed dried fruit
- 100 g nuts (a combination of walnuts, pecans, almonds)

Instructions:

Prepare the fruit Wash your dried fruit and leave for an hour to soak in hot water. Add 50 grams of rum to hot water, **and you can substitute the rum by water. Strain the fruity liquid and hold it so you can use the flavored water in the recipe! Cover the bowl with a wrap and allow the fruit to remove the residual moisture overnight so that the fruit is moist but not sticky when you use it the next day. If you want to cut the fruit into pieces, you will decide for yourself. We don't do that because we cut thin slices from it when the loaf is**

ready, and the fruit and nuts dice anyway, plus it looks more appealing to us this way. Making the dough. The whole cycle will take more than 9 hours on this day, so it is wise to prepare and maybe start early.

Measure the fruity water and add more water from the soaked fruit **so you'll have the right amount of water (200 grams) for the dough. Combine sourdough starter, bread flour, rye flour, salt, spices, and fruit water into your dough in the bowl of your standing mixer and combine for a minute until it comes together (of course, you can do it by hand as well). Cover and leave for 1 hour to rest.**

Knead the dough now for 5 minutes (10 by hand) until you have a smooth and slightly sticky dough (it will adhere to the bowl's bottom). The dough should feel more like a paste than normal bread dough, because of the large amount of rye flour. Cover again, and leave for 1 hour to rest.

Remove the dough from the bowl and press it to a flat rectangle. The soaked fruit and nuts should be spread uniformly around the dough. Pull the dough up and press the dough **to ensure well-distributed fruit and nuts (see pictures). Cover, and leave for 3 hours to rest.**

Divide the dough into two equal parts, and shape, if you want, into balls or oval shapes. Place the balls on a baking-paper tray**, or as we did in bake-able baskets. Cover the loaves and leave for the final proof.** Based on room temperature and flour, this will take about 3 hours.

Preheat your oven to 390F / 200C. Place a metal baking tray on your oven floor when you preheat the oven and pour in half a cup of hot water directly after placing the bread in the oven. Set your oven door to add some steam 5 minutes before the bread is ready **(maybe with a wooden spoon or oven mitt).**

**Switch the oven down to 170C/340F after putting the bread in the oven (starting higher and then turning down, it is done so you can lose heat very easily by oven door opening and steam adding).

After baking your loaves for 55 minutes, they are finished. Place them up to cool on a rack. Place the bread after cooling in a paper bag and leave for around 12 hours before slicing to set and ripen. Slicing that way would be easier, and the flavor will have further improved.

Fruit and nuts loaf time table Day 1: Evening: wash, soak and strain the dried fruit Leave for 12 hours till next morning Day 2 00:00 – Mix dough ingredients and knead for 1 minute 60 rest 01:05 – Knead for 5 minutes 60 rest 02:15 – Add filling to dough 3 hours rest 05:15 – Form into two balls 3 hours final evidence 08:15 – Bake for 55 minutes 09:10 – Ready and let c Mix to a shaggy dough, cover with plastic loosely and place in the refrigerator for 20-30 minutes.

Place the dough on a smooth bench and knead it to a smooth ball. Oil the bowl gently, add the dough then return it to the refrigerator for 40 minutes.

Tip the dough onto the bench again, but this time don't use any flour. Extend the dough in a big, very thin oblong, then fold the dough in both directions in 3. Give the dough back to the refrigerator overnight.

Remove the dough from the refrigerator the next day, tip it onto the unfloured bench, and then stretch it out into a big, very thin oblong. Scatter the figs and walnuts over the cough evenly then sprinkle on top with the sugar and cinnamon.

Fold the dough in both directions in 3, then fold again in 3 so you get a strong, thick sausage.

Make the dough into a ball with a smooth surface without ant fruit or nut in poppy seeds protruding the roll.

Place it on a baking paper sheet and join side down. Cover the loaf loosely with plastic and leave for 1 1/2-2 hours to grow.

Preheat the oven to 225C, after 1 1/4 hours.

When the oven reaches temperature, cut the top surface, raise the dough into a covered roasting pan on its baking paper and bake for 20 minutes at 225C.

Reduce the temperature of the oven to 200C and remove the pan lid. Bake until the loaf is golden brown for another 25 minutes and sounds hollow when you knock on the crust.

Nice, on a rack of wire. Cut to cool

12. Sourdough bread with rye and linseed:

Ingredients:

- 100% starter 300g
- Warm water 655g
- Strong white flour 1250g
- Golden linseed 100g
- Chopped rye 150g
- Salt 30g
- Boiled water 350g

Instructions:

Place the chopped rye and linseeds in a pot, then pour on the boiling water just off. Shake well. You shall see the mucilage formed by the linseeds. The smell may be strange at this point; don't let that put you off. Put a little to one side to cool. When you can do this without burning it, it's Cool.

Combine the starter, solid white flour, and remaining water in a shaggy layer. Leave for 10 to 30 minutes at any spot. The apply salt and a mixture of linseed/rye.

You will have to work the mix in the dough for a while until it's completely mixed together. If you are big enough to have a mixer, it will help.

Then at half an hour, do a stretch & fold and then hourly after that until it proved to be around four hours of bulk.

Then break up and shape your dough. Divide and shape the dough into flat balls, and then let the dough rest for 10 minutes.

Then cover with oiled film/bags of plastic and require proof until it is ready. It could take two to four hours or so, depending on the weather.

Preheat to 240 ° C your oven.

Slash your loaves and pop in the oven as you wish. If you like, spray with water. Shift the oven lower to 200°C after about 10 minutes or so, about 30-40 minutes.

7.4 13 Sweet and Savory Treat Recipes

1. Sourdough Coffee Cake:

Ingredients:

Streusel Topping:

- 1/4 cup sugar
- 1/2 cup flour
- 1/4 cup butter
- 1/8 teaspoon **cinnamon**

Cake:

- 1/3 cup oil
- 1 cup flour
- 1 egg

- 3/4 cup sugar
- 1/2 teaspoon salt
- 1 cup sourdough starter (fed, see note)
- 1 teaspoon **baking soda**
- Optional: 1/2 cinnamon teaspoon (ground), 1/4 teaspoon cardamom (ground)

Instructions:

Note: The starter will be as thick as a pancake batter, **or around 50% flour, 50% water. Normally, remove half the starter and** feed each one with equal quantities of flour and water, by weight, then wait until it bubbles (approx. 4 hours) **and then place one jar back in the fridge for another week. You can give a friend the extra sourdough starter, or use it in a recipe like this one.**

In a bowl, mix the streusel topping first by mixing flour, sugar, and cinnamon, then Rub the cold butter with your fingertips until crumbly **and sticks together when you press it between your fingertips. If you like, you can use a mixer.**

Put crumbs away. Place the sourdough starter in a bowl to make the cake, then add the remaining ingredients and stir until combined.

Load the batter into a rectangular 8- or 9-inch pan **or an 8-inch, round, sheet cake pan, buttered and floured. Smooth rim, and scatter uniformly over the batter reserved crumbs.**

Let the cake rise in a warm position for some 30 minutes.

Bake for around 35 minutes at 375 F, or until cake is set and the sides start pulling away from the oven.

Remove, and enjoy it.

2. Sourdough Pancakes:

Ingredients

- 1/2 cup **sourdough starter**
- 1 1/4 cups all-purpose flour
- 1 cup whole milk
- 2 eggs (beaten)
- 2 tablespoons granulated sugar
- 2 tablespoons butter (melted)
- 1 teaspoon baking powder
- 1/2 teaspoon salt
- 1/2 teaspoon vanilla extract
- Garnish: syrup, berries, powdered sugar, or melted butter

Instructions:

Combine the starter sourdough in a large bowl with the milk and the flour. A good-sized bowl is required to allow the mixture to grow.

Place a plastic wrap over the bowl and leave it overnight on the table. Its sourdough flavor needs to grow and continue to evolve. It will be your sponge overnight, the pancakes' foundation.

To the sourdough starter mixture, add the beaten eggs, baking powder, sugar, and salt after you let it sit overnight. Whisk the ingredients together until smooth and soft.

Whisk the butter and vanilla extract melted in. When applying it to the batter, make sure the melted butter has cooled slightly. When you're finished mixing, it will be really thick and almost bread-like.

Steam up and grease a cast-iron skillet or griddle. If you have a griddle, you can simultaneously cook several pancakes. Cooking pancakes are best on non-stick surfaces.

Turn the heat to medium-low, add the batter to the skillet and cook for several minutes or until the bubbles begin to form. These pancakes can be made as big or as small as you wish. Even the big ones flip easily.

Turn over the pancake, then take another minute to cook the other side. On the other hand, it doesn't take as long, so just watch it carefully.

Serve with new fruit, butter, and maple syrup. Experience

3. Sourdough Waffles:

Ingredients:

- 190 grams sourdough starter
- 100 grams of milk
- 2 large eggs
- 100 grams flour
- 1 1/2 teaspoons baking powder
- 30 grams of sugar
- 5 grams of salt
- 20 grams of butter (melted)

Instructions:

Preheat your medium or dark waffle iron and preheat your oven to 200 F. Whisk the sourdough starter, milk, and eggs together in a wide bowl until completely incorporated.

In another cup, add the flour, baking powder, sugar, and salt. Apply to wet-dry ingredients. Stir in the melted butter and blend until it is all finished.

Ladle onto the waffle iron, preheated. Cook until golden brown and fragrant, for about 4 minutes. Depending on your particular waffle iron, the times can differ.

Hold the first waffles warm inside the oven while the rest of the batter is cooking. When all the waffles are finished, remove, and serve directly from the oven. Place the leftovers for up to three days in an airtight container and heat before serving.

4. Sourdough English Muffins:

Ingredients:

- 125 grams bread flour
- 50 grams whole wheat flour
- 60 grams sourdough starter
- 120 grams of milk
- 30 grams of honey
- 1 egg white
- 5 grams of salt
- **Cornmeal** (for dusting)

Instructions:

To a big pot, add the bread flour, whole wheat flour, sourdough starter, milk, sugar, white eggs, and salt. Blend well before combined.

Cover and cure at room temperature for 4–5 hours.

Prepare a muffin pan (preferably the wide pecan roll-type) by sprinkling six of the cups with cooking spray and cornmeal dusting and using a large spoon to place about 1/6 of the dough inside each cup—Stab the dough over with more cornmeal. Cover the plastic wrap over the pan and refrigerate for 12 to 16 hours.

Place over medium to high heat a large griddle or cast-iron skillet. Sprinkle with oil over the pan.

Remove the muffin pan from the refrigerator. Using a small spoon or rubber spatula when the casserole is hot to gently remove any muffin from its cup and put it in the skillet.

Grid the muffins until well browned, maybe with a few tiny spots close to black, then turn over and repeat. Remove to cool rack. Serve as you wish.

5. Sourdough Biscuits:

Ingredients:

- 200 grams all-purpose flour
- 60 grams white whole wheat flour
- 2 teaspoons granulated sugar
- 2 teaspoons baking powder
- 1/2 teaspoon baking soda
- 6 grams of sea salt
- 120 grams cold whole milk, plus more for brushing the tops
- 100 grams cold starter discard
- 1 stick cold unsalted butter

Instructions:

Oven preheats to 400 F.

Attach the flours, sugar, baking strength, baking soda, and salt in a wide blending tub. Stir to combine.

Whisk the milk and sourdough starter together in a separate medium mixing cup, until mixed.

Attach bits of butter to the dry ingredients. Mash all-butter bits once through the tines of a fork or pastry mixer. Attach the wet ingredients to the air, and stir until the dough is shaggy.

Turn the raw dough out onto a floured surface and shape it into a rectangle 1 inch thick. Tuck the rectangle like a letter in thirds. Stab the dough loosely with flour and roll it out to 1 1/2 inches thick using a rolling pin. Do the letter fold and roll the dough over again, this time about 3/4 of an inch thick.

Cut the dough into the form you want. We recommend square biscuits because there is no remaining leftover dough.

Layer the biscuits on a parchment baking sheet, and brush the tops with milk. Bake for about 15 minutes, or until well-rested and golden. Serve straight away.

6. Sourdough Cinnamon Rolls:

Ingredients:

For the Dough:

- 300 grams bread flour
- 160 grams whole milk
- 100 grams **sourdough starter**
- 1 large egg
- 30 grams unsalted butter (softened)
- 30 grams of sugar
- 7 grams of sea salt

For the Filling:

- 1 tablespoon cinnamon

- 1/2 cup light brown sugar
- 3 tablespoons butter (melted)

For the Icing:
- 1/2 cup whipped cream cheese
- 1/2 cup powdered sugar
- 2 tablespoons unsalted butter
- Milk (as needed, to adjust consistency)

Instructions:

To make the dough, add all the ingredients to a stand mixer bowl that is equipped with a dough hook. Mix for about 2 minutes at low speed, or until mostly combined, then turn to second or third speed (it should be vigorous but not fast) and mix for 4 to 5 minutes more. The dough should be fluffy and smooth. If it's a little sticky, it's perfect.

Move the dough to a larger, shallower pot, using a dough scraper. Cover with a damp towel or plastic bag over the cup. Rest for 20 minutes, then take a stretch and fold to the dough.

Ferment the dough for 4 to 5 hours at room temperature then refrigerate for 12 to 16 hours.

Clear the dough from the fridge and turn onto a surface that is lightly floured. Roll the dough gently into a smooth rectangle, about 16 inches long and 1/2 inch wide, using a rolling pin.

Within a small bowl, combine brown sugar and cinnamon and add to create the filling.

Brush the dough surface with the melted butter all over, then coat evenly with brown cinnamon sugar. Beware of having as much cinnamon sugar as possible inside the dough, roll it up like a pillow. Cross-screw into eight sections.

Grease any appropriate baking pan with a little oil or butter (anything that can go into the oven and match the rolls, plus extra space for rising) and put the rolls in with their swirls facing upwards. Cover with plastic tape, loosely. When you need to touch the dough with the plastic wrap, brush the wrap or dough with a little oil to avoid sticking. Placed in a warm position (approx. 80 F) for two hours to rise.

Preheat the oven to 375 F when the rolls have risen to one and a half times its height. Bake for about 30 minutes or to brown until golden.

Prepare the icing while the rolls bake. In a cup, put butter and cream cheese, fitted with a wire whisk attachment. Whip up until fluffy, and mix well.

Start the blender. Sew the powdered sugar inside the pot. Mix to blend at a low pace. Change consistency, if necessary, by adding a splash of milk or two. Scrape down the bowl sides and whip for 1 minute.

When the cinnamon rolls are cooked, remove from the oven and allow the cream cheese icing to cool for a few minutes before spreading — serving hot.

7. Sourdough Starter Scallion Pancake:

Ingredients:

- 2 teaspoons neutral cooking oil
- 1/2 cup **sourdough starter**
- 1 tablespoon diced scallions
- 1/2 teaspoon sesame seeds
- 1/4 teaspoon salt + more to taste

Instructions:

Heat up the oil in a small, non-stick skillet over medium heat. Attach the starter to the hot pan with sourdough discard.

Sprinkle into a batter with scallions, sesame seeds, and 1/4 teaspoon salt. Let the pancake brown for 3 minutes, then turn over and brown for another 2 to 3 minutes on the other side. Sprinkle salt. Serve with your favorite dipping sauce. (like a simple combination of soy sauce, rice vinegar, and crunching chili)

8. Seeded Sourdough Crackers:

Ingredients:

- 3 tablespoons/25 grams of whole wheat pastry flour + more to spread out
- 1/4 cup/60 grams unfed starter discard
- 1/2 cup flaxseed meal
- 4 teaspoons/20 ml olive oil
- 1 tablespoon/11 grams seeds (poppy, sesame, sunflower, fennel, nigella, or a mix)
- 1/2 teaspoon/2 grams sea salt

Instructions:

Oven preheats to 350 F. Cover a sheet pan with a liner of silicone or a parchment leaf.

Place the starter, flour, flaxseed meal, butter, salt, and seeds into a medium-sized cup. Remove with a wooden spoon or rubber spatula until mixed properly, around 1 minute.

Put the cracker dough in the center of the pan and press downwards to a rectangle—dust more flour on top of the dough. Roll the dough into a paper-thin rectangle using a rolling pin (it is ok if the shape is not perfect). You are seeking thicknesses of at least 1/16-inch.

Using a pizza wheel to "rank" the dough into squares (so they quickly break apart after being baked).

Bake until golden and crisp, for 15 to 18 minutes. Let cool for 15 minutes before disintegrating.

Serve right away, or store up to 1 week in a tightly sealed container or box.

9. Savory Mushroom Toast Recipe:

Ingredients:

- 1 tablespoon butter
- 1 medium shallot (diced)
- 1 garlic clove (minced)
- 8 ounces fresh **mushrooms** (sliced)
- 1/2 teaspoon fresh thyme leaves (optional)
- 1 teaspoon soy sauce
- Salt and pepper
- 2 teaspoons fresh parsley (chopped)
- 1/3 cup gruyere cheese (or grated Swiss cheese, approx. 1 1/2 ounces)
- 1 tablespoon olive oil
- 4 Small or 2 large slices (sourdough, wheat or multigrain) of rustic bread

Instructions:

Preheat medium-heat a large skillet. Remove the butter once hot and allow it to melt. Stir in shallot and sauté 1 minute. Remove the garlic and then stir. Remove the mushrooms and sauté for about 5 minutes, or until the mushrooms have browned lightly and become tender. Remove the soy sauce, then stir. Cook for 1 to 2 minutes, stirring periodically or until cooked off mainly by the oil. Remove thyme, and then salt and pepper to season. Delete, and rising to low heat.

Brush all sides of the slices of bread with the olive oil. Place under the broiler on a baking tray and toast for 2 to 3 minutes, or until browned around the edges and slightly crispy. Switch to the other side and repeat toast.

Fill every slice of warm bread with the grated cheese. Top with the parsley followed by the mushrooms and serve.

10. Pain au Leaven-the quintessential French Sourdough:

Dough temperature 76°

Leaven Starter:

- 45 g stiff Leaven starter
- 95 g Type 55 -style flour or all-purpose unbleached flour
- 5 g stone-ground whole wheat flour
- 50 g water

Ingredients:

- 350 g Type 55 style- or all-purpose flour (I used the T 65)
- 120 g stone-ground whole wheat flour
- 30 g fine or medium rye flour
- 350 g water
- 125 g stiff Levain
- 10 g salt

Instructions:

Take the leaven out of the fridge, measure the correct amount of starter, and mix the leaven with the water in a bowl with a whisk. Attach the flours and mix until it gets together with a spatula. Turned onto the surface of the job and kneaded to add flours.

Place the Leaven in a sealed jar and let it sit for 8-12 hours at room temperature (70 to 76°) or until it has doubled in volume, and the surface is dome-dome.

Note: Make sure to use the correct amount of Leaven needed in the recipe; the remaining quantity can be refreshed and preserved for future use in the fridge.

Pour water into a large bowl or mixer to the bowl stand. Combine the rice, whole-wheat flour and rye flour until all of the ingredients are added. Cover it for 20 minutes while the flour starts to hydrate, and gluten is formed.

Hand kneading: turn the dough onto the surface of your work. Flatten the dough into a wide rectangle; sprinkle the leaven over the dough. Knead a few strokes with floured or oiled hands to completely absorb the starter, flatten the dough out, spread the salt evenly, and continue to knead for 12 to 15 minutes. If the dough is very wet to start, use a combination of the French kneading technique and that process.

For the first few minutes, it will be a sticky mess on your work surface, so don't succumb to the lure of adding more flour. Stop from time to time, and use your bench scraper to pick any stray dough off your board. Continue until you grow well in gluten. You should be able to stretch one piece of the dough softly into a thin layer you can almost see through without breaking it.

By machine: Add the salt and leaven and mix the medium velocity until the dough cleans the bowl, and you get strong growth in gluten.

The dough is then moved to a lightly oiled tub. Cover and make fermentation for 1 hour (70 to 75 °) at room temperature. (I keep the dough throughout at a constant temperature of 76 ° C.) 3. Turn the dough onto the work surface that is lightly floured, fold the dough and return it to the oiled bowl with folds on the bottom and cover. Let the dough cure for another

2 to 3 hours. After 50 minutes, you can add another fold if you're dough doesn't appear to have energy.

Split into two parts similar, approx. 500 g and pre-form gently into a boule or a log form. Flour the dough lightly, cover, and allow to rest for 10-15 minutes.

Make each piece of dough into a 12 "long batard and place the seam side up onto a floured couche or into floured bannetons. Cover with one plastic bag or plastic wrap and evidence for one hour at room temperature. 6. (70 to 75 degrees). Preheat the oven to 475 ° with a baking stone and a steam tray at the bottom of the oven, about an hour before baking. Add a cup of water to the bottom tray, or a cup of ice cubes, a few minutes before placing the loaves in the oven to create a moist atmosphere for the bakery with the tested loaves.

Switch the tested loaves gently on to parchment paper or floured peel. Loaves score. Slide the loaves onto the baking sheet, turn the oven down to 400 °, and then start baking for 20 to 25 minutes.

Let them cool on a rack of wire before digging in.

11. Sourdough cinnamon and chocolate twist bread:

Ingredients:

Starter

- 100 g water
- 1 tablespoon of your (active) sourdough starter
- 100 g white wheat flour (bread flour)

Dough:

- 1 egg yolk

Starter (200 g)

- 370 g white wheat flour (bread flour)

- 180 g warm milk
- 1 tablespoon of sugar
- 2 tablespoons of melted butter
- 6 g salt

Filling:

- 100 g soft butter
- 50 g of grated chocolate
- 2 teaspoons of cinnamon
- 60 g sugar

Instructions:

Sourdough starter: Throughout the evening, have your sourdough starter prepared first. Mix 100 g of white flour, 100 g of water, and 1 spoonful or base starter. Leave it to ferment until it's risen, puffed, active and bubbly, so the next morning you can mix it into the dough.

Beat the dough into the morning. Second, dissolve your whole starter into 180 g of water. Stir in egg yolk and butter melted. Remove the whole flour (370 g), salt and sugar, then fold. Mix well and knead the dough, until smooth, for 10 minutes. Form it into a ball and placed it in a pot. Cover and ferment with a plastic wrap until doubled in volume.

Only prepare the filling when you see the dough is about to be finished. Mix the soft butter, sugar, cinnamon, and chocolate seasoning.

Get your Dutch oven and add a piece of parchment paper and grind it with butter.

Roll the dough to a depth of 5 mm or around 3045 cm (1218 inches). Drop the filling over the rolled dough and spread the dough thinly, leaving 2 cm (1 inch) from either side. Roll-off the longest side of the dough, then tuck the ends below. Split the rolled dough halfway in length. You can cut leaving some portion of the dough uncut, or you can cut it in half entirely. Flip the halves of cut outwards.

Start to braid two strands over each other. Tuck together the ends to form a circle. Place the twisted bread and let it rise in the Dutch oven. Leave the dough to rise (doubled in volume) until puffed up. It may took 1.5 hours to complete.

Let the oven heat to 375°F or 200°C 30 minutes before it bakes. **Once the dough is ready, bake it for 30-40 minutes, until well cooked.**

12. Sourdough Fruit Buns:

Ingredients:

- 1530 g white bread flour
- 800 g active
- 40 g salt
- sourdough starter
- 800 ml of water
- ¼ cup honey, warmed for glazing
- Spices such as cinnamon to taste
- 360 g of dried fruit combined, soaked up overnight in water, and then drained. use raisins, currants, barberries, and minced figs

Instructions:

The starter, flour, and water are mixed either by hand or in an electric mixer with a dough hook until it shapes a raw dough. Cover with plastic wrap, and take 20 minutes of rest.

Stir in the water. Mix for 6 minutes, or until a smooth, elastic dough forms, when using an electric mixer. For 20 minutes or until a soft, elastic dough forms when mixed by hand knead.

If using add the fruit and spice. Use your hands to work the fruit into the dough gently.

Place the dough in a lightly greased container and allow it to prove bulk for approximately 1 hour. Knock the dough back and enable it to test mass for another 1 hour.

Place the dough on a clean, lightly oiled or floured surface. Divide the dough into roughly 30 balls of dough with a dough divider, each weighing about 120 g. Perhaps it's a little sticky, but don't be tempted to add too much extra flour; it'll work!

The dough is molded into balls. Place the buns between each bun on large sheets of baking paper, leaving a little space. Use two pieces of baking paper to make sure that every piece of paper fits onto my bread/pizza shovel, which means that you can slip your shovel under the whole thing to make it easier to put in the oven. Enable the buns to prove themselves before they meet each other and have expanded by about two thirds. Leave them to show overnight in the cold weather.

Preheat the oven to its optimum temperature. In your oven, use a layer of unglazed terracotta tiles for baking the bread. Once you start preheating, make sure that the tiles are put in a cold oven. Place the buns in the oven, carefully. Sprinkle the buns with a mist of water before closing the door to the oven.

Bake for 20 minutes, then turn around the loaves and bake for another 10 minutes. If you hit them, the base of the buns will sound hollow. Glaze the buns with warmed honey when they're dry, use a brush. The honey glaze makes the buns sticky to handle but gives them a beautiful shine, giving a touch of extra sweetness.

13. Sourdough Hot Cross Buns:

Sponge:

- 1/2 cup active (fed) sourdough starter
- 1/2 cup milk

- 1/4 cup all-purpose flour
- 1/2 tablespoon raw sugar

Dough:
- 2 3/4 cups of all-purpose flour plus extra to sprinkle
- 1/2 teaspoon cardamom
- 1/2 teaspoon nutmeg
- 1 teaspoon cinnamon
- 1/4 teaspoon ground allspice
- 1/8 teaspoon ground cloves
- 1/8 cup raw honey
- 1 egg
- 3/4 cup soaked and drained currants or raisins
- 3 tablespoons milk
- 1/4 cup of candied orange peel, chopped finely and packed
- 1/2 teaspoon sea salt
- 4 tablespoons unsalted butter, softened

Glaze:
- 1 T Honey
- 1 orange juice

Prepare the Sponge: add the sourdough starter, milk, all-purpose flour, and sugar and blend until smooth. They're going to be short. The temperature required is 80 degrees F. Place plastic wrap over the sponge and let it stand for 1-2 hours. Everything should be light and bubbly, but some structure should be there.

Mixing the Dough: In a big bowl, place the sourdough starter, flour, and spices. Beat the eggs gently with the raw honey and milk, then add to the mixture of sourdough and flour. Mix until thoroughly mixed and form a very sticky dough. Cover for 20 minutes, then let it sit.

Sprinkle the salt over the batter. Knead until the dough begins looking smooth and light. The dough is going to be very wet, but at this stage, try not to add any flour. Knead until the dough is formed, then knead into the dried fruit and candied orange peel. To assist with this method, I used the bowl scraper. It keeps the dough from being stuck to your fingers and keeps the bowl clean.

Attach the butter, slightly at a time. Knead before the butter is completely packed in. The finishing dough should be very fluffy but not sticky at all. If at this stage it's too sticky, then add a little extra flour.

Enable the dough to sit for 1 hour. Fold it on a floured board or in the bowl after an hour, and allow it to rise for another hour. You can carry on with the shaping below after two hours, or place it in the refrigerator to delay overnight. If the dough has been delayed overnight, remove from the fridge and bring up to room temperature (1-2 hours) before splitting and forming.

Divide and form: divide the dough into 12 parts and form about 2.7 ounces each into a small round ball. Place the rolls in one even arrangement on a greased sheet plate. Cover with plastic wrap to ensure the crust does not form on the surface. Let them grow for 1-2 hours at room temperature. When you hold your rolls in the refrigerator, they probably won't double in size during the final rise, but after they're baked, they will have a pretty decent spring oven.

Baking/Glazing the Buns: Use icing to make the crosses, as described. Bake the buns, and then, while they were dry, glazed them with the honey/orange glaze.

Bake the rolls for 20-30 minutes in a 375 degree Fahrenheit oven until the rolls are golden and within at least 190 degrees.

Heat the orange juice and the honey over medium heat **for the glaze until it begins to boil quickly. Clear the glaze from heat and brush it over the rolls as soon as it is removed from the oven.**

7.5 8 Gluten-Free Bread Recipes

1. Gluten-free starter:

Ingredients:

To make The Starter:

- 1 cup (approx. 120 grams) of whole-grain gluten-free flour per day for 5 to 7 days * 1 cup (8 fluid ounces) spring water or distilled water
- The best whole grain flours for a gluten-free wild yeast starter are: a mixture of sweet white sorghum flour & teff flour; brown rice flour; buckwheat meal.

To Refresh The Starter:

- Every week, forever, and before/after using 1/2 cup (about 70 grams) gum-free gluten-free flour
- 1/2 cup (4 fluid ounces) spring water or distilled water
- You will continue to use the same whole grain flour to refresh and sustain the starter, but it will change the taste and color of the baked goods you create with it.

Instructions:

Make the Morning of Day One starter: Off. Layer 1/2 cup (approx. 60 grams) of whole-grain gluten-free flour(s) and 1/2 cup (4 fluid ounces) of spring or distilled water in a non-reactive container like a glass or ceramic pot. Mix to blend together using a non-reactive mixing spoon (like a wooden or silicone spoon). Cover the container loosely and allow for 8 to 12 hours of sitting on the counter at room temperature.

Day 1 evening: Construct. Remove the bottle cover and add 1/2 cup (about 60 grams) of whole-grain gluten-free flour(s) and 1/2 cup (4 ounces of fluid) spring or distilled water. Mix to blend together using a non-reactive mixing spoon (like a wooden or silicone spoon). Cover the container loosely and allow for 8 to 12 hours of sitting on the counter at room temperature.

Day 2 Morning Building. Remove the bottle cover and add 1/2 cup (about 60 grams) of whole-grain gluten-free flour(s) and 1/2 cup (4 ounces of fluid) spring or distilled water. Mix to blend well using a non-reactive mixing spoon (like a wooden or silicone spoon). Cover the container loosely and allow for 8 to 12 hours of sitting on the counter at room temperature.

Day 2 night out Building. Remove the bottle cover and add 1/2 cup (about 60 grams) of whole-grain gluten-free flour(s) and 1/2 cup (4 ounces of fluid) spring or distilled water. Mix to blend together using a non-reactive mixing spoon (like a wooden or silicone spoon). Cover the container loosely and allow for 8 to 12 hours of sitting on the counter at room temperature.

Days 3 to 7 morning and evening, and beyond: Building and/or Discarding / Loading: remove the bottle cover and check the contents by tapping the jar on the counter to see if bubbles are starting to breach the mixture's surface and sniff it to see whether it has any scent. When it bubbles and has a scent, remove any liquid that has formed on top (called "hooch") + around 1/3 of the amount.

Then feed it: Add 1/2 cup (about 70 grams) of gum-free gluten-free flour and 1/2 cup (4 ounces of fluid) spring or distilled water. Mix to blend together using a non-reactive mixing spoon (like a wooden or silicone spoon). If it is not bubbling and has an odor, do not discard but feed with 1/2 cup of whole-grain flour and 1/2 cup of water as above.

Cover the container loosely and allow for 8 to 12 hours of sitting on the counter at room temperature.

When is the starting starter ready to use? The starter is ready when you've been feeding and discarding for at least one day, and it has doubled in size ever since. Nevertheless, the doubling is quickly interrupted and usually does not last for long. It only has to have happened for you to use it in a bread-baking recipe with confidence (coming soon). You should have fed it within about the previous 12 hours before using the starter. Refresh it after using the properly fed starter (see next step for instructions), allow it to sit on the counter covered for about 12 hours, then refrigerate it until it is ready to be refreshed or used.

Refreshing your starter in practice. An active starter in your refrigerator can be used for baking, then refreshed and stored, covered for about a week. You should refresh it after about a week by extracting it from the refrigerator, discarding around 1/3 of the volume (including any clear liquid or hooch from the top), add 1/2 cup (70 grams) of gum-free gluten-free flour and 1/2 cup (4 fluid ounces) spring water or distilled water, and combining with a non-reactive spoon. Cover the starter and allow it to sit on the counter for approximately 12 hours before returning to the fridge. Repeat the cycle for starter life every week.

2. Seeded Multigrain Gluten-Free Sourdough Bread:

Ingredients:

For the Soaker:

- 3 Tbsp. Whole Rolled Oats
- 3 Tbsp. Whole Flax Seeds
- 3 Tbsp. Hulled Sunflower Seeds
- 3 Tbsp. Red or Tricolor Quinoa rinsed
- 1/3 C (80g) Water room temperature

For the Bread:

- 1/3 C + 2 Tbsp. (100g) Gluten-Free Sourdough Starter previously fed and doubled in size
- 1 C (150g) Millet Flour
- 3 Tbsp. Maple Syrup or Honey
- 1 C (145g) Brown Rice Flour
- 2 1/2 C + 2 Tbsp. or 605g Water 80F (27C)
- 3 Tbsp. Psyllium Husk Powder
- 1 1/4 C (130g) Oat Flour gluten-free
- 1/2 C + 1 Tbsp. or 80g Tapioca Flour
- 1-2 Tbsp. Whole Rolled Oats, gluten-free to sprinkle on top
- 3 1/2 tsp. Fine Sea Salt

Instructions:

For the Soaker: Prepare the soaker by putting the seeds of flax, oats, quinoa, and sunflower in a small cup. Pour water over the top of the soaker to the room temperature. Leave on for around 6-8 hours at room temperature. If you forget to do so, you can pour hot water (hot to the touch) over the soaker before beginning to prepare the bread ingredients.

For the Dough: Trace the inwards of a 9"x5 (3.5 cm X 2 cm) loaf pan with a crisscrossing parchment on all sides to help shape the dough later and to be used as handles to remove the bread from the pan. Use them if you have clips to clamp the parchment to the sides.

Mix the Dough: Add the starter, water, and maple syrup (or honey) into a large mixing bowl. Whisk before the starter is put in. Deposit back.

Whisk the brown rice flour, millet meal, oat flour, tapioca flour, psyllium husk powder, and fine sea salt in a medium mixing bowl. Mix thoroughly so it won't clump when the psyllium husk powder hits the water.

Attach the flour mixture to the water/starter mixture. Using a fork to mix the flour into the water, about a minute, before the dough starts to stiffen. The dough feels like a dense paste. Attach the soaker and knead the dough with your hand and add the soaker for about one minute, until the mixture is uniformly distributed. Scrape any extra dough off your hands and fingers using the fork. The dough would be completely sticky. Place the bowl aside to rest for about 10 minutes. It will get a little stiff as it rests.

Shape and Pan the Dough: Two ways of approaching shaping.

a. When you happen to be in a rush

b. When you've got a little of patience and energy, both will work

A. Scrape the loaf batter into the oven. Use a moist rubber spatula (moist as needed) to gently form the top nudging the loaf's edges inward to produce a beautiful loaf bread in the form of a dome. This needs a bit of practice and finesse. Only make the most of it. Using the parchment 'handles' and draw opposite sides inwards towards the middle of the dough, making the edges round and form. Moisten your fingers or little spatula and smooth the surface to get rid of any lumpy areas.

B. For this method, a bench scraper is required. Moisten with a touch of water on the work surface. Nudge the dough out of the bowl with moistened fingertips, and onto the damp floor. The dough becomes quite sticky. Use the bench scraper as needed to move the dough to moisten your hands and pat the dough into a rough rectangle/log slightly smaller than the loaf pan size. Using wet hands (no flour here), pat and smooth the edges as needed, rocking the dough back and forth to help shape it, smoothing and rounding the top into a rectangular dome. This takes a bit of practice and finesse; just do the best you can.

Scoop the formed dough with a bench scraper and transfer it to the loaf pan in one swift step. Using the parchment 'handles' and draw opposite sides inwards towards the middle of the dough, making the edges round and form. Do several times. Moisten your fingers or little spatula and smooth the surface to get rid of any lumpy areas. Using a moist rubber spatula to gently form the top by nudging inward the loaf's edges to create a beautiful bread loaf in the dome shape.

It's time to refresh (feed) and store your starter for next time.

Bulk Ferment: If you are using delete the clips from the pan. Top with a wet tea towel and allow the dough to ferment overnight at room temperature (if the wet tea towel reaches the top of the loaf, its ok). Depending on the way your starter is involved and the ambient temperature, fermentation can take 12 to 14 hours anywhere.

This recipe is not confirmed after bulk fermentation goes straight into baking the loaf.

Once the dough grows to 1 1/2 times in size, the loaf is ready to bake and has risen to about 1.1/2 (3.8 cm) above the pan lip in the middle. The dough should spring back when pressed gently on top. Bake the loaf: place an oven rack in the middle of the oven and preheat the oven to 550F (288C).

3. Gluten-free sourdough:

Ingredients:

- 1 Tbsp. gluten-free starter
- 8 grams of salt

- 30 grams psyllium husk (not the powder)
- 30 grams of flour (rice, sorghum, millet, and buckwheat) to feed the starter
- 575 grams of water
- 460 grams of flour (use 115g each rice flour, sorghum flour, millet flour, and buckwheat flour)

Instructions:

Start feed the starter! Take out a Tbsp. on your mix the morning. Add about 30 grams of flour and 30 grams of room temperature water to your refrigerator. Cover for about 12 hours, and let ferment. Ideally, it will be at 7 a.m.

Measure 70 grams of it (you'll probably have one more smidge) along with the rest of your ingredients after the starter is beautiful and healthy. Gather a mixing bowl and either a parchment-lined loaf pan or a thinly greased pot.

Making the Loaf: Make the loaf, add the water and the starter to the pot. Push the starter around with your hands to help it dissolve in the mud. Remove the husk of the flour, salt, and psyllium and work the dough together very quickly. When the psyllium hits the liquid, it is going to jell up, and before that happens, you want to combine all the ingredients. You do not worry about over-mixing because there is no gluten in this bread. Ideally, this combination will occur at 7 p.m. If you fed the starter at 7:00 a.m. (Step 1),

Then push your dough into either a loaf pan (for a sandwich loaf) or a greased bowl (for around). Cover with a plastic or a damp towel and allow to rest for about 12 hours on the counter.

Baking the loaf: The next morning: Preheat your oven to 260 C (500 F) if you bake a loaf pan. Uncover your loaf once the oven is preheated, and put into the hot oven. Switch the heat down to 230 C (450 F) when the loaf is in the oven. Bake for 50 minutes or until the sound is hollow. **Take the loaf from the pan carefully, and let it cool on a rack.**

Pull out one of the racks from your oven **to make space while you are baking around. Place the Dutch oven in the oven and preheat it to 260 C (500 F) (or up to 500 F as hot as your oven can go). Leave it to heat for another 30 minutes after the oven has reached temperature to get the Dutch oven completely cooked.**

Invert the dough gently onto a slice of parchment paper **after the 30 minutes is up, which is large enough to lift your bread into the Dutch oven. Running easily, carefully remove your Dutch oven from the oven. Remove the lid and raise the parchment and bread gently into the bowl, taking great care not to touch the bottom. Cover the pot (be careful, it's hot!) with the lid and place the whole Dutch oven back in the oven.**

Switch the heat down to 230 C (450 F) and bake 30 minutes. Take the lid off the Dutch oven gently after 30 minutes (be mindful of steam) and bake for another 20-25 minutes (I like mine a little darker, personally). When baked, remove the pot from the oven and raise the loaf gently by removing the parchment paper.

Cooling: Both loaves would be moist (like a rye loaf), so let it cure (or rest) on the counter for a day before slicing is recommended. It could be cut the same day but is going to be a little softer. Like all gluten-free bread, I suggest that this loaf be toasted for optimum flavor and texture. When cut, it frosts and frozen perfect toasts!

Gluten-Free White Sourdough Bread: Put one tablespoon of flour and one water in a 500ml glass bowl on the first day, and blend together. Cover loosely with cling movies and leave for about 12 hours in a warm location.

Upon passing the 12 hours, add another tablespoon of flour and two more of water, blend together, shield loosely, then leave for 12 more hours.

Stir in one-third tablespoon of flour and one-third of water on day two (24 hours from the start) to blend, cover loosely and leave in a warm place for 12 hours.

Add a tablespoon of flour and water for second feed on day two, blend in to blend, cover loosely and leave in a warm place for 12 hours.

Boost feed by adding two tablespoons of flour and two of water, Combine to blend, Cover, and leave for 12 hours in a warm place for the first day three feed (36 hours after start).

For the second day, three fees add two tablespoons of flour and two more of water, blend together, and loosely cover for another 12 hours.

Your starter should be bubbled at this stage and ready to ferment. Repeat the 12-hour flour and water feeding cycle, unless the starter shows bubbles, and ensure the starter is kept in a continuously warm spot.

Ferment: When the starter is bubbly, pour the starter into a large mixing bowl and then weigh 100 g of the starter.

Apply 150 g flour and 200ml water, mix to make a paste, cover loosely with cling film and leave for 4-12 hours in a warm place before bubbles appear. Your ferment is ready to use when bubbly (you can either dispose of any unused starter after making bread or hold it and feed it regularly before your next baking session).

Dough Dust the inside of the floured banneton, and line a large parchment oven tray.

Attach the white flour, salt, and water to the fermentation bowl and whisk to blend.

Continue to mix to form a sticky mass of dough. Eviting to add flour.

Drizzle the oil over the dough, then turn the mixture in the bowl a few times.

Transfer the dough into the banneton, cover it with an oiled cling film and leave until doubled in size in a warm spot, which can take 4 – 12 hours.

Preheat the oven to heat.

Take off the cling film and turn the bread out of the banneton very gently onto the prepared oven tray.

Bake inside 50-60 minutes. If the base sounds hollow, you'll know the bread is baked.

Cool the loaf over a rack of wire.

4. Gluten-free Sourdough Boule:

Gluten-free Sourdough Starter:

- Millet Flour
- Buckwheat Flour
- Tapioca Flour
- Rice Flour
- Xanthan Gum
- Salt
- Extra virgin olive oil
- Sugar
- Apple Cider Vinegar

Make sure that your sourdough starter is at least a week old and solid because there's plenty of bubbling in it, and it bubbles up a few hours after feeding. If you have a mature starter, feed it twice a day, at least before you bake the bread.

Knead the bread until all the flours are well mixed in. You don't have to knead sourdough bread too long, but I like to offer it in the stand mixer for at least three or four minutes to ensure I have the right texture.

The boule dough's proper texture should be slightly tacky but not so sticky or loose that you cannot work with it.

The gluten-free bread only requires one rise, unlike wheat bread or other gluten-free flours. Within the oven, you will need to preheat your dutch oven to get it to the right temperature for your bread.

5. Easy Gluten-Free Sourdough Bread:

Ingredients:

- 2 cups gluten-free flour blend
- 1/2 c sourdough starter
- 1 1/2 tsp. Kosher salt
- Water as required

Instructions:

Put the dry ingredients in a bowl and whisk. Remove water and starter sourdough. You want a flour, like a pancake batter, warm.

Allow it to grow at room temperature for 12–24 hours. Put aside a few to use for another time as your starter. In a greased loaf pan, bake at 350-400 for 1 hour.

Until slicing, cool.

6. Gluten-Free Sourdough Bread:

Ingredients:

- Gluten-Free Starter 100g/ 5 Tablespoons
- Water 600g/ 2⅔ cup
- **Gluten-Free Flour 450g/ 2¾ cup**

- **Buckwheat Flour 45g/ ⅓ cup**
- **Psyllium Husk 35g/ 3 Tablespoons**

Instructions:

Feed your thriving starter generously with flour and water the evening before you intend on baking, taking it to a thicker consistency of pancake batter.

Scale all of your ingredients into a bowl, and stir until the dough has come together with your hand or bowl scraper. It will be very sticky, but a moist cookie dough will have the texture. To get it there, if you need to add flour or water, add it one tablespoon at a time.

To prove this, transfer the dough to a vessel of your choice. Using a parchment-lined bowl to test your flour, wrapped in plastic to keep it moist, if you want to make a round loaf; Move your dough to a well-greased or parchment-lined 9x5 "loaf pan, if you want a sandwich.

Proofing-You can prove your bread in two ways.

The faster way: Set your oven to 100 ° F and put the rack in the middle of the oven that you would like to bake unhindered. Leave the dough in the oven for about 4 hours to prove and test its progress every hour or so. Let the dough rise until double. Remove the dough from the oven, then set it to 425 ° F for 30 minutes to preheat.

The slower way: cover your dough with oiled plastic wrap, and let sit for 8-9 hours at room temperature. Preheat your oven at 425 ° F for 30 minutes, until the dough has nearly doubled. This method yields a more developed smelly flavor.

If you bake a round loaf, the dough will be raised by the parchment and put directly on a sheet tray, baked stone, or lowered gently into a pre-heated Dutch oven with a lid for baking. When baking in a loaf pan, remove the plastic and put it directly into the oven.

Bake within 30 minutes. You can remove the Dutch oven lid at this stage and start cooking for 20-30 more minutes. Gently tap on the dough, listening for a hollow echo.

Before slicing, let the bread cool down, then enjoy it!

7. Amazing Gluten-Free Bread:

Ingredients:

Sourdough Ferment

- 2 cups of active gluten-free sourdough starter
- 1 cups of filtered water (chlorine-free)
- 2 1/2 cups of the gluten-free bread flour mix

Other Ingredients

- 1 tsp. baking soda
- 1 tsp. salt
- 1/4 cup psyllium husk
- 3 eggs

Instructions:

Mix the starter with water and flour, then keep it warm for 2-12 hours to ferment. That is necessary to hydrate the flour thoroughly. The sourdough starter also helps break down the complex carbohydrates, thereby enhancing this bread's texture.

Sprinkle the psyllium husk, salt, baking soda over the sourdough ferment, when you are about to bake bread. The split in the shells and everything blends together. The sourdough can be very hard, so you'll have to beat the eggs in it.

Drop into the pan of a well-oiled sandwich. The acidic sourdough mix will instantly cause the baking soda to start working, so allow it to rise for just 30 minutes before baking.

Bake 60-75 min at 400F (until fully cooked and browned).

8. Gluten-Free Sourdough Bread:

Ingredients:

- 2 teaspoons xanthan gum
- 3 cups all-purpose gluten-free flour blend
- ¼ cup sugar
- ¼ teaspoon cream of tartar
- 2 teaspoons active dry yeast
- 1½ teaspoons kosher salt
- 3 Tablespoons of unsalted butter or dairy-free substitute butter, melted and cooled
- 1½ cups warm milk (about 100°F)
- 1 cup "fed" Sourdough Starter

Instructions:

A 9x5-inch loaf pan is generously greased. Deposit back. Mix the flour, xanthan gum, tartar cream, sugar, salt, and yeast in the bowl of a stand mixer fitted with the paddle attachment. Add Starter Sourdough and butter and blend.

Put in the milk in a slow, steady current, with the mixer on low. After the flour has started to absorb the liquids, beat the ingredients for 4 to 6 minutes at a minimum medium pace. The dough is going to be pretty sticky-thicker than the cake batter, not as thick as the cookie dough. In the greased loaf pan, scrape the dough and smooth the top with wet hands.

Enable the dough to rise for 30 to 45 minutes in a dry, humid place or till it has about doubled in size. (This may take longer in a colder, more sterile environment. If the atmosphere is warm and humid, it will take less time.) Preheat the oven to 400 ° F as the dough goes up.

Bake, the loaf for 40 to 45 minutes in a preheated oven or until a suitable, golden-brown crust, has formed on top.

Conclusion

Dating back tens of thousands of years, Sourdough is the oldest type of leavened bread in the world. And if it has something of a revival, it's neither modern nor a fad. Indeed, the only reasonably new thing about sourdough is how it is talked of today since sourdough was known as "bread" once upon a time.

The leavening (or rising) of dough has, for centuries, been a by-product of an essential process called fermentation. Fermentation sees natural bacteria and yeasts digesting the carbohydrates present in a batter made of flour and water, creating carbon dioxide bubbles that cause it to rise. The process also produces lactic and acetic acids, which account for the natural fermented bread's tangy, sour aroma and flavor.

'Natural fermentation' begins with a starter-a pre-fermented, highly active flour mixture that the baker cultivates and preserves. Once that starter is introduced into a higher quantity of flour, water, and salt, with all its yeasts and bacteria, it becomes an airy, tangy dough, which can be baked into what we now know as sourdough bread.

The sourdough has one more important ingredient: work. Baking with natural yeasts is not something that well translates precision ingredients, timings, and temperatures into the modern recipe format. It's much freer than that, an environmentally and personally special thing.

For this reason, you can rarely get the results you want after a recipe. The problem with the early days is that you are afraid if you had to step away from the method and unable to understand what it should be.

While baking can sound daunting in this way, it is an advantageous and exciting skill to learn. This will guide you away from the recipes and trust your intuition.

Instead of a strict recipe, this book has included all the basics of sourdough starter and science behind its working, so that you can make changes as you want to, knowing that it will not turn out as a disaster.

When you hate carbs but enjoy bread, sourdough may be the answer to your wishes. However, not all bread is created equal. Sourdough bread goes through a long cycle of fermentation that breaks down starches, so it is lower than other types of bread on the glycemic index. In a study comparing white bread, whole wheat bread, whole grain wheat barley bread, and white sourdough bread, the lowest levels of blood sugar and insulin in people who consumed sourdough bread were found. Also, their decreased glucose levels remained until the next meal.

For most people to eat more sourdough bread, they don't need much convincing. Reason enough is the dynamic taste, the crusty exterior, and the airy interior. But even if you're fond of sourdough bread, making it at home can be overwhelming, particularly if you've never taken care of culture before.

It is possible to buy sourdough loaves made traditionally, but they are most often sold at artisan bakeries and can be costly. Many of the bread in the grocery store branded as sourdough is made with commercial baker's yeast, with a little sourdough added for flavoring.

Don't worry: Making sourdough bread at home isn't that hard. It is much easier to maintain a healthy sourdough culture than many people make it, and no-knead sourdough bread takes time but minimal effort.

Sourdough fans (and other artisan food) spend weeks brewing their perfect culture-some do it for health benefits, while others do it for the pure joy of making great bread.

Sourdough bread provides a perfect alternative to regular bread. Its lower levels of phytate make it nutritious and more comfortable to digest.

Sourdough bread also tends to raise blood sugar levels less, making it a choice for those who track their sugar in the blood.

Given anything, it's worth a try.

Only note that sourdough bread can be made from nearly any kind of flour, so pick a whole variety of grains.

It will be the principal takeaway, don't let your starter go hungry. Do feed it, and make it ferment a little until it goes into the refrigerator. If you drop it out, it'll eat all of the sugar quickly and become sourer, but it will also be starving and might not be as involved and happy.

It means you can now make your bread, crackers, pancakes, waffles, biscuits, muffins, tortillas, pasta, pastry crust, cookies, cakes, English cupcakes, and quick bread all with your trusty and very happy home starter.

One final note: don't worry about playing and having fun — after all, what's the worst thing that can happen? In almost every case, no matter what comes out of your microwave, it's completely edible and delicious. Many of your significant baking changes came from events that were opportunities for you to learn and develop as a baker.

Bread Machine Cookbook for Beginners

Learn how to make homemade bread with over 50 quick recipes for baking pizza, sweet sourdough pastry and gluten free bread

By

Timothy Collins

© **Copyright 2020 by Timothy Collins- All rights reserved.**

This document is geared towards providing exact and reliable information in regard to the topic and issue covered. The publication is sold with the idea that the publisher is not required to render accounting, officially permitted, or otherwise, qualified services. If advice is necessary, legal or professional, a practiced individual in the profession should be ordered.

From a Declaration of Principles which was accepted and approved equally by a Committee of the American Bar Association and a Committee of Publishers and Associations.

In no way is it legal to reproduce, duplicate, or transmit any part of this document in either electronic means or in printed format. Recording of this publication is strictly prohibited and any storage of this document is not allowed unless with written permission from the publisher. All rights reserved.

The information provided herein is stated to be truthful and consistent, in that any liability, in terms of inattention or otherwise, by any usage or abuse of any policies, processes, or directions contained within is the solitary and utter responsibility of the recipient reader. Under no circumstances will any legal responsibility or blame be held against the publisher for any reparation, damages, or monetary loss due to the information herein, either directly or indirectly.

Respective authors own all copyrights not held by the publisher.

The information herein is offered for informational purposes solely and is universal as so. The presentation of the information is without contract or any type of guarantee assurance.

The trademarks that are used are without any consent, and the publication of the trademark is without permission or backing by the trademark owner.

All trademarks and brands within this book are for clarifying purposes only and are the owned by the owners themselves, not affiliated with this document.

Table of content

CHAPTER 1: INTRODUCTION OF BREAD MAKING MACHINE 12

1.1 What is a Bread Machine? 12

1.2 How does Bread Machine Work? 16

1.3 Difference between a Classic Bread and Homemade Bread 17

1.4 Pros and Cons of Bread Machine 21

1.5 Golden Rules of Using a Bread Machine 23

CHAPTER 2: COMMON INGREDIENTS TO MAKE BREAD 32

2.1 Different Types of Flours 34

2.2 Selection of Best Type of Yeast 36

CHAPTER 3: SOURDOUGH BREAD 39

3.1 Understanding the Basics of Sourdough Bread 39

3.2 Benefits of Sourdough Bread 41

CHAPTER 4: BENEFITS OF SOURDOUGH BREAD FOR CELIAC DISEASE 45

4.1 What is Celiac Disease? 45

4.2 Benefits of Sourdough Bread for Celiac Disease 46

CHAPTER 5: BREAD MACHINE SALTY RECIPES 49

5.1 Simple White Bread Recipe 49

5.2 Whole Wheat Bread Recipe 51

5.3 Basil bread with Tomato and Mozzarella cheese recipe 52

5.4 Barley Bread Recipe 53

5.5 Black pepper onion bread recipe 55

5.6 Blue Cheese Potato Bread Recipe 56

5.7 Rye Bread Recipe 57

5.8 Bacon Onion Cheese Bread Recipe 59

5.9 Asiago Cheese Bread Recipe 61

5.10 Basic Plain Bagel Recipe 62

5.11 Boule bread recipe 64

5.12 Light Oat Bread Recipe 65

5.13 Steakhouse Wheat Bread Recipe: 66

5.14 Bread Machine Pretzels 67

5.15 Bread Machine Pizza Dough 69

5.16 Recipe Bread Machine Italian Bread 69

5.17 A recipe for Ciabatta bread 70

5.18 Dill Bread Recipe: 71

5.19 Bread Machine Onion and Olive Bread 72

5.20 Breakfast Pastry Recipe 74

5.21 Cheese and Beer Bread Recipe 76

5.22 German Dumplings Spätzle Recipe 77

5.23 Fettuccine Alfredo Recipe 78

5.24 Ginger Bread Recipe 79

5.25 Garlic Bread Recipe 81

5. 26 Herb and Parmesan Bread 82

5.27 Indian Naan Bread 83

5.28 Mozzarella Cheese and Pepperoni Bread 85

5.29 Peanut Butter Bread Recipe 86

5.30 Rice Bread Recipe 87

5.31 Semolina Bread Recipe 88

5.32 Shepherd's bread Recipe 90

5.33 Sourdough Buns Recipe 91

CHAPTER 6: BREAD MACHINE SWEET RECIPES 93

6.1 Sourdough Bread Recipe 93

6.2 Sourdough Nut Butter Cookies 95

6.3 Sourdough Banana Bread in the Bread Machine 96

6.4 Buttery Butternut Squash Bread Recipe: 97

6.5 Apricot Bread Cake Recipe 98

6.6 Almond Bread Cake Recipe 100

6.7 Chocolate Pumpkin Bread Cake Recipe 101

6.8 Cinnamon Applesauce Bread Recipe 103

6.9 Date Nut Bread Recipe 104

6.10 Fruit Bread Recipe 105

6.11 Lemon Bread Cake Recipe 106

6.12 Red Velvet Cake Recipe 107

6.13 Sweet cinnamon coffee cake 109

6.14 Cinnamon Raisin Bread 110

6.15 Orange Nut Cake Bread Recipe 111

6.16 Pina Colada Bread Recipe 112

6.17 Banana Chocolate Chip Bread Recipe 113

6.18 Carrot Cake Recipe 115

CHAPTER 7: BREAD MACHINE GLUTEN-FREE RECIPES
.... 117

7.1 Gluten-Free Pear Cake Bread Recipe 117

7.2 100% Buckwheat Bread (Gluten-Free) Recipe 118

7.3 Corn Bread Gluten-Free Recipe 120

7.4 Gluten-Free Banana Bread Recipe 122

7.5 Gluten-Free Vegan Bread Recipe 123

7.6 Gluten-Free Chocolate Chip Cookies Recipe 124

7.7 Gluten Free Pizza Dough Recipe 125

7.8 Gluten-Free White Bread 126

7.9 Gluten-Free Bagels Recipe 127

7.10 Gluten-Free French bread Recipe 130

7.11 Gluten-Free White Bread 131

7.12 Gluten-Free Nut and Seed Bread Recipe 132

7.13 Gluten-Free Crusty Boule Bread Recipe 133

7.14 Easy Gluten Free Dairy Free Bread Recipe **135**

7.15 Easy Gluten-Free Sandwich Bread **136**

7.16 Cinnamon Raisin Bread-Machine Bread Recipe [Vegan / Gluten Free] Yields 1 ....**138**

CONCLUSION 140

REFERENCES 142

Introduction

A bread machine or bread maker is a home appliance designed to convert raw ingredients into baked pieces of bread. It consists of a bread pan (or "tin"), with one or more built-in paddles at the bottom, placed in the center of a small special-purpose oven. This small oven is normally operated by a control panel via a simple built-in device using the input settings. Some bread machines have specific cycles for various styles of dough — including white bread, whole grain, European-style (sometimes called "French"), and dough-only (for pizza dough and formed loaves baked in a traditional oven). Some also have a timer to enable the bread machine to work without attendance from the operator, and some high-end models allow the user to program a customized period.

The first bread maker was launched by Matsushita Electric Industrial Co. (now Panasonic) in Japan in 1986, based on a year of work by project engineers and software developer Tanaka, who trained with the head baker at Osaka Hotel to know how to knead bread optimally and involved inserting special ribs inside the machine. The machines of the Funai Electric Company added a fan for cooling bread and claimed to make the first automatic bread machine.

How a bread machine works: you put the paddle inside the pan. You weigh the ingredients with tin out of the oven and load them up. Then you need to do is, pick the setting you want to use from the electronic control panel, close the lid, and wait. If you have a glass lid in your bread maker, you can see what they are doing.

If the cover is opaque, the imagination will have to be listened to and used. One of the first sounds you will hear is the motor whirling on the pump as the paddle turns round, kneading the dough.

Then, during the rising phase, everything will go quiet. Next, during the proving, you can hear more kneading and another time of stillness. Finally, the oven turns on, you will see steam coming up through the exhaust vent, and a few minutes later, you will start smelling the delicious aroma of baking bread. The basic process of bread making is mostly automatic, but most devices come with books of the recipe to make more sophisticated types of dough.

Main ingredients of bread are water, salt, sugar, flour and yeast. Different types of flours are available like whole wheat flour, white wheat flour, bread flour and all-purpose flour. Three types of yeast are available: active dry yeast, instant yeast and rapid rise yeast.

Yeast bread is a bread whose dough rises as a result of the gas being created as the grain ferments during the bread-making process.

Most leavened bread uses industrial baker yeast to assist the rise of the dough. Traditional sourdough fermentation, however, relies on "wild yeast" and lactic acid bacteria, which naturally occur in flour to leaven the bread.

Wild yeast avoids acidic conditions more than baker's yeast. That's what helps it to work with bacteria that generate lactic acid to help the dough rise.

The mixture of wild yeast, lactic acid bacteria, flour, and water used to produce sourdough bread is called a "starter." The starter ferments the sugars in the bread dough during the bread-making process, allowing the bread to rise and develop its characteristic flavor.

Sourdough bread must ferment and grow much longer than other types of bread, which is what produces its distinctive texture.

Celiac disease is a severe autoimmune disease that occurs in genetically predisposed people, where gluten ingestion causes damage to the small intestine. One in every 100 people worldwide is estimated to be affected. Two and a half million Americans are undiagnosed and are at risk for complications of long-term health.

If anyone with celiac disease eats gluten (a protein found in wheat, rye, and barley), their body mounts an immune response which attacks the small intestine. These attacks result in damage to the villi, small finger-like projections that line the small intestine that facilitates the absorption of nutrients. When the villi get damaged, nutrients cannot be properly absorbed into the body.

Sourdough breads is very useful for celiac patients.

Chapter 1: Introduction of Bread Making Machine

Bread is a baked meal that can be made from various types of flour. The dough usually consists of water and flour. Bread is made in hundreds of shapes, sizes, characteristics, and textures. Proportions and forms of flour and other ingredients vary, as do preparation methods.

Bread has been one of the essential foods in history, as it is one of the oldest artificial foods, too. In fact, people made bread from the dawn of farming.

With every meal of the day, people of all cultures eat the bread in various ways. It can be eaten as part of the meal, or as an individual snack. Bread can be baked in the oven or can be made in bread makers. People usually bake bread in the oven. Yet more and more people turn to special bread machines at home to bake fresh bread.

1.1 What is a Bread Machine?

A bread maker, or bread machine, is a kitchen gadget. The tool consists of a bread pan or tin with built-in paddles, placed in the center of a small multi-purpose, special oven.

Different types of bread machines

Majority of bread making devices would be a little different. This is because every variation of a bread maker is built to serve a specific purpose. Below we'll be addressing the most common types of bread makers available in the modern market.

Vertical

Most bread machines bake loaves, which are placed vertically, as the shape of baking tin is vertical. This bread machine style features one kneading paddle only.

Horizontal

Some bread makers have two kneading paddles inside the pot. These bread machines bake horizontal bread, just like the one that you get from the store's bakery.

Small

Small Bread makers are perfect for the limited space in the kitchen or if you don't eat much bread. These little helpers in the kitchen do not take much of the counter space and just produce enough bread for a couple or a person.

Large

Large bread machines come in handy in big families – when you have a lot of people at the table, bread can disappear quite fast. Big bread makers making 3 lb. of bread loaves are capable of feeding a large family.

Gluten free

With the great abundance of bread maker models on the market, there are definitely those designed to meet the needs of safe eaters

What kind of bread can a bread machine produce?

Bread making machine control panel: most bread makers, have several different programs for making a loaf of many different kinds. When using various kinds of flour and mixing the other ingredients, you can make white bread, whole-meal, or special loaves. On its display panel, you can see the various options. For different loaves of bread, at the outset, you simply put a slightly different mix into the tin and pick a different program from the panel, and the bread maker can automatically manage different kneading, rising and baking times, and so on. (Like French loaves get longer rising time, whole-meal loaves get more preheating, sweetbreads have longer kneading and rising times, and dark, crusty bread get extra baking time.) Some bread makers also give a "fast-bake" (energy-saving mode) that delivers your loaf in about half the time, but you'll get a slightly less perfect results. Baking bread takes time and patience and, if you hurry it, you can't expect perfect results.

How is a bread machine manufactured?

The bread maker consists of several pieces. The bread machine is basically a compact electric oven that holds inside a single, large tin of bread. The tin itself is a bit different – it has an axle underneath, which is connected to an electric motor below.

At the bottom of the box, a small metal paddle is attached to the axle. The paddle is responsible for having the dough kneaded. The axle itself is coated with a wax impervious to salt. Let's look in-depth at each of the bread machine parts:

The lid on top of the bread machine comes either with the viewing window or without it the control panel is also placed on top of the bread machine for comfort purposes

There is a steam vent in the center of the lid that exhausts the steam in the baking process. Some of the bread machines also have an air vent on the side of the cooker so that the dough may rise in the tin.

Baking tin cover built into the folding frame, folding, lid, in the middle, contains steam exhaust vent.

The exhaust port allows steam to flow through the cover and escape from the baking tin.

The air vent allows air to rise up into the dough.

The whole where tin screws firmly into a position where the motorized axle that turns the kneading paddle is located at its center

The outer plastic case insulates the oven and makes it secure to reach the bread maker during service.

Easy LCD monitor, and touch control panel wipe-clean

Recessed groove, where the lid's bottom locks in

Removable baking tin can simultaneously bake one loaf.

Detachable kneading paddle clicks on an axle in a waterproof cover, slotted across the middle of the container

The first bread maker was launched by Matsushita Electric Industrial Co. (now Panasonic) in Japan in 1986, based on a year of work by project engineers and software developer Tanaka, who trained with the head baker at Osaka Hotel to know how to knead bread optimally and involved inserting special ribs inside the machine. The machines of the Funai Electric Company added a fan for cooling bread and claimed to make the first automatic bread machine.

A decade later, they became famous in the U.K., Australia, and the U.S. Because of the fixed loaf shape and the short service cycle, bread machines are not feasible for industrial use, but they are very suitable for home use, delivering their best performance when handling kneaded doughs.

1.2 How does Bread Machine Work?

The great thing about an automatic bread machine for you is that it performs all these processes. A bread making machine is essentially a small electric oven that holds one large, single tin of bread. The tin is special: it has an axle at the bottom underneath, which connects to an electric motor. A tiny metal paddle clicks on the inside tin axle. A waterproof seal protects the hinge so that none of your bread mixtures can escape.

So how does all of that work? Next, you put the paddle inside the pan. You weigh the ingredients with tin out of the oven and load them up. Then you need to do is, pick the setting you want to use from the electronic control panel, close the lid, and wait. If you have a glass lid in your bread maker, you can see what they are doing. If the cover is opaque, the imagination will have to be listened to and used. One of the first sounds you will hear is the motor whirling on the pump as the paddle turns round, kneading the dough. Then, during the rising phase, everything will go quiet. Next, during the proving, you can hear more kneading and another time of stillness.

Finally, the oven turns on, you will see steam coming up through the exhaust vent, and a few minutes later, you will start smelling the delicious aroma of baking bread. The basic process of bread making is mostly automatic, but most devices come with books of the recipe to make more sophisticated types of dough.

Some bread makers have other features, such as an integrated memory so they can withstand a few minutes of short power outages ("blackouts"): they recall what they were doing and start when the power returns. Many bread making machines also have the ability to make a delayed start, so you can put in the ingredients before going to bed and wake up in the morning to a freshly baked loaf. (It's worth noting, though, that if you leave a loaf in a hot machine after it's done, it's going to go on cooking and the crust gets noticeably harder — perhaps to your taste, maybe not.) (Woodford., 2019).

1.3 Difference between a Classic Bread and Homemade Bread

Classic bread

The bread was baked in the same way for thousands of years, using whole grain flour and leaven. Not only was this bread delicious, but it also, covered, and healed the body. A method of increasing the shelf life of flour was discovered in the 19th century by extracting the wheat germ and bran coating, leaving only the starchy endosperm portion of the grain behind. This flour lasted a lot longer, but it also lost much of its nutritional value. All bran and germ healthy proteins, fats, vitamins, minerals, and fiber were removed. Dry yeast was also produced at that time, replacing the traditional leaven blocks. Technology "improved" white flour through the 20th century by introducing chemicals, sugars, fats, and other additives.

And now we've got fresh bread of the 21st century. Our modern bread is inclusive of additives and preservatives, a far cry from what our ancestors ate. Even with those additives, after three days, modern bread begins to mold. It is, moreover, often overcooked, dehydrated, frozen and thawed, and extruded by special machines. All this leads to a product that, although cheap to produce, can be difficult to digest, and can have devastating effects on the body if consumed regularly. Organic bread, which fared marginally better than "natural" bread but still is far from being a healthy food.

Unlike whole grain flour, "refined" flour does not have healthy fats or high-quality proteins but is mostly plain fiber-free sugars. Some vitamins and minerals are applied back to the food, seeking to make it look healthier. These empty calories are not filling up, and because of that, people tend to eat too much of it.

2. Sticks to the intestines:

Wheat gluten is practically indigestible and can gradually decompose in the intestines. It can eventually lead to intestinal coating, which creates an atmosphere in which yeasts and fungi can develop. That can lead to smoke, eczema, shortness of breath, and arrhythmia of the heart. This can also cause you to eat more, particularly simple sugar food. Because of these fungal growths, the intestines may also consume fewer nutrients.

3. Clogs the blood:

Clogged intestines produce blood toxins. These toxins are often expressed in skin conditions such as acne, eczema, dermatitis, and allergic rashes. Such contaminants in the past can be the product of stuff we ate and drank for up to three months. What you eat determines your blood condition to a large degree.

Limiting processed food can result in cleaner intestines, leading to cleaner blood. Pureblood leaves you feeling fresher and healthier, with greater strength. This can be seen in your skin condition – these issues also tend to clear up soon after your diet changes.

Body acidification:

A strongly acidic condition produces a surplus of intestinal gluten and leaven. This causes the intestinal mucous to get disturbed. This can contribute to compounds that enter the bloodstream, such as undigested protein, milk caseins, and gluten itself. This acid condition also makes burning fat more difficult for the body. Furthermore, it provides a more favorable atmosphere for unhealthy species to survive. Acidity is often cited as a major cause of cancer. Lastly, the acid removes calcium, which can contribute to osteoporosis.

Homemade bread with bread machine

1. Using a Bread Maker is cheaper than buying your bread in a store. Making bread using the bread maker is really cheap, about 30p-50p per simple loaf made including ingredients and machine running. You get a lot better quality loaf of bread for this than if you bought the bread at the supermarket. You can, of course, get discounts and cheap bread offers at the end of the day if you make the right time.

2. There are easily seen health benefits when you make your own bread by using a bread maker or a cooker, you have much more control over the ingredients that go into it than if you shop in a supermarket. The Ingredients for a plain white loaf you make yourself would be: Strong white bread flour, salt, sugar, butter or oil, leaven, and warm water.

You often have to fly when you buy a pre-packed loaf from the supermarket, so it isn't so new. It is added to keep things fresher.

The ingredients of a shop-bought pre-wrapped loaf (Note these are the ingredients are of a similar loaf others may be different) Wheat Flour with Calcium, Iron, Thiamin (B1), Niacin (B3) Water, Seed Mix (13 percent), malted barley flour, yeast, vegetable oil, sugar and salt, wheat gluten, and then the additives: Emulsifiers: E471, E472e, E481, Soya Flour, Preservative: Flour treatment

The Bread Machine is easy to use

The machines are very easy to use themselves. Just need to be correct in your measurements.

4. Making bread is much simpler. You will find it much easier to make bread that way. You just weigh the ingredients out and pop them into the machine.

No sloppy kneading or mixing.

Accessibility Note: If you have and have trouble making bread with your muscles, this way is less of a strain on your muscles.

448

6. The bread consistency & superior taste!! The taste-poor. There is nothing like turning off, still warm and enjoying a piece of freshly baked bread. Sweet, so fuzzy and so new in your mouth, it just dissolves.

You can add ingredients of your own choice while making your own bread.

1.4 Pros and Cons of Bread Machine

Advantages:

Cleaning

Quite simple-it's just the baking dish that needs to be cleaned, but because the bread still let go quickly, it's always pointless to do something other than removing the piece of bread that sits on the shaft to the dough hook.

Most bread machines are equipped with Teflon coating, so it is easy to remove the pieces, so generally place them in the dishwasher.

Kneading.

The bread machine is also used to knead dough in the bread maker for certain forms of bread you don't want to bake in. you manage to knead the dough into buns, cookies, and cake with success.

Odor to fresh bread

It's great that you can be sure with the timer that your cup of coffee will still be with freshly made bread in the morning or evening. The smell of freshly baked bread from the baking machine definitely makes getting out of bed in the morning easier.

Master Baking

If you want to play with making various new bread and create new recipes, so you feel like a true champion of baking, then a bread maker is an absolute success. You can try with Graham flour, cracked wheat kernels, walnuts, mixed rye bread and a lot more.

It makes healthy bread

It's easy to clean, and setup is incredibly easy. Someone will soon find their favorite recipes, but playing with kneading/raising / baking times and ingredients is also very enjoyable.

Disadvantages

Noise.

The kneading process is a rational noisy affair that lasts a total of 30-40 minutes. It might not be possible to stop all the bread maker's noise, but if you live in a tiny apartment or home, it won't bother you anywhere.

This means you'll most likely be awakened by the noise if it starts kneading the dough 3 hours before you need to get up to the delicious freshly baked bread in the morning.

Holes in bread

You will just got used to it. In the beginning, there will be a hole in your bread, but latter you will get used to it, so you won't even call it a drawback, because it's so small. If it was because of this that people had to waste the bread, they must have done something wrong.

Top of bread not fully baked

Obviously, the top is not baked as much as the sides and the bottom but baked enough. You can't make bread on top because it's baked with a golden-brown crust.

Form

Bread baked in a bread machine is square and not like the bread from the bakery or supermarket. It took you and your family a little to get used to.

The size of a sandwich. If you're a big family, you need to be mindful that regular on-the-market equipment probably won't bake a big enough bread. However, some bread makers are big enough in size and can meet most family needs, but sadly the price is always higher too.

1.5 Golden Rules of Using a Bread Machine

How to use a bread machine for perfect results?

The baking cycle is pretty much the same everywhere, regardless of which bread machine you pick. You load ingredients into the tin, then put the bread pan inside the machine and pick the setting you need.

Depending on the model, the standard baking cycle takes between 2 and 5 hours. It is recommended that a loaf be put on a wire rack at the end of the baking process to cool down before eating it. Just like the handmade bread recipe, you'll need four key ingredients:

- Yeast (or starter)
- Flour Liquid (usually water or milk)
- Salt (for flavoring and fermentation control)
- In addition to the main ingredients, you add and any other extras you want, including raisins, nuts, chocolate chips, etc.

Although bread baking may seem very basic and simple, there are some tips to make you a bread baking pro with a bread machine:

- Check the instructions / manual and follow them. The dry ingredients should be added first with some bread makers; with others, the wet ingredients go in first.

- In addition, when reading bread baking recipes, keep in mind that not all bread makers are created equal – some products make loaves of 1 pound, others make loaves of 1, 5 and 2 pounds. Some versions of the bread machine will bake 3-pound loaves.
- When trying out a new recipe, the amounts of ingredients must be matched with the recipes usually used in the bread machine. It is important that you don't exceed the bread machine pan capacity.

Pouring Flour in Bread Maker

The use of a delayed mix cycle is not recommended in the event that the recipe calls for milk.

Mix the warm water, olive oil, salt, flour, and yeast in the bread pan, if you need to make pizza dough in your bread machine.

Set the bread maker to program 'Pizza Dough' according to your bread maker's manual. When your dough is ready for further processing, you can move it to a lightly floured surface.

Maintenance and cleaning your bread machine?

Caring for your bread maker

The bread maker has certainly revolutionized kitchen life. You don't need to do the hard work anymore to get the lovely scent of fresh bread all over your house. However, the fact it has made it so convenient for us means we still fail to take care of it properly.

In fact, routine maintenance is very easy and should be performed frequently. Perhaps that's why we are inclined to forget that often. In reality, after each new loaf is baked, routine machine cleaning will take place.

Do you make sure that your bread machine works to its best?

Eventually, you'll get used to doing this maintenance and have your bread machine for years and years.

Here are some basic steps you should do routinely to keep your bread baking machine at its best.

- The main step is to always read the manual.
- Each model of a bread machine is slightly different, so be sure to obey any clear guidelines given in the instructions.
- Taking the time to read the instructions and try to execute them. Reading the fine print can be a little tedious, but it's much better to prevent any problems than trying to address them in the future.

General cleaning

1. Always keeps your bread maker clean

2. Careful cleaning should ensure your bread machine runs smoothly after use.

3. Even before doing any cleaning or repairs, make sure that the system has cooled and unplugged completely.

Put the bread maker NOT in water or a dishwasher. The majority of bread pans are not suitable for dishwashing. It is due to the bearing, which needs some lubrication on the underside of the plate. Even though there are many brands that market their pans and removable parts as a secure dishwasher, that will surely damage the pan finish and the other parts. Cleaning the pans and parts with mild dish soap, rinsing them, and drying them very well. When the non-stick coating surface produces a slight, unintentional mark, the heat, moisture, and detergent in a dishwasher will ensure its demise.

Tip: Do not use benzene, scrubbing brushes, or chemical cleaners because this can cause harm to the equipment. To clean the bread maker using only a mild, non-abrasive cleanser. Never clean the interior of your machine with something abrasive. It will scratch it and not only makes it less appealing but will make it harder to clean up next time, you are using the bread maker, NOT metal utensils. This damages the non-stick pan, as well as other pieces.

To prevent rusting of your bread machine, it is important to dry all parts of the bread machine.

It is not recommended to soak pieces of bread, making machines for more than 30 minutes. Excessive soaking can cause bread maker parts to become rusty and corrosive.

Cleaning inside bread machine

The first step is to unplug and let the bread machine cool. When you've baked for the day, and the bread maker's cooled down.

Remove the baking pan from the bread maker when the unit is cool and unplugged. Then, when the pan is removed, take the time to look at the bottom of your bread machine and take a brief moment to brush or dab the crumbs and the leftover flour from the bottom of the machine. Since your bread machine includes heating elements, these "meal-bits" start baking and re-baking for every new loaf. They will burn over time and can affect your machine's efficiency, and give your freshly baked loaf a burnt smell.

Stop these ending up as burnt scraps by making sure you remove them all before you reuse your bread maker. The best way to do so is to use your vacuum cleaner, which has a hose attachment to clear much of it (carefully). You should then wipe everything left and stuck on breadcrumbs from the bottom of the machine carefully by wiping them away with a paper towel or a slightly wet, non-abrasive cleaning cloth. Be gentle surrounding the product. Remove all the debris with care.

Do NOT pour water into the cavity of the oven to avoid damage to the heating function. The most significant thing to stop is getting your bread machine's gears wet. Only make sure when cleaning it, you never spill water or other liquids directly into the machine's rim. The bread pan that contains liquids such as water and milk, but the machine's bottom is not designed for liquids of any sort. These gears work the kneading blade, and having them moist will seriously harm your bread machine's service.

Caution: Do not bend the heating device that is in the bread maker's interior.

Cleaning the top or sides of the bread maker

If the bread has risen high and baked to the top or sides of the oven, remove the pan and leave the oven open to allow it to stick on the dough to dry up. It will come off pretty easily then. For anyone not coming off, just dampen a paper towel and put in over the doughy area and let the dough soften and then wash it away. Wipe the glass top carefully with glass cleaner and a non-abrasive moist cloth or use a wooden spoon or plastic spatula to extract bread dough baked-on lumps Rinse or wipe dry with a clean cloth.

Cleaning the bread machine body

The exterior of the unit can be washed with a damp rag.

Don't worry if the bread pan changes color over time. The change of color is a result of steam and other moisture and does not affect the performance of the machine.

Cleaning the baking pan is where the dough gets mixed and baked (also called bread pan basket or bucket).

Baking pan and the kneading blade are the pieces of the bread dough that come into contact.

Use anything that is not abrasive when you clean the bread pan by hand. Most pans and parts made by bread makers have a non-stick coating. The non-stick coating does not reduce the need for clean-up but simplifies it. Teflon and abrasive coatings will erode the finish. The non-stick coating is particularly susceptible to deterioration unless properly cared for.

If you need help extracting your delicious creation from the non-stick pan, it's completely imperative that you use some sort of soft utensils like wood or silicone. When a scratch is applied, the pan coating may begin to deteriorate. You certainly don't want to feed your family bits of chemicals as they flake into your delicious bread off the oven. Replace it with immediate effect.

Anti-stick cooking spray on your non-stick pan is completely avoided. The pan can produce a gummy mess that can hardly be removed without destroying the pan. It can totally destroy the pan's non-stick quality, too.

Never use a spatula in metal to extract any excess dough. To prevent damage, opt to plastic or silicone. You should finish the job with a warm wet cloth giving the pan a final run through.

Caring for the kneading blade,

Which kneads the dough is the bread machine Kneading Blade (also kneading paddle). Take good care.

The kneading blade of bread is one of the most important elements of any bread machine.

It is essential to cleanse the kneading blade. Doesn't your bread soar like it used to? Your kneading blade may be the problem. Make sure every loaf you make is cleaned properly.

Most devices provide removable blades for the kneading. The exterior surface is simple to clean with its non-stick finish.

A common lament with kneading blades is their tendency to either come off in a baked loaf or stick in the bottom of the pan to the kneading blade-spindle. When the kneading blade in the loaf comes off. Remove is simple, and usually clean it by hand. The temptation to apply a little vegetable oil to the spindle to make the kneading blade easier to remove. The oil can burn and thicken over time, which could cause the kneading blade to become stuck-fast. Just note after each loaf, to clean the kneading blades and the spindles. If the kneading blades get stuck, add 30 minutes of hot water to the tub, and try to extract the kneading blade carefully.

Remove any kneading dough from under the blade. Checking inside the kneading blade is necessary to ensure it's clean. Soaking it in a few minutes of soapy water will make the job much easier.

Get rid of the little bits of bread trapped between pieces using a cleaning brush rather than a sponge. If that doesn't fit, try a toothpick. It's much more powerful, and it will ensure your bread machine continues to properly mix the dough. Dry the blade to the kneading

Assemble the bread machine parts after cleaning

Assemble the bread machine parts, so they are ready for further use.

After the removable parts have been washed and inside cleaned, please leave the unit open to dry out completely. Enable for proper dissipation of the moisture from baking and washing.

Before returning them to the bread maker and closing the cover, make sure your pan and kneading blades are fully dry.

Bread machine to clean basics It's a joy to own a bread machine before it's time to clean it. Many owners of bread machines aren't sure how to clean a bread machine safely. Some aren't sure if cleaning is (it is) even necessary.

Crumbs and flour

Ensure your bread machine is totally cool. Flip it upside down and use a small paintbrush or butter basting brush to sweep the crumbs out of the unit gently. For this mission, do NOT use water.

Dough

Don't seek to remove moist dough from your bread machine's cover or sides. Instead, open the lid and let dry out the dough. It will come off quickly when it's completely dry. If you find the dough has dropped on the heating element when baking, immediately shut off the oven.

Follow the same method described above, and when extracting the dough, be very gentle.

Use a slightly dampened microfiber cleaning cloth if you have trouble. Place the cloth on top of the hardened dough for a few minutes before the dough can be extracted quickly by gently wiping away.

Cleaning the Heating Element

When the heating system of your bread machine is dirty, it poses a fire hazard. Clean it with NO detergent. Many bread makers' heating elements are very delicate and require a gentle hand. Moist a sponge cloth or microfiber, and wring it out. Wipe the sponge or cloth all over the heating element's length. Repeat that until it's clean.

Cleaning the Bread Pan and Dough Hook

It will usually be an easy job to clean the bread pan and dough hook. Just clean a moist soapy rag in the inside of the tub, rinse and let air dry. If there is dough or bread inside the dough hook, use a pipe cleaner to extract it gently, then wash it gently with moist, soapy water and a rag. Let the hook dry in upright sand.

Chapter 2: Common Ingredients to Make Bread

Water

Water is the liquid component used most in bread. It is one of the essential ingredients, just as flour is.

Heat, which allows the gluten to form in contact with flour This also helps dissolve other ingredients such as sugar, salt and it plays a very important function Water should be lukewarm, about 100F – you can feel it warm inside your wrist (get an instant thermometer if necessary). Some bakers propose boiling the water and letting it cook until it reaches 100F. If you don't always have the patience to do so, but you can use a basic Brita filter to clean your water. This way, you make sure the impurities are eliminated from the drinking water.

Mineral water is not recommended for bread making as the minerals present in water slow down the fermentation cycle.

Milk

Apart from water, milk is the second liquid product that is used the most. It's totally up to you, can it be full fat, skimmed or fat-free. The fat percentage is not as significant in bread as it is in pastries.

Milk for adding flavor. It enriches the dough and gives a creamy color, a fluffy crumb, and a golden crust to the bread.

Like water, milk used in recipes for bread must be lukewarm, particularly when mixed directly with yeast.

Many liquids used in bread, such as buttermilk, yogurt, sour cream, coconut milk, fruit juice, vegetable juice, beer, coffee, and so on

Salt

While there is only one salt, less bread, Tuscan Bread, all other bread recipes involve salt. Salt is an important ingredient. It is used for improving the flavor and also for managing fermentation, strengthening gluten, and preventing too much / blooming and collapsing of the dough during baking.

You have to keep one basic rule in mind when applying salt – keep it away from the yeast. If sugar helps ferment the yeast, the salt can destroy the fermentation.

Sugar

Is one of the optional bread-making ingredients?

While some say it's best to add a touch of sugar when the yeast is dissolved, the bread will work very well without it otherwise. Let it melt on its own, even if it takes another 3-5 minutes, but if you do, know your bread will have more flavor.

Still use a bit of sugar in plenty of bread recipes, but adding it after the yeast has been dissolved, even though it's wonderful bread. Sugar stops the bread from going stale faster in limited amounts (not that it would last too long anyhow). This also affects the color of the crust in some way. The more a bread calls for sugar, the darker the crust gets. Normally around 1-3 tbsp. is called per 4 cups of flour, but you'll find bread recipes that need up to one cup or even a little more per 4 cups of flour.

Keep in mind that even while a little bit of sugar speeds the fermentation process, it will stop too much sugar. Contrary to other assumptions, bread recipes that need about 1 cup of sugar such as this Romanian swirl bread) will take a long time to rise than those that use 1/4 cup.

2.1 Different Types of Flours

There are four types of wheat flour, which are most widely used in bread recipes. : All-purpose meal, bread meal, whole wheat meal, and whole wheat meal.

All-purpose flour is

One of the most frequently used flour in bread recipes. It has 9-11 percent gluten content. It usually consists of a combination of soft and hard wheat and comes in two varieties. Clean and unbleached.

Naturally, unbleached flour is aged to oxidize the proteins and bleach the natural yellow pigment in freshly milled flour. The unbleached meal has more nutrients to it.

Bleached flour with chlorine dioxide gas is aged rapidly. Bleaching also eliminates other chemicals that interfere with the production of gluten. When you look closely, you will find that some bleached flour is enriched, this means that some nutrients (mostly iron, B vitamins and occasionally calcium) are added back to the flour after the bleaching process to match the unbleached flour nutritional value.

All flours can be used with no problems in the bread recipes. You will not find any difference with bleached or unbleached baking, so don't worry over it.

Bread flour

This type of flour is used as the name states to make the bread white. Unbleached bread flour is made from hard spring wheat red aged without preservatives or chemicals. (So low price). Many national flour brands sell lower-price bread flour, flour, which was aged faster and enriched when the process was completed.

The high percentage of gluten, generally about 11-14 percent, makes the dough more elastic and simpler to work with making bread with a light texture.

Bread flour may be replaced with all-purpose flour, but you must bear in mind that bread flour needs more liquid, as it has a higher gluten content. You can either add more (usually 1 tbsp. per 1 cup flour) or add less water when using all-purpose flour.

Whole wheat flour

Is made from the whole wheat berry plus the bran and germ rich in oil. You will test the label to see that it is 100 percent whole wheat flour, indicating nothing has been added or removed. The flour comes straight from the mill as naturally as possible. Whole wheat flour produces strong nutty tastes and a range of fine to coarse textures that bakes up into chewy, crusty bread.

Whole wheat flour has the highest concentration of gluten, sometimes up to 16 percent. Now you might wonder why the whole wheat bread isn't the most fluffy of all; in fact, it's heavy and dense, particularly 100 percent whole-wheat bread. That's a good question, and since the whole wheat flour isn't as finely ground as the bread or all-purpose flour, the hulls found in the whole wheat flour tent harm the gluten strands, making it less efficient.

White whole wheat flour

It is made from a fresh, light-colored, and sweet form of white spring wheat. It is about 12 percent of gluten that makes this type of flour a good substitute for all-purpose flour without any loss of light texture. It is as nutritious as the wheat flour as a whole, but with a milder flavor.

Measuring the dry ingredients correctly makes a difference for baking (and not just for bread) around the world. You can either add too much (in most cases) or add so little that results in unsatisfactory results at all.

2.2 Selection of Best Type of Yeast

Yeast is the only living ingredients that are used in bread (sometimes that is why some people are afraid). It consists of the single-celled microscopic fungus, Saccharomyces cerevisiae. When it comes in contact with a warm liquid (water or milk), and feeds on sugar and flour, it starts to give off tiny carbon dioxide gas bubbles. This gas, trapped between the webs of gluten, is what makes bread rise and attain its light texture.

Yeast is the leavening agent most common for baking bread. It is really easy to use, and there's no going back to the store-bought bread once you've learned it. It's easy to bake your own bread.

As most of you probably know, at any supermarket, there are three types of yeast that are readily available.

- Active dry yeast
- Rapid dry yeast rises
- Instant dry yeast

People say fast yeast rise and instant yeast are the same and although they make the dough rise faster, the instant one is more forgiving.

Active dry yeast

The dry yeast is probably the most commonly used dry yeast on the market. Most of the bread recipes use active dry yeast unless otherwise specified. It looks like tiny granules that were dehydrated and put to sleep before they were packed. After mixing it with water, it wakes up.

Active dry yeast must be proven before mixing it with the other ingredients, unlike rapid rise and instant leaven. Upon proofing, it can be added a little sugar or honey to jump its production.

Active dry yeast is mostly available in 3 envelope strips (7 grams each) or 4 oz. jars made with Red Star Yeast and Fleischmann's.

Rapid rise yeast

As the name suggests, another form of dry yeast can make your dough rise faster, sometimes in half the time. It is a bit finer milled than active dry yeast. As the granules are smaller in size, you can combine them directly with the flour, without first having to prove it. Sometimes this form of leaven is also found under the name "bread machine yeast."

Instant dry yeast

Instant dry yeast is another kind of fast-acting, much finer milled yeast. Compared to active dry yeast, instant yeast accelerates the time of increase by half. It is intended for direct mixing with the dry ingredients. Not only can you skip the proofing when you use instant yeast, but you can also skip the first rise, forming the bread as soon as you knead it.

There are only a few times in bread recipes that you choose to use rapid rise or instant yeast. As with these baked croissants, when the dough requires a lot of rest time. Or you may also use it in pizza crust because as soon as you shape them, they are baked.

Instant dry yeast is completely the most forgiving. If you are still afraid to bake with yeast,

It does not matter what type of yeast you use, you know your leaven is alive that way. If the yeast is dead, you have wasted your time, and the other ingredients.

Proofing yeast

Proofing is the method of combining lukewarm water (or other liquid) with yeast before it is mixed with the rest of the ingredients. This method can be conducted in a separate bowl, mixing just the liquid with the yeast and waiting about 5 minutes until the surface of the foam emerges.

Like all living things, yeast requires four things to survive: water, humidity, food, and oxygen.

There are other ways to prove yeast, one of which is the sponge process.

The yeast is combined to create a batter with a small amount of water and flour. This can be achieved in a separate bowl, or in the middle of the flour by creating a well. The better is left aside for about ten minutes before bubbles appear on the surface and a spongy texture in the mixture. You will need to remember that a wet sponge (one that uses more liquid) rises faster than a firm one (one that uses more flour).

Chapter 3: Sourdough Bread

3.1 Understanding the Basics of Sourdough Bread

Sourdough bread is an old times favorite that has gone up in popularity lately.

This is considered by many to be tastier and safer than traditional bread. Some even say that your blood sugar is easier to digest and less likely to spike.

What is Bread Sourdough?

Sourdough is one of the oldest fermentation types of cereals.

It is believed to have originated around 1,500 BC in ancient Egypt and remained the usual form of bread leavening until it was replaced by baker's yeast a few centuries ago.

Yeast bread is a bread whose dough rises as a result of the gas being created as the grain ferments during the bread-making process.

Most leavened bread uses industrial baker yeast to assist the rise of the dough. Traditional sourdough fermentation, however, relies on "wild yeast" and lactic acid bacteria, which naturally occur in flour to leaven the bread.

Wild yeast avoids acidic conditions more than baker's yeast. That's what helps it to work with bacteria that generate lactic acid to help the dough rise.

In several other fermented feet, lactic acid bacteria can be found, including milk, kefir, pickles, sauerkraut, and kimchi.

The mixture of wild yeast, lactic acid bacteria, flour, and water used to produce sourdough bread is called a "starter." The starter ferments the sugars in the bread dough during the bread-making process, allowing the bread to rise and develop its characteristic flavor.

Sourdough bread must ferment and grow much longer than other types of bread, which is what produces its distinctive texture.

The making of sourdough bread remains popular in Mediterranean and Middle Eastern countries, as well as in the US area of San Francisco Bay to this day.

Many store-bought sourdough breads is not made using the conventional sourdough process, so their health benefits are diminished.

Buying sourdough bread from a baker or from a farmer's market increases the likelihood that it will be "actual" sourdough.

Nutrition quality

The nutritional composition of sourdough bread depends on the type of flour used to produce it — whether whole or processed.

Even the nutrient profile of sourdough resembles that of most other breeds.

On average, one medium slice weighing approximately 2 ounces (56 g) contains (2): calories: 162 calories Carbs: 32 grams Fiber: 2-4 grams Protein: 6 grams Fat: 2 grams Selenium: 22% RDI Folate: 20% RDI Thiamin: 16% RDI Sodium: 16% RDI Manganese: 14% RDI Niacin: 14% RDI Iron: 12% RDI Sodium: 16% RDI Manganese: 16% RDI Manganese: 14% RDI Niacin: 14% RDI Iron: 12% RDI.

The basic nutrition profile of sourdough is close to that of other breads, but it does have a few unique properties that make it more nutritious.

3.2 Benefits of Sourdough Bread

While sourdough bread is mostly made from the same flour as other forms of bread, the fermentation process enhances its nutritional profile in many ways.

For example, whole-grain bread contains a good deal of minerals, including potassium, phosphate, magnesium, and zinc.

The absorption of these minerals is sadly impaired by the presence of phytic acid, commonly known as phytate.

Phytates are considered ant nutrients, because they bind to minerals, limiting the capacity of the body to absorb them.

Interestingly, the bacteria of lactic acid found in sourdough bread lower the pH of the bread, which helps to degrade phytates. This results in a bread with a slightly lower phytate content than other bread types.

One study showed that sourdough fermentation could reduce bread's phytate content by 24–50 percent more than traditional yeast fermentation.

Lower levels of phytate improve mineral absorption, which is one reason that sourdough bread is more nutritious than traditional bread.

In fact, studies show that the lactic acid bacteria in sourdough bread are capable of releasing antioxidants during sourdough fermentation.

Sourdough fermentation often raises folate levels in the bread, although certain nutrient levels, such as vitamin E, maybe slightly decreased in the process. It is also easier to digest sourdough bread than bread fermented with brewer's yeast.

Researchers think this may be due partly to the prebiotic quality of sourdough bread and probiotic-like properties.

Prebiotics are non-digestible fibers that feed into your gut's beneficial bacteria, while probiotics are beneficial bacteria contained in certain foods and supplements.

Eating both regularly will help improve your bowel health and ease digestion.

Sourdough fermentation can also more degrade gluten than baker's yeast.

Gluten is a form of protein found in certain cereals. In people who are prone or allergic to it, it can cause digestive problems.

Gluten tolerance varies across individuals. Some have no obvious problems digesting gluten, while others may cause stomach pain, bloating, diarrhea, or constipation.

The lower gluten content of sourdough bread can make it easier to tolerate for people who are sensitive to gluten.

Better for blood sugar regulation

Sourdough bread can have a stronger effect than other forms of bread on blood sugar and insulin levels, but the explanation for this is not yet well understood.

Researchers believe the sourdough fermentation can alter the carb molecules' structure. It decreases the glycemic index (GI) of bread and increases the rate at which sugar reaches the bloodstream.

The GI is an indicator of how blood sugar influences a diet. Foods with a lower GI are less likely to produce a spike in blood sugar.

Additionally, the lactic acid bacteria present in the dough during fermentation produce organic acids. Some researchers believe that these acids can help delay the emptying of the stomach and prevent a blood sugar spike similar to vinegar.

The sourdough fermentation method is also used to produce rye bread because rye does not contain enough gluten to work effectively with the baker's yeast.

One study found that participants who ate rye bread had a lower spike in insulin levels compared with those who got the same amount of traditional wheat bread.

Further, several other studies compared the glucose response of the participants.

Chapter 4: Benefits of Sourdough Bread for Celiac Disease

4.1 What is Celiac Disease?

Celiac disease is a severe autoimmune disease that occurs in genetically predisposed people, where gluten ingestion causes damage to the small intestine. One in every 100 people worldwide is estimated to be affected. Two and a half million Americans are undiagnosed and are at risk for complications of long-term health.

If anyone with celiac disease eats gluten (a protein found in wheat, rye, and barley), their body mounts an immune response which attacks the small intestine. These attacks result in damage to the villi, small finger-like projections that line the small intestine that facilitates the absorption of nutrients. When the villi get damaged, nutrients cannot be properly absorbed into the body.

Celiac disease is inherited; that is, it occurs within families. The first-degree relative with celiac disease (parent, infant, and sibling) has a risk of developing celiac disease 1 in 10.

Celiac disease can evolve at any age after humans start consuming gluten-containing foods or medicines. Remain untreated, and celiac disease may cause further serious health problems.

Long-term health consequences People with celiac disease have a 2x higher risk of developing coronary artery disease, and a 4x higher risk of developing small bowel cancers.

The burden of care for celiac disease is comparable to end-stage renal disease, and the family burden is comparable to caring for a cancer patient.

Untreated celiac disease can lead to the development of other autoimmune disorders such as type I diabetes and multiple sclerosis (MS), and many other conditions including dermatitis (an itchy skin rash), anemia, osteoporosis, infertility and miscarriage, neurological conditions such as epilepsy and migraines, short stature, heart disease, and intestinal cancers.

4.2 Benefits of Sourdough Bread for Celiac Disease

The invention of industrial rapid-rise yeast has been replacing the way we have cooked bread from the start. But now, sourdough bread's increasing popularity tells us something: It's easier to digest.

Throughout the ages, sourdough was a kind companion to our hearts.

We made bread with a sourdough starter before commercial yeast, or "baker's yeast," got popular in the 1960s. It is a mixture of fermented grain and water that absorbs the wild yeast that lives in the soil, on our bodies, and in the flour itself all around us. A sourdough starter's complex, symbiotic environment works to leaven, flavor, and create the dough structure. The slow fermentation cycle attracts a magical mix of wild yeast, bacteria, and enzymes, and lactobacillus (the same yogurt bacteria) releases lactic acid to produce the sour flavor, which is used for sourdough. The enzymes activate minerals that are otherwise inaccessible to us in the wheat. The yeast that feeds on complex starches emits CO_2 as a by-product. And gluten, Satanized as it may be, traps the CO_2 and produces the loaf's rise and texture.

Our ancestors, of course, knew that, to some extent. The bread-baking mystery was known long before we knew the science thereof.

Bread-baking was a remarkable innovation of its time, as the author Michael Pollan points out in Cooked: It converted a previously indigestible grass into a healthy, satisfying meal. But, it turns out, fermentation was necessary.

So what exactly is this science miracle which makes sourdough easier to digest?

Tara Jensen lays a ball of bread dough under running water at her workshops in Marshall, North Carolina. After the starches are removed and rinsed off, what remains is pure gluten: a sticky, gluey protein mass that has a bubble feel. Keep the hard gluten glob, and it's clear that it might be difficult to digest

But sourdough — the only bread— has a trick that will help us digest gluten. It uses natural fermentation. The more the dough ferments, the more we break down the gluten.

This occurs through a process called hydrolysis, in which large, indigestible proteins break down into smaller amino acids.

Other studies point to phytic acid, an acid contained in wheat flour, which is also broken down during fermentation with sourdough.

Work about exposure to non-celiac gluten is complicated. We still do not know exactly what causes the non-celiac allergy to gluten-containing foods.

Several recent reports point to fructan, a compound found in bread, as well as bananas and garlic, among other things. Many people prone to gluten have sought digestive relief from avoiding foods containing fructans (also called FODMAPS). When it goes through fermentation, sourdough bread does not contain fructans. Some reports point to phytic acid-an acid present in wheat flour-that breaks down during fermentation with sourdough.

In both of these experiments, materials that are believed to be harmful to people susceptible to gluten are made digestible during fermentation with sourdough. As a result, plenty of people think they can eat gluten again.

The tests, however, aren't enough to draw a specific conclusion when it comes to celiac disease. Those diagnosed with celiacs are warned not to consume any gluten-containing foods, including sourdough, until consulting their doctor.

The research is, however, fascinating. Those with mild digestive problems or sensitivities to non-celiac gluten would almost certainly find relief with the properly made sourdough.

Properly refers to the bread that is leavened with a sourdough starter and left before baking to ferment. Many loaves of bread called "sourdough" at the grocery store have a sour taste added but are leavened with industrial yeast, avoiding fermentation. If uncertain, ask your bakery if the bread is naturally leavened.

Luckily, sourdough bread is easier to find. Part of the sourdough revival is going back to those ancient traditions and working toward inventions (like fast-rise yeast) that we never wanted in the first place. And as a result, we could be making gluten friends again (Severson, 2018).

Chapter 5: Bread Machine Salty Recipes

5.1 Simple White Bread Recipe

To make white bread less dense

Prep time: ten mins

Cook time: three hrs. 15 mins

Total time 3 hrs. 25 mins

The bread is of good form, tall and not thick. A simple recipe for a bread maker.

Course: Side Dish

Cuisine: American

Servings: 6 people

Calories: 313 kcal

Ingredients

- One cup and three tablespoons of water
- Two tablespoons of vegetable oil
- 1 1/2 teaspoons of salt
- Two tablespoons of sugar
- 3 1/4 cups of white bread flour
- Two teaspoons of active dry yeast

Instructions

Important note on the correct calculation of flour by means of measuring cups: It is accomplished either by sifting or aerating meal by fluffing it up and whisking it well, then spooning it into the measuring cup, then scraping any excess meal with a knife carefully. If you just put the measuring cup in the meal bag and scoop some out, you'll get a lot more flour than the recipe demands. Do aerate the flour, or you'll end up drying the dough!

How to make the bread in a bread machine:

Add the bread pan with water and oil stir in water, and add sugar then add flour.

Create a slight indentation on top of the flour and make sure that the ingredients do not touch wet ingredients. For the indentation, add the yeast.

Don't let the yeast touch the salt.

Put the pan into the bread maker and click to snap it down. Put the cover.

Use Simple bread, 1.5 lb. loaf, medium crust process (3 hrs. 15 minutes)

Remove the bread pan with oven mitts when the bread is cooked. Turnover and shake the bread pan to free the loaf. Let the loaf cool for some thirty minutes on a wire rack.

Nutrition Facts

Amount per Serving

Calories 313Calories from Fat 54%

Daily Value * Fat 6g9%

Saturated Fat 4g25%

Sodium 587mg26%

Potassium 105mg3%

Carbohydrates 54g18%

Fiber 2g 8%

Sugar 4g 4%

Protein 9g 18%

Calcium 10mg 1%

Iron 0.7 4%

Be sure to remember these points when making bread in a bread machine: – When you measure flour using cups, make sure that you don't pack flour too thick in a measuring cup. Otherwise, you'll end up with much more flour than you need, and thus the bread will come out denser. The right measurement of the flour can solve several "dense" problems. The trick that works is that you use 1/3 measuring cup to carefully scoop in the bread machine all the flour you need (usually around 3 cups) without over packing it. It will be another way to measure flour, which you don't do, but it's a solution.

Use bread flour, not standard all-purpose flour for all recipes made from bread machines. Bread meal contains a higher percentage of gluten than a regular all-purpose meal. We will produce bigger, less dense loaves using bread flour. Using all-purpose flour (which has a lower percentage of gluten than bread flour) can make your loaves flatter and denser. Make sure you add the yeast last, then apply it to the dry ingredients (flour) on top (JULIA, 2012).

5.2 Whole Wheat Bread Recipe

This strong, sweet loaf of golden whole wheat bread, ideal for sandwiches and toast

Prep 5 mins

Cooking 1 hr. 15 mins

Total time 3 hrs. 5 mins

Yield 1 loaf

Ingredients

- 1 1/4 cups (283 g) lukewarm water
- Two tablespoons (25 g) olive oil or vegetable oil
- 1/4 cup (85 g) honey or 1/4 cup (78 g) maple syrup
- 3 1/2 cups (397 g) King Arthur white wheat flour
- 1/4 cup (35 g) sunflower, sesame or flax seeds, or a mixture, optional
- One tablespoon essential wheat gluten;

Instructions

Program for simple white bread (or whole wheat bread, if you have a whole wheat setting on your machine), and press Start

When done remove the bread from the machine Just move it out of the pan onto a rack to cool, or move it out of the pan, put it back in the oven (atop the frame holding the pan), open the lid about 1 "and let it cool right in the cooling-down system. It helps keep the crust from wrinkling as the loaf cools.

5.3 Basil bread with Tomato and Mozzarella cheese recipe

Let's just have fun. Making a simple bread and adding basil is easy and that is all right. Fresh basil is a beautiful herb, but if it's not available in winter, fear not simply add more dried basil, and let's tell you how many. But there's another possibility: I added some sliced tomatoes and mozzarella cheese with either fresh or dried basil to this bread recipe, and it has the flavor profile of a Margherita pizza or a classic New York-style pizza. This is not about making pizza dough for the record, but rather a traditional white bread loaf with some pizza ingredients.

You can go the simpler route and simply add dried basil or fresh basil as indicated, but we'll send you some additions to the list of INGREDIENTS you might want to consider as an experiment.

Ingredients:

- 1 cup of 80 ° F. / 27 ° C hot.
- 3 tbsp. of olive oil
- 1 cup of chopped, tomatoes drained
- One-fourth cups of shredded mozzarella cheese (optional)
- 2.50 tbsp. of sugar
- 1.75 tsp of salt
- Four cups of bread flour 2 tsp of shredded fresh basil or four teaspoons of dried basil 2 1/4 teaspoon of bread maker yeast

Instructions:

1. Place the ingredients into the bread pan as shown in the list of ingredients and select the simple or white course, 2-pound bread, medium crust.

2. If the dough appears a little loose due to the addition of tomatoes, apply some flour one tablespoon a time during the kneading process to obtain the right consistency. You may also sprinkle basil on top of the loaf before beginning the growing process.

3. When the loaf has finished, remove it from the bread pan and let it rest for 10 minutes on a cooling rack, cut it in slices, and then serve it.

4. Great to eat alone and great with a pasta course or a big green salad.

5.4 Barley Bread Recipe

Minutes to Prepare: 15 Minutes

Cooking time: 150

Number of Servings: 18

Barley is an ancient grain and barley-based bread recipes that date back to Sumerians and Egyptians. It was also the standard flour for Middle Eastern and African bread recipes in medieval Europe. Unlike popular belief, the flour in barley is not gluten-free. In fact, there is a relatively high amount of gluten that helps both to get up and to bake.

However, the amounts of gluten are less than bread flour, so we'll combine barley flour and bread flour to give this bread its best lift. Brown sugar also feeds on the yeast, giving a good color and taste to the loaf. Barley bread is perfect with a stew-like, hearty meal or a thick, gravy meal or sauce.

Ingredients

- 1 1/2 cups of water (100 degrees F/38 degrees C)
- One tablespoon of olive oil
- 3 cups of bread flour
- 1 cup of barley flour
- Two teaspoons of brown sugar
- 1teaspoon of salt
- One and a half tsp of active dry yeast or bread machine yeast

Directions:

1 Add all bread ingredients in the order specified and select the whole wheat cycle, 2-pound loaf, and medium crust.

1 Cool down on a wire rack for fifteen minutes, slice, and serve (Nubie, 2017).

5.5 Black pepper onion bread recipe

Full of flavor the black pepper onion, bread is perfect with soups, stews, or gravy-based meals. It is also very good as a side dish or as a sandwich, toasted and buttered. The addition of the onions into both the dough and slightly sweet as a crispy, caramelized topping out The pepper is a great accent to the flavor, and depending on your taste for pepper, you can increase or reduce the amount.

You can make this bread in your bread machine from start to finish, but you'll need to glaze the top quickly with the egg yolk, ground black pepper, and slivered onions before it enters the final baking cycle. You have to do this immediately, or the bread may lose its rise and fall or collapse. If you want to keep it easy, you could skip that step too. The loaf still tastes great.

One choice is to use dehydrated onions, but especially on top, fresh onions are preferred. An option is to use the dehydrated onions as a topping in the dough and the fresh, slivered onions. Dehydrated onions will carry the day in both the dough and as a topping if you're out of the onions. If you are using dehydrated onions on top, however, be sure to rehydrate them in cold water for ten minutes before sprinkling on top.

Ingredients:

- One cup of water 110 degrees F. or 43 degrees Centigrade
- One tablespoon of butter at room temperature
- One teaspoon of salt
- One tablespoon of sugar
- Three tablespoons of non-fat dry milk powder
- A one-fourth teaspoon of garlic powder

- A three-fourth teaspoon of powdered pepper for incorporation into the dough
- One medium onion diced for incorporation into a dough or two teaspoons of dehydrated onions
- Three cups of bread flour
- Two tsp of active dry yeast

Glaze and topping

One egg yolk mix with a half teaspoon of water

Half teaspoon of black pepper for loaf topping

One medium onion silvered onion for topping

Directions

1. Put the ingredients in the machine pan, reserve ingredients for the glaze and decoration.

2. For a 1, 5-pound loaf, choose the basic white bread course; dark crust setting,

The dark crust atmosphere is what you want to help caramelize the onions on top.

3. When the process of mixing, kneading, and growing is complete, whisk the egg yolk and water together and paint the top of the loaf quickly with the glaze; crack the black pepper and uniformly distribute the slivered onions or rehydrated dry onions.

4. When finish, let it cool for ten minutes on a wire rack and then slice and serve.

5.6 Blue Cheese Potato Bread Recipe

If you're fond of blue cheese, you'll love this recipe for pizza. We only add a 1/2 cup of blue cheese, but you can add up to a cup or, better still, top the bread in your bread machine at the end of the baking process to give the loaf a blue-cheesy finish.

We have also added a few potato flakes to this recipe to give a bit more body to the loaf. The overall ingredient combination makes for a highly flavorful bread that you can make in your bread machine from start to finish.

Ingredients:

- One plus 1/4 cup water (110 ° F. /43 ° C.)
- One egg (room temperature)
- One tablespoon of melted butter
- 1/4 cup of non-fat dried milk powder
- One tablespoon of sugar
- 3/4 teaspoon of salt
- Half teaspoon onion powder
- 1/2 cup of crumbled blue cheese
- 3cups of bread flour
- 1/3 cup of mashed potato flakes or buds
- One teaspoon of active dry yeast or bread machine yeast

Directions:

1 Adding ingredients to the bread machine and select white bread 1.5-pound loaf and dark crust button.

2. When preparing to serve.

5.7 Rye Bread Recipe

Rye bread is a traditional recycle of Eastern European bread. Still popular throughout Russia, Germany, and the Baltic states. This was largely because of that the rye grains were easy to grow in bitter climates and were growing well not only on farms but also in the wild.

We will look at a rye bread made with 100 percent rye flour for this recipe. Thanks to the fact that ryegrass was hardy and quick to grow in harsh weather.

You should know that there is no significant amount of gluten in the rye flour, which causes the yeast to develop and raise a loaf of bread. The effect is a very large and dense loaf of bread you'll end up with. It will still have an outstanding taste, but if the loaf doesn't rise and is quite thick, don't be disappointed. You should also be aware that rye flour is not gluten-free; it also lacks the same amount of gluten you find in bread flour, all-purpose flour, and wheat flour.

This recipe for rye bread can be made using the whole wheat setting on your bread machine if you have an entire wheat environment of 100 percent that's even better. It has a great flavor and works very well as an appetizer or canape base and should be sliced thinly.

One warning is that this recipe doesn't coalesce into a ball of dough in your bread machine like other bread made from more conventional flours. During the early kneading process, you will have to lift the lid and occasionally push the rye dough toward the kneading paddle to form the dough ball. Stick with the kneading cycle throughout. Remove the dough ball from the pan if necessary and shape it with your hands into a dough ball and drop it back into the bread pan.

Ingredients:

- 1 cup of water at 110 degrees Fahrenheit
- Two teaspoons of salt
- ¼ canola or olive or vegetable oil
- 1/4 cup of honey
- Two eggs at room temperature
- Three tablespoons of dry milk (optional)
- 4 cups of rye flour
- Two plus 1/4 teaspoons of bread machine yeast or active dry yeast

Topping:

One teaspoon of caraway seeds (optional)

Directions:

1 Add all ingredients to the machine.

2 Use the whole wheat setting for a 2-pound loaf (1-pound loaf if half of the recipe has been split) and a medium crust. If your bread machine has one, select the 100 percent whole-wheat configuration.

3 Remember to open the lid during the kneading process and to push the dough with a plastic spatula against the kneading paddle. When kneading stops and you still don't have a ball of dough, remove it from the bread pan and shape it in your hand until you have a ball of dough and fall back into the bread pan.

4 Sprinkle the reserved teaspoon of caraway seeds over the top after the kneading cycle and before the rising cycle if you choose to use them.

5 Remove from the bread pan when finished and allow it to cool for 10 minutes on a wire rack. : slice and enjoy

5.8 Bacon Onion Cheese Bread Recipe

Serves: 8

Prep: 10 Min

Cooking time: 4 Hour

Method: this is an easy-to-make bacon-onion cheese bread beginning with the dough setting on your bread machine. You finish it in the oven because the bacon, onion, and cheese are to be rolled up as a filling. This bread is a little tricky to make and takes some time, but it's worth it. This bread is perfect as a basis for French toast grilled cheese sandwiches and is perfect for eating as a side dish with soup or with a salad. The trick is to ensure that the bacon is crisp and that the onions are caramelized to give it a punch of flavor.

Dough ingredients:

- 1 cup of a 110 ° F milk. /43 degrees.
- 1 tsp salt
- 2 tsp onion powder
- 2 tbsp. Softened butter
- 3 1/4 cups of bread flour
- 2 tsp. Bread machine or active dry yeast

Filling ingredients:

- 16 ounces (one pound) of sliced bacon
- 1 1/2 cups of finely diced onions
- 1/2 teaspoon black pepper
- One teaspoon of paprika
- One cup of shredded parmesan or asiago cheese

For glaze and pan:

- One large egg with 1 tbsp. Of water for the glaze.
- One tablespoon bacon fat to glaze pan

Directions

1 Put the ingredients for the bread dough into the bread machine pan and choose the setting for the dough. Add the ingredients in the order set out in the list of ingredients.

2. Prepare the bacon/onion/cheese stuffing while the bread machine is making the dough.

3. Cook the bacon till it is crispy and drain away to a plate covered with paper towels. Reserve the bacon fat for three tablespoons. Cut the bacon into pieces, and put it in a dish.

4. Cook the onions until crispy and caramelize the bacon drippings in 2 teaspoons. Drain on the paper towels and apply the pepper, paprika, and shredded cheese to the bacon in the bowl and shake. Book it until later. Put aside 1/3 of this mixture, after glazing with egg wash, to cover the crust.

5. Roll the bread dough out to an 8 x 18-inch rectangle after the dough process is complete. Clean some of the egg wash and scatter some of the fillings over the floor. Roll the dough and put in a baking pan of 9 x 5 inches of bread, which was oiled it with some of the bacon fat.

6. Glaze the top of the bread and top with the remaining topping at letting it rise for 45 to an hour. Preheat the oven to 350 ° F/ 145 ° C and bake until browned for 30 minutes.

7. Let rest and slice for 10 minutes, and serve.

5.9 Asiago Cheese Bread Recipe

Asiago cheese is similar to Parmesan cheese, which is strongly fragrant. It is a hard cheese, and when used in recipes, it browns well, particularly bread. This recipe requires the introduction of the Asiago into the dough and as a topping. At the end of the rise cycle and before the baking process, you top off the bread with a small cup of grated asiago cheese. Asiago cheese bread goes good with a soup or salad or a glass of wine or beer on its own. It's also a perfect accompaniment to robust offerings such as roasts and barbecue, making great bread for the sandwich.

Ingredients:
- One ¼ cup of 110 ° F/43 ° C milk.
- 1 1/2 Tsp salt
- One tsp of sugar
- ¼ tsp pepper
- Two tablespoons of butter
- One large egg
- 4 Cups of bread flour or all-purpose flour
- 1 1/4 cup shredded asiago cheese (topping save 1/4 cup)
- 1/2 tsp. OF Bread-machine yeast or active dry yeast:

Direction:

1 Place the ingredients to the machine pan in the order specified in the ingredients section and pick basic white-bread, 2-pound loaf, and medium crust framework. Reserve a 1/4 cup of the Asiago grated cheese.

2 Top the risen dough with the remaining 1/4 cup of shredded asiago cheese after the rising process and before the baking cycle starts, and close the lid quickly.

Let the bread cool for ten minutes, slice, and serve.

5.10 Basic Plain Bagel Recipe

Bagels are the favorite of all and can be found all over the world. They are a little difficult to make and bake, but the process can be made easier by your bread machine. Once again, the dough environment comes to rescue, but you'll have to finish these on the counter and then go through a boiling phase until you finish in the oven. It's worth the effort and usually makes a big bunch because they keep well and can be refrigerated to extend their shelf life too.

This recipe is for a simple bagel, but there are plenty of variants. Regardless of how you make bagels, they're great whether they're overwhelmed with something as simple as cream cheese or loaded with, onions, and capers. So, just roll up your sleeves, and let's continue.

Ingredients:

- One cup of water (80 ° F. /27 ° C.)
- 1 1/2 tablespoons of sugar
- 1 1/2 teaspoons of salt
- 3 Cups of bread flour
- Two teaspoons of active dry yeast (1/4 cup of malt syrup for boiling water bath) optional

For glaze

Whisk together: 1 egg yolk one tablespoon of water

Instructions:

1 Place the ingredients to the bread pan in the order specified and pick the dough process. Upon completion of the dough, cycle transfers the dough to a lightly floured surface and divide the dough into eight equal pieces.

2 Each piece of dough has the shape of a sausage, and then it forms a ring. To remove the seam a bit, press the joined ends together and roll lightly through the ring with your fingers. Repeat with remaining pieces of dough until eight circular pieces of dough are in place.

3 Let the bagels stand up for 15 to 30 minutes. Line a baking sheet or lightly coat it with parchment paper.

4 Bring to a boil four quarters of water and preheat the oven to 475 ° F/245 ° C. You can add a 1/4 cup of malt syrup to the boiling water if you wish. That will give a chewier texture to the bagels. The syrup can be omitted too.

5 Boil the bagels, three at a time, before they rise to the water-pot level. Place a slotted spoon over them. You should be boiling them one side for about 1 minute.

6 Take them carefully to the baking sheet and glaze them with a mixture of yolk and water—Bake for between 15 and 20 minutes or until brow

5.11 Boule bread recipe

Boule Bread is a traditional recycle from France. This is an artisanal bread with a thick, dark crust and a coarse baked texture. It's a very complicated bread to make from a baking perspective, especially as it relates to the rising process, but use the simple dough setup, your bread machine can facilitate part of the process. The dough is allowed to rise for some time and baked in the oven for part of the baking process in a sealed Dutch oven.

Parchment paper is very important for the baking process as it will allow you to raise the risen and unbaked dough and lower it before baking into the preheated Dutch oven, and also remove the baked loaf from the Dutch oven.

With soups and stews, boule bread is wonderful, a fine bread to dip into olive oil and a perfect accompaniment for any heartfelt meal. It's decent sandwich bread, and due to the strong but elastic texture and crust, it can contain a range of ingredients, toppings, and condiments.

Ingredients:

- 1 1/2 teaspoons of salt
- 3/4 cup of flat beer at room temperature
- 3/4 cup of water at 110 degrees Fahrenheit/43 degrees Celsius
- 2 1/2 tsp of yeast
- Four cups of bread flour or unbleached all-purpose meal
- 1 1/2 teaspoons of apple cider vinegar
- One egg yolk whisked for glazing

Instructions:

1 Add the ingredients to the pan of the bread machine in the order stated in the ingredient list. Pick and start the setting of the base dough. If the dough appears too soft, add a spoonful of flour and give it one minute. If it looks too hard, add a tablespoon of warm water and give it one minute again before you have the consistency of a dough ball.

2 Take out the dough to a sheet of parchment paper on a baking sheet when the dough setting is complete, dust the top with flour and cover with plastic wrap, and let it rise for two hours.

3. Preheat the oven to 350 degrees F or 176 centigrade.

4 Whisk the egg and sprinkle the dough on top after it has risen.

5 Bake at 350 degrees F. or 175 C for 30-35 minutes.

6 Let it cool for ten minutes, slice, and serve.

5.12 Light Oat Bread Recipe

Light Oat Bread Recipe:

This next recipe encourages you to explore the addition of oats and some of the all-purpose flour baking nuances as opposed to bread meal. Also, the sum of yeast and salt is a crucial success factor here. This recipe decreases the amount of salt and raises the yeast in order to ensure a successful "up," provided that all-purpose meal has less gluten than bread flour. You can also substitute the margarine with two tablespoons of softened butter if you like.

Ingredients: Makes 1 -1/2 pound loaf

- 1 1/4 cups water
- Two tablespoons margarine
- 1/2 teaspoon salt

- 3 cups of all-purpose flour
- 1/2 cup rolled oats
- Two tablespoons of brown sugar
- Two teaspoons of active dry yeast

Instructions:

Place ingredients to the bread maker pan in the order recommended by a list of ingredients or by your manufacturer. Using the setting "normal/bright."

5.13 Steakhouse Wheat Bread Recipe:

The ingredient that gives this bread its special flavor is instant coffee and cocoa crystals. Establish a subtle tone to the bread color and a robust flavor that is comparable to the traditionally served bread in steak house restaurants. Although this is wheat bread, the smaller percentage of wheat flour allows for a simple process setting such as setting white bread or whatever your instruction book says.

Ingredients:

- Original recipe makes one loaf
- 3/4 cup of warm water
- One tablespoon butter,
- 1/4 cup of honey
- 1/2 teaspoon salt
- One teaspoon of instant coffee granules
- One tablespoon of unsweetened cocoa powder
- One tablespoon of white sugar
- 1 cup of bread flour
- 1 cup of whole wheat flour
- 1 1/4 teaspoon of bread machine yeast

Directions:

put warm water, butter, honey, salt, coffee, coffee, wheat flour 1 1/4 teaspoon of bread machine yeast Put light crust on daily or simple loop.

5.14 Bread Machine Pretzels

Soft and chewy baked pretzels, use your bread machine.

Ingredients

- 1 cup of water room temperature
- 1 cup of butter room temperature
- Two tablespoons of sugar
- 1 tsp of salt
- 2 3/4 cups of all-purpose flour
- 2 tsp of active dry yeast
- 6 cups of water for cooking water
- 1/3 cup of baking soda for cooking water
- One egg to brush on before baking
- 2-3 cups of melted butter
- 2 tsp of coarse salt for topping

Instructions

Position 1 cup of water, butter, sugar, salt, flour, and dry yeasts don't mix in.

Select setting to dough and press start

Cut the dough and switch to a lightly floured surface when the process is complete.

Oven preheats to 400F, Cover a baking sheet with parchment paper and cooking spray lightly.

Divide the dough into six parts, which are equal.

Roll every piece of dough into an 18-20 "chain.

Form the rope in U, take two ends, and cross 1 or 2 times over. Bring to an end, fold-down, leaving ends a little overhang. Push a little down to the bottom where the dough intersects.

Prepare the baking water with soda. Using a big pot, bring 6 cups of water to easily simmer. Slowly add baking soda to the bowl, then stir to dissolve. Reduce heat to maintain a simmer.

Placed 1 to 2 pretzels in the water, do not put more than two

Cook for 30 seconds, then turn over and cook for 30 seconds.

Remove pretzels and switch to the baking sheet using a wide slotted ladle.

Prepare egg wash with 1 tsp of water, whisking the egg together.

Clean the egg wash with the pretzels. Sprinkle with oil. Coarse sea salt is a preference.

Bake for 10-12 minutes at 400oF, until golden brown.

Remove the melted butter from the oven, and clean generously.

Nutrition

Calories: 291kcal |

Carbohydrates: 48g |

Protein: 7g | Fat: 7g |

Saturated Fat: 3g |

Cholesterol: 42mg |

Sodium: 3064mg |

Potassium: 90mg | Fiber: 2g | Sugar: 4g | Vitamin A: 215IU | Calcium: 20mg | Iron: 2.8mg (King, 2019).

5.15 Bread Machine Pizza Dough

This pizza is fast and simple to make in New York City! Put all of the ingredients into your bread machine pan and bake a thick crust brick oven style pizza once it's baked!

Cooking time: 1 hour 30 minutes

Total time 1 hour 30 minutes

Ingredients

- 3/4 cup water
- One tablespoon of olive oil
- 2 1/4 cups of bread flour
- 1 1/2 tablespoon of sugar
- 1 1/2 teaspoon of salt
- One teaspoon of active dry yeast

Instructions

Put all ingredients in your baking pot, as suggested by the manufacturer of your bread machine.

Click the Bread / Pizza course button, and then Continue.

Remove dough and form into a ball after the bread machine has finished. Place the dough in a bowl, cover with a towel and allow to rest in a warm spot for 20 minutes.

Put the bread dough on a floured surface and roll out into a circle with a diameter of about 12 inches.

Bake dough just as you would normally.

5.16 Recipe Bread Machine Italian Bread

These simple step-by-step instructions demonstrate how to make crusty Italian bread in your oven. You can make this homemade family bread every day!

Preparation time: 5 minutes

Cooking time: 3 hours

Total time 3 hours 5 minutes

Serving 8

Ingredients

- 3/4 cup of cold water
- 2 cups of bread flour suggested King Arthur or Bob's Red Mill
- One tablespoon of sugar
- One teaspoon of salt
- One tbsp. of olive oil
- One teaspoon of dry yeast

Instructions

Put water, bread flour, sugar, salt, olive oil, and active dry yeast in the bread machine jar.

If you have a Bread cycle in Italy, click that. Pick a simple bread process, if you don't—press Release.

The machine is going to make the bread now. When baking is finished, remove from the oven and serve.

Nutrition information: 135kcal calories (7 percent)

5.17 A recipe for Ciabatta bread

The homemade bread is crusty and full of holes! Turning in a bread machine is fast. Serve it for a sandwich, soup, or a side dish for dinner!

What's Bread from Ciabatta?

Ciabatta bread is white Italian bread, somewhat like a French baguette but more elongated and thick. The texture is normally chewy and lined with crumbly air holes. Great for soup dipping, sandwich eating, or just sliced eating with a little bit of butter!

Ingredients

- 1 1/2 cup of water
- Half teaspoon salt
- One teaspoon of sugar
- One tablespoon of olive oil
- 3 1/4 cups of bread flour
- 1 1/2 teaspoon of active dry yeast
- Two tablespoons of dried rosemary

Directions

Place all the ingredients in your bread machine as needed by your dough machine. Pick and continue the Dough process.

Fill a counter surface with a generous amount of flour and put the dough on it. Cover with plastic wrap, and take 20 minutes of rest.

Divide the dough into two parts, each forming the shape of a bread loaf. Place the dough on a baking sheet with a nonstick put some flour on the top.

Preheat oven to 425oC. Spritz the bread loaves with water, using a water bottle. Don't skip this step, please-that makes the bread crispy! Bake bread for twenty to 30 minutes, or brown until warm.

5.18 Dill Bread Recipe:

(Making a 1.5-pound loaf) Five dills whole loaf bread it is a perfect bread to have with a hearty meal from pasta with sauce to meats and poultry. Either fresh dill or dried dill can be used. If fresh dill is used, strip the leaves from the stems and finely chop it. Certain ingredients may be used too. To this recycle, add some dried onions. What's best about dill bread is that it's going to fill the kitchen with the new, dill scent as its growing and baking.

The introduction of chopped dill pickles, which makes a perfect hot dog or hamburger bun, is another interesting variety. Choose the dough course and shape for that variation into the bun shape you like, and let it rise on an oiled baking sheet — Bake to 375 ° F. For 20 minutes or until it browns. Keep things simple and go to the bread machine with the basic dill and onion recipe.

Ingredients:

- Two eggs at 110 ° F/43 ° C
- + 1 cup and one tablespoon of water.
- Two tablespoons of oil or melted butter
- Two tablespoons of sugar
- 1 1/2 teaspoons of salt
- 3 cups of bread flour
- One tablespoon of dill (fresh or dried)
- One tablespoon of dehydrated onions
- Two teaspoons of bread machine yeast

Instructions:

Place all the ingredients into your bread maker pan in the order indicated in the ingredients and pick the base or white bread package, 1.5 loaves, medium crustacean. When the bread is completely done, take it out from the bread pan and leave it to rest for one minute on a cooling rack. Cut and serve.

5.19 Bread Machine Onion and Olive Bread

This savory bread machine recipe with onion and olive is artisan bread made right in your bread maker with staples such as frozen, sliced black olives, dehydrated onions, dried thyme, and all-purpose flour.

Cook Time2 hours

Total Time2 hours 20 minutes

Servings 8 serving

Calories 199kcal

Ingredients

- 8 oz. water
- Tbsp. olive oil
- Two cups of all-purpose flour
- 1 1/2 tbsp. white granulated sugar
- 1 tsp salt
- 3/4 tsp dried thyme
- 200 ml can of sliced black olives
- 1/4 cup dried onions chopped

Directions

Add all the ingredients according to the list

Pour it over the outer edge of the mixture, away from the yeast when applying salt.

Yeast should be added last when adding sugar, pour it around the outer edge of the mixture, away from yeast (opposite to the salt). In the center of the flour, dig a small hole, away from the salt, sugar, and water.

Set bread machine to fit the most suitable setting-make it the "standard model" setting for bread (the same setting you would use to make a daily white bread loaf).

It is very important to follow your bread machine manufacturer's operating instructions while trying to make some bread.

The time varies from one bread machine to another, too.

NOTE: This recipe is for 1 lb.

Nutrition Facts

Bread Machine Onion and Olive Bread

Sum Per Serving Calories 199Calories from Fat 63% Daily Value * Fat 7g11% Saturated Fat 1g6% Sodium 682mg30% Potassium 81mg2% Carbohydrates 28g9% Fiber 2g8% Sugar 3g3% Protein 4g8% Vitamin A 100IU2 perc.

5.20 Breakfast Pastry Recipe

The typical Cornish pasty is made from puff pastry, but we will keep it simple, and we will use a basic pie crust. The filling includes protein combinations like other Cornish Pastry recipes, from eggs to bacon or ham. We will make a version of the breakfast with some classic tastes of the breakfast combined and sealed in the dough. It makes for a great breakfast on the go before work or school, or a nice breakfast weekend treat.

We will start by making a simple pie crust in the bread machine and then roll out the pie crust and top it with the breakfast toppings and folding, sealing, glazing with egg yolk, and baking in the oven.

Ingredients: Pie Crust:

- 2 1/2 cups of all-purpose flour
- 1/2 teaspoon salt
- 3/4 cup butter cut into 1/2 tablespoon slices (total 1 1/2 sticks to freeze for 15 to 20 minutes)
- 1/2 cup of very cold water (allow the ice to stay in the water and then weigh the 1/2 cup)

Breakfast Pasty Topping Ingredients:

- Two tablespoon butter
- Six eggs + 2 eggs for glazing.
- Four breakfast sausages cooked and chopped or you can use one cup of ham
- Half cup diced onion
- Half cup diced sweet bell pepper

- One cup cheddar cheese
- Four to eight-inch round pie crust

Pie crust Directions

1. Select the pasta dough button and add all the ingredients in the bread machine pan according to the list.

2. When the dough is cooked, wrap the dough in plastic wrap and cool for 30 minutes.

3 Cut into four balls of the same size after 30 minutes, place each between two pieces of waxed paper and roll out until the piece is 6 to 8 inches in diameter.

4 Remove the wax paper carefully, and place the bowl as a guide over the crust so that you can cut a circle.

5 Put the crust on the baking sheet, oiled. You're now ready to top up your tea.

Breakfast pastry topping directions:

Cook the sausage or ham and set aside, sauté the butter with the peppers and onions until the onions are translucent.

In a cup, whisk the eggs and add the peppers and onions to the pan, and scramble, then mix in the sausage or ham.

Season with salt and pepper.

Oven preheats to 400 ° F/205 ° C.

A thin line of egg yolk is painted around the edge of each round pie crust.

Place the pie dough filling in the middle and sprinkle with 1/4 of the cheese and fold over.

Close the crust securely with your fingertips around the bottom, and then gently crimp with a fork.

Beat the remaining two eggs with a spoonful of water and glaze the egg yolk with the pastries.

Bake at 205 ° C/400 ° F. 15 to 20 minutes, or before golden brown is dark

Immediately serve or tie, and go.

5.21 Cheese and Beer Bread Recipe

Cheese and beer seem to go hand in hand, and this recipe blends them to make a salty, savory crust. After the rise and before the baking process begins, the cheese is mixed into the dough and sprinkled on top too.

You can use any type of cheese or beer, and the beer does help with the bread's rising and overall texture and taste.

Ingredients:

- Ten ounces of beer, at room temperature
- Four ounces of shredded or diced cheddar cheese
- 4 ounces of shredded or diced Monterey Jack cheese
- One tablespoon of sugar
- 1 1/2 tsp of salt
- Three cups of bread flour
- One tablespoon of butter at room temperature divided into opposite corners of the bread pan
- One teaspoon of active dry yeast or bread machine yeast

Directions:

1 On the top of the stove or in your microwave, heat beer and cheese, there's no need to melt the cheese. Remove to mix and pour the mixture into the bread pan.

2 Let it cool again down to 110 ° F/43 ° C.

3 In the order specified in the recipe, add the remaining ingredients, unless your manufacturer suggests a different order.

4 Select a simple white, 11.5-pound loaf, and medium crust framework press start.

5 Remove the loaf from the bread pan when done, and let it cool on the rack and serve.

5.22 German Dumplings Spätzle Recipe

Famous in parts of Europe, and Germany Spätzle is a popular dumpling recipe. It is a simple recipe that is either formed into a larger dumpling or cut into smaller pieces by pushing the dough through a cheese grater's holes. There is also a Spätzle press that resembles a potato ricer.

Typically the spätzle is baked in a chicken broth or just boiling water, and melted butter is the usual serving topping. If you like, you can also sprinkle herbs over the top and, of course, season them with salt and pepper.

Ingredients:

- 1/4 cup of milk
- Two eggs
- 1/2 teaspoon of ground nutmeg
- One pinch of white pepper
- 1 cup of all-purpose flour

For the cooking process:

- 1 gallon of water
- 1/2 teaspoon of salt

Topping:

- Two tablespoons of melted butter
- Two tablespoons of parsley

Directions:

1 Apply the base spätzle ingredients to the bread pan and pick the dough environment.

2 Formed the dough into canoe shapes when finished, or press it through the holes of a metal grater to a finer size or use a spätzle ricer.

3 Carry the gallon of salted water to a moderate boil and drop the spätzle in the water for a few minutes, then cook for 5 to 8 minutes.

Cut the spätzle with a slotted spoon and apply the butter and parsley to top and serve.

5.23 Fettuccine Alfredo Recipe

Many bread machines have set for pasta dough. This environment can be used to make different types of pasta like fettuccine. We'll cover the simple recipe for fettuccine and some of the steps involved in actually rolling out and cutting the Fettuccine noodles. Also, we'll cover a simple Alfredo sauce so you can make a perfect Alfredo Fettuccine.

If your bread machine has no pasta dough setting, look to see if it has a dough setting for pizza, you are going to get the same result. You can also try the simple dough setting, but make sure that you take the dough out before the dough setting begins the rising process. There is no yeast used in pasta dough, so the rising process is not necessary.

Dough fettuccine:
- 3/4 cup + 1 tablespoon water 80 ° F/27 ° C.
- Four big eggs room temperature
- 1 1/2 tablespoons oil
- 1 1/2 tsp salt
- 1 1/2 cups Semolina Flour
- 2 1/2 cups of all-purpose

Alfredo Flour Sauce:
- 1 1/2 cups of heavy cream

- One tablespoon butter
- 1/2 teaspoon salt
- 1/2 teaspoon pepper
- 1 cup of rubbed Parmesan cheese

Fettuccine Dough Instructions

1 Place the ingredients in the bread maker and pick the course of pasta dough.

2 Once finished, roll out as thinly as possible on a floured surface with a rolling pin. Slice thin strips with a large knife or a pizza wheel into 1/4 "to 1/8" inch.

3 Hang and dry, or set aside for immediate use.

Fettuccine Alfredo Recipe:

Boil four fettuccine in 2 quarts of salted boiling water until it is cooked.

5 Heat the ingredients of the Alfredo sauce in a saucepan to a light boil except for the Parmesan cheese.

6 Throw the fettuccine in the cream sauce and apply the parmesan, then throw on. Support.

5.24 Ginger Bread Recipe

This is an interesting recipe, in the sense that it is not about making a typical gingerbread cookie, but about making gingerbread ginger as an ingredient that results in a "Ginger" bread. Typically, this is a bread cake, or "batter." You can still tell a batter bread since instead of yeast, it uses baking soda and/or baking powder.

You also have the ginger flavor alternative. You can use fresh ginger in a food processor that has been peeled, sliced and processed to mash, or use powdered, ground ginger from a jar if you don't have fresh ginger on hand or you don't want to add the processing phase to the recipe. Both approaches produce a decent ginger flavor though the fresh ginger approach provides the bread with a slightly stronger ginger flavor note. With this recipe, if your bread machine has one, you can either use the cake bread setting or use the pasta dough or pizza dough setting to make the batter and finish it in the oven. Batter bread does not rise before baking, unlike the yeast bread. That's why you're not using the normal setting to the dough. The regular setting of the dough has a period of rising, which is not appropriate for a batter bread. At the end of the cooking phase, they grow in the refrigerator or in the oven. This bread is perfect for breakfast or a cup of tea or coffee at tea-time. Especially during the holidays, it also serves as a great dessert.

Ingredients:

- 3tbsp of white sugar
- One cup of water (110 ° F. /43 ° C),
- One and a half teaspoon of baking soda
- 1 cup of molasses
- Half cup of butter at room temperature
- 1/2 teaspoon of salt
- One teaspoon of ground cinnamon
- one tsp of ground ginger or one tsp of fresh ginger mashed in a food processor
- 1/2 teaspoon of ground cloves
- One egg at room temperature
- 2 1/2 cups of all-purpose flour

Directions

Whether powdered, ground ginger or fresh ginger may be used, but the fresh ginger needs to be peeled and sliced and processed in a food processor until it is a pulpy, mash. Whole chunks of ginger can give a slice a harsh taste when not processed enough.

2 Choose 1-pound loaf and medium crust cake-bread setup.

3 Pizza dough or pasta settings can also be used to make the batter and then move to a greased dish and bake at 425 ° F or 218 ° C. 40-45 minutes. Place a knife or toothpick in the middle of the crust, and test for doneness. If it comes out hot, keep baking for another 5 minutes and then test again. Repeat if need be.

3. Let the bread rest for 10 minutes, whatever the baking process, and serve.

5.25 Garlic Bread Recipe

For garlic lovers, this is a perfect recipe. It is filled with garlic as both an ingredient and a topping, through and through. Garlic powder is applied to bread dough, and after rising and before baking, sliced garlic is put on top of the loaf.

A traditional accompaniment to pasta dishes and sauces, or only eaten with a salad on the side

Ingredients:

- One cup 110o F. /43o C hot.
- 1 tbsp. of sugar
- 1 tsp of salt
- 1 tbsp. of room temperature butter
- 1 tbsp. of garlic powder
- One Tbsp. of minced garlic
- Three cups of bread flour

- Two tsp of bread machine yeast
- Three tablespoons of thinly sliced garlic cloves

Direction:

1 Place the ingredients to the bread machine pan in the order listed in the recipe and pick the base or white bread cycle for a 1, 5-pound loaf and dark crust environment.

2 Start the cycle, but be careful about the end of the kneading process. Lots of machines are going to beep at this stage. Redistribute the dough in the bread pan to an even shape and top with the sliced garlic before beginning the rising process.

3 Remove the bread from the bread pan when the bread is finished and allow it to rest for 10 minutes. Slice and enjoy

You might need to run a rubber spatula around the sides of the pan to remove any bits of garlic that have caramelized and stuck to the surface of the pan.

5. 26 Herb and Parmesan Bread

This recipe is a cinch as you can start by adding all the ingredients and letting it go for a great result. Every mixture of herbs you like can be mixed and matched as long as they don't exceed three tablespoons, as the recipe says.

This bread is perfect with a salad, soups or as a side dish of pasta or other savory food. The parmesan is added to the dough and gives it a slightly salty richness. It is also a nice olive oil bread with your favorite additions such as pepper flakes or yes – more parmesan.

Ingredients:

- One plus a one-third cup warm water (110 ° F.)
- Two tablespoons olive oil
- Two cloves of chopped garlic or one tsp of dried garlic

- Three tablespoon combination of basil, chives, oregano, and rosemary (can be fresh or dried but double up to Six tablespoons when using fresh. You can use any combination of herbs you want but remain true to the measurements)
- 4 cups of bread flour
- One teaspoon salt 1
- One tablespoon sugar
- Four tablespoons of grated parmesan cheese
- 2¼ tsp dry active yeast

Direction

Use the process of wheat, medium crust, and loaf arrangement of 2 pounds. You can start by adding all the ingredients, including the savory ingredients, so you don't have to wait for a signal to add the parmesan and herbs.

5.27 Indian Naan Bread

Naan bread is a traditional Indian rendered flat-bread. - Culture has its flat-bread version from pita to lavash, and in India, Naan is the flat-bread of choice. It's a very simple recipe and using a basic dough system, and you can make the basic dough in your bread machine. On a very heavy, cast-iron skillet, the dough is then removed and formed into flats and quickly cooked and seared.

For this kind of bread, a tandoor is a traditional method of cooking in India. A tandoor oven is a big, clay oven in the form of a tiny barrel, and the flat-breads are stuck to the tandoor sides to bake. Very few people at home have something that resembles a tandoor oven, but the hot cast-iron works just as well.

Naan bread is used in a host of different ways. Several toppings are sometimes put on top, and the bread is folded to make a sandwich. A piece of bread can be pinched from a plate between two fingers to pinch some rice and beans, or the bread can simply be dipped in a sauce.

Ingredients:

- 3/4 cup of water
- 2 table cups of plain yogurt
- One egg
- Two teaspoons of salt
- 1 table cup of olive oil
- 3 cups of flour
- 1 1/2 table cups of bread machine yeast or active dry yeast

Direction:

1. Put the ingredients listed above into the bread maker pan in the order indicated in the recipe and choose the basic dough system.

2 Bring the dough out on a floured surface when the dough setting is complete and cut into 6 bits of equal size.

3 Shape the dough into a flat-bread about 6 to 8 inches in diameter, using your hands and fingers.

4 Let the pieces of dough rise for some 15 minutes. Meanwhile, heat an ungreased cast-iron skillet over high heat until very dry.

5 Throw the Naan flat-bread onto the skillet one after the other for around 2 to 3 minutes or until you have some browning on it.

6 Stack the flat-breads as you go and, when done, serve.

5.28 Mozzarella Cheese and Pepperoni Bread

This may sound like pizza bread, but it does have the bread texture incorporated into the dough with the mozzarella cheese and pepperoni. A little oregano rounds out the flavors of Italy. At the beginning of the process, the mozzarella cheese is added, but the chopped pepperoni is added to the end of the kneading cycle, much like fruits or nuts. You can add the pepperoni to the hopper if you have a fruit and nut hopper, but make sure that you dust the pepperoni with flour, so it doesn't stick to the hopper's sides.

This is a great snack bread after school, and it also goes well with pasta or lasagna.

Ingredients:

- 1 cup of water + 2 tablespoons (110 ° F/43 ° C)
- Half cup of medium shredded mozzarella cheese
- Two tablespoons of sugar
- 1 1/2 teaspoons of garlic salt
- 1 1/2 teaspoons of dried oregano
- 3 1/4 cups of bread flour
- 1 1/2 teaspoons of active dry yeast or bread machine yeast
- 2/3 cup of pepperoni (1/4 inch or 1/2 centimeter)

Instructions:

1. Put the ingredients to the bread pan in the order as listed above.

2. Choose the setting for white bread, 1.5-pound loaf, and medium crust.

3. Add in the diced pepperoni at the beep after the first kneading process after baking, let cool, slice, and serve.

5.29 Peanut Butter Bread Recipe

To make this peanut butter bread in your bread machine, you will need warm water, white bread flour, brown sugar, salt, peanut butter, and active dry yeast. You'll need a bit more peanut butter, icing sugar, and water to make the glaze that goes over after baking. Add that little smear of peanut butter or cream cheese, if desired. And is it toasted? This bread is amazing {just skip the glaze if you plan to toast it}.

This simple bread machine recipe is a favorite around our house and makes a delicious breakfast or snack. If you like to get really adventurous and start the day with something special, try making French toast with it!

Ingredients

- 1 1/4 cup plus four teaspoons warm water
- Three cups of white bread flour
- 1/4 cup brown sugar
- Half teaspoon salt
- Half cup plus one teaspoon peanut butter
- Three teaspoons active dry yeast
- 2/3 cup powdered sugar

Instructions

1. Layer 1 1/4 cups of water, white bread flour, brown sugar, salt, 1/2 cup peanut butter, and bread machine yeast, as instructed by the manufacturer.

2. Set machine at basic/white setting.

3. Let bake according to the machine setting, then remove from the baking pan and allow it to cool.

4. Stir together one tablespoon creamy peanut butter, powdered sugar, and four teaspoons water and drizzle over the cooled bread.

5. If desired, place the bread in the fridge for a few minutes to harden the glaze a bit.

6. Slice and serve (Dukes).

5.30 Rice Bread Recipe

Although rice flour is used to make many gluten-free loaves of bread, this is not a gluten-free bread. It does not, in reality, use rice flour but cooked rice as an optional ingredient, either white, wild, or brown. Here again, the added rice ingredient added a hearty ingredient to give the bread more body and texture, which helped to increase the amount of flour required when the supply of flour was reduced.

The main success factor for this recipe is to cook the rice in the bread pan before adding it to the other ingredients. Hot, uncooked rice will never get enough moisture and will leave you in every bite with rough, chewy rice nuggets. Try this if you like it, but I prefer bread with strong texture and mouthfeel.

Ingredients:
- 1/2 cup of cooked rice
- One plus one-fourth cup of warm water (110 ° F/ 43o C.)
- 1 1/2 cup of salt
- One teaspoon of sugar
- Four cups of bread flour
- Two plus 1/4 teaspoons of bread machine yeast

Directions:

1 1 1/2 cup of cooked rice add 1/2 cup of rice to one cup of water boiling, cover and simmer until rice is finished.

2 In the order specified, add ingredients to the bread pan. Before adding the flour and finishing with the yeast, stir the cooked rice into the water/salt/sugar mixture to form a slurry.

3 Pick a white or simple course of bread for a 2-pound loaf and a medium crust.

4 Let rest and slice for 10 minutes, and serve.

5 Rice bread is sometimes served in main courses rich in gravy or dipped in soups or stews.

5.31 Semolina Bread Recipe

Semolina bread is made of added semolina flour to the all-purpose flour. Semolina flour is made from a very hard grain of wheat called durum. The meal is traditionally used to make pasta in Italy, but it was in Sardinia that the bread of semolina originated. You might have some trouble finding Semolina flour in your local grocery store's standard baking section, but many supermarkets have specialized sections where you can also find more varied and obscure flours. Don't buy this recipe's large package, since it only needs one cup. The good news is it's a simple bread to make in your bread machine from start to finish.

The recipe for this bread includes a single cup of semolina flour to 3 cups of the all-purpose meal. However, if you want bread with a more golden color and a firmer texture, you can raise the proportion to 2 cups of semolina added to 2 cups of all-purpose flour.

Semolina bread is a perfect sandwich bread and is also good when soaked in olive oil or any sauces usually accompanying an Italian dish.

A favorite Sardinian combination is a soft cheese and olives spread or the traditional Sardinian sardine's accompaniment. If rolled, the bread can keep for days, and longer if frozen or refrigerated. This recipe produces a 2-pound loaf. If you want a 1-pound loaf, just split the ingredient ratios into two.

Ingredients:

- 1 1/2 cups of 110 degrees Fahrenheit or 43 degrees Celsius
- Two teaspoons of sugar
- 1 1/2 tablespoon of olive oil
- One teaspoon of salt
- 1 cup of Semolina flour
- 3 cups of all-purpose meal
- Two plus 1/4 tsp of bread machine yeast or active dry yeast

Directions:

1 Add all ingredients to the bread pan of the bread machine in the order indicated in the bread machine ingredient.

2 Press start and, as normal, open the lid to double-check the consistency of your dough during the kneading process. If, after 5 minutes of kneading, it begins to dry, try scraping some flour down from the side of the bread machine pan with a plastic spatula to help absorb the flour. If it is still too dry, add a spoonful of water at one time until you see the right consistency. If the dough tends to be wet or loose, add a spoonful of flour at a time until the desired result is achieved. You want a whole, cohesive ball of dough with no flour sticking to the sides of the pan.

Remove the loaf from the pan when the bread is finished and let it rest on a wire rack for 10 minutes. Cut and wrap or serve, and stock.

5.32 Shepherd's bread Recipe

Shepherd's bread was, in fact, a staple for shepherds in Western Europe, especially the Basque shepherds of Spain. There were several of reasons it appealed to them. For one, they had made the recipe very simple and quick. The use of whole wheat flour, they also enjoyed the bread's sturdy and crusty appearance—finally, the bread held in a backpack or over-the-shoulder bag very well, without getting crushed.

This bread is simple to make in your bread machine, and it goes well on a cold, chilly night with hearty soups, stews, or any dinner. It is also perfectly toasted with a soft butter smear, or with a spoonful of jelly or jam at breakfast.

Ingredients:

- 2 1/2 teaspoons of salt
- Half cup of butter at room temperature
- One cup of water at 110 ferenhite. Or 45 grades C.
- Three cups of whole wheat flour
- Two and a half teaspoons of bread machine yeast or active dry yeast

Directions:

1 Add all ingredients to the bread pan in the order specified in the recipe ingredient section.

2 Choose a 1.5-pound loaf and a dark crust for the Wheat Bread table. If your machine has one, you can use the 100 percent whole-wheat bread configuration.

3. Allow the bread to cool for ten minutes on a rack until its cold, then slice and serve or throw the entire loaf into your backpack.

5.33 Sourdough Buns Recipe

In traditional sourdough bread, sourdough buns are crispy and have the sour piquancy you would find. You have started with a sourdough starter that you can either buy or make. Using the dough method, you can also mix the sourdough into your bread machine and form the buns on the countertop to end up in the oven.

Those buns are perfect for sturdy burgers and sandwiches and can stand up to the messiest pile of toppings and condiments. Better still, every sandwich has its own flavor applied to the bun's texture.

Ingredients:

- 1/4 cup of milk, warmed (100-110 ° F/37 ° C to 43 ° C),
- One teaspoon salt
- Three tablespoons of melted butter
- One egg, room temperature
- Two tablespoons of sugar
- 2 3/4 cups of bread flour or all-purpose flour
- 1/2 cup of whole wheat flour
- One teaspoon of bread machine yeast or active dry yeast
- 2 cups of sourdough starter

For glazing and topping:

Two egg yolks two tablespoons of water sesame seeds

If the dough looks too hard, apply one spoonful of water at a time and scrape the flour with a spoon from the corners of the bread pan. If the dough is too hot, add one tablespoon of flour at a time until you have the consistency of a dough ball.

2 Take out the dough from the bread maker pan to a lightly floured work-surface when the cycle is complete. Cut the bread dough into eight equal pieces, and shape the dough into a bun. Place the buns on a lightly greased cookie sheet and cover them with plastic wrap, allowing for 1 hour of rising. Oven preheats to 350 ° F/175 ° C.

3 Remove the plastic wrap and glaze the glazed buns made of 2 eggs mixed with two spoons of sugar. Top with sesame seeds on each bun.

4 Bake for twenty to 25 minutes or until golden brown buns is on. Let it rest for ten minutes, then serve.

Chapter 6: Bread Machine Sweet Recipes

6.1 Sourdough Bread Recipe

Sourdough bread has been in use for centuries and is a popular and conventional recipe for bread. It features a bubbling, mass of flour yeast typically held in a crock that allowed somebody to have access to an endless supply of yeast. This involved feeding the sourdough yeast starter with added flour and sugar, but it kept them supplied with all the yeast they wanted for settlers who couldn't buy yeast readily.

The sourdough bread is a finely textured bread with a crispy crust and a vinegar-like piquancy. There is no vinegar in the recipe, but the sour taste stems from the fermentation of the yeast over time and the high levels of carbon dioxide to induce the rise.

In some grocery stores, you can buy sourdough starters, or make your own. It is not very difficult to do it yourself, but it takes some time and energy. It's basically a mixture of warm water, yeast, sugar, and flour stored in a crock or jar and allowed for a long period of time to bubble and thrive. For hundreds of years, some sourdough starters in San Francisco have gone solid.

Ingredients:

Sourdough starter ingredients:

- 1 1/2 teaspoons bread machine or fast active dry yeast
- cups of lukewarm water (105 ° F to 115 ° F)
- cups of all-purpose flour or bread flour
- Four teaspoons of sugar

Sourdough bread Ingredients:

- 1/2 cup water

- cups of bread flour
- Two tablespoons of sugar
- 1 1/2 teaspoons of salt
- One teaspoon bread machine or quick active dry yeast
- One cup sourdough starter
- One yolk of an egg and a teaspoon of water for glaze

Sourdough starter direction

You'll need to start your sourdough at least one week before you make your first loaf of bread. So many people choose to buy their already produced sourdough starter.

2. Dissolve one and a half teaspoons of yeast in warm water in a wide glass bowl

3 to make it yourself. Whisk in the 3 cups of flour and four teaspoons of sugar and either start whisking or beating at medium speed with an electric mixer for around one minute or until the batter is smooth.

4. Cover lightly with a damp washcloth and let stand for around one week at room temperature, or till the mixture is bubbly and has a sour fragrance.

5. Do not think about having the washcloth moistened again; just keep the bowl covered as much as possible. The starter bubbles you'll see are caused by carbon dioxide emissions. This is what yeast releases every time we bake, and it causes bread to grow.

6. Move the starter to a non-metal bowl or large glass jar with a lid of 2 quarters or larger. Cover tightly, and cool the starter until ready to use.

7. You can replenish it after you've used the starter by adding a tablespoon of sugar and about three-fourth cup of flour, 3/4 cup of water, and mixing it all together. Cover loosely, and store at least one day in a warm spot. Refrigerate again after a day.

8. Also, note to let any refrigerated starter arrive at room temperature prior to use, this is going to grow a bit because it warms up, and that's all right.

9. Once you've developed your sourdough starter, you're ready to bake your first loaf of sourdough bread in your bread machine.

Directions for the Sourdough Bread:

10. Add the ingredients to the bread pan according to the order given

11. For the 2-pound loaf and a medium crust, pick the simple white process. After the loaf has risen, glaze the top quickly with the wash of the eggs, cut the upfront of the bread with a knife and let the maker finish the process of baking.

12. Allow it to cool on a wire rack for ten minutes when the bread is finished, and serve.

6.2 Sourdough Nut Butter Cookies

Tailored to your tastes!

Chocolate peanut butter cookie coconut can be added to the batter and mixed in, or you can make cookie balls and roll into the coconut before baking. Makes 1-1/2 inch cookies by two dozen

Ingredients

- One cup natural peanut butter or nut butter of choice
- Half cup dry unrefined sweetener of choice, to taste
- 1/4 teaspoon sea salt
- One teaspoon vanilla extract
- One organic or pastured egg
- 1/4 cup cocoa powder
- 1/3 cup sourdough start
- 1/4 teaspoon baking soda

- Unsweetened shredded coconut

Instructions

Preheat oven to 350 degrees Fahrenheit.

Prepare layer cookies.

Combine all ingredients, except for a big bowl of unsweetened shredded coconut.

Blend well.

Cut, or stir in coconut before baking.

Roll onto the prepared cookie sheet and click it.

Bake for 12 minutes, or so

After 10 minutes, check it out.

Enable to sit for 5 minutes on a cookie sheet.

Switch to rack for cooling.

Once completely cool, store on the counter, refrigerator, or freezer in a sealed container.

6.3 Sourdough Banana Bread in the Bread Machine

Ingredients

- 1/3 cup butter, softened
- 1/2 cup honey
- One egg
- 1 cup of whole wheat flour
- 1 cup of bread flour
- Half teaspoon of baking soda
- One teaspoon of baking powder
- 1 cup of mashed bananas
- One teaspoon salt
- 1 cup of sourdough starter
- One teaspoon of vanilla extract

Direction

Step 1 Place butter, honey, egg, whole wheat flour, vanilla extract, baking powder, baking soda, and sourdough starter in the bread machine pan according to the order as listed.

Move 2 choose fast cycle bread. After the last kneading, dip the clean fingers into the dough and remove the paddles so that they do not hole in your loaf. After baking, removes dough from the oven, around 1 hour 35 minutes. Before slicing, cool (Melody).

6.4 Buttery Butternut Squash Bread Recipe:

(Making a 2-pound loaf) Squash abounds from zucchini to acorn to butternut squash during harvest time. Butternut squash is used as a basis for this recipe. It is naturally sweet with some of the pumpkin features and colors. This specific recipe is a batter bread that you can either finish in the bread machine or pour it into a saucepan and finish in the oven.

Ingredients:

- 2/3 cups of water
- Four eggs
- 2 2/3 cups of white sugar
- 1 1/2 tsp of salt
- One teaspoon of ground cinnamon
- One teaspoon of ground cloves
- 2/3 cups of shortening
- Two cups of pureed and cooked butternut squash
- Three and a 1/3 cups of all-purpose flour
- Two teaspoons of baking soda
- Two tsp of baking powder

Directions:

Add all ingredients in the order indicated in the bread pan. Grease two loaf pans measuring 9 inches. Bake in the preheated oven for about one hour till a toothpick inserted in the middle comes out neat if you want to bake it or else you can make it in your bread machine. Cool down in the pan for ten minutes before putting on a wire rack to cool completely.

6.5 Apricot Bread Cake Recipe

Apricots are a small, flavorful fruit. Unfortunately, apricots are extremely seasonal, and at some times of the year, they can be one of the toughest fruits to find in a grocery store or market. However, when rehydrated, dried apricots perform equally well, and this recipe uses dried apricots.

Typically, this bread is a batter or cake-bread. Batter bread begins with a batter that looks like a pancake batter, unlike yeast bread that starts with a dough ball that is left to rise. Usage of baking soda and/or baking powder instead of yeast is the typical measure for a batter bread. It is vital to remember in mind that before baking a batter or cake, bread doesn't rise. At the end of the baking step, the bread rises in the pan and wants to finish in the oven by selecting a pizza dough, pasta dough, or cookie dough. If only you have a dough setting and you want to finish in the oven after the kneading process has ended and before the rising cycle starts, take the batter out of the bread pan into a greased baking pan.

Ingredients:
- 1 cup of dried apricots
- 2 cups of warm water
- 1 cup of sugar
- Two tablespoons of butter or margarine,
- One egg
- 3/4 cup of orange juice

- 2 cups of all-purpose flour
- Two teaspoons of baking powder
- 1/4 teaspoon of baking soda
- One teaspoon of salt
- 3/4 cup of chopped nuts

Instructions

1 Put apricots in warm water for 30 minutes cut to bits. Keep aside the apricots and nuts and put all the other ingredients to the bread pan and either choose the cake bread setting to bake from beginning to end in the bread maker or the pasta or pizza dough setting.

2 Brush the apricots with flour and add the fruit and nuts to the hopper, if you have a fruit and nut hopper. If you do not have a fruit and nut hopper, add the fruit and nuts to the batter when you hear an audible beep at the end of the kneading process. This is the fruit and/or nuts signal to add. Set the machine in a bread machine to the setting for a 1-pound loaf and medium crust for Cake Bread.

3 Bake the bread in a bread machine and let it rest for 10 minutes before eating. Pour the batter into a bread pan with butter and bake for 40 to 50 minutes if you want to bake it in the oven. When you think it's finished, the normal test for any batter bread is to put a knife into the middle of the bread. If the knife or skewer is wet, add 10 minutes of baking time and repeat until the knife or skewer has dry appearance.

If you have a panel of cake bread, you can make this recipe in the bread maker from start to end, or you can finish it in the oven by using the bread machine to mix the batter. Do not use the setting for dough if you can help.

The regular setting of dough has a growing process that warms the dough with the presumption that the recipe includes yeast.

This rising cycle can actually start baking the bread when the rising agent is baking soda or baking powder and compromise the end result when it is fully baked if you have no cake-bread setting.

6.6 Almond Bread Cake Recipe

Almond bread is bread or batter bread that gets its almond flavor from almond paste and a slivered almond topping. Like all cake bread, the dough is more like a pancake batter than the normal dough ball. That is because it uses baking powder instead of yeast.

Because there is no yeast, the dough of the batter will not rise before baking, unlike a dough of yeast bread that can double in size when rising. If you have a cake setting on your bread making machine, or else you can use the bread machine to mix, knead and blend the batter and then end up in the oven or in a buttered bread pan, you can make this recipe from start to finish.

You should use a setting for pizza dough or pasta dough if you are going to end up in the oven. Following the kneading process, they don't have an up process, and a batter bread doesn't have to rise before baking. Towards the finish of the baking process, it should grow in the oven once the batter is in the machine or in the bread pan with the almonds ready top.

Ingredients:

- 1 cup of milk
- 1/2 teaspoon of vanilla extract
- 1/2 teaspoon of salt
- 2/3 cup of granulated sugar
- Two tablespoons of butter softened
- Two tablespoons of canola oil
- Two large eggs
- 1 (7-ounce) pack of almond paste

- 1 1/2 cup of flour
- 1 1/2 teaspoon of baking powder
- 1/4 cup of slivered almonds

Direction:

1. Place all the ingredients to the bread pan in the order stated but reserved if your bread machine has a fruit hopper and put the almonds in the hopper.

2 Pick the setting for a 1-pound loaf cake bread. If your bread machine does not have a cake bread setting, use the pasta or pizza dough setting to blend and knead the batter.

3 If you have is a dough setting, after the kneading process, but before the increasing process, place the batter out into a greased bread pan. Oven preheats to 350 ° F. Then bake for about 45-50 minutes.

Do the test with a skewer or knife in the middle and, if still wet, place it in the oven again and add 10 minutes of baking time. When done, let it rest for a few minutes, then slice and serve.

6.7 Chocolate Pumpkin Bread Cake Recipe

This is another batter bread which you can create using the cake set in your bread machine. As normal in the recipe, it replaces yeast with baking soda and baking powder. Most cake recipes are common to this. You can make this bread in the bread machine from start to finish, but you also have the option of using the process of pizza dough and finishing in the oven. The reason you used the process of pizza dough is that it doesn't have a long time of heating and growing, which is not necessary for a batter crust. At the end of the process, the bread must come up in the oven.

The chocolate chips will be applied at the end of the mixing/kneading process so that during the mixing step, they are not crushed. If your machine has one, you might use a fruit and nut hopper to add it at the right time if you're in the kitchen, or simply fold it into the batter before placing it in the bread pan and the oven.

Ingredients:

- Two large eggs
- Two tablespoons of unsweetened almond milk or regular milk
- 1 3/4 cups (one 15-ounce can) pumpkin purée
- Three tablespoons of unsalted butter,
- 1/2 cup of softened organic dark or light brown sugar
- 1 3/4 cups of all-purpose or gluten-free flour
- One teaspoon of baking soda
- One teaspoon of baking powder
- Two teaspoons of pumpkin pie spice
- 1/4 teaspoon of sea salt

One cup of semisweet chocolate those at the end of the kneading process or after the beep, if you have an automatic machine, it will give a beep.

Instructions

1. Put all the ingredients as listed above in the bread machine pan and use a gluten-free or whole wheat bread option if your machine has.

2 Preheat the oven until 350 ° F/175 ° C.

3 In a greased bread pan, pour the batter and bake at 350 ° Fahrenheit or 175 ° C. For forty minutes, or till a wooden skewer or toothpick comes out from the center, clean and dry.

1 Let the bread rest on a plate, for at least ten minutes slice, and serve. The sour cream and a mint leaf are optional toppings while serving.

6.8 Cinnamon Applesauce Bread Recipe

This is a robust combination of cake bread and yeast bread that catches autumn's flavors as a compliment to dinner on a brisk fall night. It results in a batter-like consistency, but in addition to baking powder, the addition of yeast gives it a lightness which balances the robust ingredients.

The traditional recipe includes raisins but, if you prefer, you can add Raisins, also known as dried cranberries. Because of the addition of yeast, you use the white bread process, although it won't rise much like most yeast bread. If you have a cycle of cake-bread that could work too, but with the White-bread cycle, similar success can be achieved.

Ingredients:

- 2/3 cups warmed to 110 ° F/43 ° C fat-free milk.
- 2 tbsp. of vegetable oil
- 0.25 tsp of salt
- One egg
- 1 cup of chunky applesauce
- One cup of firmly packed light brown sugar
- 2 tbsp. of ground Cinnamon
- 2.50 cups of bread flour
- 1 tbsp. of baking powder
- 1 tbsp. of bread machine yeast
- 1 cup of chopped walnuts
- 0.50 cup of raisins or (dried cranberries)

Direction:

1 Add all the ingredients to the bread machine pan in the order indicated.

2 Select the 1.5-pound loaf white bread process and the dark crust.

3 Once done, let it rest on a wire rack for 10 minutes.

6.9 Date Nut Bread Recipe

Dates are an ancient fruit that goes back 4,000 years and has a syrupy sweetness that makes this recipe special for bread. Dates have pits, so make sure you buy pitted dates or remove them before you slice. The dates are extremely nutritious, just as the almonds in this recipe are. The blend of wheat flour rolled oats, and bread flour is high in fiber and adds to the nutritional profile.

This is a good all-purpose breakfast, lunch, or dinner bread. The loaf's integrity makes it a perfect sandwich bread for beef or poultry, and, like many pieces of bread, it's great for French toasting or just toast and buttering. While the chopped dates are meant to be incorporated into the dough, after its growth, you can also top the dough to add a pleasant accent with a dispersion of sliced dates.

Ingredients:

- 1 cup of water
- Half tbsp. of vegetable oil
- Two tbsp. of honey
- Half tsp of salt
- 1/3 cup of rolled oats
- 0.75 cup of whole wheat flour
- 1.50 cups of bread flour
- 1.50 tsp active dry yeast
- 0.50 cup dates, pitted and chopped.
- Half Cup of almonds hacked.

Direction:

1 Place all the ingredients in the machine pan in the order of the ingredients that are listed or recommended by the producer.

2 Select the setting for the Fruit Bread, and start.

3 Dates and nuts can be added for better distribution at the very beginning or added after the beep. If you've got a fruit and nut hopper add the dates and nuts, but first dust the dates with flour, or they may stick in the hopper.

4. Top the loaf with sliced dates if you like, before the first rise.

5. Allow it cool for ten minutes then slice, and serve.

6.10 Fruit Bread Recipe

This is called an everyday fruit bread since it uses any season fruits, including mixed dried and candied fruits. This has the characteristics of a fruit cake in some ways, but conventional fruit cake has the consistency of a batter. This is a yeast bread starting as a dough and finishing with the texture and consistency of a white bread loaf.

You may use any combination of dried or candied fruits. Just make sure that you do not reach 2/3's of a cup for any combination of fruits. You'll also want to add the fruits after the initial kneading process at the first beef or use your fruit and nut hopper if you have one. If you are using the hopper, make sure that you brush the fruits with flour. Dried fruit and especially candied fruit can get very sticky and remain in the hopper until tossed and powdered in some flour.

Ingredients:
- One egg
- One cup of water plus two tablespoons
- Half tsp of ground cardamom
- 1 tsp of salt
- 1.50 tbsp. of sugar
- 0.25 cup of butter, softened
- Three cups of bread flour
- One tsp of bread machine yeast
- 1/3 cups of raisins

- 1/3 cups of mixed candied fruit

Direction:

1 Place all ingredients except raisins and fruit cakes mix in bread machine pan in the order indicated by the manufacturer or recommended.

2 In fruit/nut beep, add raisins and candied nuts, or 5 to 10 minutes before the last kneading process finishes. If you have an automatic fruit hopper, it will immediately happen. Set for a 1.5-pound sandwich, and set the simple white setting either to the Fruit and Nut setting if you don't have a setting for fruit and nut. Using the color Medium Crust.

6.11 Lemon Bread Cake Recipe

This is a cake-bread made with a decent quantity of lemon juice and zest. Zesting is easy to do if you have a "zester," but if you don't have one, you will have very thinly cut off the top skin of the lemon and then julienne or slice it very thinly. Zesting means having just the top layer of the lemon skin that has the most oils and the most strong lemon taste.

The lemon would then have to be juiced. If you have a lemon juicer to do lemon juice, but the seeds still need to be taken out? You can also squeeze the lemon with your hands and let the seeds capture your fingertips.

Ingredients: For Cake-Bread:

- 1/2 cup of milk
- Two large eggs
- 1 cup of sugar
- 1/8 teaspoon of salt
- One teaspoon of baking powder
- Two tablespoons of lemon juice
- 1 1/2 cup of all-purpose flour
- One tablespoon of rubbed lemon peel

- 1/2 cup of melted butter

For glazing:

- 1/2 cup of sugar
- Two tablespoons of lemon juice

Direction:

1 Add all the ingredients in the machine pan and select a 1 pound loaf cake bread setting with medium crust.

2 Let it cool for ten minutes, and then slice and serve.

3 Prepare the ingredients in glaze and drizzle immediately with glaze.

6.12 Red Velvet Cake Recipe

Red Velvet cake is a dramatic-looking cake usually overlapped with white icing to act as a contrast to the cake's bright red color. You have the choice of slicing the finished red velvet cake and layering before frosting a combination of strawberries and strawberry jelly in one-to-one proportion.

This specific recipe uses a mixture of red velvet cake and is cooked in the bread maker. Traditionally red velvet cakes are eaten with a frosting of buttercream or cream cheese. For this recipe, we have included cream cheese frosting.

Ingredients:

- One box red velvet cake mix
- 1 cup water 250 ml
- Three eggs, lightly beaten
- 1/3 cup vegetable oil –

Cream Cheese Recipe:

- 1 cup of cream cheese, softened (8 ounces/225 grams)

- 0, 50 cups of unsalted butter, softened, or Mascarpone cheese, at room temperature (65 to 67 ° F) (1 stick/4 ounces/115 grams)
- 1 lb. of sugar, sifted (4 cups/455 grams)
- 1 tsp Vanilla extract

Strawberry filling

One cup strawberries chopped and mixed with half cup sugar

Instructions

1. Put cake ingredients in the bread maker pan according to the order listed.

2. Insert pan into the machine and select the cake cycle or Batter cycle Bread; 1 pound loaf and light crust.

3 Use a rubber spatula to rub-down the sides of the baking pan and knead the paddle halfway through the mixing.

4 When the signal sounds indicating the duration of the baking process are complete, check the wooden skewer for doneness. Delete the baking pan from the bread machine if it is ready. If not, if you have it on your machine until baked, keep it in the bread machine or place it on the warm cycle for 10 to 30 minutes, or on the Bake Only Cycle.

Cream cheese frosting:

5 To frost the cream cheese: Beat the cream cheese and butter in a medium bowl until it is smooth, about 1 minute. Gradually add the sugar and beat for about 5 minutes, until fluffy. Stir in coffee.

6 Trim the cake and either slice it into layers or simply cut the form and frost you want.

Strawberry filling:

7 Rest to glaze strawberries for 20 minutes and then spread before frosting onto the middle layer of the cake.

6.13 Sweet cinnamon coffee cake

A yeast bread starts with the setting of the dough and is finished in a bread pan in the oven. That makes this bread different is the toppings, and you can choose your combination of nuts along with brown sugar, butter, and cinnamon.

Allow it to rise in the machine pan before covering it with butter, sugar, cinnamon, and nuts, but if you're in a rush, you can top it up before the rise. This is a beautiful dessert bread and is a great foundation for French toast.

Ingredients:

- 7/8 cup of milk
- 1/4 cup of sugar
- One teaspoon salt
- One egg yolk
- One tablespoon butter
- 2 1/4 cup of bread flour
- Two teaspoons of active dry yeast or bread machine yeast

Topping:

- Two tablespoons of melted butter
- 1/4 cup of brown sugar
- One teaspoon cinnamon
- Half cup of chopped nuts

Direction:

1 Place all the ingredients into the machine pan, as listed above. Set the dough timer at the dough cycle.

2 Fill a glass baking dish with the dough into the bowl and grease the dish with butter before adding the dough. Keep the dough to rise for about 10 minutes and then brush it with melted butter.

3 In a cup, blend brown sugar and cinnamon, then sprinkle on top and finish with a chop nut coating if you choose to add it.

4 Oven preheats to 375 ° F/190 ° C.

5 Let the overhanging dough rise for another 30 minutes.

6 Bake for 30 to 35 minutes or until clean and dry come out the wooden skewer inserted in the middle. Make sure that you put a baking sheet under the baking dish, as both the nuts and the brown sugar make the cake fall as it continues to rise in the oven.

7 Let it rest in the dish for 10 minutes when finished. Cut the coffee cake carefully, then slice and serve.

6.14 Cinnamon Raisin Bread

The scent of raisin bread from freshly baked cinnamon could attract just about anyone into the kitchen. Making homemade cinnamon raisin bread in the bread machine in just a few minutes is simple.

Cinnamon can prevent raising on a bread loaf, so be careful not to add too much. One teaspoon brings just enough flavor to this bread, without too much hampering the yeast. Even, you'll find that the crumb on this bread is denser than most, meaning it's good for butter toasting and slathering with butter. Through the baking process, it remains soft and moist, and the raisins add just enough sweetness. There you have it, a very easy to make cinnamon raisin bread from the bread machine that the whole family can enjoy. Now the actual trick is waiting until it's cool before slicing.

This soft, tender cinnamon raisin bread can be made easily in a bread machine.

Ingredients
- 3/4 cup milk, lukewarm

- 1/4 cup water, lukewarm
- 2 tbsp. butter softened
- 1/2 cup raisins
- 1/2 cup rolled oats, old-fashioned (not instantly)
- One-fourth cup brown sugar
- One and a half tsp salt
- Three cups All-Purpose Flour
- One tsp cinnamon
- Two and a half tsp instant yeast or bread machine yeast

Direction

Put all ingredients in the bread machine in the order indicated.

Set the "basic white" bread machine and press Start.

Before cutting, allow the bread to cool completely (Adamant, 2019).

6.15 Orange Nut Cake Bread Recipe

This is an orange flavoring cake bread recipe. It is also served as a tea-meal, a sweet meal, or bread for breakfasts. For this cake bread, you won't get a dough-like consistency you'll end up with more of a batter as a cake-bread.

It can be done in the bread machine, or you can pour the batter into a bread pan with butter. Use the setting for pizza dough to simply make a batter that mixes and kneads but doesn't have a period of rising. There's no need for a bread batter to rise as it'll do that while it's baking in the oven. In the following instructions, the instructions for baking this recipe are described in both ways.

Ingredients:

- Two-third cup Water at 110 ° F/43 ° C
- Half cup Orange juice

- Half tsp salt
- Two tbsp. Salt butter
- One cup granulated white sugar
- One teaspoon baking powder
- Half tsp Baking soda
- One tsp Vanilla extract
- 1 Egg at room temperature
- 2 cups all-purpose flour
- 0.50 cup Cut walnuts
- One tablespoon of grated orange rind

Direction:

One place all the ingredients to the bread pan in the bread machine in the order given above.

2 Add it into a greased pan and bake at 350 ° For 175 ° C, if you want to finish it in the oven. It can be inserted into the middle for 45 minutes or until a toothpick, or wooden skewer comes out dry.

3 Let rest for ten minutes and slice and serve.

6.16 Pina Colada Bread Recipe

This bread has all the flavor of a Pina Colada, as the name implies. It combines the recipe's unique flavor notes, including crushed pineapple, pineapple juice, shredded coconut, and even some rum. When you don't want to use rum, you can use a combination of water and molasses.

This is a perfect dessert sandwich, and during weekend barbecues or cookouts makes for a great side-dish. It is very popular on cruise ships and at Caribbean resorts. Best of all, using the standard white bread setting is simple to make in your bread machine.

Ingredients:

- 3/4 cup water at 110 F. Or 45 grades C.
- Three tablespoons of rum or 1 1/2 tablespoons of molasses combined with 1 1/2 tablespoons of water
- Two tablespoons of white sugar
- Two tablespoons of butter at room temperature
- 1/2 teaspoons of salt
- 2/3 tablespoons of crushed pineapple with juice
- 1/4 cups of bread flour or all-purpose flour
- 1/2 cup of flaked coconut plus
- 1/4 teaspoons of flaked coconut covering
- 1 3/4 teaspoons of the active dry leaf.

Instructions

1. Put all the ingredients as listed above in the bread machine pan. Keep ¼ cup pf coconut to put on top

2 Pick a 1.5-pound loaf and a medium crust base white bread arrangement.

3 Once done, let it rest on a wire rack for 10 minutes, then slice and serve.

6.17 Banana Chocolate Chip Bread Recipe

Prep Time: 5 mins

Cook Time: 2 hrs.

Total time: 2 hrs. 5 mins

This recipe for the banana chocolate chip in a bread maker is so simple! Simply put the ingredients into your bread maker, push the button, and go forward. Your home will smell divine two hours later, and you'll be slicing up some hot, delicious homemade banana bread!

For this banana chocolate chip recipe, you will need, the following ingredients

- Two eggs
- 1/3 cup melted butter
- 1 ounce of milk
- Two mashed bananas
- 2 cups of bread flour
- 2/3 cups of sugar
- 1.25 tsp baking soda
- 1/2 tsp baking soda
- Half teaspoon salt
- 1/2 cup chopped walnuts
- 1/2 cup of chocolate chips

Instructions

Pour eggs, butter, milk, and bananas into the bread pan and set aside.

Banana bread ingredients in the bread machine next add all your dry ingredients in a bowl of medium size and stir until well combined.

Fill the bread pan with the dry ingredients.

On your bread machine, click the "Fast Bread" button.

The loop runs on your bread machine for 2 hours.

Insert a long knife or skewer into the bread at the end of the process to see if it is cooked.

If you need a few more minutes for your banana chocolate chip bread, check your control panel to see if you've got a "Baking only" option. It works in increments of 10 minutes, so if appropriate, you can increase the baking time by 10 minutes. When the baking process is complete, remove the bread from the pan and allow to cool on a baking rack. Cut, sprinkle with butter, and enjoy! (Currie).

6.18 Carrot Cake Recipe

This carrot cake recipe can be made from start to finish in the bread machine if your machine is set to a cake-bread or batter-bread. If not, you could use the setting of pizza dough or pasta dough and finish it in the oven. The regular dough setting could work too, but before the normal rising cycle begins, you'll want to remove the batter.

The reason you don't want the dough setting to start is that this is not a yeast bread but a recipe for batter bread or cake bread. A cake bread or batter bread is usually suggested by adding the baking soda and or baking powder instead of yeast. If you don't have a cake bread setting, after the bread machine has mixed and blended the batter, you can finish this recipe on the oven.

A common test to decide if a cake bread is finished or not is to insert a wooden skewer or knife into the bread, and if either comes out wet, it means the interior is not baked, and more time is needed. You can just close the lid on a bread machine and let it sit in the oven for ten t0 15 minutes. Turn off the heat in the oven and close the door, and do likewise. This will finish the batter inside, which is unbaked. You should also leave it to rest after either the bread machine or the oven is removed to give it the final finish.

Ingredients:

- 3/4 cup buttermilk
- Three large eggs
- Two teaspoons of soda
- 1/2 teaspoon salt
- Two teaspoons of cinnamon
- 2 cups of sugar
- 3/4 cup of vegetable oil
- Two teaspoons of vanilla extract

- 2 cups of grated carrot
- 2 cups of all-purpose flour
- 1/2 cup of flaked coconut plus another half for topping

Glaze

Two tablespoons of water

Adequate powdered sugar to make a smooth glaze

The other 1/2 cups of flaked coconut

Instructions

Add all the ingredients in the bread machine pan as listed above and select the setting for 1, 5-pound loaf cake-bread. After completion of the process, insert a wooden skewer or knife into the middle of the loaf. Let it stay in the bread machine or add up to the baking cycle for 5 minutes and test again.

Take it out into a platter and glaze, and top with coconut if you like.

Glaze

In a bowl, add two tablespoons of water and gradually mix in powdered sugar until you have a syrupy consistency.

Brush the top and sprinkle with the coconut, if you like. Slice and serve.

Chapter 7: Bread Machine Gluten-Free Recipes

7.1 Gluten-Free Pear Cake Bread Recipe

This particular recipe is gluten-free cake bread. A great flour can be easily found in several stores' specialty baking section called "Gluten-free all-purpose flour." There are many flours that are gluten-free, but with the gluten-free all-purpose flour, you will have nice results. Another significant factor is whether your bread machine has a Gluten-free setting or not. If not, and you really want to follow a gluten-free diet with that environment, you should consider purchasing a new unit. You may try the simple setting of white bread, but in any loaf of bread, you may not get the raise you would like.

Pear cake bread is a nice dessert bread, breakfast bread, and also perfect for coffee or tea at tea-time. A soft butter pat is also good when it's still dry. Making in your bread machine is simple, but just make sure you follow the list of ingredients to add to the bread pan and peel and shred your pears in advance. You will also want to add your pecan later after the bread has risen and before the baking process begins, as the instructions suggest and top with your sliced pear. This recipe makes a 2-pound bread. If your bread machine does not have the ability, simply cut the ingredients for the recipe in half.

Ingredients:

- Three eggs
- Two teaspoons of vanilla extract
- One teaspoon of salt
- One teaspoon of ground cinnamon
- 3/4 cup of vegetable oil
- 2 cups of peeled and sliced pears
- 2 cups of white sugar

- 3 cups of gluten-free all-purpose flour
- 1/4 teaspoon of baking soda
- One teaspoon of baking powder

Additions:

One cup of chopped pecans but hold until after beep for the addition of nuts or use nut and fruit hopper.

1 Peeled and thinly slice pear topping

Direction:

1 Place the ingredients to the bread pan in the order specified in the recipe and choose gluten-free, 2-pound loaf and medium crust. If you have the ingredients on your bread maker to suit the settings, then change accordingly.

2 Pu6t the pecans to the dough mixture when the system beeps for the addition of nuts. When the bread with thin pear slices has risen in the top of the machine, and the lid is quickly closed.

3 Allow the bread rest on a wire rack for ten minutes, then remove from the pan and slice.

7.2 100% Buckwheat Bread (Gluten-Free) Recipe

Buckwheat is a plant that is often confused. For one thing, that's not wheat related. In addition, like most other sources of flour, it is not even grass or grain. Buckwheat is, in reality, a flower that produces a seed that can be milled into flour when dried to produce a variety of baked goods, including bread.

Buckwheat has one advantage that it is gluten-free. Like other sources of gluten-free flour, however, it is struggling to grow as a bread dough because of the lack of a primary yeast fuel: gluten.

As a result, this recipe is supplemented with other ingredients to compensate for the lack of gluten as a fuel for growth. Like other gluten-free recipes, this gets a little complicated from an ingredient point of view, but you should get an excellent result if you follow the instructions.

This recipe does what other gluten-free recipes do too. It blends other sources of gluten-free flour plus lecithin that improves the dough and helps the rise. To find any of those items, you will need to visit a natural food store or a store that provides a range of baking products such as Whole Foods or other high-end groceries. If you are gluten intolerant, or someone you know, you are probably familiar with those resources anyway. If you want to go along the pure buckwheat route, simply add 3 cups of buckwheat flour to the bread pan and ignore the other flours and the potato starch. A few bread machines also have a gluten-free setting. You can use the setting certainly if yours does. Otherwise, use the simple setting in white and hope for the best.

Ingredients:

- 3 tbsp. of butter
- Three eggs
- 1 tbsp. of gum xanthan
- 1 tsp. Sea salt
- 1 1/2 cup of milk (110 ° F/43 ° C)
- 1 tsp. Soy lecithin
- 1/2 cup of buckwheat flour (or 3 cups of pure buckwheat bread)
- 1/2 cup of tapioca flour (excluding if pure buckwheat bread)
- 1 1/2 cup of brown rice flour (excluding if pure buckwheat bread)
- 1/2 cup of potato starch (excluding if pure buckwheat bread)

Direction:

Apply the ingredients to the bread machine in the order indicated and preferably pick the gluten-free setting or the normal white bread setting for a 1.5-pound loaf, medium crust.

Let the bread rest 10 minutes after its finished, then slice and serve.

7.3 Corn Bread Gluten-Free Recipe

For thousands of years, cornbread has been made and baked by cultures and civilizations. This happened in South, Central, and North America, where the corn plant had its roots. In the southern United States, it is a very popular bread and is a traditional accompaniment to chicken, fish, and almost any barbecue. Many people do not know is that 100 percent gluten-free maize meal. This makes it a good ingredient for gluten-free baking, and in your bread machine, it is simple to do.

This recipe is a recipe for batter bread or cake bread. In the bread machine, you won't see a dough ball shape but rather a batter that looks wet and loose. Do not add dry ingredients any more to get a ball of dough. When you see baking soda and/or baking powder in the ingredient list, you can always say a batter sandwich. No yeast, so this bread batter won't rise until baking. The rise happens towards the end of the cycle of baking.

Ingredients:

- 2 cups of cornmeal (make sure it is granular cornmeal and not a combination of corn or corn ground to a flourishing consistency)
- 1 tsp. salt
- 2 Tsp baking powder

- One teaspoon baking soda
- 1 Egg
- Four tablespoon butter
- 1 1/2 tablespoon of plain yogurt or sour cream, buttermilk or milk.
- You can also combine them to a total of 1 1/2 cups, any way you want.
- Four tablespoon honey
- Add water to create a batter-like consistency up to one cup

Instructions

1 Place all ingredients in the bread machine bread pan, as stated in the order. Pick the setting for a cake bread or batter bread. If your unit does not have one, pick the setting of the dough but take the batter out before the setting of the dough begins the process of rising. If you have a dough setting for pizza or pasta, you could also use that setting. Those two settings have no period of increase.

2 Preheat oven to 205 ° C/400 ° F.

3 Generously butter a glass baking dish measuring 12 x 12 inches, and pour the batter into the pot. Once the oven reaches temperature on the baking rack in the center, bake for 15 to 20 minutes. After 15 minutes, check the cornbread and measure the center with a toothpick and if it comes out dry remove from the oven. If not, give him another 5 minutes. Take out the bread and allow it cool down for ten minutes, then slice and serve.

7.4 Gluten-Free Banana Bread Recipe

Banana bread is a popular breakfast bread that can be eaten either as a dessert or with coffee or tea at a time. What is special about this recipe is that it's gluten-free. Gluten-free bread can be a challenge as they don't rise like most bread, but they're different from a cake bread like this banana bread. This is due to baking powder replace the yeast, and the bread rises in the bread machine as it cooks. But that gives a question: does your bread machine have a dedicated gluten-free setting, and should you use it for a cake bread?

The simple answer is: NO. Gluten-free settings have a rising cycle, which is unnecessary for a cake bread. In fact, a gluten-free setting will make your bread dense and heavy. You need to use a cake bread setting or finish the loaf in the oven. Ultimately, it's the ingredients that make this gluten-free, not the bread machine setting. If you do not have a cake bread setting, you can use a pasta dough or a pizza dough setting that does not have a rising cycle or uses the normal bread setting but take out the batter before the rising cycle starts and finishes in the oven.

Recommended a buttered baking bread pan and an oven setting of 350 degrees F (175 degrees C). Cook for 20 to 35 minutes until a knife or cake tester emerges from the center dry. If wet, bake a further 5 minutes until they emerge dry.

Another secret to success for this bread is that the use of quite ripe bananas. The darker the skin on bananas, the better. They are very soft and integrate easily into the batter. Too fresh bananas are too firm, and will not mix with the batter.

Ingredients:

- Two eggs
- Three tablespoons of maple syrup
- 1/2 cup of softened butter

- 1/2 teaspoon salt
- One teaspoon of baking powder
- 1/2 cup of sugar
- Three very ripe bananas mashed
- 2 cups of gluten-free all-purpose flour

Direction:

One is to use the bread machine from beginning to end, as long as you have a cake-bread setting, or you can bake it in the oven. Choose the cake-bread setting on your bread machine for a 1.5-pound sandwich, medium crust.

2 In the oven, grease a baking pan and preheat the oven until 350 degrees F. A 9x5 loaf pan is the best metal or glass. Bake for 25 to 30 minutes. When done for either approach, let stand for 10 minutes and remove and serve afterward.

7.5 Gluten-Free Vegan Bread Recipe

This recipe for bread represents a double challenge. It requires both gluten-free ingredients as well as vegan ingredients, but using the dough setting of your bread machine is surprisingly easy to make.

What distinguishes a gluten-free food is a number of flours where gluten is absent. Gluten-free all-purpose flour is the easiest to use, and can usually be found in most grocery stores' specialty, baking section.

Ingredients free of vegan substances essentially involve the omission of certain ingredients such as eggs, milk, butter, or buttermilk. It's pretty easy to replace water with milk, coconut oil, butter, or olive oil and just skip the eggs entirely.

This recipe also requires the use of Xanthan gum, which helps with the process of rising up. It can also be found in your grocery store's specialty baking section, but you might need to ask someone where they are located.

If you have a gluten-free setting, this bread can either be baked in the bread machine from start to finish, or you can use the dough setting and finish in the oven in a buttered bread pan with a 350 ° F preheated temperature setting. Thirty to thirty-five minutes.

Ingredients:

- Warm water 1 1/2 cups
- Two tsp xanthan gum
- 1/2 tsp kosher salt
- Three Tbsp. Sugar
- Two tsp of coconut oil or olive oil
- 3 cups of gluten-free all-purpose flour
- 1 tsp of a bread machine or active dry yeast

Instructions:

1 Put the ingredients in the order specified in the Ingredients section and select a gluten-free setting for a 1.5-pound loaf and medium settings. If you do not have a gluten-free setting, you can select the dough setting and bake at 350 ° F in a preheated oven in a buttered bread pan —

2 Let the bread rest for about 10 minutes, then slice and serve.

7.6 Gluten-Free Chocolate Chip Cookies Recipe

Some bread machines are set to cookie dough. You may use the pizza dough setting if yours does not. The configuration of the pizza dough combines and kneads the dough but does not have a growing period that is excessive for cookie dough.

The cookies are done on a baking sheet in the oven, and it's a good idea to mix gluten-free flours to make the cookies again.

Ingredients:

- 1 1/8 Light buckwheat flour
- Half tsp Baking soda

- Half tsp salt
- Half cup (1 stick) unsalted butter
- 1/3 cup Brown sugar
- Half tsp Vanilla extract (using one teaspoon peppermint extract for chocolate mint cookies)
- One large egg
- One cup of gluten-free chocolate chips (6 ounces)
- Half cup Chopped nuts (optional)

Instructions:

1 Preheat oven to 375 ° F/190 ° C

2 add the ingredients to the bread machine pan and select the cookie dough button

3 Use 2 wide parchment paper baking sheets, or light oil.

4 Use a tablespoon and dollop onto the baking sheet for two dozen small cookies.

5 Bake 9-11 minutes in a preheated oven or until the cookies are crisp on the edges and slightly soft in the middle. Cool on the baking sheet then moves to finish plate or cookie screen.

7.7 Gluten Free Pizza Dough Recipe

Pizza dough is a popular preparation for gluten-free cooking. You are using the setting on your bread machine for pizza dough. The environment of pizza dough has no period of rising, which is excessive for pizza dough. Do not use the gluten-free environment, and the ingredients will provide you with the gluten-free dough you want.

Usually, leave the rest on the baking sheet after you have rolled it out. It isn't going to grow a lot, but you're going to get some yeast boost. You can then top it up and finish it in the oven with your favorite pizza toppings.

Ingredients:

- Buttermilk 1 cup, or rice milk.
- Four teaspoons of apple cider vinegar keep for fifteen minutes at room temperature
- At room temperature one whole large egg
- Three large egg whites, at room temperature
- 0.25 cup of water at room temperature
- tsp apple cider vinegar and rested for 15 minutes
- 0.25 cup of extra virgin olive oil
- 1 cup of brown rice flour
- 1 1/2 cup of starched potato.
- 0.50 cup of corn starch
- 1 tsp of fine sea salt
- One tbsp. of sugar
- One tbsp. of xanthan gum
- One tablespoon of yeast

Instructions

1 Add to the machine in the order specified or specified by your cookbook manufacturer and select "pizza dough" setting or "dough" setting

2 Remove when finished and divide and roll out to create a pizza round the shape you like and top with your favorite setting. Before the crust browns gently. That'll depend on your pizza's size or diameter.

7.8 Gluten-Free White Bread

Many machines for bread have gluten-free settings. This setting has numerous rising and kneading cycles in various gluten-free flours to compensate for the lack of gluten. And the use of more than one of the gluten-free flours is a secret to success without gluten.

Rice flour is the most common gluten-free flour, but adding other gluten-free flours will improve the flavor and texture of gluten-free bread. Adding sugar or honey also helps the yeast grow and elevate the bread, and warm water is also critical to making the most of the elevation.

Ingredients:

- Three eggs
- One tablespoon of cider vinegar
- 1/4 cup of olive oil
- 1/4 cup of honey
- 1 1/2 cup of buttermilk, at room temperature
- One teaspoon of salt
- One tablespoon of xanthan gum
- 1/3 cup of cornstarch
- 1/2 cup of potato starch
- 1/2 cup of soy flour
- 2 cups of white rice flour
- One tablespoon of active dry yeast

Instructions:

1 Add ingredients in the bread machine pan in the order of indication.

2 Prefer 'gluten-free' process.

3 Check the consistency of the dough for five minutes in the cycle. If necessary, add extra rice flour or liquid.

Remove the bread and let it finish on a baker's rack or platter.

7.9 Gluten-Free Bagels Recipe

If you've made bagels before you may be shocked to hear that boiling is one of the steps before baking

That's Okay. Boiling down, they're dropped in boiling water for a minute or two before going into the oven after the bagels are formed and risen. The boiling phase is what gives glazed shine and chewiness to bagels. But the boiling step as strange as it sounds is actually pretty easy. Kneading the dough is the hard part since some bagel recipes result in a dough that appears to be a little heavier than normal bread dough. That is where our bread machines help facilitate the process. We will, by the way, use the dough cycle of the bread machine for the bagel recipes and finish baking them in your oven. These bagels do happen to be gluten-free using all-purpose gluten-free flour.

The bagel is thought to have originated in 16th century Poland. The hole in the center helps the cooking process, and sometimes a string or a wooden dowel was inserted into a bundle of bagels to make them easier to transport and display in the windows of the bakery. The standard bagel is simple, and typical toppings are both sesame seeds and onion flakes.

This bagel recipe comes with two critical components. One is the use of all-purpose gluten-free flour. The other is to add a sweetener such as sugar, honey, or malt syrup to the boiling water. Often these ingredients are added to the boiling water as well, but that's more of a grace-note than a necessary move. Adding a sweet ingredient to the water is making the bagels a little chewier. Leavening is done with yeast. The times of increase vary from 20 to 30 minutes to 12 hours.

We'll be trying three kinds of bagels: simple, sesame and onion. You can experiment with other types of toppings or fruits once you understand the basics of those three approaches.

Ingredients:
- Three and a half-cup (490 g) Gluten Free Bread Flour and a little more for sprinkle

- Two teaspoons (6 g) instant yeast
- Two tbsp. sugar
- 1 1/2 teaspoons kosher salt
- One cup plus one tablespoon (8 1/2 fluid ounces) warm water (95 ° F)
- Six tablespoons (84 g) unsalted butter, at room temperature
- Egg wash (1 egg beaten at room temperature one tablespoon milk)

Instructions

Line and set aside a broad, rimmed baking sheet with unbleached parchment paper. Bring the water (six cups of water, one table cubic molasses, and one teaspoon of kosher salt to a boil in water over medium-high heat in a medium-sized covered saucepan.

2 Make the hitter. Put the bread flour, yeast, and sugar in the bread machine pan, and use the basic setting for dough. Add salt and water and butter, and let knead again. The dough is a smooth dough but very dense. Sprinkle a silicone spatula lightly with a spray of cooking oil, and scrape the sides of the pan. Let them grow during the normal upward period.

3 Shape the rolls. Remove the dough from the bread saucepan and transfer it to a lightly sprinkled bread flour surface. Sprinkle the dough with more flour very lightly, and turn it over a few times until the dough becomes smoother. Cut the dough into eight pieces, using a bench scraper or sharp knife. Shape the pieces into dough rounds and place them some 2 inches apart on the prepared baking sheet. Put a floured finger in the center of each dough round, press down to the bottom, and push in a circular motion to create a whole at least 1 1/2 "deep.

4 Those bagels boil. Put as many of the raw, shaped bagels in the boiling water as you can fit without crowding and boil them for nearly 46 seconds in total, gently turning over the bagels to ensure that they boil even. Remove from the water bath the boiled bagels, and return to the baking sheet. Brush the egg wash on the tops and sides and either scatter or dip into the sesame seeds or onion flakes if used.

1 Cook Place the baking sheet in the center of the preheated oven and bake until all the bagels are golden brown and the internal temperature reaches approximately 180 ° F (18-20 min). Remove from the oven and momentarily allow to cool before serving.

7.10 Gluten-Free French bread Recipe

Ingredients

- 1 cup of sorghum flour
- 1 1/2 cup of potato starch
- 1/2 cup of tapioca starch or flour
- 1 1/2 teaspoon of salt
- One teaspoon of sugar
- One teaspoon of xanthan gum
- One teaspoon of guar gum (or xanthan)
- 1 1/2 tablespoon of instant or bread machine yeast
- One tablespoon of olive oil
- Three big egg whites
- One tablespoon of cider vinegar
- 1 cup of warm water (105-115 degrees)

Directions

Add all the dry ingredients in the mixing bowl

Incorporate the olive oil and the egg whites and blend.

Stir in the vinegar and much water. Beat for two minutes, then add the remaining water to make a soft dough if necessary.

Spoon the dough into the saucepan and form with a spatula carefully. Owing to the softness of the dough, it should move through the tiny holes in the pan. Do not click hard while shaping.

You may brush the top with egg white pounded if you like.

Use a sharp knife to cut into the top of each loaf, several slits.

Place the pan onto a middle rack in a cold oven. Turn on the oven to 425 degrees and start timing 30-35 minutes.

Before slicing the loaves cool down on a wire rack (Etherton).

7.11 Gluten-Free White Bread

When making gluten-free bread, it is necessary to carefully measure these ingredients, and not forget anything. Swap the white egg to chickpea flour for a vegan version of this gluten-free white loaf bread machine.

Ingredients

- Small Loaf 2.4lt pan *
- Egg whites (or Chickpea Flour + water) 2 (or 20 g + 60ml)
- Sugar 2 tbsp.
- Salt 1 tsp
- Oil 6 tbsp.
- Vinegar 1 tsp
- Tepid water 350ml
- White bread flour 500g
- Farm Fast Yeast 2 tsp

Instructions

Fill your pan with water to decide your bread tin capacity

Method: Put the egg whites (or chickpea flour + water), oil, sugar, vinegar, salt, and water and mix together

Pour that into the pan of the machine.

Attach the flour, and sprinkle over the yeast.

Whenever possible, close the lid and start the machine on the gluten-free bread system, alternatively use the simple, fast setting with a high bake option.

Remove the bread from the pan when cooked and allow it to cool before slicing completely.

7.12 Gluten-Free Nut and Seed Bread Recipe

Ingredients

Change Servings:

- 1 1 tbsp. linseeds
- 1 tbsp. pumpkin seeds
- 1 tbsp. of sesame seeds
- 1 tbsp. of millet seeds
- 1 tbsp. of walnuts
- 350ml of water
- 1 tsp of cider vinegar
- tsp of vegetable oil
- Two medium eggs
- 1 tsp of salt
- 1 tsp of honey
- 450 g of gluten-free bread flour
- 1 1/2 tsp of yeast

Instructions

Who do not eat gluten will never skip the pleasure of moist, freshly cooked bread flour. This sweet, fluffy bread is making delicious sandwiches and great toast! The nuts and seeds give it the extra snap, and a few nutrients added. Another advantage of baking your bread is that you know exactly what's going into it, with no harmful chemicals or preservatives there. Making in your bread maker is so simple, you will never miss out on fresh sandwiches for work or for school!

Steps 1 roast the nuts and seeds before making the bread to improve its nutty flavor. Sprinkle with a bit of salt and allow it to cool. (We recommend you buy a pack of seeds and nuts, cook them all together and store them in airtight containers as they are perfect for baking or stirring through salads to offer texture and taste).

2 Put water, vinegar, olive oil, eggs, salt, and sugar in the pan.

3 Add the flour, seeds, and yeast to the gluten-free setting and set your bread maker with the dark crust.

7.13 Gluten-Free Crusty Boule Bread Recipe

Ingredients

- Three ¼ cups gluten-free flour
- One tablespoon active dry yeast
- 1 1/2 teaspoon kosher salt
- One tablespoon guar gum
- 1 1/3 cup warm water
- Two large eggs, room temperature — place them in a bowl of warm water to speed up the process two tablespoons + 2 teaspoon oil of choice
- One tablespoon honey

Use a variety of options: brown rice, sorghum & tapioca starch, also homemade all— if you use a mix that already contains gums, don't add to the dough any additional, as a final product, it may become gummy. The King Arthur Flour mix contained quinoa flour, which gives the bread a bitter taste, If you like quinoa flour, Instead of using xanthan or guar gum, you can also substitute one tablespoon of ground flaxseed, combined with two tablespoons of boiling water, add this to the wet ingredients.

Guidelines

1. Mix the dry ingredients in a wide cup, excluding the yeast — whisk the flours, salt, and guar gum (or flax) together and put the yeast to the side.

2. Thoroughly whisk the water, eggs, oil, and honey together in a medium cup. (Add that to wet ingredients now, if you used the flax method.)

3. Put the ingredients wet into the bread maker. Don't forget to position the stirring little blade in the first place.

4. Carefully add the dry ingredients to the machine's wet ingredients — you can do this simply by using a 1/4 cup scoop measuring scoop and gently scooping the dry ingredients in, forming a layer on top of the wet ingredients. Instead, the yeast over the top

5. Set the gluten-free setting of your bread machine (2 lb. loaf), and get a rubber scraper. While the machine begins the cycle of mixing, scrape down the sides of the pan to ensure that all the loose flour is incorporated into the dough. (Skipping this step will sometimes leave flour on top or on the sides of the loaf, a may make bread maker newbie complaint)

6. Let the magic begin in no time does your home smell like freshly baked bread. It's going to sound really gourmet. Maybe you never want to buy overpriced GF bread again at the supermarket.

7. Remove the bread when the baking process is complete! While there is a warming time, in the end, to keep things nice and toasty, this is too much of the bread maker, so immediately remove it and place it on a cooling rack.

8. If you want the bread to have a nice crusty top, you'll have to take the extra phase, and the bread maker won't give you a brown top like baking it in the oven will. But it's Simple to do — just rub a little butter on top (it's going to be easy to melt as the bread is still hot) cover the sides (but leave the top open) with foil and place it in the oven for a few minutes.

9. Before cutting and serving to allow the bread to cool completely (if you can!). Just enjoy every bite.

7.14 Easy Gluten Free Dairy Free Bread Recipe

Quick Gluten-free Dairy-free Bread in your Bread Machine the best to make gluten-free bread loaf!

Preparation time: 10 minutes

Cooking time: 3 hours 30 minutes

Total time: 3 hours 40 minutes

Ingredients

- 1 1/2 cup warm water (105-110 °)
- 2 tsp. Active dry yeast
- Two teaspoon Sugar
- Two eggs
- One white egg (room temperature)
- 1 1/2 Tbsp. apple cider vinegar
- 1/2 Tbsp. Olive oil or grapeseed oil
- 420 grams Manini multi-purpose gluten-free flour

Directions

Heat one and 1/2 cups of water in a glass measuring cup until it reaches 105-110

Add the sugar and yeast and stir to blend. Set aside for about 8-10 minutes until it is foamy.

Using a fork or whisk to beat the two eggs and one white egg together, then add to bread machine pan.

Add in the baking pan apple cider vinegar and oil.

Add on the mixture of foamy yeast/water to the baking pan.

Finally, add the Manini's gluten-free Multi-purpose flour to top.

Place the baking pan in the bread machine and set aside and start for a gluten-free bread setting.

Your system will beep after mixing cycles, just before the ascending process starts. You are using a spatula to whisk in any leftover flour that may be trapped in any angle or pan. At this time, you can also remove the mixing blade, so if you want, it won't be left in the baked bread.

When the bread is cooked, remove pan immediately and invert it onto a cooling rack to remove the bread from the baking pan. Enable to absolutely cool to store before slicing or covering.

Notes Tips: maintain the correct temperature of your water. Too cold, and your yeast won't be active too hot, and it could kill your yeast.

Make sure that your leaves are good. If your yeast does not make foam, then you need new yeast using the method listed. Keep your yeast in the fridge, so it lasts a long time.

Use the eggs at room temperature. If they're cold, your bread won't go up that far.

7.15 Easy Gluten-Free Sandwich Bread

This simple gluten-free sandwich bread to your next lunch

Preparation time: 15 minutes

Cooking time: 1 hour 5 minutes

Additional time: 1 hour 15 minutes

Total time: 2 hours 35 minutes

Ingredients for the yeast:

- One and 1/4 cup water between 95 ° F-110 ° F
- Two tablespoons (25 g.) sugar (or honey)
- Two and 1/4 teaspoons dry active yeast (7 g. packets worth)

For the bread:

- 1 cup (145 g.) white rice flour
- 3/4 cup (85 g.) tapioca starch
- 3/4 cup (9 g.)Potato starch
- Half cup millet flour
- ¼ cup flax seeds ground
- One teaspoon baking powder
- Two ½ tsp xanthan gum
- One fourth cup oil
- Three egg whites
- One tsp cider vinegar

Instructions

Add the sugar and yeast (95-110 degrees F) to your warm water and stir; set aside for 5-10 minutes, but no longer.

When the yeast is being proofed, add the flours, flaxseed meal, xanthan gum, baking powder, and salt in the mixer with the paddle attachment. Switch your mixer to low and blend until all together.

Add the butter, egg whites, vinegar, and tested yeast mixture with the mixer still running.

Switch the mixer to medium velocity and mix for a further 2 minutes. The dough is getting thick and sticky.

Using a rubber spatula, apply the dough to your prepared loaf pan, making sure that the sides of the pan are filled and the top level. Wet your fingertips, and make the top smooth.

Cover the dough with an oiled piece of wrap and keep it to rise for 46 to 61 minutes in a warm place, or until it rises slightly above the loaf pan.

Preheat the oven to 350 ° Fahrenheit, when the dough is at the top of the pan.

Remove and bake the plastic wrap for 60-65 minutes. Halfway through baking, cover with a piece of foil over the bread loaf to prevent it from over-browning.

Take out the bread from the oven and allow to cool before slicing full.

Slice the entire loaf and store in a refrigerator for up to 4 days at room temperature, or in a freezer for up to one month (Chrystal).

7.16 Cinnamon Raisin Bread-Machine Bread Recipe [Vegan / Gluten Free] Yields 1

Ingredients

Wet

- 3/4 cup dairy milk
- Two tablespoons of flax meal + 6 tablespoons of warm water, combined and let stand for 5 min
- 1 + 1/2 tsp. apple cider vinegar.
- Two Tbsp. Vegan butter (earth balance)
- One plus half Tablespoon maple syrup

Dry

- 1 + 2/3 cups of brown rice flour
- 1/4 cup maize starch
- 2 Tbsp. Starched potato
- 1 + 1/2 tsp. Xanthan gum
- One cinnamon tablespoon
- 1/2 tsp. Salt
- 1 tsp. active dry yeast

Instructions

In a separate dry bowl, mix dry ingredients (brown rice flour, maize starch, potato starch, xanthan gum, cinnamon, and salt)

Place wet ingredients to the bread machine (milk, eggs, flex, apple cider vinegar, vegan butter, and maple syrup) Add the dry mixture to the bread machine. Until storing in an airtight bag, placed on the cooling rack to cool fully. If stored in the fridge, it will keep about four days or longer. Serve with light toast.

Conclusion

Bread making machine or bread maker is a home appliance that transforms uncooked ingredients into bread. It is made up of a bread pan (or "tin"), with one or more built-in paddles at the bottom, present in the center of a small special-purpose oven. This small oven is normally operated via a control panel via a simple built-in computer using the input settings. Some bread machines have different cycles for various forms of dough — including white bread, whole grain, European-style (sometimes called "French"), and dough-only (for pizza dough and formed loaves baked in a traditional oven). Many also have a timer to enable the bread machine to work without attendance from the operator, and some high-end models allow the user to program a customized period.

In order to bake bread, ingredients are measured in a specified order into the bread pan (usually first liquids, with solid ingredients layered on top), and then the pan is put in the bread maker. The order of ingredients is important because contact with water triggers the instant yeast used in bread makers, so the yeast and water have to be kept separate until the program starts.

It takes the machine several hours to make a bread loaf. The products are rested first and brought to an optimal temperature. Stir with a paddle, and the ingredients are then shaped into a flour. Use optimal temperature regulation, and the dough is then confirmed and then cooked.

When the bread has been baked, the bread maker removes the pan, leaving a slight indentation from the rod to which the paddle is connected.

The finished loaf's shape is often regarded as unique, with many early bread machines producing a vertically oriented, square, or cylindrical loaf that is very different from commercial bread; however, more recent units typically have a more conventional horizontal pan. Some bread machines use two paddles to form two lb. loaf in regular rectangle shape.

Bread machine recipes are often much smaller than regular bread recipes, and are sometimes standardized based on the machine's pan capacity; most popular in the US market is 1.5 lb./700 g units, and most recipes are written for that capacity; however, two lb./900 g units are not uncommon either. There are prepared bread mixes, specially made for bread makers, containing pre-measured ingredients including flour and yeast, as well as flavorings and sometimes dough conditioners.

Bread makers are also fitted with a timer for testing when bread-making starts. For example, this allows them to be loaded at night but only start baking in the morning to produce a freshly baked bread for breakfast. They may also be set only for making dough, for example, for making pizza. Apart from bread, some can also be set to make other things like jam, pasta dough, and a kind of Japanese rice cake. Some of the new developments in the facility for automatically adding nuts and fruit from a tray during the kneading process. Bread makers typically take between three and four hours to bake a loaf. However, recent "quick bake" modes have become standard additions, many of which can produce a loaf in less than an hour.

References

Adamant, A. (2019). BREAD MACHINE CINNAMON RAISIN BREAD. pp. https://adamantkitchen.com/bread-machine-cinnamon-raisin-bread/.

chrystal. (n.d.). GLUTEN-FREE BREAD RECIPE FOR A OVEN OR BREAD MACHINE. pp. https://www.glutenfreepalate.com/gluten-free-bread-recipe/.

Currie, J. (n.d.). banana chocolate chip bread machine recipe . pp. https://happyhooligans.ca/banana-chocolate-chip-bread-machine-recipe/.

Dukes, R. (n.d.). Peanut Butter Bread Recipe for the Bread Machine. pp. https://dukesandduchesses.com/peanut-butter-bread-for-the-bread-machine/.

etherton, l. (n.d.). French Bread. pp. https://glutenfreehomemaker.com/gluten-free-french-bread-recipe/.

Harjak, H. (2018). Breadmaker vs store-bought bread: Which is best? pp. https://www.trustedreviews.com/opinion/breadmaker-vs-store-bought-bread-3632620.

JULIA. (2012). HOW TO MAKE BASIC WHITE BREAD LESS DENSE IN A BREAD MACHINE. pp. https://juliasalbum.com/how-to-make-basic-white-bread-less-dense-in-a-bread-machine-recipe/.

King, L. (2019). BREAD MACHINE PRETZELS. pp. https://www.artandthekitchen.com/bread-machine-pretzels/.

Melody. (n.d.). Sourdough Banana Bread in the Bread Machine. pp.

https://www.allrecipes.com/recipe/272376/sourdough-banana-bread-in-the-bread-machine/.

Nubie, S. (2017). Barley Bread Recipe. pp. https://www.breadmakermachines.com/recipes/barley-bread-recipe/.

O., A. (2010). Bread Machines - Pros and Cons. pp. https://ezinearticles.com/?Bread-Machines---Pros-and-Cons&id=5523825.

Roxana. (2013). BREAD BAKING 101 – INGREDIENTS. pp. http://atreatsaffair.com/bread-baking-101-baking-with-yeast/.

Severson, K. (2018). How Sourdough Bread Is Helping People Eat Gluten Again. pp. https://www.huffpost.com/entry/sourdough-bread-gluten-celiac_n_5b213232e4b0adfb82702959.

Taking care of your bread maker. (2018). pp. http://fast2eat.com/breadmaker-care/.

Woodford., C. (2019). Breadmaking machines. p. https://www.explainthatstuff.com/breadmaker.html.

Made in the USA
Columbia, SC
04 December 2024